THE POLITICAL THOUGHT OF JOHN LOCKE

AN HISTORICAL ACCOUNT OF THE ARGUMENT OF THE 'TWO TREATISES OF GOVERNMENT'

THE POLITICAL THOUGHT OF JOHN LOCKE

AN HISTORICAL ACCOUNT OF THE ARGUMENT OF THE 'TWO TREATISES OF GOVERNMENT'

JOHN DUNN

Fellow of King's College, Cambridge

CAMBRIDGE UNIVERSITY PRESS

CAMBRIDGE

LONDON NEW YORK NEW ROCHELLE

MELBOURNE SYDNEY

Published by the Press Syndicate of the University of Cambridge
The Pitt Building, Trumpington Street, Cambridge CB2 1RP
32 East 57th Street, New York, NY 10022, USA
296 Beaconsfield Parade, Middle Park, Melbourne 3206, Australia

First published 1969
Reprinted 1975
First paperback edition 1982

Printed in Great Britain at the
University Press, Cambridge

Library of Congress catalogue card number: 69-14394

British Library Cataloguing in Publication Data

Dunn, John
The political thought of John Locke.
1. Locke, John—Political science
I. Title
320'.01 JC153.L87

ISBN 0 521 07408 8 hard covers
ISBN 0 521 27139 8 paperback

FOR SUE

CONTENTS

PREFACE

The claim that the account given here of Locke's argument in the *Two Treatises of Government* is 'historical' implies that its status depends upon the adequacy of its identification of Locke's *own* meaning. It is often assumed that there is little serious problem about identifying the meaning of the argument of such a book—that we can see readily enough what Locke meant or, at the very least, what Locke *said*.[1] In so far as the present work resembles an attempt at an extended archaeological excavation of Locke's mind, it may seem at first glance that the entire enterprise is supererogatory, that it is an exercise in the painful excavation of what is already wholly above the ground. However plausible such an expectation may be *a priori* it will, I hope, be disconfirmed by a reading of the ensuing work.

By 'historical', then, is meant an account of what *Locke* was talking about, not a doctrine written (perhaps unconsciously) by him in a sort of invisible ink which becomes apparent only when held up to the light (or heat) of the twentieth-century mind.[2] More precisely, what I attempt is to give an account of what Locke was maintaining in the central argument of the *Two Treatises*.[3] It is not a critique of this argument and, in particular, it does not expand on the theme of how inadequate Locke's argument is to resolve the puzzlements of contemporary political theory. There are two separate reasons for this. The first is that a large proportion of the scholarly, and more especially the journal, literature on Locke has been preoccupied with this task, a succession of determined philosophers mounting their scholastic Rosinantes and riding

[1] Cf. Alan Ryan, 'Locke and the Dictatorship of the Bourgeoisie', *Political Studies* XIII, 2 (June 1965), 219. I have commented on the oddity of this claim in an article, 'The Identity of the History of Ideas', *Philosophy* (April 1968), pp. 85–104.

[2] Cf. C. B. Macpherson, *The Political Theory of Possessive Individualism* (Oxford, 1962); Leo Strauss, *Natural Right and History* (Chicago, 1953); Richard H. Cox, *Locke on War and Peace* (Oxford, 1960).

[3] In the *central* argument of the *Two Treatises*, not of course in *all* the arguments of that prolix work, which would require a text several times longer than Locke's own and strikingly more boring than its original.

forth to do battle with a set of disused windmills, or solemnly and expertly flailing thin air. In this dimension what it hopes to achieve is simply to restore the windmill to its original condition, to show how, creakingly but unmistakably, the sails used to turn. Even at the level of preserving ancient monuments it is perhaps a service to recondition these hallowed targets. There seems little purpose in recording hits on a target that has no existence outside our own minds—and even if there is thought to be point in such an activity, it can scarcely entitle us to dignify our targets with the identity of a historical figure like Locke.[1]

The second reason is more personal. At one level all that can be said about this pastime is that if you like tilting against those kinds of windmill, those are the kinds of windmill against which you like to tilt. But a less unbending subjectivism normally maintains that the point of such commentaries is the illumination which they bring to contemporary philosophical issues. Clearly it is at least logically possible that Locke might have been talking about very different issues and yet the critical reactions to his words of a philosopher today still provide a powerful illumination of contemporary philosophical issues. In this sense, the reasons why I have confined my attention to giving an effective exposition of Locke's argument and refrained from systematic formal criticism are bleakly autobiographical. I simply cannot conceive of constructing an analysis of any issue in contemporary political theory around the affirmation or negation of anything which Locke says about political matters. The only argument in his entire political philosophy which does seem to me still to be interesting as a starting point for reflection about any issue of contemporary political theory is the theme of the *Letters on Toleration*,[2] and in

[1] Cf. John Passmore, 'The Idea of a History of Philosophy', *History and Theory*, supplement 5, 'The Historiography of the History of Philosophy', pp. 1–32. 'Too often, indeed, such polemical writings consist in telling men of straw that they have no brains' (p. 13). One reason, thus, why I have not presented an extended critique of Locke's argument and expanded on the theme of how inadequate it is to resolve the puzzlements of contemporary political theory is that on historical examination it becomes clear that he was not talking about these.

[2] Cf. also, possibly, Viano's construction of Locke's bequest to the enlightenment as the insistence on a form of social freedom essential to the advancement of science, making Locke the Michael Polanyi or Karl Popper *de ses jours*. See Carlo Augusto Viano, *John Locke: Dal Razionalismo all'Illuminismo* (Turin, 1960), esp. p. 608: 'Riconoscere il primato dell'intelligenza significa riconoscere la necessità di pro-

Locke's thought this rests firmly upon a religious premise. Indeed one of the central expository points made throughout this book is the intimate dependence of an extremely high proportion of Locke's arguments for their very intelligibility, let alone plausibility, on a series of theological commitments.

I have set out the type of issue on which I hope to throw light in the introduction below, as well as throughout the book, and have provided more formal justifications of some implicit assumptions elsewhere.[1] In crude outline what is aimed at is a more coherent and historically accurate account of what Locke was maintaining in the *Two Treatises* than has yet been given[2] and a more coherent explanation of why he should have wished to maintain this. The most important single novelty in the account is probably the stress

muovere un rinnovamento di tutta la società per istituere in essa le garanzie che possono permettere il lavoro dell'intelligenza e preparare gli uomini ad accoglierne i risultati. Il problema della condotta dell'intelligenza diventava cosí un problema di organizzazione di tutta la vita umana nel suo complesso, ivi comprese le forme di coesistenza tra gli uomini.' It is difficult to make out just what the historical status of this analysis is intended to be. It could, at most, be an inference from the trend of Locke's thought. It is assuredly not something which he *said*.

1 I have given an outline account of the relationship between what I call 'causal' and 'rational' analysis in understanding what a man is talking about in an article, 'The Identity of the History of Ideas', *Philosophy* (April 1968), pp. 85–104. One sketch of how a concept in the book would appear if subjected to somewhat more formal analysis in this spirit is presented in 'Consent in the Political Theory of John Locke', *The Historical Journal*, x, 2 (July 1967), 153–82. This could be duplicated for a large number of other concepts, 'trust', 'property', the 'state of nature', the relationship between executive and legislative powers, etc. But to do this would require a work of much greater length and one not necessarily matched by a corresponding increase in illumination. In any case such an operation would be logically posterior to the enterprise attempted in this book. I have also provided an example of the type of historical oversimplification generated by such powerful recent interpretations of Locke's politics as those of Professors C. B. Macpherson, Leo Strauss and Raymond Polin in 'Justice and the Interpretation of Locke's Political Theory', *Political Studies* (February 1968), pp. 68–87. I hope that these convergent ventures will provide a clear enough definition of the nature of my intentions and will avoid an intolerable level of repetition.

2 I have attempted to grasp the logical coherence of Locke's arguments throughout. Where I have noted their incoherence in the text this has been at points in which it appears to me that what Locke was maintaining was not internally consistent. The criterion of what Locke was in fact maintaining is necessarily historical. The criterion of its internal consistency is a matter of contemporary philosophical judgement. All the claims made in the text which follows are at risk in both of these dimensions. The criterion of the *status* of Locke's entire analytical enterprise is equally a matter of contemporary philosophical judgement. But, as said above, this is not discussed at all here because once the precise character of this enterprise has been grasped it is difficult to see how the issue of its status could exercise the meanest intelligence for very long.

on the theoretical centrality of Locke's religious preoccupations throughout the work. Many elements of the interpretation have been perceived by others at some point. Since there has been a great deal of recent work on the Locke materials and since much of it, particularly that by Von Leyden, Laslett and Abrams, has been of a very high order, this is inevitable. However, nothing very like the whole attempt has been made before. Laslett never gave a systematic full-length account of his interpretation of Locke's meaning[1] and Polin's account, brilliant though it is, is often tenuously related to the historical Locke.[2] It will be evident that the present reading differs from both of them, as from most other Locke interpreters, on a great many points. But whatever importance it may have lies less in such novelties of detail than in the historical rationale which it sets out for *why* these readings should be judged correct and why many others must be judged definitely mistaken.

I should like to acknowledge a large general debt to recent Locke scholarship, affirmed throughout where I have simply followed in the footsteps of particular predecessors,[3] and an especially heavy debt to Mr Laslett, who has done so much to restore the *Two Treatises* to the condition in which Locke himself would have wished to bequeath it to posterity and who has supervised my work throughout with generosity. Three institutions have supported the research on which this work is based: the Harkness Fellowships of the Commonwealth Fund; Jesus College, Cambridge; and over a longer period of time, King's College, Cambridge. I should like to express my gratitude to all of them, most particularly the last. Many scholars have helped me generously at various points in the work and I am greatly in their

1 Laslett's interpretation has to be pieced together from the section of his introduction, *Two Treatises of Government*, ed. Peter Laslett (Cambridge, 1960), pp. 92–120, with the addition of his notes to the text throughout.

2 Raymond Polin, *La Politique Morale de John Locke* (Paris, 1960) and 'Justice in Locke's Philosophy', in *Nomos VI, Justice*, ed. Carl J. Friedrich and J. W. Chapman (New York, 1963), pp. 262–83. Polin's interpretation throughout sees Locke's thought as altogether more coherent than the surviving materials suggest it to have been.

3 I have not thought it appropriate, in view of the bulk and heterogeneity of the literature on Locke, to mention contrary interpretations throughout except where the arguments advanced in their favour seem impressive or when it is possible to bring out some feature of my own interpretation by doing so.

debt. More personally, I should like to record what I owe to Moses Finley, who first made me understand that the role of historian has a moral seriousness. To him is due the ambition behind this work, however caricatured this may be by its many deficiencies of execution and conception in this instance. Over several years Joanna Ryan and Robert Young have helped me more than they can know in different ways, by their kindness and perception, to understand and express what I wished to say. My greatest and most persistent debt in writing it has been to Quentin Skinner for his unfailing patience, kindness, intellectual taste and analytical rigour.

NOTE. In quoting from Locke manuscripts I have not retained the contractions of the original and I have in most cases not retained oddities in the highly erratic spelling. But I have retained the use of capitals and such punctuation and emphases as Locke himself included, unless noted to the contrary. I hope that this will guard against losing stresses which Locke himself intended to mark, without imposing upon the reader the full disorder of the original notes.

J. D.

Cambridge
March 1968

AUTHOR'S NOTE

In the references to each of John Locke's major works, the edition I have used is described in full at the first mention only. A full list is to be found in the Bibliography under Locke.

Manuscript sources prefixed by 'MS Locke' are in the Bodleian Library, Oxford; those prefixed 'MS Film. 77' are in the *Commonplace Book, 1661*, which is in the possession of Arthur J. Houghton Jr.

Happiness. Happiness is a continuation of content without any molestation. Very imperfect in this world. No body happy here certain. May be perfect in an other world possible probable.

Law. The original and foundation of all Law is dependency. A dependent intelligent being is under the power and direction and dominion of him on whom he depends and must be for the ends appointed him by that superior being. If man were independent he could have no law but his own will no end but himself. He would be a god to himself and the satisfaction of his own will the sole measure and end of all his actions.

John Locke (Ethica B. MS Locke c 28, p. 141)

PART I

I

INTRODUCTION: JOHN LOCKE IN HISTORY—THE PROBLEMS

In the portrait gallery of history, Locke is a man who has worn many faces. In the studies of professional historians and philosophers these faces still remain discrete—so many masks. No simple story will draw them together or fit them to the single man whose refracted image they all must be. There are so many clear analyses of the different roles—only begetter of the Enlightenment,[1] self-conscious and dedicated ideologist of the rising bourgeoisie,[2] greatest of the exponents of English liberal constitutionalism, kept intellectual, freethinker turned *dévot*, majoritarian populist,[3] most shifty and esoteric of the treasonous clerks.[4] Some of these place him as a key figure in a story which reveals the hidden truth of European history. But the hidden truths, whether Whig, Marxist, or Straussian, are only mechanistic superstitions, models as inept to explain the microcosm of John Locke as they are the macrocosm of the 'Historical Process'. Others are more simply biographical. Yet these, too, seem more arbitrary abridgements of a complexity than analytic simplifications of one: still others are merely false.

[1] This role, one of the earliest to be assigned to him, has a considerable degree of truth. We can see this role taking definition in the attitudes of contemporaries and acquaintances like Jean Le Clerc, Anthony Collins, William Molyneux, Jean Barbeyrac, and John Shute; in the vast reputation of the *Essay concerning Human Understanding* in France and the American colonies in the eighteenth century and in the degree to which its doctrines were accepted, especially in France in the simplified form of Condillac's *Origine des connoissances humaines* (1746); and most unequivocally in such leading declarations of intellectual allegiance as Voltaire's in the thirteenth letter of the *Lettres Philosophiques* (1734, first published in 1733 in English translation) or Condorcet's in the *Esquisse d'un tableau historique des progrès de l'esprit humain*, ed. O. H. Prior (Paris, 1933), pp. 155–7 (published posthumously in 1795). Where the remaining roles listed seem simple (and not false) comments on facets of Locke's life, I have not included references to scholars who have suggested them.

[2] C. B. Macpherson, *The Political Theory of Possessive Individualism* (Oxford, 1962).

[3] Willmoore Kendall, *John Locke and the Doctrine of Majority-Rule* (Urbana, Ill., 1941).

[4] Leo Strauss, *Natural Right and History* (Chicago, 1953), pp. 202–51.

The account which is given here of Locke's political doctrines is not, it is hoped, of any of these types. It is indeed analytical in ambition. But it is intended as an attempt to explain what needs explanation—to present an intelligible account of one facet of one man's intellectual experience, however vulgar; to elucidate why it was that Locke said what he said, wrote what he wrote, and published what he published in the *Two Treatises of Government*. It is a matter of resolving an incoherence in biographical explanation, not one of denying the presence of incoherence in Locke's own thought or of inflicting an illicit explanatory coherence upon the historical world as a whole. This may seem to be both a simple and a trivial enterprise. Against its triviality I shall argue in the conclusion (though in a sense the whole book is intended to counter such a claim). Against its simplicity, the whole brake of tangled and thorny commentary may be left to speak for itself.

It is unnecessary to demonstrate at any length the scale of Locke's reputation or the ambiguity of his heritage. From Voltaire and Jonathan Edwards, from Condillac and Thomas Jefferson, from Thomas Hodgskin or the Marquis de Condorcet, the testimonies are clear, eloquent and contradictory. The man whose portrait bust ornamented the arbour of Queen Caroline and whose company in his lifetime delighted great Whig magnates like Pembroke, Mordaunt, or Somers, was the man in whose name the American Revolution was made, the man whose doctrine in his own lifetime was seen as the indictment of the British ascendancy in Ireland,[1] the man whose name stood between the leader of the

[1] See [Simon Clement], *An Answer to Mr Molyneux, his Case of Ireland*...(London, 1698), preface, for its comments on the implications of Molyneux's use in his *The Case of Ireland's being Bound by Acts of Parliament in England* (Dublin, 1698) of Locke's attack upon the derivation of political rights from conquest. Clement argued that Molyneux must have been mistaken in applying Locke's arguments in such a case; but he was clearly wrong as to the logic of Locke's concepts, however correct he may have been as to the psychology of Locke himself. Molyneux's 'plausible Arguments for the Liberty and Right of all Mankind; that Conquests cann't bind posterity etc are wholly misapply'd in this Case, and he abuses Mr Lock, or whoever was the Author of that Excellent Treatise of Government, in referring to that book on this occasion; for that Worthy Gentleman doth therein argue the Case of People whose just Rights are violated, their Laws subverted, and the Liberty and Property inherent to them by the Fundamental Laws of Nature (which he very accurately describes) is invaded and usurped upon, and that when this is as Evident and apparent as the Sun that shines in a clear day, they may then take the best occasion they can find to right themselves. This is a doctrine that all

first British working-class political organization and the gallows,[1] the man above all whom hysterical conservatives all over Europe would blame for the collapse of the Ancien Régime.[2] The story of how the *Two Treatises of Government* was causally responsible (for what other sorts of responsibility could it bear?) for the direction of American political theory in the eighteenth century is, of course, largely false.[3] Very similar judgements appear to be correct for

good Men may assent to but this is in *no* wise the Case of Ireland' (Clement, *An Answer to Mr Molyneux*, p. 30). See also [John Cary], *A Vindication of the Parliament of England in Answer to a Book Written by W. Molyneux*...(London, 1698), p. 103. The best general description of the background to this situation is a fine article by H. F. Kearney, 'The Political Background to English Mercantilism, 1695–1700', *Economic History Review*, 2nd ser., XI, 3 (April 1959), 484–96. Locke's role can be followed to some degree in his correspondence with Molyneux published in *Some Familiar Letters* (*Works*, IV (1768), 267–383), together with a single hitherto unprinted letter from Molyneux to Locke (with important enclosure from James Hamilton), October 1698, in the Carl H. Pforzheimer Library, New York (seen by kindness of Dr E. S. de Beer). See also MS Locke c 30, pp. 65–75 and 82–5.

1 See Thomas Erskine's speech in defence of Thomas Hardy, the leader of the London Corresponding Society, at his trial for high treason. 'One of the greatest men that this country ever saw considered universal representation to be such an inherent part of the constitution as that the King himself might grant it by his prerogative even without the Lords and Commons...The maxim that the King might grant universal representation as a right before inherent in the whole people to be represented stands upon the authority of Mr Locke, the man, next to sir Isaac Newton of the greatest strength of understanding which England, perhaps, ever had; high too in the favour of King William, and enjoying one of the most exalted offices in the state.' *The Trial of Thomas Hardy for High Treason...taken down in shorthand*...(London, 1794), III, 243.

2 'While the age abounds with affected declamations against human authority, there never was a time when men so meanly submitted their understandings to be led away by one another. It is an honour to submit our faculties to God who gave them, but it is base and servile to submit to the usurpations of men in things pertaining to God. And...I ask...whether the doctrines of Mr Locke, whom the world is gone after, will prepare any young man for preaching the doctrine of Jesus Christ, when he was the oracle to those who began and conducted the American Rebellion, which led to the French Revolution; which will lead (unless God in his mercy interfere) to the total overthrow of Religion and Government in this kingdom, perhaps in the whole Christian World; the prime favourite and grand instrument with that mischievous infidel Voltaire; who knew what he was about when he came forward to destroy Christianity as he had threatened, with Mr Locke in his hand.' (Rev. William Jones, in *A Letter to the Church of England* (1798), cited in William Stevens, *Life of the Rev William Jones*, *The Theological, Philosophical and Miscellaneous Works of Rev William Jones* (London, 1801), I, l).

3 It was this story which I spent the first three and a half years of my research in attempting to unravel. Parts of it still remain remarkably obscure. But it is now possible, for instance, to say with confidence (on the basis of all relevant printed works available in the *Evans Microcard Series*, a very high percentage of the total, published between 1700 and 1775, all American newspapers and magazines printed

the French, and to a lesser degree even for the English, experiences also. It is certainly untrue, despite the wealth of secondary testimony, that many people read the *Two Treatises of Government* in France in the first half of the eighteenth century. We do not even have evidence in all the vast corpus of his surviving materials that Voltaire ever opened the book, and Montesquieu's indebtedness to it for the doctrine of the separation of powers in the form in which he held it is a historiographical myth. Detailed study of the composition manuscript of *L'Esprit des Loix* reveals that the only part of the famous chapter 6 of book XI in which there is any reason to suppose that Montesquieu specifically followed Locke was the interpolated and inconsistent formulation at the beginning of the chapter.[1] Even in England the book at no time secured the sort of unquestioned acceptance and esteem which it is customary to assert for it today. But if the prominence of the role, and more especially its causal efficacy, has been exaggerated, its ambiguity has, if anything, been understated. How could a work which was ideologically acceptable to Whig lords like Somers or Chesterfield or Chatham express the political ambitions of a revolutionist like Spence or a Socialist like Hodgskin? How could it serve as the unthinking moral apologia for the American Revolution, if it could be cited after careful reading by a leading New York politician as the ground for the illegitimacy of such a revolution?[2] All

before 31 December 1775, a wide variety of manuscript sources (particularly those which bear upon the reading of students at the colonial colleges), and an analysis of most surviving American library catalogues, private or institutional, and booksellers' lists, manuscript or printed before 1780), that the American story, as still in general enunciated today, is largely false and, where not actually false, frequently highly misleading. I have discussed these points in an extended article, 'The Politics of Locke in England and America in the Eighteenth Century', in *John Locke: Problems and Perspectives*, ed. J. W. Yolton (Cambridge, 1969).

1 Noted perceptively by Robert Shackelton in his *Montesquieu: A Critical Biography* (Oxford, 1961), p. 287, n. i. But cf. p. 276, n. v. See the manuscript, Bibliothèque Nationale (réserve), nouvelles acquisitions français, 12832–6, *loc. cit.* For the system of dating the manuscript by the handwritings of Montesquieu's secretaries see Shackleton's study in *Œuvres Complètes de Montesquieu*, ed. André Masson, 3 vols (Nagel edition, Paris, 1950–5), II, xxxv–xliii. I could not have begun to carry out my investigations in the very intricate field of Montesquieu scholarship without the aid of Mr Shackleton's seminal researches and his extraordinary personal kindness; but he should not be held in any way responsible for what might seem to him a rather rash inference.

2 H. C. Van Schaack, *The Life of Peter Van Schaack, Ll D...*(New York, 1842), pp. 54–8.

such puzzles—and these should be understood to be paradigmatic for very many others—must needs be explained by the historical psychology of the reader as much as by the content of the book. But they cannot be explained by the psychology alone.

The ambiguity of its incitement to political action greatly exceeds that of any other work of political theory written in the seventeenth century. It is the degree of definition in the book itself which determines the limits of possible projection. No one, after all, has mistaken the *Leviathan* for an anticipation of John Stuart Mill's *On Liberty*. Yet to read Professor Macpherson, Professor Kendall, Professor Strauss and Mr Gough on the *Two Treatises* is to acquire a picture of works differing almost as widely as these, sharing indeed almost nothing but their title. At best the present study would resolve two different sorts of problem within this incoherence. It would explain how a book could mean so many things to so many people, would set the work within the history of its interpretation, so that the latter could be rendered comprehensible instead of inexplicable. It would also set it inside its own history, the specific focus of Locke's mind at the times of the composition of the work, in so far as we know this, so that it can be seen that in the circumstances that prevailed this was the work that Locke would have written.[1] It is a scheme of explanation in which the premises must needs be psychological and sociological (however ineptly) as well as simply conceptual. Most crudely, it is an account of what Locke's political thought was, why it was what it was, why people might (and did) think it to be other than it was. It attempts above all to identify the odd balance of recklessness and cowardice, quietism and radicalism, disingenuousness and sincerity which is at the heart of all Locke's enterprises and

[1] This looks a rather causal claim. I do not mean to suggest that one can establish regularities by the examination of a single instance; rather that by the sustained analysis of particular examples of some complexity one is most likely to discover what sorts of regularities one could in principle establish. What I attempt here is the effort of following the rationality of an individual intellectual project in the specific biographical and historical context in which it bore such rationality. It would be delightful to be able to state the necessary and sufficient conditions for the composition of the *Two Treatises of Government* but such projects, I fear, are hardly as yet available to the psychologist or the sociologist of knowledge, let alone to the historian of seventeenth-century ideas. The notion of following the rationality of an intellectual project, being more abstract, seems more possibly within our grasp.

which is at the same time the condition of his achievement and the blemish which flaws all his efforts. Only when this has been clearly grasped does it become possible to identify the intricate sense in which all those who claimed his mantle were in part correct to do so and how in consequence there could be to him no true Elisha, no wholly authentic inheritor. In order to follow how this flaw arose, it is necessary to begin with the man himself, in fact with the first extended pieces which he wrote.

2

THE DEVELOPING MIND

The first of Locke's writings on politics which remain extant derive a single normative conclusion from a theological axiom. The axiom is simply that there exists a benevolent God who provides a set of sufficient rules for the direction of human beings throughout their lives. The pieces in question are assured and a little insensitive, almost glib—the work of a clever and slightly shallow young man. From this confident beginning Locke's literary career travels a long and subtle journey and its development is rich and sophisticated. It was a career which ended in an extraordinary eminence, which left him in his own lifetime as one of the luminaries of the European intellectual scene and, after his death, as the symbolic forerunner and philosophical foundation of the Enlightenment and of what it has become fashionable to call the Age of the Democratic Revolution. It was a glittering trajectory in social as well as intellectual terms and it made him a figure of substance in the political as well as the learned world, a friend of Pembroke, to whom he dedicated his greatest work, and of Somers and Peterborough, as well as of Sydenham, Boyle and Newton. It was not a smooth ascent, though, and we mistake its meaning when we look upon it too readily from the standpoint of those honoured last years in what John Edwards inimitably called 'the Seraglio'[1] at Oates, surrounded by the adulation of brilliant young men and the flattery of the great. Part of the frailness and contingency of the line can be recaptured simply enough when we recall that we should scarcely know the name today, and care little if we did, had its bearer died, as he well might have, in self-imposed exile in Holland in, say, 1685. In that year he would have been fifty-three, an academic expelled from his post by royal command, an expatriate hanger-on of a dead and discredited politician, a forcibly retired civil servant, a minor intellectual who had published nothing of note.

[1] MS Locke c 23, p. 200. (For the identification see John Harrison and Peter Laslett, *The Library of John Locke*, Oxford Bibliographical Society Publications, N.S. XIII (1965), 8.)

But such a hiatus in the public life of the man is only a crude qualification to the triumphant tone of the story. There are deeper and less trivial strains elsewhere. The career of the mind did not run in any simple parallel with the public life. The glib self-assurance of the brilliant young academic, his pleasure in the use of the mind as a supple and responsive instrument, the ease, control and energy of the writing alter in quality over the years. In some dimensions the assurance increases. The academic learns to live among the great, to play a role in the world of public affairs and to do it with a certain ease—even if the ease was always purchased at a cost. But the gay, self-conscious wit disappears, the language becomes flatter, the tone less controlled. The simple, perfunctorily sketched shapes of the argument begin repeatedly to blur. The closed academic game of definitions and their consequents falters and a more demanding task forces itself forward. The repetitive character of the first writings, the tone of a clever student ensuring the completeness of his exercises, changes to the painful, anxious wrestling of a tired old man to hold the world together with his mind. Display gives way to struggle, ease to a sort of exhausted patience. The confidence of the young man came mostly from the restricted challenges of his environment, the exhaustion of the old man partly from having learnt too much. The progress from the one to the other is dramatically obvious. But the links between them were more than merely biographical and in these links we touch upon some of the most profound structures of Locke's final intellectual achievement. Some of these, a facile constitutionalism, a notably inconsequential treatment of the necessity for a sovereign power, are specific to the political writings. Others, most notably the axiomatic centrality of the purposes of God, dominate the entire intellectual construction. Still others, like the blinkered, relentless exposition of a single argument as the means of resolving a complex dilemma, delineate the shape of each subsequent project. The problem of comprehending the nature of Locke's intellectual life is the problem of grasping the relationship between these rigidities and the achievement which they made possible.

The first two political writings, one in English and one in Latin, are designed as treatments of the same issue. Though they differ somewhat in the formality and systematic quality of their presentation, both expound the single proposition that there does exist an area of religious duty which is not explicitly defined by divine positive law and which it lies within the authority of the magistrate to determine. This purpose of the writings has been finely analysed in Dr Abrams' edition[1] and needs no extended discussion here. What needs to be noted, rather, is the set of premises, implicit and expressed, on which the argument is based. The whole position starts unhesitatingly from the fact of an existing political order which it presumes to be legitimate, but the treatment of this point is astonishingly airy. It is claimed as axiomatic that the supreme power in any legitimate polity has the right of unrestricted legislative activity (in all religiously indifferent matters)[2] and the English constitution on the restoration of Charles II is treated as a paradigm of legitimacy.[3] But it is quite unclear in the writings whether or not England had had a legitimate government in the preceding eleven years, in the midst of 'our late miseries',[4] or how such a question could be resolved. The highly authoritarian conception of law which is expounded (and held to be applicable to any form of legitimate polity) is combined with the most banal type of constitutionalist cant. The whole idea of legitimacy is left in an entire theoretical vacuum made possible only by the happy historical contingency of Charles II's restoration. This penchant for the formulations of an evasive constitutionalism remains throughout Locke's discussions

[1] *Two Tracts on Government*, ed. Philip Abrams (Cambridge, 1967).

[2] *Ibid.*, Preface, pp. 122–3; English Tract, pp. 125, 129–30, 156–7, 171–2, 175; Latin Tract, pp. 187–8, 192, 194, 197, 198–9, 200–1, 202–3, 205–6.

[3] 'All the *freedom* I can wish my country or myself is to enjoy the *protection* of those *laws* which the prudence and providence of our ancestors established and the happy return of his Majesty hath restored: a body of laws so well composed, that whilst this nation would be content only to be under them they were always sure to be above their neighbours...' (*Ibid.*, Preface, p. 121). Cf. for the continuity claimed above, Locke's letter to Edward Clarke of 8 February 1689, '...the settlement of the nation upon the sure grounds of peace and security...can no way so well be done as by restoring our ancient government; the best possibly that ever was, if taken and put together all of a piece in its original constitution. If this has not been invaded men have done very ill to complain...' (*The Correspondence of John Locke and Edward Clarke*, ed. B. Rand (London, 1927), p. 289). See also *Two Tracts*, preface, pp. 122, 123 (and note by Abrams *loc. cit.*), English Tract, pp. 125–6.

[4] *Ibid.*, English Tract, p. 125. Cf. the difficulties of relating a functionally authoritarian and theologically guaranteed account of human authority to any coherent criteria of legitimacy faced even by Sir Robert Filmer. See chapter 6 below.

of substantive political issues (though it does gradually disappear from the writings on toleration) and it muddies much of the already opaque exposition of the *Second Treatise*. But never again is it employed with such nonchalance to evade such fundamental issues.

But there are more important continuities between these writings and their successors.[1] The argument for the extremely wide scope of political authority is presented as a consequence of the relationship between God and the created universe, a functional prerequisite for the execution of God's purposes for man.[2] This forms the basic structure of the argument and, while numerous descriptive statements about human behaviour appear in the exposition, they serve the function of explicating the reasonableness of the divine prescriptions in the form in which these apply to sinful men, rather than act as an alternative basis for these prescriptions. There is a certain dialectical necessity for this, since the subject matter is the extent of political authority in religious affairs, and the implications of the fact should not be exaggerated. God appears throughout much more as a guarantor of order, an effective focus of repression, than as a source of a particular sort of valuable experience. What is made most obvious is His tactical availability for Locke's purposes—not the veneration He might be supposed to elicit. But it would be a mistake to sneer at the hypocrisy of such ready manipulation; for to do so supposes altogether too much of a capacity in the young man to stand outside the boundaries of his own experience. The memory of barren political instability, the sense of success achieved by merit in his own life, the triviality of the constant bickering over the forms of religious worship, and the degree to which the sole language available in his environment for the training of the emotions was the language of Christian homiletic,[3] would make

[1] I have not distinguished between the two works in my exposition because the differences between them (which are largely in manner of presentation and in points of detail) do not affect the considerations which I wish to advance. The differences are excellently treated by Philip Abrams, especially in *John Locke as a Conservative* (unpublished Cambridge Ph.D. dissertation, 1961).

[2] 'Voluit deus inter homines societatem ordinem et regimen esse, quam rempublicam nominamus, in omni republica debet esse aliqua suprema potestas sine qua res publica esse non potest', etc. (*Two Tracts*, Latin Tract, p. 201).

[3] The only other rhetoric which we know Locke to have employed at this time, the teasing, fantasticated array of conceits with which his relationships with his young

the assimilation of all human responsibilities to the disciplined and deferential performance of Christian duties a simple one. The virtues of the way of life would be defined not by the keenness and splendour of its own satisfactions but by the unpleasing contours of the disorder which it rejected. It was the crudity of the historical situation and not just the manipulative insincerities of the individual which gave such bland political utility to his religious and moral sentiments.

It is God who constitutes the order of law which instructs men in their duties at all points in the world. But the duties are made actual, converted from hypothetical aesthetic aspirations to effective sanctions for conduct, by the institutions of political communities. Men because of their historical lapse are notoriously sinful. Though this regrettable attribute in no way affects the set of substantive moral duties which the law of God prescribes for them, it does impair the degree to which they are likely autonomously to respond to these, and hence has consequences for the ways in which this law is articulated in the world. The cognitive insouciance and the insubordinate disposition of fallen men[1] necessitate an elaborate structure of human authorities to bring this law to bear upon their diverse situations. Some areas of conduct, those covered by divine positive law, revealed religious truth, do not require (or indeed permit) authoritative human determination. But all other dimensions of human action, because of their powerful tendency to promote dissension and disorder, must be subjected to univocal control. Human society is subjected to constant and violent centrifugal forces; and of these religious dispute is the most dangerous precisely because of its moral plausibility.[2] Social control is the central problem of politics

Oxford friends, and more especially with women, were conducted, seems better designed to hold emotion at a respectful distance than give it too concrete an embodiment. If the deployment of religious notions for the purposes of political suppression seems often disagreeably bland, it is certainly harder to feel the careful formality or self-congratulatory pyrotechnics of the private correspondence as sincere and deeply committing.

[1] *Two Tracts*, English Tract, pp. 137, 149, 153–6, 158–9, 160–1, 169–70; Latin Tract, p. 198.

[2] *Ibid.*, English Tract, esp.: 'almost all those tragical revolutions which have exercised Christendom these many years have turned upon this hinge...there hath been no design so wicked which hath not worn the vizor of religion, nor rebellion which hath not been so kind to itself as to assume the specious name of reformation,

because of men's inherently rebellious nature. Toleration cannot be conceded as a religious principle because *any* exemption of religious practice from human authority can be made an excuse for terrestrial misbehaviour on the pretext of conscience. None of these specifically political precepts are themselves explicated as *a priori* deductions from divine law.[1] They are merely treated as empirical concomitants of the problem of making this law operational among recalcitrant human beings. Intolerance is not touted as a religious *virtue* but toleration is rejected as a religious right because such a concession would be incompatible with those rights necessarily vested in human authorities for the control of men's iniquities.

There are some important consequences of this position. It makes inquiries into the origins of government, that nagging historico-philosophical preoccupation of the inheritors of the legalism of the decaying feudal order, wholly irrelevant. The question of these contractual, patriarchal or directly divine origins does not receive any serious examination because the contractual theory, the formulation traditionally most threatening to Locke's position, is effectively insulated by the rest of the analysis from any practical implications.[2] The contractual theory is treated most extensively because it is the theory which holds most potential embarrassment. It may also be[3] that it was the theory which Locke himself adopted; but the texts in their rather inadvertent handling of the issue scarcely show more than Locke's awareness of this embarrassing potential. The hypothetical treat-

proclaiming a design either to supply the defects or correct the errors of religion ...none ever went about to ruin the *state* but with pretence to build the *temple*, all those disturbers of public quiet being wise enough to lay hold on religion as a shield which if it could not defend their cause was best like to secure their credit, and gain as well pity to their ruin as partisans to their success, men finding no cause that can so rationally draw them to hazard this life, or compound for the dangers of a war as that which promises them a better, all other arguments, of liberty, country, relations, glory being to be enjoyed only in this life can give but small encouragements to a man to endanger that and to improve their present enjoyments a little, run themselves into the danger of an irreparable loss of all' (p. 160).

[1] Despite the fact that they are asserted to *be* such, asserted to be consequences of the positive prescription to obey the powers that be, set out in Romans, XIII; and despite the fact that their moral authority, their obligatory force, derives from their role in promoting God's purposes for man.

[2] *Two Tracts*, English Tract, p. 125, etc.

[3] *Ibid.*, pp. 25–7.

ment *may* have been a strategy to evade the expression of heterodox opinion, but it seems more likely to have been intended simply to lend the greatest polemical force to the argument.

This evasive quality is not confined to the treatment of the origins of government; it extends also to its form. It is not clear whether the insistence that the nature of political authority is unaffected by its constitutional form is in fact an assertion of the equal legitimacy of every existing political order or whether it too is merely a device for maximizing the polemical purchase of the arguments. The assertion of the central role of the sovereign legislative in government perhaps suggests the former. Certainly it gives the discussion a more functional analysis of legitimacy than Filmer, for instance, would have appreciated. The assertion of the ruler's duty to execute the interests of the subjects,[1] and the assertion that security of property depends upon the efficacy of the sovereign are common to both authors,[2] merely, in this form, the conventional banalities, though they were later to become the axis of a very different Lockean position. But the character of the discussion, the specific quality of the legalism displayed, is already more academic and theological in tone and farther from the historical nexus of English constitutionalism than in the works of Filmer. It stems from the ecclesiastical and intellectual preoccupations of the university, not the social and legal concerns of the county community of the gentry. This certainly does not make any more appealing the ease with which all religious beliefs which imply a duty of disobedience to prevailing regulations about public behaviour are discounted. But it gives more sense of the social locus, that intricate and parochial historical conditioning which made all the constitutionalist clichés so effortlessly available to the young academic. When all the problems which a man is set can be solved, and most of the rewards which the world provides for him earned, by the manipulation of intellectual categories, it is easy to learn a certain glibness about the relation of these to the world. Because nothing in Locke's life had involved him in the

[1] *Ibid.*, Preface, p. 119; English Tract, pp. 126, 136, 137, 145, 150, 151, 152, 156, 162; Latin Tract, pp. 191–2, 206; and cf. chapter 6 below.

[2] *Ibid*, *passim*, for the dependence of human security on effective political authority, and English Tract, p. 138, Latin Tract, p. 199, for the complete dependence of property on positive law. Cf. chapter 6 below.

world of political manipulation, the world in which problems are solved by the controlling of men, there seemed nothing odd in the notion that one could meet the demands of social action by the exposition of a scholastic theorem. And the conceptual peculiarity of such a notion would be even more submerged by the sensitivity with which the theorem articulated all those values by which Locke himself had learned to live: order, learning, diligence, control, a comfortable and well-esteemed place in the world well protected from the storms outside. The touchy, exhibitionist,[1] ambitious young man who knew the costs of his own role would hardly feel the ambiguities of the values which gave to it its rewards. It is easy to see how all claims to religious toleration, all claims of subjects against the state, are ruled out of account. It is not by the assertion of one's idiosyncratic needs that a man can rise in safety but rather by their relentless control—and one does not readily see the point of the values one is trained to deny. What is needed above all if a man is to make sense out of this structure of repression, the demand which he must make of the world, is not exuberant and unrestricted emotional indulgence but merely stability. And so settlement is the great aim[2] and authority the mode of its attainment. Religion as such appears only as a coercive, never as a creative force. The yearning is for peace and the strategy is the assertion of a symmetrical order of repression.

[1] 'This John Lock, was a man of turbulent spirit, clamorous and never contented. The club wrot and took notes from the mouth of their master who sat at the upper end of a table, but the said J. Lock scorn's to do it; so that while every man besides of the club were writing, he would be prating and troublesome.' (*The Life and Times of Antony Wood*, ed. Andrew Clark (Oxford, 1892), I, 472.) Wood is here commenting on Locke's behaviour at Peter Stahl's lectures on chemistry. Dewhurst's qualification, that Locke's boredom may have reflected simply the fact that he knew most of what Stahl was teaching already (Kenneth Dewhurst, *John Locke (1632-1704): Physician and Philosopher. A Medical Biography* (London, 1963), p. 10) hardly affects the assessment of the personality portrayed in this vignette.

[2] *Two Tracts*, Preface, pp. 118, 119–20, 121–2; Latin Tract, pp. 186–7.

3

THE 'ESSAYS ON THE LAW OF NATURE'

With the *Essays on the Law of Nature* more interesting developments begin. The shift from a polemical to a more academic purpose allows a greater speculative freedom. It is no longer necessary to subsume all conceptual possibilities under a single practical precept, and the resulting relaxation generates a more dispassionate and discriminating inquiry. It becomes easier, too, to pick out the more idiosyncratic features of Locke's picture of the world, his own peculiar balance of assurances and anxieties, and to sense how this constricts or enhances his thought. The movement of the pieces is internal, a development from a conventional muddle to a more poised and differentiated intellectual confidence. They are exploratory, moments in the activity of thinking, and not merely apodictic. They do, that is to say, actually *develop* a position, instead of merely embellishing a single argument. In fact, in the course of their composition, Locke changes his mind about an issue which was to become one of the major themes of his thought—indeed, precisely to set him that general problem which his later works were predominantly attempting to resolve. The foundation of the law of nature in the general consent of men, while difficult to reconcile with the thrust of Locke's thought from the beginning,[1] does make an appearance in the rather off-hand listing of its grounds at the beginning of the *Essays*. But the text is altered in the course of composition and the fifth essay is devoted to a refutation of this argument.[2]

Just what Locke's intentions were in writing these *Essays* we do not know with any great precision. At the time when he wrote the first *Tracts* we learn in a letter from his friend Gabriel

[1] See the constant stress on men's domination by custom and their moral nescience in *Two Tracts on Government*, *passim*.

[2] *Essays on the Law of Nature*, ed. W. Von Leyden (Oxford, 1954), cf. p. 282 with p. 112. The revised position is stated at pp. 176–8.

Towerson[1] that they had been considering together the ways in which the law of nature can be known. We also know that, as Censor at Christ Church, Locke was obliged to lecture to undergraduates, presumably on ethics.[2] Yet how far the interest in ethical theory arose directly out of the first writings on toleration, how far they constituted a project which the problems raised by this first enterprise had made mandatory, is obscure.[3] But the issue is in some fashion a central one. From the *Essays* onwards it is possible to represent the development of Locke's thought as the unfolding of an internal dialectic, not, of course, in a biographical vacuum, but with all its varied historical cruces to be resolved within a unitary intellectual context. To some extent the reasons for this appearance are quasi-literary, a matter of eliciting a set of particular coherences from a highly indeterminate matrix. And the initial traverse which we are here asserting to be problematical certainly represents no crude doctrinal or political break (that comes perhaps between 1660 and 1667 but scarcely between 1660 and 1664). What happens in it is, rather, an autonomous extension and elaboration of Locke's intellectual development or perhaps, more extravagantly, a transformation from the pragmatic deployment of an intellect to an authentically intellectual enterprise, from politics to philosophy. In part this impression results from the enclosed and insulated character of the first writings, their sustained exposition of a single theme, a theme effortlessly located in the most rigid cadre of theological and social

1 Towerson to Locke, n.d. MS Locke c 22 p. 3. The relevant section is printed in *Essays*, pp. 8–9. Von Leyden dates conjecturally to 1660. Abrams prefers 1661 (*Two Tracts*, p. 15). Further on Locke's relationship with Towerson, see *Essays*, pp. 82–5.

2 See his valedictory speech as Censor of Moral Philosophy, *ibid.*, pp. 220–42, and also pp. 11–12.

3 Von Leyden, rather disappointingly, does not concern himself with precisely this issue, beyond noting the fact that Locke had the *Essays* recopied into a notebook dated 1663 (a dangerous method of inference with Locke—cf. MS Film. 77) and citing the Towerson correspondence (which can hardly shed very precise light on Locke's intentions in 1664). His treatment of the relationship between these *Essays* and Locke's other writings is superb; but it is a relationship of doctrine, not one of intellectual genesis, with which he is concerned. On the latter topic his preoccupation in the traditional manner with sources and influences is not always very illuminating. It is only just to note, though, that beyond the critical Towerson letter (see above, n. 1) we have virtually no evidence for Locke's *intentions* outside the texts themselves.

convention. Far more than because of the rigidity of the expository style itself, it was because this line of argument needed so little intellectual imagination that there is so little sense of intellectual exploration in the pieces. He scarcely needed to use his mind to set out the theme, with the whole array of traditional English social values to say it for him. It is hardly conceivable that they were written to resolve Locke's own mind about the issue. But in the *Essays* we do undoubtedly see something of the sort. More than in any other of Locke's works, with the single exception of the great *Essay concerning Human Understanding* itself, they present the mind at work and not merely the finished results of such work. The stimulus for this sudden extension of his range and ambition may have been the conversations with his friends or the requirements of his academic post or it may have been the development of his own private intellectual puzzlement. From the point of view of the result it does not greatly matter which, but the contours of the story are hazier here than elsewhere. If we could see them more clearly, we might understand much which is now obscure.

Still, if this lack of definition in his purposes is puzzling, the groping quality of the performance must not be exaggerated. It was no searching investigation into substantive morality, no deep and Kierkegaardian inquiry into how men should make their lives. We are all assumed to know that already. Justice (no theft), chastity (no fornication), honesty (no lies), the moral virtues touted, can have offered no surprises to the most unthinking of contemporary students—and even *they* are less commended than assumed, indeed merely mentioned as examples of moral duties. Even the very existence of a binding morality does not seem to demand much defence. The ground that we have for believing in a law of nature is the existence of God. And the grounds we have for believing in the existence of God (never one of Locke's more impressively orchestrated themes) seem flaccid in the extreme. It is not here certainly that the authentic intellectual searching comes. The argument is intellectually perfunctory and emotionally flat. But however placid one's allegiance to the values of the Christ Church authorities, there is an irreducible intellectual problem in the question of how one knows these values to be correct. It is not in the ethical question of how to live or the theological question of what God, if any, there is, but only in the epistemological question of how one can *know* something to be good or the psychological question of how men *do* derive their moral values that Locke's thought begins to be more adventurous.

These questions are rather insecurely separated in the writing. The first is really treated thoroughly only in a negative way. Two common accounts of how men come to know the obligatory character and the content of moral duties, through inscription, a sort of unitary genetic heritage, or tradition, are shown to be inadequate. But the account of how one can know the obligatory force of the law of nature through rational reflection upon sense-experience is once again predominantly theological in its argument and deals only very tangentially with the question of *what* one would know oneself obliged to do as the result of this devout reflection. Neither tradition (because it is imperfect as a criterion) nor the general consent of mankind (because it doesn't exist) can tell us what the law of nature prescribes. But by extended reflection in the right frame of mind[1] one can come to know what one's duty is; and one's duty, unsurprisingly, seems to consist of a few simple maxims and a highly differentiated exercise in obedience. One barely needs to know for practical purposes what the law of nature prescribes; all one needs to know is whom to obey—and the answer to that question in *Restoration* England is seldom very puzzling. The obligatory authority of the law of nature is mediated through a hierarchy of terrestrial authorities, and their derived legislative authority, as kings, parents, or masters,[2] tells us most

1 And just possibly, though this issue is never explicitly faced here, in the right country (? a Christian country). It is quite consistent to believe that the law of nature is only likely to be known as obligatory at all widely in a Christian country, even though it could in principle be known anywhere and is in fact obligatory everywhere. This is the position which Locke sustains in the *Reasonableness of Christianity* (1695) and nothing is said in the *Essays* which is incompatible with such an expectation about pre-Christian men's cognitive capacities in the field of ethics. However, the *Reasonableness* is precisely concerned with the overwhelming significance of this depressed expectation: and there is no sign that Locke realized its significance with any acuteness as early as 1664, even if the problem is raised in principle by the ever-handy Brazil and Saldanha Bay. Cf. *Essays*, p. 174, with *An Essay concerning Human Understanding*, ed. J. W. Yolton (London, 1961), I, IV, §§ 8 and 12, and *Two Treatises of Government* II, § 14 (first state of first edition; see Laslett's collation, p. 474).

2 '... Deus cujus omnia sunt partem imperii sui in aliquem transtulit et jus imperandi tribuit, ut primogenitis et monarchis' (*Essays*, p. 184). See also pp. 186, 202, and for

of what we need to know about how to act. The *Essays* would not have helped greatly to resolve people's consciences. Their briskness of tone suggests a view in which few men have much excuse to need their consciences resolved. It is all a long way, in its lack of urgency, from Great Tew or even the carefully copied Bishop Sanderson.

But if there is little sense of strain in the literary objectives of the writing, there is a great deal more in the picture which it suggests of the nature of human existence. The dominating character of the human condition, the experiential situation in which men find themselves, is one of internal tension and external conflict. Why this should be so is not made clear (the presumable theological explanation, the Fall, receives no emphasis).[1] The essential unease is presented simply as a fact. Economically the human condition is one of scarcity, and consequently one in which men's interests intrinsically and permanently conflict.[2] Their natural attitude towards one another may not be one of hostility, but the duty of right action is experienced by them as coercive, not as instinctually satisfying.[3] Were it not for one

the relativist problem in this context see p. 170. In general see pp. 118, 126, 180–6, 196.

[1] The precise meaning of the Fall of Man for the relationship between ethical values and existing human psychology is of overwhelming significance for a Christian natural-law ethic, with the particular cognitive problems which this poses. Locke's sole reference to the issue (in the *Essays*, p. 138) merely points out that the Augustinian position does not in any way help to solve the epistemological problems of deriving a coherent natural law from man's conflicting moral intuitions. This demonstration gives no clear indication of what Locke thought of the relationship between the ethical content of the law of nature and the condition of prelapsarian man, though cf. the conventional formula 'Aeterna sunt hujus legis vincula et humano generi coaeva, simul nascuntur et simul intereunt' (*ibid.* p. 192). This suggests a chronological relation but hardly clarifies the psychological one. In later writings he does seem to assume that human conflict derives from the Fall of Man (MS Locke c 28, fo. 113v) but it is not clear how this doctrine relates to that expounded in the *Reasonableness of Christianity*. Locke's interpretation of the doctrine of original sin changed in the course of writing this work (MS Locke c 27, p. 101) and the degree of muddle which he exhibits over this embarrassing theme indicates how difficult he found it to reconcile with the rest of his thought.

[2] *Essays*, pp. 210, 212, esp.: 'neque cuivis licet nisi per alterius damna ditescere' (p. 210). It is, of course, Locke's reversal of his position on this issue, made most explicit during his final revisions of the *Two Treatises*, which has enabled that work to be presented as 'the incarnation of the spirit of capitalism'. See *Two Treatises* II, 37, ll. 10–29 and notes.

[3] See *Essays*, pp. 162 and 282 (deleted), but cf. 168, 170, 200 and the more vehement characterizations in Abrams (1967).

particular feature of their situation they would exist in a condition of total anomie.[1]

This single feature is the existence of God. From this one great fact all else follows.[2] Roughly what seems to follow (and the word is not used in any approbation of the rigour of the logical proceedings) is the contemporary English (Christian) morality. Because this is what follows[3] we can see that the law of nature, rationally understood ethical truth, is not reducible to the practice of self-preservation or to an individualist hedonism.[4]

The world belongs to God and its right disposal is determinable solely by his authority. There can be apparent conflicts of duty engendered by his intervention in history—just as there can be apparent conflicts of duty within a hierarchy of terrestrial authority[5]—but these indicate at most that the ethical quality is not intrinsic to a particular piece of behaviour but merely to the observance of a particular command.[6] Though natural law is rationally intelligible and possibly even demonstrative,[7] its determination is essentially carried out for the most part through a hierarchy of authorities, rather than through an order of morally obligatory acts.[8]

God, the guarantor of this order of values, is also the epistemological key to its understanding. A predominantly naturalistic ethic can be overwhelmingly relativist without much cost. The

1 *Essays*, pp. 108, 118–20, 188, 200.

2 *Ibid.*, pp. 108, 132, 152, 156, 172–4, 182–8, 200–2, etc.

3 The inference is, of course, very informal. In form it is almost completely open-ended, excluding merely perhaps Hobbesian ethics, among those ethical positions which Locke saw himself as addressing.

4 *Essays*, pp. 126–8, 180 ('si sui ipsius cura et conservatio sit omnis hujus legis fons et principium, virtus non tam officium hominis videretur quam commodum, nec homini quid honestum erit nisi quod utile, neque legis hujus observatio tam munus nostrum esset et debitum ad quod natura obligamur quam privilegium et beneficium ad quod utilitate ducimur...'), 204–14.

5 *Ibid.* p. 202. It is an axiom that there cannot be *real* conflicts (see p. 212).

6 *Ibid.* pp. 200–2.

7 *Ibid.* pp. 198–200 and see Von Leyden's searching discussion of the implications of this, pp. 54–8.

8 'plurima legis hujus praecepta diversas hominum inter se relationes respiciunt et in iis fundantur...' (*Essays*, p. 196). The very distinctive features of an ethic based upon (rationally intelligible) divine command and their curiously continued dominance of much contemporary ethical thought is brilliantly brought out by G. E. M. Anscombe in 'Modern Moral Philosophy', *Philosophy*, XXXIII, 124 (January 1958), 1–19.

only pressing questions which it poses arise over its obligatory force. But, given the existence of God, a theologically based ethic does have a certain *a priori* stability. In such an ethic ethical judgement is clearly a cognitive matter. The critical distinction between knowledge and belief is easy to maintain, though just as difficult to indicate with any definition. There is also less possibility that the epistemology of ethics will collapse dispiritedly into mere psychology. The psychology of morals does make its duly subordinate appearance in these *Essays*, in the form already favoured in the first writings. Men are predictably loath to observe those moral norms which they do recognize as such and there is no reliable consistency from society to society in their recognition of even the most fundamental norms.

But the central preoccupation of the *Essays* is this issue of just how one can *know* the content of the law of nature. Several reassuring answers have to be discarded. One cannot know it as an innate idea because this conveniently unitary genetic endowment is simply not to be found reflected in the consciousness of men as they are. Even more plainly one cannot learn from a non-existent uniformity of moral sentiment or opinion.[1] One cannot know it through tradition because the acceptance of a tradition is either simply a belief (and hence not a possible ground of *knowledge*) or a belief judged by certain criteria (in which case the cognitive status comes from the application of the criteria, not from the belief itself). It is impossible for traditions to be self-validating.[2] The way in which knowledge is in fact held to come, the operation of reason upon sense-experience, is promising enough but its mechanics are not sketched with great clarity.[3] The problem of relating this epistemological mechanism and the theological guarantee of a stable ethic was to remain the central feature of Locke's ethical thought and it was one which he never went any great distance towards solving.[4] But at this point it did not appear especially problematic. The assertion of the law of nature was the assertion of the existence of an order of value. It was not an

[1] *Essays*, pp. 136–44; 160–78.

[2] *Ibid.* pp. 126–30.

[3] *Ibid.* pp. 130–4; 146–58.

[4] For the excellent reason, among others, that it happens not to be soluble. See, classically, David Hume, *Dialogues concerning Natural Religion*, ed. Norman Kemp Smith (2nd edition, London, 1947).

attempt to manipulate that order. It needed no greater degree of definition because it had so exclusively a philosophical (or at the rudest a pedagogic) rather than a practical purpose. In the first *Tracts* what was being affirmed was an 'official' ethic of authority. In the *Essays* this ethic still sufficed. It was only when he set himself explicitly to challenge some component of this traditional ethic that the epistemological issue was to become acute. Dialectically, the problem which it posed was one of extreme delicacy and it is scarcely surprising that Locke should have gone to some lengths in his subsequent writings to separate both in place (different books) and in manner (the substantive arguments were all published anonymously) substantive ethical arguments from discussions of the cognitive basis of ethics.

There is no reason to suppose that he ever concluded that there were discrepancies in principle between the two operations but his successive efforts to elaborate a convincing and determinable account of the cognitive basis of ethics proved increasingly abortive. In the course of his attempts to contrive this integration, he elaborated a number of subtle variations. Yet in one respect they all showed a striking continuity. Whenever he began to sketch out the contours of an ethic and searched for the fundamental form which it must take, the touchstone which he set up was always the relation between Creator and created. Somehow all human values were to be elicited from this inexhaustible matrix. The abstracted and rather emotional religious focus was a powerful guarantee for the existence of a moral order, but it hardly expedited a precise delineation of this order. In this crude and ineluctable caesura, we can see very sharply how completely moral experience was, for Locke, a derivative of religious experience, how wholly lacking in autonomy of value he saw and felt the human condition to be.

4

THE 'ESSAY ON TOLERATION'

Between the composition of the *Essays on the Law of Nature* and that of the *Two Treatises* Locke's life changed in many different ways. It is not here appropriate nor would it for these purposes be particularly illuminating to examine these developments at length. But the main axis of the change is of the greatest importance. It can be identified with some assurance in the geographical transition from Oxford to Thanet House and in the occupational transition from academic medicine to political and administrative service in the Shaftesbury household and thus at times in the national government. The academic world was deserted, at least as major focus of interest and activity, for the diplomatic and then for the political. Interpreting the world as an activity was henceforth always to be conducted as a part of the attempt, however modestly, to change it. It was not that the academic roles, the studentship at Christ Church, the medical research, the investigation of the cognitive basis of morals were abandoned. Rather, their rationale was subtly altered and the purchase of his mind upon the world correspondingly transformed. We do not really know just what caused this change. There is a good deal of circumstantial evidence and some points are clear enough—most notably Locke's lack of enthusiasm for remaining in a fully academic and more especially an ecclesiastical role. It is also clear, more abstractly and evasively, that there is some sort of harmony between the venture from the academy into diplomacy and the world of politics and his shift from the rigid and authoritarian legalism of the first political writings to the more dominantly prudential emphasis of the *Essay on Toleration*. But the evasion here cannot simply be ignored, for it embodies the most urgent of all the explanatory problems over Locke's intellectual life. For more than fifteen years Locke belonged to the household of Antony Ashley Cooper, the first Earl of Shaftesbury. It was while he was in Shaftesbury's entourage that he wrote what we may, with a certain looseness, regard as the first drafts of his three greatest works, the *Essay concerning Human Understanding*, the *Two Treatises of Government* and the *Epistola de Tolerantia*.[1] Two of these expound a particular type of 'liberal' political position,[2] a type which in the world of political action during these fifteen years was advocated by Shaftesbury himself. Yet all that we know of Locke's political opinions before he entered Shaftesbury's service was sharply opposed to this position. Why then did he join the Shaftesbury entourage and why did he change his opinions? Was the first a consequence of the second or the second a consequence of the first? To put it at its most offensive, are we to see Locke's 'liberal politics' as simply a fortuitous mode of upward social mobility or are we to see what was eventually his undoubted social ascent as a 'deserved' consequence of his devotion to 'liberal politics'? Was it a purely arbitrary historical accident (or a natural, non-ideological, consequence of his west country connections and background) that it was Shaftesbury's service that he entered or was this a mode of social ascent made independently inviting by his initial and considered ideological affiliations? This is a startlingly crude question, involving the most profound issues of continuity and authenticity in Locke's intellectual life. It is raised here in this simple-minded form because we do not at the moment apparently (and may never) know the answer to it.

Towards the end of Shaftesbury's life and after his death this issue may lose much of its salience, and we may agree flaccidly both that Shaftesbury was a brilliant, sophisticated, and inordinately persuasive man, a *politique par excellence*, and that the bulk of Locke's collected works, being written after Shaftesbury's death in 1683, can hardly be expropriated from their author. A man's intellectual ambience is all very interesting but it never wrote *that* many pages for him. But then it is not merely agency which is at issue at this point. We can accept, without its altering the force of most expository hypotheses, both that it made an

1 The 1667 *Essay on Toleration* bears no direct textual relationship to the 1689 work. But it does contain the central argument of the latter and there does not seem to be significantly less thematic continuity between it and the latter than between the drafts *A* and *B* of the *Essay* (ed. B. Rand (Cambridge, Mass., 1931) and ed. R. Aaron and J. Gibb (Oxford, 1936)) and the completed form of the *Essay*.

2 For an account of how barren this ascription of liberalism is as a mode of explanation of Locke's political ideas and of how unilluminating it must necessarily be as an analytical category, see below, chapter 15.

important difference to Locke's intellectual life that he was employed by Shaftesbury[1] and that it was very much Locke's own intellectual life that he scribbled out over so many pages. The latter is, indeed, self-evident. But when we recur to 1667 and ask just why it was that Locke wrote in the fashion that he did in defence of toleration, the opacity returns.

The precise balance of causality and rationality remains obscure. Surely, we might say, this is just the way Locke would have 'expressed' Shaftesbury's policy—and perhaps we might add that doubtless most of Shaftesbury's intimate acquaintances, for even so short a time as Locke himself had then been such, would have come to see the force of his viewpoint on this issue. But whether in Locke's own reflections the categories of the *Tracts* and the *Essays* had already undergone this metamorphosis in the face of the Clarendon Code[2] is still unclear. We do not know, to insist again, whether what we owe to Locke's role as 'kept intellectual' is simply the publication of the various books in their eventual form, the availability to us of his perspective on the world in all its definition, or whether it is indeed the very shape and structure displayed in this perspective. And it is no mitigation of this ignorance to claim that there was in Locke's past reflection the potential basis for this reassessment of the world. The fact that someone's views are incoherent at one time can never be a sufficient explanation of the fact that they become more coherent at another time. Many men's ideas always remain totally disordered and, as we insist throughout, Locke's own ideas remain for his entire life profoundly and exotically incoherent. No explanation of why the older Locke adopted his 'liberal' incoherence in place of his earlier 'conservative' incoherence can be purely conceptual. To have an explanation of this transition, it is necessary to make claims within the severely causal domain of psychology. Since such an explanation, at least at the moment, seems

[1] As Laslett and Viano have urged so powerfully. See *Two Treatises of Government*, pp. 25–37, and Peter Laslett, 'Locke and the first Earl of Shaftesbury', *Mind*, no. 241 (January 1952), pp. 89–92; Carlo Augusto Viano, *John Locke: Dal Razionalismo all'Illuminismo* (Turin, 1960), esp. pp. 180–209, and 'I rapporti tra Locke e Shaftesbury e le teorie economiche di Locke', *Rivista di Filosofia*, XLIX (1958), 69–84.

[2] Philip Abrams (*Two Tracts on Government*, pp. 30–6) stresses the very specific context of the first writings. For a more detailed treatment see his *John Locke as a Conservative*, unpublished Ph.D. dissertation (Cambridge, 1961).

inaccessible, we must insist that we have no adequate and established explanation of why Locke should have become the particular sort of liberal that he did become.

But even if no full account can be given of what Locke was doing in altering his position, there is little obscurity about the ways in which he did alter it. The first two political works expound the argument that the sociological conditions of human existence necessitate there being a locus of unrestricted authority over all human behaviour, answerable to God alone. This authoritarian theorem is also presented as a scriptural injunction but the main structure of argument for it is, at least hypothetically, utilitarian. And the utility of this power is alleged to lie precisely in its lack of terrestrial accountability. It is only because it is not in this way answerable directly to the human beings over whom it is exercised that it can do them this service. What Locke does in the *Essay on Toleration* is simply to reverse the purchase of this argument. Instead of considering the extent of the behavioural domain over which the power may be employed (which remains identical) he examines which instances of its exertion are intrinsically legitimate. The criteria for its legitimate exercise must be logically congruous with the general ground of its existence. Attention is shifted from the issue of what subjects are obliged to do (obey) to the question of what obligations of obedience a ruler is justified in exacting. Neither the logical structure of the theory nor its implications for the legitimate behaviour of subjects has altered greatly but its practical persuasions and its moral alignment seem very different. The first writings were concerned with the affirmation of a structure of authority and clearly presupposed that the assertion of the rights of authority was a real way of handling the problems of politics. The new work sees the problems of politics as problems of 'policy', as issues in the effective manipulation of the world. Both presuppose that the correct answer to a moral question is an important component in effective manipulation of the world but, in the second, issues of right merge readily into those of prudence. Moral reflection is conducted in a more intimate and relaxed relationship with a world open to manipulation. If the first writings often seem an exercise in the exorcising of a nightmare of social disintegration, the new *Essay* seems altogether more detached and bland in its handling of the moral issues. It remains oddly poised between the committed authoritarian rigidity of the first writings and the committed 'liberal' rigidity of the *Epistola de Tolerantia*, as though for Locke at this time not very much was at stake in this issue, as though it was genuinely, if temporarily, an issue of policy rather than an issue of right, a separation which, because he wrote increasingly of issues of right, it is easy to lose sight of later in his life, but which remains at all points of the last importance if we wish to understand why he thought as he did.

But, even if prudence does have this salience, the main argument remains also legalistic. It *is* a dispute over 'titles'[1] as well as a debate about prudential action; and the form of the argument mediates skilfully between these two disparate themes. It begins from a teleological account of the nature of government and not from a structure of existing authority. Having in this way based the authority of government on its particular utility, it simply restricts this authority to instances of such utility. Indeed it restricts its title to interfere more specifically and more drastically than any other piece of Locke's writing—going so far as to designate any effort by the state to enforce personal morality as 'injustice'.[2] It is perhaps hardly surprising that this, the most extreme 'liberal' doctrine to be found in all his writings, should occur in the last among his sustained political pieces in which it is axiomatic that the community outside the structure of political authority is morally inert and devoid of any right to take autonomous political initiatives. But the fact that he does not in later works point up the implication so sharply does not necessarily mean that he did not continue to hold precisely the same position.

In this form, in any case, the purpose of political society seemed

[1] H. R. Fox Bourne, *Life of John Locke* (London, 1876), I, 174, 186, etc. Locke uses 'title', 'claim', 'right', and even at times 'liberty' as synonyms throughout this work.

[2] Fox Bourne, *John Locke*, pp. 176–7 and cf. 181–2. But it is not entirely clear how serious a restriction Locke intended this to be, cf.: '...toleration conduces no otherwise to the settlement of a government than as it makes the majority of one mind, and encourages virtue in all, which is done by making and executing strict laws concerning virtue and vice, but making the terms of church communion as large as may be' (p. 194).

startlingly simple and intelligible. Without political society men could not live together in peace and security.[1] Hence the end of political society must be the maintenance of peace and security. Any exercise of political power over individual behaviour which did not threaten peace or security was an exercise of power unjustified by the end for which that power existed. In other words, it was an illegitimate exercise of power. Whatever the origin of political power and indeed whatever its form, absolutist or constitutionalist, all the theoretical possibilities which Locke had been willing previously to contemplate[2] and whatever the mode of its operation, its legitimate *field* of operation, since this depended solely on its end, remained the same. Only if a religious commitment constituted a direct threat to the public peace could a political authority have any right to interfere with it. Beliefs and ways of worship were intrinsically privileged from political interference. Only in so far as they were contaminated by particular subversive human motives could they come within the notice of rightful human authority at all.

But almost any form of overt religious behaviour[3] could under some circumstances constitute a threat to public order.[4] Since the political sovereign must be the judge of the threatening character of the behaviour and since he is not directly accountable to individuals and indeed not necessarily accountable to anyone but God[5] for his behaviour, the restrictive definition of the purpose of political society may seem a flimsy protection.

To sharpen this analysis Locke pursues a further line of argu-

[1] 'For, if men could live peaceably and quietly together, without uniting under certain laws, and growing into a commonwealth, there would be no need at all of magistrates or politics, which were only made to preserve men in this world from the fraud and violence of one another; so that what was the end of erecting of government ought alone to be the measure of its proceeding' (Fox Bourne, *John Locke*, I, 174).

[2] Cf. *ibid.* I, 174–5 with *Two Tracts*, pp. 125–6, and with MS Film. 77, side 2 (not paginated by Locke). Cf. MS Locke c 28, fo. 157v: 'Jus paternum/Consensus Populi/Arma.'

[3] It is unusual for men to be persecuted for beliefs which make literally no difference to overt behaviour, it being impossible to identify them as holding the beliefs except through their behaviour.

[4] Burning oneself to death in the Golden Temple at Amritsar being about as seditious conduct as is open to a prominent Indian citizen at the moment. It is the context of an action and not merely its behavioural content which defines its quality.

[5] Fox Bourne, *John Locke*, I, 179, 180–1.

ment which converges on the same conclusion. The end of government is preservation and such of its projects as do not derive from this end have no real legitimacy. But it is not just a contingent sociological matter that government has no intrinsic authority over religious beliefs and observances. Rather, it is a necessary feature of the individual religious predicament that this should be so. Individual religious behaviour, if it is to attain its end, is necessarily defined by subjective conviction. Such conviction cannot in principle be generated by governmental action.[1] Indeed such belief is not causally manipulable at all except by direct divine action.[2] Alterations in overt religious behaviour procured by the threat of political coercion and unaccompanied by subjective conviction are both pointless from the perspective of the coercing authority. They are religious actions performed in such a way as to destroy the purpose of religious actions. They are

[1] This claim was at the heart of Locke's controversy with Jonas Proast. Cf. *Epistola de Tolerantia; Second Letter concerning Toleration; Third Letter for Toleration; Fourth Letter for Toleration* (*Works* II (1768), 315–713), with Proast, *The Argument of the Letter concerning Toleration, Briefly Consider'd andAnswer'd* (Oxford, 1690); *Third Letter concerning Toleration*...(Oxford, 1691); *A Second Letter To the Author of the Three Letters for Toleration*...(Oxford, 1704). (The latter also contains comments on the work of Locke's young friend and admirer John Shute, *The Rights of the Protestant Dissenters*...) Proast argues throughout that religious establishments do over a period of time exert a causal influence on the religious beliefs of those subject to them. As Locke repeatedly complains, he is often slightly disingenuous in his discussion of the means which they may employ to further this end. But the argument, if crudely positivist, is not a weak one and Locke handles it pretty feebly. His case rests on the empirical claim that it is impossible to change men's beliefs by coercion. But he also wishes to argue as a sort of logical truth that it is a defining characteristic of a religious belief that it be not the product of human coercion. The falsity of the first of these claims becomes increasingly obvious and the force of the second has diminished with the lower status accorded to religious beliefs in the contemporary world. Hence it has become difficult to see why Locke found his own argument so convincing. But in the historical context the first was a plausible extrapolation from the religious and political history of England over the preceding thirty years and the second is almost the central axis of Locke's own distinctive development of Puritan religious individualism.

[2] 'But if God (which is the point in question) would have men forced to heaven, it must not be by the outward violence of the magistrate on men's bodies, but the inward constraints of his own spirit on their minds, which are not to be wrought on by any human compulsion; the way to salvation not being any forced exterior performance, but the voluntary and secret choice of the mind; and it cannot be supposed that God would make use of any means which could not reach, but would rather cross, the attainment of the end' (Fox Bourne, I, 177). However, 'courtesy, friendship and soft usage' (*ibid.* I, 191) are commended for their efficacy in producing just such an alteration by external, non-logical influence.

necessarily irrational and vicious from the point of view of the coerced because they involve sacrificing eternal happiness for temporal relief, infinite and eternal goods for purely finite benefits.[1] To put it more sympathetically, they involve sacrificing religious duty for terrestrial advantage. Various tactics are employed to make this point more salient. Where the status of an institution depends upon the hypothetical consent of its participants given because of its advantages to them, the institution can hardly claim to be legitimate when its behaviour damages them. Less felicitously for Locke's purposes, no man has a right to compel someone else to an action for which, if it turns out to be misconceived, no adequate compensation can be given.[2]

But, even if these arguments are not entirely cogent or coherent and even if the explicit separation between issues of legitimacy and issues of policy appears glib and imperfectly maintained, the central thrust of the argument is extremely effective and its reversal of the more rationalist authoritarian arguments (including Locke's own in the *Tracts on Government*) impressively deft. Having argued so forcibly that there could be no crude behavioural criterion for freeing acts of individuals from political authority—and being concerned, perhaps at Shaftesbury's behest, to persuade the government of the day—he could hardly have conducted his first 'defence' of individual right by an explicit advocacy of conscientious subversion. The threat of resistance which he

[1] 'Nor can it be thought that men should give the magistrate a power to choose for them their way to salvation, which is too great to give away, if not impossible to part with; since, whatever the magistrate enjoined in the worship of God, men must in this necessarily follow what they themselves thought best, since no consideration could be sufficient to force a man from, or to, that which he was fully persuaded was the way to infinite happiness or infinite misery' (Fox Bourne, *John Locke*, I, 177). Here again it is not clear whether the necessity is one of psychological impossibility, logical impossibility or moral outrage.

[2] The magistrate 'ought not to prescribe me the way, or require my diligence, in the prosecution of that good which is of a far higher concernment to me than anything within his power; having no more certain or more infallible knowledge of the way to attain it than I myself, where we are both equally inquirers, both equally subjects, and wherein he can give me no security that I shall not—nor make me any recompence if I do—miscarry' (*ibid.* I, 176–7). The parenthesis, if taken seriously as a restriction on the power which one man can exercise over another, would presumably make it difficult to justify the infliction of the death penalty or indeed any form of mutilation. It seems unlikely that Locke's 'liberalism' extended nearly as far as this.

flourishes in an admonitory fashion[1] appears exclusively in the prudential section of the work. It is only the sort of response which *will* greet the persecuting sovereign, not the sort of response which should greet him. Men ought to be subservient but are recalcitrant.[2] The rights which conscience has are only to a small extent rights to behave in a particular manner—specifically in worship—and even this restricted right is liable to invalidation by a suspicion on the part of the magistrate that it is, however contingently, connected with further behaviour which threatens the purposes of organized society. And this prohibition of interference on purely religious grounds turns in the course of argument from a religious taboo almost into an injunction against gratuitous governmental action of any sort. A magistrate may interfere with a sect whose overt religious behaviour makes him fear for his eventual control over them in the same way as he may interfere with a group united by wearing a particular sort of hat, if he supposes that the latter may come to threaten his authority.[3] It is not just the outrageousness of political interference in purely religious matters but almost equally its categorical irrelevance that drives the argument home.

But even to assert the point in this fashion as a necessary truth about the character of religious belief could carry much emotional force in the context. The most socially specific locus of resistance to political claims for which Locke argued in the *Two Treatises*, the institution of property, seems here still to be as much at the disposal of the political sovereign as it was in Locke's first writings.[4] It is only in the context of religious worship that

[1] '...let divines preach duty as long as they will, 'twas never known that men lay down quietly under the oppression and submitted their backs to the blows of others, when they thought they had strength enough to defend themselves' (Fox Bourne, *John Locke*, I, 190).

[2] *Ibid.* I, 190.

[3] *Ibid.* I, 184–5.

[4] *Ibid.* pp. 182–3: 'God does sometimes (so much does he take care of the preservation of government) make his law in some degrees submit and comply with man's; his law forbids the vice, but the law of man often makes the measure of it. There have been commonwealths that have made theft lawful for such as were not caught in the fact, and perhaps 'twas as guiltless a thing to steal a horse in Sparta as to win a horse-race in England. For the magistrate, having a power of transferring properties from one man to another, may establish any, so they be universal, equal and without violence, and suited to the interest and welfare of that society, as this was at Sparta, who, being a warlike people, found this no ill way to teach their citizens vigilancy, boldness, and activity. This I only note, by the by, to show how

Locke seems at this time to have felt any inclination to inquire into political legitimacy. It is hard to believe that he could have been moved to do so by a sympathy with gratuitously persecuted wearers of hats.

But even if the protection of conscience is given no real political viability in a concrete historical situation and even if no empirical feature of this world is granted an autonomous legitimacy against the will of the sovereign, the authoritarian structure of the theory has been critically disturbed. Furthermore, the fulcrum on which the structure is turned is an epistemological argument, if rather a crude one. Religious duties are intrinsically dependent on conviction. Conviction cannot be generated by coercion—or can only be so in the very special sense of divine psychological compulsion. It is not possible to make a claim against the specifically religious status of another man's religious beliefs on grounds of one's own convictions.[1] For it is a logically necessary characteristic of any man's religious beliefs that he considers them correct. Belief is a subjective, not an objective, matter. This does not mean that one is not responsible for one's own beliefs, that one does not have cognitive duties.[2] But it does mean that however strenuously and responsibly one arrives at and holds one's beliefs, neither the quality of the effort nor the social or political status of the individual can permit or enable the substitution of his beliefs for those of someone else. Beliefs are not like that.

Yet the protection of religious beliefs as such lends no support to subversive activities on the part of religious enthusiasts. What mediates between the toleration of beliefs and the rigid order of political control is the conscience of the ruler. But it is his official and not his private conscience, his duty as a ruler, not his faith as an individual,[3] the devotion and care with which he carried out

much the good of the commonwealth is the standard of all human laws, when it seems to limit and alter the obligation even of some of the laws of God, and change the nature of vice and virtue.' Cf. *Two Tracts*, English Tract, p. 138, etc. and cf. the version in the Huntington Library copy of the 1667 *Essay* quoted by Laslett, *Two Treatises*, § 120 n., and Introduction, pp. 103–4. Laslett seems here almost to assimilate the power of 'regulating' property to a right to tax redistributively. But it seems important to note Locke's subsequent explicit disjunction between this power and any right of non-consensual expropriation for however admirable motives (*Two Treatises*, II, § 140, ll. 1–11).

[1] Fox Bourne, *John Locke*, I, 179.

[2] *Ibid.* I, 178 and esp. p. 181.

[3] *Ibid.* I, 179.

this public duty in the public realm for which he answered to God. The protected area of human behaviour was not a concrete set of acts which could legitimately be identified by any observer as such. It was a jural abstraction from history in much the same way as the 'state of nature' in the *Two Treatises*. It was not whatever an individual conceived to be an example of his relationship to God which was protected but only such a part as in no way appeared to the sovereign to threaten the interest of others. The logic of authentically religious beliefs prevented them from threatening the interests of others.[1] But religious beliefs in the form in which human beings hold them are frequently contingently connected with a range of overt behaviour which directly threatens others. To worship one's God is a private 'concernment' between oneself and the deity in question. But to worship one's God in a Catholic rite in a Protestant country amounts to constructive subversion.[2] The judgement of whether or not religious behaviour remains a successfully private transaction must be left to the conscientious decision of the sovereign.[3] It is the duty of the sovereign to confine his interference, whatever the strength of his personal detestation, only to those instances of religious behaviour which he judges to threaten the interests of others in the community. The duty is to be exercised in the most careful and conscientious fashion and it will often be difficult to

1 Since Locke here argues repeatedly and at length that Catholicism does threaten the interests of others directly it should imply that he regards the state of being a Catholic as intrinsically morally corrupt. But it is not clear that he held any such extravagant doctrine. Yet he could only take refuge in the 'politique' argument from divided allegiance by tacitly assuming the failure of the claims to legitimacy of one of the authorities—and the claims to legitimacy of the Catholic Church are *religious* claims. To reject them in favour of the claims of the terrestrial sovereign is to dismiss their status as authentic religious revelations.

2 Fox Bourne, *John Locke*, I, 187–9.

3 '...any actions flowing from any of these opinions, as also in all other indifferent things, the magistrate has a power to command or forbid so far as they tend to the peace, safety, or security of his people, whereof though he be judge, yet he ought still to have a great care that no such laws be made, no such restraints established, for any other reason but because the necessity of the state and the welfare of the people called for them, and perhaps it will not be sufficient that he barely thinks such impositions and such rigour necessary or convenient unless he hath seriously and impartially considered and debated whether they be so or no; and his opinion (if he mistake) will no more justify him in the making of such laws than the conscience or opinion of the subject will excuse him if he disobey them, if consideration and inquiry could have better informed either of them' (*ibid.* I, 180).

determine its precise implications in practice. The religious duties of subjects likewise demand the greatest conscientiousness in their own assessment. Every man is obliged to worship his God in the way which he believes to be right (Locke treats this as a tautology) and is obliged to assess the precise character of this duty with such care because he is fully responsible for his correctness or incorrectness in this assessment. In so far as his motives are purely devotional, he has a right not to be interfered with in his manner of worship.[1] This right empowers men to refuse to engage in religious practices which they believe to be wrong. It does not empower them to resist political authority but it does empower them to disobey it.[2] In so far as their assessment of their religious duties is theologically correct and their motivation purely religious, they have indeed an absolute duty to disobey it. In so far as they err in their theological apprehension or in the purity of their motivation, they retain a *prima facie* obligation to do what they see as obligatory—even if in the final judgement they are to be divinely punished for their responsibility for the erroneous assessment of their duty.[3]

[1] But quite apart from the contamination of all theologies as they are actually held by individual men, there are, as we have already noted, complete theologies which exclude the possibility of *purely* devotional commitment. Being a Catholic commits you constructively to treason under certain circumstances according to Locke's interpretation.

[2] Fox Bourne, *John Locke*, I, 180–1.

[3] Locke normally employs motive concepts to refer to fully conscious wishes. It seems to be an implication of this position that Roman Catholics had a *prima facie* obligation to be treasonous or Fifth Monarchy men an obligation to rebel, if only they were sufficiently 'enthusiastic' in their devotion (though of course he supposed that they would suffer eventually in heaven for the folly of their beliefs). It is not very clear how far Locke regarded such systematic and culturally generated examples of (what he saw as) moral error as instances of moral viciousness and how far of individual stupidity or complete psychological heteronomy. It seems unlikely that he had a consistent view on this issue. It seems that, taking a jaundiced view of humanity in general, he employed human iniquity as an explanatory axiom to account for divergences between his simplistic rationalist law of nature and his empirically, though not perhaps morally, sophisticated consciousness of human moral diversity. But although his inordinate suspicion of other men's goodwill might explain particular outrageous moral beliefs, it could hardly explain the existence of systematic structures of moral belief of which he disapproved. It is likely that he might suppose that men are sometimes Catholics for malign motives. But even for him malign motives could hardly be an explanation for the origin and widespread acceptance of moral beliefs which are, at least superficially, often highly inconvenient for those who hold them. No doubt success in explaining this area of human behaviour could only be bought by somewhat diminishing the force of his cognitive voluntarism. The future role of the 'association of ideas', a

Thus the limits on the legitimacy of the conscientious religious claims of individuals and the limits on the sovereign's duty to tolerate such subjectively apprehended religious obligations are both set by their compatibility with the goals of organized human society, its 'end', those human purposes which could not be served without its existence. Locke's account of these purposes in this *Essay on Toleration* is more crisply reductivist than in his other writings. If men did not need political society to live together in peace, there would be no need of government. Hence this and nothing else is the end of government.[1] And what this seems to be in practice is preservation, peace, liberty, prosperity, riches, power, and population,[2] with the ruler merely an 'umpire between man and man',[3] without the least right to impose upon or devise for others any form of virtue. Not surprisingly, the work also contains Locke's most unequivocal assertions of the conscientious primacy of *raison d'état* as a criterion for the ruler's duty.[4] But if it combines in this way a secular, manipulative role for the ruler and a totally instrumental view of political society with passive obedience for the subjects, it had already defined the basis for a more subversive politics. The necessary autonomy of individual religious judgement had been proclaimed to the world of politics. The transposition of this theme from theology and epistemology to sociology and politics made each individual man the final judge of how far the society in which he lived had succeeded in avoiding force, the 'way of beasts', the avoidance of which was its sole end.[5]

notion which made its appearance in the later editions of the *Essay*, has been prominent for longer in psychological theory than it was in epistemology but it was for Locke himself perhaps his most successful if inadvertent attempt to confront part of this problem.

1 Though cf. again Fox Bourne, *John Locke*, I, 194 (6) for what seems to be a commendation of a type of government for its efficacy in the fostering of virtue.

2 *Ibid.* I, 174, 175, 178, 180, 181, 182, 185, 187, etc.

3 *Ibid.* I, 176.

4 Under such circumstances the magistrate 'may endeavour to suppress and weaken or dissolve any party of men which religion or any other thing hath united, to the manifest danger of his government, by all those means that shall be most convenient for that purpose whereof he is to be judge, nor shall he be accountable in the other world for what he does directly in order to the preservation and peace of his people, according to the best of his knowledge' (*ibid.* I, 185). Cf. *ibid.* p. 179 and see chapter 12 below.

5 Fox Bourne, *John Locke*, I, 185 (avoidance of force), 189 (to impose on reason is to attempt to reduce men to beasts). The use of the suicide taboo in the *Two Treatises* should be contrasted with the argument used here for the ineluctability of

intellectual autonomy: 'Besides, no man can give another man power (and it would be to no purpose if God should) over that over which he has no power himself. Now that a man cannot command his own understanding, or positively determine today what opinion he will be of to-morrow, is evident from experience and the nature of the understanding, which cannot more apprehend things, otherwise than they appear to it, than the eye see other colours in the rainbow than it doth, whether those colours be really there or no' (I, 176). This argument is clearly more effective than that in the *Two Treatises* (see below, chapters 8 and 13).

PART II

'...the original freedom of mankind being supposed, every man is at liberty to be of what kingdom he please, and so every petty company hath a right to make a kingdom by itself; and not only every city, but every village, and every family, nay, and every particular man, a liberty to choose himself to be his own King if he please; and he were a madman that being by nature free, would choose any man but himself to be his own governor. Thus to avoid the having but of one King of the whole world, we shall run into a liberty of having as many Kings as there be men in the world...'

Sir Robert Filmer (*Patriarcha and other Political Works of Sir Robert Filmer*, ed. Peter Laslett (Oxford, 1949), p. 286)

''Tis true (who would have his conscience imposed upon?) and 'tis as true, who would pay taxes? who would be poor? who almost would not be a prince?'

John Locke (*Two Tracts on Government*, p. 138)

'If Man in the State of Nature be so free...Why will he give up this Empire, and subject himself to the Dominion and Controul of any other Power? To which 'tis obvious to Answer, that though in the state of Nature he hath such a right, yet the Enjoyment of it is very uncertain, and constantly exposed to the Invasion of others. For all being Kings as much as he, every Man his Equal, and the greater part no strict Observers of Equity and Justice, the enjoyment of the property he has in this state is very unsafe, very unsecure.'

John Locke (*Two Treatises of Government*, II, §123)

'Every man a King.'

Governor Huey Long of Louisiana

5

THE 'TWO TREATISES' AND EXCLUSION

In the late 1670s the English political community was bitterly divided on a number of different issues. The lines of division did not run in quite the same places from one issue to another and individual politicians on occasion crossed the lines for distinctly private advantages. But between 1679 and 1681 political attitudes and activities came increasingly to polarize around two consolidated political groups, each with its own more or less systematic ideology.[1] The names applied to the two groups at the time, Whigs and Tories, the Court and Country parties, are in themselves at least as misleading as they are revealing. The leaders of the Country party were struggling self-consciously to be admitted to office under the crown and the initial leader of the Court party, the king's chief minister, the Earl of Danby, was a robust Protestant who certainly believed himself to have the interests of the country at heart and supposed himself to be exercising his office in accordance with the constitution. The ideology of the Country party at times sounded stirringly populist but few of its leaders showed in practice much inclination for a re-enactment of 1649.

[1] The best single study of the politics of the Exclusion crisis is J. R. Jones, *The First Whigs, The Politics of the Exclusion Crisis 1678–1683* (London, 1961). There are also helpful general accounts in Keith Feiling, *A History of the Tory Party 1640–1714* (Oxford, 1924) and David Ogg, *England in the Reign of Charles II* (paperback edition, Oxford, 1963). The constitutional issues are well treated by Clayton Roberts, *The Growth of Responsible Government in Stuart England* (Cambridge, 1966), chapter 6, 'The Crisis of Confidence', pp. 197–244. The basis of Whig ideas about the constitution is discussed in B. Behrens, 'The Whig Theory of the Constitution in the Reign of Charles II', *Cambridge Historical Journal*, VII, 1 (1941), 42–71, and the content of the Whig Exclusion pamphlets themselves is described by O. W. Furley, 'The Whig Exclusionists: Pamphlet Literature in the Exclusion Campaign, 1679–81', *Cambridge Historical Journal*, XIII, 1 (1957), 19–36. There are useful but not entirely convincingly presented materials on Shaftesbury himself in W. D. Christie, *A Life of Anthony Ashley Cooper, First Earl of Shaftesbury, 1621–1683*, 2 vols. (London, 1871), and Louise Fargo Brown, *The First Earl of Shaftesbury* (New York, 1933). The account given here is merely a conventional outline based predominantly on these materials and without pretence to originality.

Perhaps the most authoritative statement of the Tory ideology was held to be Sir Robert Filmer's masterwork *Patriarcha*. Yet such an unyielding upholder of the royal prerogative as the Marquis of Halifax thought even Sir William Temple's mild patriarchalism injudicious as propaganda and can only have regarded Filmer himself as a rather laboured joke.[1] Nevertheless it remains true that the politics of the Exclusion controversy mark one of the critical stages in the elaboration of the Whig constitutional theory of responsible government[2] and in the political struggle of the English gentry and aristocracy to establish effective control over the monarch's conduct of policy.

The Whigs were spurred on by a variety of fears. The threat of popery, represented by the prospect of James, Duke of York's accession, and the menace of arbitrary power which was inextricably linked with it,[3] lent greater intensity to their anxiety over Charles's relationships with the French king and to their disapproval of the energetic administrative measures of the king's servants in Ireland and Scotland. As the struggle progressed it became increasingly a struggle to establish permanent controls over the prerogative for the Whigs and a struggle to preserve the autonomy of the executive and the hereditary succession to the throne for the Tories. It was fought out in the king's council and on the floor of parliament, in the countryside in a series of fiercely contested and skilfully organized elections in which more men voted probably than ever before in an English election,[4] on the

[1] H. C. Foxcroft, *The Life and Letters of Sir George Savile, Bart., First Marquis of Halifax*, 2 vols. (London, 1898), I, 152–3.

[2] See esp. Roberts, *Growth of Responsible Government*, pp. 240–4.

[3] The key image which united these two threats was that of monarchy on the French model, the France with which Charles II was in such intimate relationship. See, for example, Sir Henry Capel, 'There are but two sorts of monarchy in the whole world: one absolute without limitation, as that of France, whose subjects are at the disposal of the King for life and limb, and to invade other nation's property for the luxury of the court: and little men of low fortunes are the Ministers of State—and whoever does that I shall suspect him of absolute monarchy. Cardinal Richelieu would not suffer so great a man as the Duke of Montmorency, but cut off his head, and all to support absolute monarchy' (7 January 1681, quoted in J. H. Plumb, *The Growth of Political Stability in England 1675–1725* (London, 1967), pp. 51n.–52n. and see, for example, Shaftesbury's speech of 25 March 1679, quoted in W. D. Christie, *Life of Anthony Ashley Cooper*...(London, 1871), II, Appendix VI, p.c.: 'Popery and slavery, like two sisters, go hand-in-hand.'

[4] '...it must be emphasized once again that more voters were involved in the elections of 1679–81 than ever before in the history of Parliament' (Plumb, *Growth*

printing presses and in the common council of the City of London, even indeed in the London streets. The rhetoric in which it was conducted grew increasingly hysterical. Even the Popish Plot, which at its initial 'revelation' had seemed merely a politically effective caricature of insecurities and hostilities already felt by the Whigs, became eventually a dubious propaganda asset. Charles's relentless imperturbability and his political skill left them committed to justifying their conduct in terms of a threat, the imminence of which became increasingly incredible. The more threadbare their justification became, the more outrageous seemed the novelty of their constitutional demands.[1] By 1683 it had become easy for the king to portray them as nothing but a group of factious grandees with a taste for Venetian oligarchy and at least an excessive sympathy for the incendiaries of 1641, attempting to impose their own arrogant private wills on the will of the king himself.

The political tactics of the Whigs were designed to force the crown to compromise by parliamentary action. They attempted to extend the device of impeachment in the case of Danby and later of Halifax so that the servants of the crown were liable to prosecution for treason not merely for actions which were actually illegal but also for those to which the Commons objected as 'offensive'. In addition they attempted to use the power of the purse to control the crown's conduct of foreign policy.[2] The

of Political Stability, p. 50). The whole of chapter II, 'Parliament Preserved', pp. 31–65, is a most illuminating account of the development of the electorate in this period.

[1] See Jones, *The First Whigs*, p. 147, and Roberts, *Growth of Responsible Government*, pp. 240–4, esp. Sir Francis North's comments on the impeachment tactics of the Whigs: 'So here is the executive part of the government taken away, and the legislative made necessary' (quoted *ibid.* p. 243 n. 2). The charge of novelty in constitutional matters was equivalent to a charge of illegality. Hence the heavy resonances of the duty of 'restoring' the government. (See, for example, George Downing's rebuke to the Commons in 1675, 'You are the restorers of the government, but this about the Chamber of London is setting up a new government' (Roberts, *ibid.* p. 227), and cf. Locke's hailing of 'our Great Restorer' (*Two Treatises of Government*, Preface, l. 5).)

[2] And eventually to force Exclusion on Charles. See Shaftesbury's speech of 23 December 1680: '...the nation is betrayed if, upon any terms, we part with our money till we are sure the King is ours. Have what laws you will, and what conditions, they will be of no use but waste-paper before Easter, if the Court has money to set up for Popery and arbitrary designs in the meanwhile' (Christie, *Anthony Ashley Cooper*, II, Appendix VI, cv).

latter was scarcely a novel manoeuvre, but the former had far-reaching implications. The determination with which the Whigs pressed the doctrine of ministerial responsibility destroyed the entire category of private counsel given to the king and thus divested the king's ministers, at least in intention, of all protection of the crown for doing the king's will. Previously prerogative had been an adequate protection for all execution of the king's will which was within the bounds of the law. The Whig position in contrast admitted it as a protection only in such cases as Parliament did not find the actions 'offensive', in effect only in those cases where protection was otiose. The result was simply to remove all autonomy from the executive power.

The novelty and subversive quality of these positions did not altogether escape the Whigs themselves. It seems likely, indeed, that only the degree of their anxiety over the linked threats of Charles's French entanglements, the establishment of arbitrary power and the popish succession could have driven them quite so far. This ambivalence in their feelings is reflected in the character of their ideological pronouncements. At the level of political tactics, their strenuous confrontation of the royal will necessarily took the form of blackmail directed at the crown. Systematic political obstruction and outraged indictment of the crown's servants were combined with obsequious protestations of confidence in the goodwill of the king himself and of humility in the face of the authority of the crown and with judicious offers of whole-hearted co-operation and the provision of extensive supplies if the crown was ready to co-operate. The political attack on the reality of prerogative power was combined with persistent ideological obeisance before the status of 'true Prerogative'. True prerogative was prerogative exercised for the true interests of the people,[1] as interpreted by the representatives of the people's will, the Whig Lords and Commons.

Partly because of the novelty of this interpretation and its in-

[1] Cf., for example, Shaftesbury's opinion of 1673: '...the King's prerogative is law, and the principal part of it: therefore, in maintaining that, you maintain the law. The government of England is so excellently interwoven, that every part of the prerogative hath a broad mixture of the interest of the subject: the ease and safety of the people being inseparable from the greatness and security of the Crown' (Christie, *Anthony Ashley Cooper*, Appendix v, lx).

compatibility with much that was known of the history of the constitution, an incompatibility recognized at one level by both Shaftesbury himself and Locke,[1] there were increasingly serious problems in mobilizing the full support of the Whigs in successive parliamentary elections. As the conflict of wills became more intense and direct and the Whig position implicitly more extreme, there was an increasing need to muffle the embarrassingly intimate resonances of the traditional rhetoric of prerogative power and point the issue in clearer and more clinical terms. The heady propaganda of the Whig pamphleteers seemed more and more to threaten anarchy,[2] and anarchy, as the French ambassador Barillon noted early in the agitation,[3] was hardly a state of affairs for which the great Whig merchants had any intuitive enthusiasm. When Filmer's *Patriarcha* was at last published in 1680 it became imperatively necessary to provide an ideological counterweight which could set out the rationale of the Exclusionist position in a way which assimilated it firmly to the solid continuous historical order of the English polity and protected it against the needling gibes of *Patriarcha*. Mr Laslett has shown effectively that Locke's workings for the *Two Treatises* date back to this political struggle and it is established beyond doubt that Shaftesbury and Locke both worked on the problems of contriving such an ideological position, though it is not known whether Shaftesbury even *knew* of Locke's writing the first draft of the *Two Treatises* and despite Mr Laslett's immensely painstaking investigations it is not clear how much of the present text or anything closely resembling it dates from this period.[4]

[1] See Shaftesbury, 'Some Observations concerning the regulating of Elections for Parliament...', *A Collection of Scarce and Valuable Tracts*...(=*Somers Tracts*), ed. Sir Walter Scott, 13 vols. (2nd edition, London, 1809–15), VIII, 398, and for Locke's recognition see the *Second Treatise*, chapter XIV, 'Of Prerogative'.

[2] See, for example, *A Just and Modest Vindication of the proceedings of the Two last Parliaments*... (anon.) (London, 1681), p. 31: 'But if there must be a War...'

[3] 2/12 January 1679: 'Since the wealthy merchants fear disorder, and above all civil war, I believe that it lies in the power of the King to prevent matters from being carried to an extremity' (quoted by Roberts, *Growth of Responsible Government*, p. 222).

[4] The circumstantial evidence as assembled by Mr Laslett makes it very difficult to believe that a large portion of the book was not written by the time that he departed to Holland in 1683. But it does not provide a clear means of discriminating which portions of the text were written at which time. It is not clear how any satisfactory logic of inference from each sentence in the text to its date of composition could be established in principle, since no trace has survived of any composition

What is clear is that at some point in 1681 at the very latest[1] Locke set himself to provide a systematic refutation of absolutist theory in its most socially plausible, though not intellectually most rigorous form, the patriarchalism of Sir Robert Filmer. It was a refutation which not merely set out logical limits to the legitimacy of royal authority but which rendered these socially operational by empowering the community to judge when they had been transgressed and to reassert them in action. In short it was a theoretical proclamation of the ultimate right of revolution.[2] At no point in Locke's previous reflection on politics had such a right been proclaimed. His earliest references to Filmer and the typology of the origins of government in his various tables of the sciences[3] do not suggest any very decisive revulsion from the Filmerian position.[4] When he discussed the obligation of penal

manuscript, such as that of *L'Esprit des loix*. The text as we have it is clearly a palimpsest of workings dating back to 1681 at the latest and continuing up to 1689 though possibly, as Laslett suggests, with a lengthy interval between 1683 and 1689 (see *Two Treatises*, p. 65). It is possible that all of Laslett's conjectures (recorded in the notes to individual paragraphs) as to the precise dates of composition are in fact correct, though not all of them seem entirely plausible. But I simply cannot see any way of *knowing* on the basis of the evidence at present available whether they are correct or not.

[1] We know that he was paying close critical attention to Filmer's writings as early as 1679 (MS Locke f 28, p. 118) but there does not become any considerable body of evidence of materials which he was *definitely* employing in the *Two Treatises* until 1681, though cf. Laslett's suggestive argument from the citation of Filmer's tracts (*Two Treatises*, pp. 57–9) that he must have reached at least § 22 of the *Second Treatise* (begun before the *First Treatise*) before the publication of *Patriarcha* itself.

[2] It was in fact a more individualist theory than this account suggests but the individualism can scarcely be attributed to the demands of the Exclusion controversy and its basis in Locke's thought can be more conveniently explored below. See chapter 13 below.

[3] MS Locke d 10 (=1659–), pp. 185, 528. MS Locke f 14 (1667–), pp. 5, 7 10, 16. For link with Shaftesbury papers see *Two Treatises*, p. 33, and for the presentation of Consensus Populi and Jus Paternum as the two possible foundations of political power in the tables of the sciences, see MS Film. 77, side 3 (not paginated by Locke, printed in *Two Tracts*, pp. 245–6 (Adversaria 1661)). MS Locke c 28, p. 41 (1672). MS Locke c 28, fo. 157v (n.d.; includes 'Arma' as a third possible foundation for political power). But none of these headings can be taken to indicate Locke's adherence to a patriarchalist theory, merely his recognition that it is a theoretical position for which some have argued. Cf. his critical comments on Samuel Parker's arguments, MS Locke c 39, pp. 7–9 (printed in M. Cranston, *John Locke, a Biography* (London, 1957), esp. pp. 132–3), and the fact that Jus Paternum, Consensus Populi and Arma are still listed as possible foundations in a 1681 division of the sciences, MS Film. 77, pp. 290–1.

[4] This did not mean that his thought was in any way close in style to that of Filmer (see chapters 2 and 4, etc. above), merely that he does not appear before the period

laws in February 1676 he denied a right of resistance[1] and when he sketched an outline of natural law in his journal in 1678 political obligation appears as an unequivocal duty.[2] Indeed in his later writings on toleration and incidental observations on morality he continued to treat the need for political order and the consequent duty of allegiance as a primary imperative of the human condition.[3] There is no doubt that he accepted the reality

of the composition of the *Two Treatises* to have seen the Filmerian position as a target to which it was necessary to address himself systematically.

1 MS Locke f 1, pp. 123–6 (printed in Peter King, *The Life of John Locke* (London, 1830), I, 114–7). Locke argues in this that although the designation of political authorities may be a function of human positive law the obligation to obey them is commanded by the law of God and hence logically prior to human law. This is an extrapolation from the category of 'indifferent things' explored by Abrams. The distinction maintained by Locke is that between the mode of obligation of human laws (necessarily penal) and the mode of obligation of divine laws (conscientious). In practice these two laws very frequently coincide. The *conscience* of men is obliged in the case of indifferent things to active or passive obedience, not by virtue of human law, 'but by that law of God which forbids disturbance or dissolution of governments'. Consequently 'he that obeys the magistrate to that degree as not to endanger or disturb the government: under what form of government soever he lives, fulfils all the law of God concerning government i.e. obeys to the utmost that the magistrate or society can oblige his conscience...'. This solution 'clears a man from that infinite number of sins that otherwise he must unavoidably be guilty of if all penal laws oblige the conscience farther than this'. But it does not threaten the preservation of civil order: 'The obligation of conscience then upon every subject being to preserve the government. 'tis plain that when any law made with a penalty is submitted to i.e. the penalty is quietly undergone without other obedience. the government cannot be disturbed or endangered for whilst the magistrate hath power to increase the penalty even to loss of life, and the subject submits patiently to the penalty which he in conscience is obliged to do, the Government can never be in danger, nor can the public want active obedience in any case, when it hath power to require it under pain of death.' The whole note should be read in the context of the moral situation of the Huguenot community in France. It is an application of the interpretation of the boundaries between civil and religious societies suggested in the *Essay on Toleration* (1667) and reasserted in the note, Excommunicacon 73/4. MS Locke c 27, pp. 29a, b, printed in King, *Life of Locke*, II, 108–19. It is not easy to see why Laslett (*Two Treatises*, p. 35), regards it as rather obscure.

2 'If he finds that God has made him and all other men in a state wherein they cannot subsist without society and has given them judgment to discern what is capable of preserving that society, can he but conclude that he is obliged and that God requires him to follow those rules which conduce to the preserving of society?' (MS Locke f 3, pp. 201–2 (15 July 1678), 'Lex Nãã', conveniently printed by W. Von Leyden in 'Locke and Natural Law', *Philosophy*, XXXI (1956), 34–5).

3 MS Locke c 28, p. 139: 'Morality' on the need for compact to determine people's rights because 'Man made not the world which he found made at his birth. Therefore no man at his birth can have no right to any thing in the world more than an other. Men therefore must either enjoy all things in common or by compact determine their rights if all things be left in common want rapine and force will

of (and in some sense approved of) the solid burden of social authority as much as Shaftesbury himself though, even before he had addressed himself so strenuously to Filmer's writings, he might not have cared to follow Shaftesbury in the latter's calm proclamation of the paterfamilias's status as a 'natural prince' with 'an absolute power over his family'[1] or household.

Yet when he came to write the *Two Treatises* the doctrine which emerged was notably more individualist than can be explained simply by his adherence to the Exclusion programme. We may explain the fact that he was prepared to justify revolution by the fact that the Whigs were certainly prepared at least to *threaten* it to get their way. But the individualism is more distinctively Lockean. The key appears to be the very intensive confrontation with the positions of Filmer. Filmer's claims were claims about the God-given rights of the crown. What appears to have gouged out of Locke his implicitly radical response was not just a prudential judgement about how extensive the rights of the crown should be but a horror at the idea that limitless royal power should be construed as a gift of God. In this sense the work is not a piece of political prudence, advice on what to do, the status of which depends upon matter of fact,[2] but a statement of the limits of political right, the status of which depends upon knowledge of the law of nature. It is not a book about how to construct governments or about just when it is desirable to resist but a book about why under some circumstances men have a *right* to resist. It was the

unavoidably follow in which state as is evident happiness cannot be had...' This treatment occurs in one of Locke's attempts to set out a purely utilitarian basis for morality. It is in interesting tension with the account of property right in the *Two Treatises*.

[1] Shaftesbury, *Somers Tracts*, VIII, 401.

[2] Cf. MS Locke f 5, pp. 77–83 (26 June 1681) (printed in *An Early Draft of Locke's Essay*, ed. R. I. Aaron and Jocelyn Gibb (Oxford, 1936), pp. 116–8), esp. pp. 81–2: '...the well management of publique or private affairs depending upon the various and unknowne humors interests and capacitys of men we have to doe with in the world and not upon any setled Ideas of things physique, politie and prudence are not capeable of demonstration but a man is principally helpd in them by the history of matter of fact and a sagacity of enquireing into probable causes and findeing out an analogie in their operations and effects. Knowledg then depends upon right and true Ideas, Opinion upon history and matter of fact, and Hence it comes to passe that our knowledg of generall things are eternae veritates and depend not upon the existence or accidents of things for the truths of mathematiques and morality are certain whether men make true mathematicall figures, or suit their actions to the rules of morality or noe' (*ibid.* p. 117).

confrontation of Locke's previously socially quietist religious individualism, clarified in presentation perhaps particularly by his recent reading of Pufendorf, with the exorbitant claims of Filmerian absolutism which led him to the assertion of a countervailing right in the conscience of every man to judge the damage inflicted by the strong and wicked upon God's world.

Thus, just as *Patriarcha* could be read by the Tories both as a moral charter for the king's defence of his prerogative and as a proclamation of God's revealed will to the world of politics, there can be read in the *Two Treatises*, oddly side by side, both a systematic moral apologia for the political attitudes of the Exclusionists and a theological proclamation of the autonomous rights of all men in the conduct of politics. It is the latter proclamation which has led theorists to talk ever since the nineteenth century of the 'political philosophy' of Locke and it is its apparent autonomy which has led many, perhaps justly, to feel some discomfiture at the description of the *Two Treatises* as an 'Exclusion tract'. It is with the analysis and explanation of this latter that the subsequent discussion is predominantly concerned, but it is necessary, in order to place this in context, to begin by giving a brief outline of the relationship of Locke's own constitutional statements to the Exclusionist position.

The *Two Treatises* asserts the superiority of the legislative power to the executive power.[1] The location of both of these powers is specified by the 'Original Constitution' and thus cannot be changed while the society subsists.[2] Locke's insistence on this point involves him at times in gratuitous problems and leads him to propound a solution at one point which was sharply in tension

[1] 'In all Cases, whilst the Government subsists, the *Legislative is the Supream Power*. For what can give Laws to another, must needs be superior to him: and since the Legislative is no otherwise Legislative of the Society, but by the right it has to make Laws for all the parts and for every Member of the Society, prescribing Rules to their actions, and giving power of Execution, where they are transgressed, the *Legislative* must needs be the *Supream*, and all other Powers in any Members or parts of the Society, derived from and subordinate to it' (*Two Treatises*, II, § 150, ll. 1–9).

[2] *Ibid.* II, § 198, ll. 1–7. '...the Constitution of the Legislative being the original and supream act of the Society, antecedent to all positive Laws in it, and depending wholly on the People, no inferior Power can alter it. And therefore the *People*, when the *Legislative* is once Constituted, *having* in such a Government as we have been speaking of, *no Power* to act as long as the Government stands; this inconvenience is thought incapable of a remedy' (*ibid.* § 157, ll. 21–7).

with the Exclusionist programme.[1] At this stage of the argument it appears that though the legislative is superior to the executive, only the executive has the authority to 'restore' the original constitution. But this appearance is probably over-strict. The teleological justification for executive action in this case would seem to apply equally aptly to the justification of legislative action. In any case, in the English constitution, the superiority of the legislative to the executive is a point with most equivocal implications. For the king is not merely the holder of the executive (and federative) power but also an essential figure in the legislative process.[2] To assert the superiority of the legislative to the executive power is only to proclaim limits to the legitimate exercise of executive authority. It is not to provide any direct political instrument within the constituted political order for enforcing these limits in practice. The only effective sanction offered by Locke against the systematic abuse of executive power by the crown is the residual threat of revolution. He proclaims the legitimacy of resistance to the servants of the crown; but only when they threaten illegal force.[3] There is no exploration of the legitimacy of parliament's practical efforts to control the conduct of royal policy by extending the device of impeachment to cases where the king's ministers were not technically in breach of the law. Similarly the

[1] *Two Treatises* II, § 158.

[2] 'In some Commonwealths where the *Legislative* is not always in being, and the *Executive* is vested in a single Person, who has also a share in the Legislative; there that single Person in a very tolerable sense may also be called *Supream*, not that he has in himself all the Supream Power, which is that of Law-making: But because he has in him the *Supream Execution*, from whom all inferiour Magistrates derive all their several subordinate Powers, or at least the greatest part of them: having also no Legislative superiour to him, there being no Law to be made without his consent, which cannot be expected should ever subject him to the other part of the Legislative, *he is* properly enough in this sense *Supream*' (*ibid.* § 151, ll. 1–12); '...it is not the *supream Executive Power* that is exempt from *Subordination*, but the *Supream Executive Power* vested in one, who having a share in the Legislative, has no distinct superior Legislative to be subordinate and accountable to, farther than he himself shall joyn and consent: so that he is no more subordinate than he himself shall think fit, which one may certainly conclude will be but very little' (*ibid.* § 152, ll. 4–10).

[3] *Ibid.* § 205, esp. 'But yet opposition may be made to the illegal Acts of any inferiour Officer, or other commissioned by him' (ll. 4–6); § 206, esp.: '...they may be questioned, opposed, and resisted, who use unjust force, though they pretend a Commission from him, which the Law authorizes not' (ll. 2–4). But '*Force* is to be *opposed* to nothing, but to unjust and unlawful *Force*' (§ 204, ll. 1–2).

constraint for which Locke argues most extendedly, the insistence on taxation as a power under sole control of the representative legislative,[1] was not a power threatened directly by the crown. Furthermore, the aspect of royal power which Locke appears to exempt most thoroughly from legislative control, the conduct of foreign policy, the responsibility of the federative power,[2] was an aspect which the Whigs were particularly anxious to control because of the political importance of Charles's relations with France. There is no doubt that if the text of the *Two Treatises* as we have it now is exclusively or even predominantly an Exclusion tract, it is often a notably ham-fisted one.

But whatever the deftness of its initial political purchase and whenever the specifically constitutional sections as they now stand were written, what cannot be doubted is that Locke chose to publish them in this form as a political charter for 'our Great Restorer, Our present King William'[3] and republished them in what, from this viewpoint, was essentially the same form twice during his own lifetime. Hence they must be supposed to contain broadly Locke's interpretation of the English constitution at this time and his conception of the rationale for it, the criteria by which it was to be judged as 'the best possibly that ever was'.[4]

[1] ''Tis true, Governments cannot be supported without great Charge, and 'tis fit every one who enjoys his share of the Protection, should pay out of his Estate his proportion for the maintenance of it. But still it must be with his own Consent, *i.e.* the Consent of the Majority, giving it either by themselves, or their Representatives chosen by them. For if any one shall claim a *Power to lay* and levy *Taxes* on the People, by his own Authority, and without such consent of the People, he thereby invades the *Fundamental Law of Property*, and subverts the end of Government. For what property have I in that which another may by right take, when he pleases to himself?' etc. (*Two Treatises*, II, § 140, ll. 1–11).

[2] '...though this *federative Power* in the well or ill management of it be of great moment to the commonwealth, yet it is much less capable to be directed by antecedent, standing, positive Laws, than the *Executive*; and so must necessarily be left to the Prudence and Wisdom of those whose hands it is in, to be managed for the publick good. For the *Laws* that concern Subjects one amongst another, being to direct their actions, may well enough *precede* them. But what is to be done in reference to *Foreigners*, depending much upon their actions, and the variation of designs and interests, must be *left* in great part *to* the *Prudence* of those who have this Power committed to them, to be managed by the best of their Skill, for the advantage of the Commonwealth' (*ibid.* § 147, ll. 7–18).

[3] *Ibid.* Preface, l. 5.

[4] John Locke to Edward Clarke, 8 February 1689, printed (not wholly accurately) in *The Correspondence of John Locke and Edward Clarke*, ed. Benjamin Rand (London, 1927), p. 289.

Two points in particular require emphasis in this interpretation, one, already noted, because it marked some deviation from the Whig programme and the other because of the great importance which it came to assume in the subsequent career of Locke's work. The first of these, the extent of prerogative power and its status, arises in fact most critically in relation to the second, the role of representation within the constitution. The essential function of representation within the constitution is to legitimize the appropriation of private property to support the public 'Charge'.[1] The right of taxation vested in a legislative that has a separate interest from the people, as in the case of an absolute monarch, is not logically compatible with the right of private property.[2] But in the English constitution, where the Legislative consists at least in part of men chosen by their communities at intervals who are in effect subject themselves to the laws which they pass,[3] there is an effective institutional check on the arbitrary appropriation of property, and an institutional check of a kind on the executive's conduct of policy.[4] In so far as the first type of restraint was

[1] *Two Treatises*, II, § 140, quoted p. 53, n. 1, above.

[2] *Ibid.* II, § 138, ll. 1–31, esp.: '...it is a mistake to think, that the Supream or *Legislative Power* of any Commonwealth, can do what it will, and dispose of the Estates of the Subject *arbitrarily*, or take any part of them at pleasure' (ll. 14–17); and: '...in Governments, where the *Legislative* is in one lasting Assembly always in being, or in one Man, as in Absolute Monarchies, there is danger still, that they will think themselves to have a distinct interest, from the rest of the Community; and so will be apt to increase their own Riches and Power, by taking, what they think fit, from the People. For a Man's *Property* is not at all secure, though there be good and equitable Laws to set the bounds of it, between him and his Fellow Subjects, if he who commands those Subjects, have Power to take from any private Man, what part he pleases of his *Property* and use and dispose of it as he thinks good' (ll. 21–31).

[3] Arbitrary expropriation of property 'is not much to be fear'd in Governments where the *Legislative* consists, wholly or in part, in Assemblies which are variable, whose Members upon the Dissolution of the Assembly, are Subjects under the common Laws of their Country, equally with the rest' (*ibid.* pp. 17–21); § 154, ll. 1–4. This point is the basis for Shaftesbury's project for confining eligibility for election to parliament to the very rich: 'Wealth and substance will also give a lustre and reputation to our great council, and a security to the people; for their estates are then pawned, and so many pledges for their good behaviour, becoming thereby equal sharers themselves in the benefit or disadvantage which shall result from their own acts and councils' (*Somers Tracts*, VIII, 400–1).

[4] By manipulation of the power of the purse—cf. the 'Instructions for Members of the Parliament, summoned for March 21st 1681', the draft of which was originally in Locke's hand, *Shaftesbury Papers*, P.R.O. 30/24/VI B.399, printed in Christie, *Anthony Ashley Cooper*, II, Appendix VII, cxi–cxii, esp. 'Lastly. Although we

concerned, all that Locke needed to assert was the dependence of legitimate taxation upon representative legislative consent—no taxation without parliaments. But in so far as a broader measure of control was envisaged,[1] it was an imperative necessity to ensure a regular meeting of parliament. The Whig stress on the constitutional status of annual parliaments was one of their most insistent themes,[2] reflected in Locke's draft of the instructions for members of the Oxford parliament in 1681.[3] But in the text of the *Two Treatises*, the issue of whether annual parliaments were a component of the 'original constitution' is never explicitly faced. The Whig and Tory interpretations of the grounds for the meeting of parliament, constitutionally fixed intervals and the prerogative right of summons, are throughout presented together.[4] Similarly,

mention these three Particulars as most necessary to us, yet there are Several others of great Importance which we leave to your Wisdoms, assuring our selves, that until you have fully provided for a Complete security against Popery and Arbitrary Power, you will not give any of our Money.' Though, as noted above, the power of the purse was never threatened directly as such by the use of prerogative taxation during the Exclusion controversy, it is only just to note that the Whigs may have *feared* that it would be so threatened.

[1] Cf. 'When the *Legislative* hath put the Execution of the Laws, they make, into other hands, they have a power still to resume it out of those hands, when they find cause, and to punish for any mall-administration against the Laws. The same holds also in regard of the *Federative* Power, that and the Executive, being both *Ministerial and subordinate to the Legislative*, which as has been shew'd in a Constituted Commonwealth, is the Supream' (*Two Treatises*, II, § 153, ll. 5–11). The equivocal phrase 'when they find cause' is the closest Locke comes to an explicit espousal of the Whig claim of a right to impeach for 'offensive' ministerial acts.

[2] Annual parliaments have been provided by the constitution, lest the Kings should 'by Passion, private Interest, or the influence of ill Counsellors, be so far misled as not to Assemble Parliaments, when the Publick Affairs require it; or Declare them Dissolved before the ends of their Meeting were Accomplished' (*A Just and Modest Vindication*, p. 1).

[3] 'That you insist upon an adjustment to be made betwixt the King's prerogative of calling, proroguing, and dissolving Parliament, and the rights of the people to have annual Parliaments to despatch and provide for those important affairs and businesses that can nowhere else be taken care of; for, without the certainty of Parliaments meeting in due distance of time from each other, and their sitting so long as shall be necessary for the despatch of the affairs of the nation, it is not possible but that our laws, liberties, lives, and estates should become in short time at the will of the prince' (*Shaftesbury Papers*, P.R.O. 30/24/VI B.399, printed in Christie, *Anthony Ashley Cooper*, II, Appendix VII, cxii).

[4] *Two Treatises*, II, § 154, ll. 1–16, esp.: '...the power of convoking the Legislative, is ordinarily placed in the Executive, and has one of these two limitations in respect of time: That either the Original Constitution requires their *assembling* and *acting* at certain intervals, and then the Executive Power does nothing but Ministerially issue directions for their Electing and Assembling, according to due

while both Locke and Shaftesbury displayed anxiety over the adequacy of representation in the English electoral system of the time, because of the over-representation of some interests and under-representation of others,[1] Shaftesbury's anxiety seemed very precisely political and the means which he suggested for remedy-

Forms: Or else it is left to his Prudence to call them by new Elections, when the Occasions or Exigencies of the publick require the amendment of old, or making of new Laws, or the redress or prevention of any inconveniencies, that lie on, or threaten the People' (ll. 7–16); cf. § 155, ll. 9–10; § 156, ll. 1–42, esp.: 'Thus supposing the regulation of times for the *Assembling and Sitting of the Legislative*, not settled by the original Constitution, it naturally fell into the hands of the Executive, not as an Arbitrary Power depending on his good pleasure, but with this trust always to have it exercised only for the publick Weal, as the Occurrences of times and change of affairs might require. Whether *settled periods of their Convening*, or a *liberty* left to the Prince *for Convoking the Legislative*, or perhaps a mixture of both, hath the least inconvenience attending it, 'tis not my business here to inquire, but only to shew, that though the Executive Power may have the Prerogative of *Convoking* and *dissolving* such *Conventions of the Legislative*, yet it is not thereby superiour to it' (ll. 30–9). § 153, ll. 12–25 appears to give to the legislative the power to fix the dates of its own summoning. But this should be read as a general statement of the derivation of the right of fixing times for the meeting of the legislature, not as a statement about the English constitution. § 154 is the application of this general position to the English constitution. The only effective sanction which Locke does set out to limit prerogative discretion is the right of the people forcibly to reinstate their legislative where the executive frustrates its meeting by force at a time 'when the Original Constitution, or the publick Exigencies require it' (§ 155, ll. 1–15).

[1] Shaftesbury, *Somers Tracts*, VIII, 399–400, esp.: 'That the parliament, as now constituted, is no equal representative of the people, is notorious'. *Two Treatises*, II, § 157, esp. ll. 14–19, 'the bare Name of a Town, of which there remains not so much as the ruines, where scarce so much Housing as a Sheep-coat; or more Inhabitants than a Shepherd is to be found, sends *as many Representatives* to the grand Assembly of Law-makers, as a whole County numerous in People, and powerful in riches'. A 'fair and *equal Representative*' (§ 158, ll. 13–14) seems to be a function of both 'Wealth and Inhabitants' (§ 157, l. 6). It is a right 'which no part of the People however incorporated can pretend to, but in proportion to the assistance, which it affords to the publick' (§ 158, ll. 7–9). It is important to read this insistence in the context of incorporated boroughs which do have members of parliament but which no longer have inhabitants, rather than see it simply as an acceptance of property as the sole basis of representation. Even Shaftesbury in his elaborate scheme for adjusting representation to constituencies of similar population and the possibility of election to members of the 'optimacy' insists that 'every individual person in the nation has a natural right to vote in this great council; but this being impracticable, they are forced to do it by proxy, [that is,] by devolving this right upon certain common representatives indifferently chosen, for certain select numbers and communities of men, in which the whole body of the people is, or ought to be comprehended' (*Somers Tracts*, VIII, 401). The point of this method is that its effect will be that 'the parliament will be perfect representative of the whole body of the people, and also of every numerical person in the kingdom' (*Somers Tracts*, VIII, 402).

ing the situation were well calculated to preserve the political power of the gentry against the crown.[1] Yet Locke adopted an expedient, the use of prerogative power, the political dangers of which Shaftesbury himself had explicitly denounced[2] and both Charles II and, later, James II subsequently demonstrated most dramatically. In constitutional terms the role of prerogative as analysed by Locke was already somewhat old-fashioned. But at the same time, in theoretical terms, the status of prerogative authority over each individual as analysed by him was startlingly novel.[3] The contrast is an apt index of the gap between Locke's conventional constitutionalism and his more distinctive religious individualism. In order to understand the stimulus which led Locke to fuse these two attitudes in a work on government it is necessary to examine the theory which he set himself to refute, the remarkable political doctrine of Robert Filmer.

1 Cf. Plumb's insistence (*Growth of Political Stability*, esp. p. 63), that this remained the purpose of the campaign for free elections throughout the later seventeenth century.

2 *Two Treatises*, II, § 158. Cf. with: 'That the King's prerogative does still extend to grant this franchise to such other towns or villages as he shall think fit, I cannot affirm' (Shaftesbury, *Somers Tracts*, VIII, 398); 'It is, moreover, a thing of very dangerous consequence to have such a power lodged in the King alone; for then he might thereby infranchise what number of vills he pleases, and by the same power place the election of their representatives in a select number, such as he should always have the power to direct and appoint, which would be in effect to chuse his own parliament, and thereby to make or repeal what law he pleases' (*ibid.* p. 399).

3 See below, esp. chapter 11.

6

SIR ROBERT FILMER

Filmer's political claims, like those of Locke in the *Two Treatises*, are set out not in a deductive philosophical system but as a critical commentary on a political theory which was charged with being distinctively novel.[1] As a commentary it is almost as coherent in argument and fully as repetitive in style as that which Locke wrote to refute it. It would be as hard to construct Locke's philosophy and theology from the *Two Treatises* as it is to construct any epistemologically coherent philosophy from *Patriarcha* or the other *Political Tracts*. This, however, scarcely constitutes sufficient reason for us to follow Professor Greenleaf[2] in elevating the latter work to the status of philosophy. For the reason why it is sensible to inquire into the philosophical location of the *Two Treatises* is not any self-evidently taut and systematic character in the work itself. The work has a place as a literary component of that historian's reification, the 'philosophy of Locke', precisely because there exist independently the most deeply etched philosophical contours within which it can be located. The precise conceptual geography may be, indeed *is*, highly dubious; but however blurred the boundaries may have been, it is clear that there must have *been* some boundaries. It is the known existence of a high degree of conceptual definition in some areas at some points in time which encourages the historian to grope for a similar definition of outline in other areas. No such high degree of definition is known ever to have existed in any of Filmer's reflections and there is no reason to suppose that it ever did exist.[3]

1 Robert Filmer, *Patriarcha and other Political Works*, ed. Peter Laslett (Oxford, 1949), p. 53 and esp. p. 277: 'Since the growth of this new doctrine, of the limitation and mixture of monarchy, it is most apparent, that monarchy hath been crucified (as it were) between two thieves, the Pope and the people,' etc. Cf. John Locke, *Two Treatises of Government*, Preface, p. 156; I, §§ 4, 5.

2 W. H. Greenleaf, *Order, Empiricism and Politics* (London, 1964), pp. 87 and 94.

3 This does not of course mean that Filmer's views can be supposed not to have made sense to him; i.e. to have been part of a coherent way of looking at the world. But such a degree of subjective rationality hardly constitutes a philosophical

The degree of coherence imposed upon Filmer's premises seems closer to the existent incoherence of a system of social values than to the formal articulations of a philosopher. The tactics of his polemic consist more in skirmishing against elevated and exposed positions from the tangled and intricate undergrowth of systematic social prejudice than in the formal array of a set of countervailing notions. This did not prevent him from adopting the tone, and indeed the pose, of the scholar.[1] Nor did it mean that he rejected scholastic procedures in his critical method: he had been educated at Cambridge at a time[2] when the curriculum was uniformly scholastic in character.[3] But there is nothing in his works which at any point suggests the sort of taxonomic effort which one can trace through Locke's manuscripts from the first surviving attempt in 1661[4] through to the finally approved text of the *Essay* in the various divisions of the sciences. Filmer's method, instead, is one of persistent attrition—to lay out what he claimed would be the implications of contractarian thought, to gibe at the gross discontinuity between these and the assumptions of the contemporary social order, and to cast derision upon the authorities produced to support these novel positions.

Such a procedure is no way demanded the support of a coherent metaphysic. The charge of novelty which Filmer, with evident sincerity, levelled against the contractarians put upon them the dialectical burden of proof. A man claiming to assert merely what others already know not only can afford to, but indeed must,

achievement, being shared in principle with any human subject of psychological, sociological or anthropological investigation whom the investigator does not presume resolutely insane (and perhaps many whom most people would so consider; cf. R. D. Laing, *The Divided Self* (London, 1960) and the whole enterprise of existential psychiatry of which that is a part).

[1] See Filmer, *Patriarcha*, p. 79, where he notes an omission from the text of Aristotle in several of the most popular editions and translations; and the statement on p. 202 that Aristotle 'breaks the rule of method, by delivering the faults of commonweals, before he teach us what a commonweal is'; 'he observes no method at all, but in a disorderly way, flies backward and forward from one sort to another ...where he comes to discourse of particular forms, he is full of contradiction, or confusion, or both...'; see also p. 303 on Aristotle's 'crabbed and broken passages'.

[2] *Ibid.* pp. 1–2.

[3] William T. Costello, S.J., *The Scholastic Curriculum in Early Seventeenth-Century Cambridge* (Cambridge, Mass., 1958), *passim.*

[4] Bodleian MS Film. 77, sides 2–5, and see *Two Tracts on Government*, pp. 54, 62.

appeal to values at a level at which they are experienced by his audience. A 'philosophical' account of the Filmerian position by its very explicitness would have been as likely to impair as to enhance its plausibility. The ideological purchase of his writing came precisely from its odd combination of tactical brilliance and strategic nescience, the capacity to express eloquently but altogether recognizably misgivings and enthusiasms of which his audience were already conscious in themselves.

The dialectical fulcrum as well as the emotional core of his persuasion lay in its interpretation of divine providence. The existent social world embodied the providence of God. It must surely have shared this embellishment with every previous stage of human history—and pre-eminently with that which immediately followed the creation of the human race in the person of Adam. Would it not, he demanded fiercely, 'derogate from the providence of God Almighty, to ordain a community which could not continue? Or doth it not make the act of our forefathers, in abrogating the natural law of community by introducing that of property, to be a sin of a high presumption?'[1] The central axiom of his argument was always the necessary continuity and homogeneity of the relationship between man and God. The law of nature specifies a unitary set of duties. No change in social or political form can alter the categorical content of duties. To claim, with Grotius, that there can be community of property at one stage and private property at another stage of social organization is explicitly to assert that God makes self-contradictory demands upon human beings.[2] Either all men never had any natural right

[1] *Patriarcha*, p. 65.

[2] 'If there hath been a time when all things were common, and all men equal, and that it be otherwise now; we must needs conclude that the law by which things were common, and men equal, was contrary to the law by which now things are proper and men subject' (*Patriarcha*, p. 262); and '...dominion, he saith, was brought in by the will of man, whom by this doctrine Grotius makes to be able to change that law which God himself cannot change, as he saith. He gives a double ability to man; first to make that no law of nature, which God made to be the law of nature: and next, to make that a law of nature which God made not; for now that dominion is brought in, he maintains, it is against the law of nature to take that which is in another man's dominion. Besides, I find no coherence in these words, by the law of nature it was right for every man to take his own by force, before laws made, since by the law of nature no man had anything of his own; and until laws were made, there was no propriety according to his doctrine' (*ibid.* p. 266); and '...Grotius saith, that by the law of nature all things were at first

to property or the legitimacy of all government is inherently defeasible by the will of any single individual.[1]

The claim is that God must have provided for human beings at every point of their existence a set of rules for social behaviour and that these rules must at all points have been embodied in institutions of social control. Furthermore, these institutions must have been subject to a single supreme authority at every point and all rights held under them must have been determinations of his will. And because *all* rights *and* all powers are determinations of his will, because it is the sole locus of legitimate human authority, his power must be transferable.[2] Dominion is a form of perpetual property.[3] It belongs to God, is conferred by him upon individual men, and transferred from one man to another by his will.

The easiest way of understanding this divine performance is to examine the history of the first, and most unequivocally direct, divine conferment of authority, the gift of the world to Adam. The simplicity of the situation and its historical authenticity make

common, and yet teacheth, that after propriety was brought in, it was against the law of nature to use community. He doth thereby not only make the law of nature changeable, which he saith God cannot do, but he also makes the law of nature contrary to itself' (*ibid.* p. 274).

1 'So that if any one man in the world, be he never so mean or base, will but alter his will, and say, he will resume his natural right to community, and be restored unto his natural liberty, and consequently take what he please and do what he list, who can say that such a man doth more than by right he may? And then it will be lawful for every man, when he please, to dissolve all government, and destroy all property' (*ibid.* p. 274).

2 It is at this sort of point that the idea of a coherent structure in Filmer's ideas becomes most misleading. The maxim of the necessary continuity of political authority is related to that of the transferability of power both as premise (it is needed to lend plausibility to the idea that the words of Genesis do in fact constitute God's political mandate to the human race) and as conclusion (why else should anyone suspect the diversity of political authority in the surrounding world to be uniformly consequent on God's bequest to Adam?). The grounds for believing in the transferability of Adamic authority are predicated on a maxim whose force depends upon there being sufficient grounds to believe in the transferability of Adamic authority. This sort of circularity is typical of Filmer's forms of argument. It would be tedious to point it out with any frequency. But it should at least be noted. Cf. Greenleaf, *Order, Empiricism and Politics*, p. 87, on 'the philosophical basis' and the grounds for the 'cogency' of Filmer's position.

3 '...Father and King are not so diverse, it is confessed that at first they were all one...fatherly empire, as it was of itself hereditary, so it was *alienable* by the parent, and *seizable* by a usurper as other goods are: and thus every King that now is hath a paternal empire, either by inheritance, or by translation or usurpation, so a Father and a King may be all one' (*Patriarcha*, p. 256).

it much easier to be clear about the nature of the event than the later and more damaged traditions of antiquity could do. It is scarcely surprising that the unfortunate Aristotle should have so confused the issues and it is not difficult to excuse him for having done so.[1] But when Christians fail to conduct any serious analysis of their privileged historical data in elaborating their political theories, the ineptness is altogether more reprehensible.[2] Yet even without the benefit of the Judaic or Christian revelations, contractarian political theories can be seen to be internally inconsistent and dangerous in more naturalistic terms. Even Filmer himself generally conceives of political institutions primarily in terms of their putative consequences for human experience on earth rather than for their predetermined theological sanction. Even theologically, they are discussed at times less as authoritarian determinations of the divine will than as instances of God's

[1] 'We cannot much blame Aristotle for the uncertainty and contrariety in him about the sorts of government, if we consider him as a heathen; for it is not possible for the wit of man to search out the first grounds or principles of government (which necessarily depend upon the original of property) except he know that at the creation one man alone was made, to whom the dominion of all things was given and from whom all men derive their title. This point can be learnt only from the scriptures' (*ibid.* pp. 203–4). For the continuity of this position see Bishop Blackall on Hoadly's conception of the state of nature: 'those *Wilderness-States*, which you make mention of two or three times in your Letter, but of which, I own, I do not know quite so much, as I think I do of the Ante Diluvian Political State of Mankind' (Offspring Blackall, *The Lord Bishop of Exeter's Answer to Mr Hoadly's Letter*...(London, 1709), p. 17) and *Divine Institutes of True Religion and Civil Government* (anon.) (London, 1783), chapters 3 and 4.

[2] 'It is not probable that any sure direction of the beginning of government can be found either in Plato, Aristotle, Cicero, Polybius, or in any other of the heathen authors, who were ignorant of the manner of the creation of the world: we must not neglect the scriptures, and search in philosophers for the grounds of dominion and property...' (*Patriarcha*, p. 187). See p. 241 on Hobbes's fictive state of nature —of men 'all created together without any dependency one of another'—'the scripture teacheth us otherwise, that all men came by succession, and generation from one man: we must not deny the truth of the history of the creation'. '...the heathens taught, that all things at first were common, and that all men were equal. This mistake was not so heinous in those ethnic authors of the civil laws, who wanting the guide of the history of Moses, were fain to follow poets and fables for their leaders. But for christians, who have read the scriptures, to dream either of a community of all things, or an equality of all persons, is a fault scarce pardonable' (*ibid.* p. 262). 'It is a shame and scandal for us Christians to seek the original of government from the inventions or fictions of poets, orators, philosophers and heathen historians, who all lived thousands of years after the creation, and were (in a manner) ignorant of it: and to neglect the scriptures, which have with more authority most particularly given us the true grounds and principles of government' (*ibid.* p. 278).

benevolent concern for the preservation of the human race. It is as embodiments of the Love as well as of the Power of God that they are acclaimed.

The framework of critical commentary in which he sets his theories lends an illusory coherence to the different styles of argument which Filmer employs. The theories of others are attacked as incompatible with a simple ahistorical reading of the Scriptures and as either internally inconsistent or disastrous in their prospective practical implications. Either their positions must be instances of a remarkable stupidity or they must be held in bad faith. If they mean what they say, their beliefs would imply anarchy. Their theories are popular precisely because the sinful mass of mankind grasps this implication—but as the theories themselves issue from men with a secure stake in the existing social order, they clearly are not intended to mean what they say. These charges, naturally, do not exhaust the range of Filmer's controversial tactics; but the remaining moves seem more purely technical or more simply polemical, scriptural exegesis or vulgar abuse. The association of non-monarchical government with the fragmentation of divine authority[1] or, more obscurely, with papism,[2]

[1] 'It is well said by J. M. [*sc.* Milton] that all liberty doth almost consist in choosing their form of government, for there is another liberty exercised by the people, which he mentions not, which is the liberty of the peoples choosing their religion; every man may be of any religion, or of no religion; Greece and Rome have been as famous for Polytheism, or multitudes of gods, as of governors; and imagining aristocracy and democracy in heaven, as on earth' (*Patriarcha*, p. 260); see also pp. 188, 207–8 (on Venice and Holland). Cf. the comment in Filmer's most brilliant expositor and Locke's earliest systematic public critic, Charles Leslie: 'The Sum of the Matter betwixt Mr *Hoadly* and Me is this, I think it most Natural that *Authority* shou'd *Descend*, that is, be *Derived* from a *Superiour* to an *Inferiour*, from *God* to *Fathers* and *Kings*, and from *Kings* and *Fathers* to *Sons* and *Servants*: But Mr *Hoadly* wou'd have it *Ascend*, from *Sons* to *Fathers*, and from *Subjects* to *Sovereigns*; nay to *God* Himself, whose *Kingship* the Men of the *Rights* say, is *Derived* to *Him* from the *People*! And the *Argument* does Naturally Carry it all that Way. For if *Authority* does *Ascend*, it must *Ascend* to the *Height*' (*The Finishing Stroke, Being a Vindication of the Patriarchal Scheme of Government*...(London, 1711), p. 87).

[2] '...what principles the papists make use of for the power of the Pope above Kings; the very same, by blotting out the word Pope, and putting in the word people, the plebists take up to use against their sovereigns. If we would truly know what popery is, we shall find by the laws and statutes of the realm, that the main, and indeed, the only point of popery, "is the alienating and withdrawing of subjects from their obedience to their prince, to raise sedition and rebellion." If popery and popularity agree in this point, the Kings of Christendom that have shaken off the power of the Pope, have made no great bargain of it, if in place of one lord abroad,

clearly had a grand ideological resonance[1] and there is every reason to suppose that it catches at the emotional heart of Filmer's picture of human life, but it is hardly worked out rationally at any point and, except in the most patronizing of senses, it would be false to say that we can still understand it today. However, such of the conceptual structure as *is* set out in sufficient detail to be intelligible can be reproduced in outline—and it is *this* structure, Filmer's explicit doctrines, to which Locke addressed himself in the *Two Treatises* and which set him the particular set of dialectical problems which his most important notions were intended to resolve.

The origin of government must be identical in character to the present basis of government.[2] Its origin as described in the scrip-

they get many lords at home within their own kingdoms' (*Patriarcha*, p. 277–8). 'What power soever general assemblies of the estates claim or exercise over and above the bare naked act of counselling, they were first beholding to the popish clergy for it: it is they first brought Parliaments into request and power: I cannot find in any kingdom, but only where popery hath been, that Parliaments have been of reputation: and in the greatest times of superstition they are first mentioned' (*ibid.* pp. 311–2).

[1] So too, no doubt, did the claim that popular government implied a standing army, 'if unity in government, which is only found in monarchy, be once broken, there is no stay or bound, until it come to a constant standing army, for the people or multitude, as Aristotle teacheth us, can excel in no virtue but military, and that that is natural to them, and therefore in a popular estate, the sovereign power is in the sword, and those that are possessed of the arms. So that any nation or kingdom that is not charged with the keeping of a King, must perpetually be at the charge of paying and keeping of an army' (*ibid.* p. 199). Though in 1652 the intelligibility and force of this appeal to English constitutionalist shibboleth is not difficult to follow.

[2] Filmer's comment on Bellarmine: 'First, he saith, that by the law of God, power is immediately in the people; hereby he makes God the author of a democratical estate; for a democracy is nothing else but the power of the multitude. If this be true, not only aristocracies but all monarchies are altogether unlawful, as being ordained (as he thinks) by men, when as God himself hath chosen a democracy' (*ibid.* p. 56). Cf., for the consequences of denying the unitary nature of the inherited authority, 'in other governments, the body of their acts and ordinances is composed of a multitude of momentary monarchs, who by the strength and power of their parties or factions are still under a kind of a civil war, fighting and scratching for the legislative miscellany, or medley of several governments. If we consider each government according to the nobler part of which it is composed, it is nothing else but a monarchy of monothelites, or of many men of one will, most commonly in one point only: but if we regard only the baser part, or bodies of such persons as govern, there is an interrupted succession of a multitude of short-lived governments, with as many intervals of anarchy; so that no man can say at any time, that he is under any form of government; for in a shorter time than the word can be spoken, every government is begun and ended' (*ibid.* p. 206).

ture was the direct providence of God. This providence continues indefinitely. No subsequent human state can be worse provided for than the Adamic state. No subsequent human state can be differently provided for.[1] God's gift of authority to Adam and God's gift of property were a single act.[2] All authority is property and all property depends upon authority. Hence authority must be thought of as a transferable object, a good distributed in a system in which the only autonomous agent is God.[3] Since

[1] Filmer is scarcely consistent on this point. He admits, with Locke, the possibility and indeed actuality of men living together outside government, of non-political societies. Even though these are clearly stated to be inferior communities, this is still hardly consistent with the principle of continuity. The providence of God appears to have dozed a little here. Significantly this admission is contained in the reply he makes to the challenge to show the patriarchal origins of the sovereignties of the Republic of Venice and the Confederation of the Netherlands. Laslett (*Patriarcha*, p. 13) perhaps does not adequately bring out this discontinuity. See Filmer, '...it is said that it is evident to common sense, that of old time Rome, and in this present age Venice, and the Low Countries, enjoy a form of government different from monarchy: hereunto it may be answered, that a people may live together in society, and help one another; and yet not be under any form of government; as we see herds of cattle do, and yet we may not say they live under government. For government is not a society only to live, but to live well and virtuously. This is acknowledged by Aristotle, who teacheth that the end of a city, is to live blessedly and honestly. Political communities are ordained for honest actions, but not for living together only' (*ibid.* p. 206).

[2] '...more absurdities are easily removed if on the contrary we maintain *the natural and private dominion of Adam* to be the fountain of all government and propriety' (*Patriarcha*, p. 71). 'The first government in the world was monarchical in the father of all flesh. Adam being commanded to multiply, and people the earth, and to subdue it, and having dominion given him over all creatures, was thereby the monarch of the whole world; none of his posterity had any right to possess anything, but by his grant or permission, or by succession from him: the earth (saith the Psalmist) hath he given to the children of men: which shows, the title comes from the fatherhood' (*ibid.* pp. 187–8).

[3] '...the paternal power cannot be lost; it may either be transferred or usurped; but never lost, or ceaseth. God, who is the giver of power, may transfer it from the Father to some other...As the power of the Father may be lawfully transferred or aliened, so it may be unjustly usurped: and in usurpation, the title of a usurper is before, and better than the title of any other than of him that had a former right: for he hath a possession by the permissive will of God, which permission, how long it may endure, no man ordinarily knows' (*Patriarcha*, pp. 231–2). See also *ibid.* p. 256 (cited above, p. 61, n. 3). Filmer's position on usurpation is extremely shifty and it is probably significant that this treatment of the theme comes in the *Directions for Obedience to Government in Dangerous or Doubtful Times* of 1652. The claim that he makes that 'though by humane laws, a long prescription may take away right, yet divine right never dies, nor can be lost, or taken away' (*Patriarcha*, p. 232), reflects some little credit on his capacity for loyalty but less on his capacity for logical coherence. It surely does 'detract from the providence of God' that his will should be sufficiently permissive to leave men with directly conflicting duties

authority is a matter of will, of the right to make choices for, and command the obedience of, others, it must be unitary—'an indivisible beam of majesty, cannot be divided among, or settled upon a multitude.'[1] The indivisibility of government and the fact that there can be no lawful criterion on earth for the exercise of supreme authority means that the idea of a tyranny is without content.[2] Thus authority in Filmer becomes curiously like property in Macpherson's interpretation of Locke, a good upon whose use no one but the possessor has any *prima facie* claim within the legal and moral order, whilst property itself, in this same legalistic sense, becomes the only conceivable relationship between man and natural objects. This centrality and paradigmatic quality of the analysis of property for the whole theory of politics[3] is the dialectical origin of the most celebrated feature of Locke's theory. Filmer forced upon him the necessity of demonstrating that property right in origin was not simply reducible to positive law; that there are more true property-holders than just the king;[4] that property is in principle an unequivocal right against forceful seizure by any individual including the monarch (not any sort of moral right against a starving man);[5] that exertion could in principle lead to property differentiation (not that it would be a sufficient justification for all particular differentials in appropria-

towards authority, the very eventuality against which the unequivocal terms of the Genetic charter purported to insure. (For a comprehensive statement of the muddle see *Patriarcha*, p. 233.)

[1] *Patriarcha*, p. 189. The passage continues, 'God would have it fixed in one person, not sometimes in one part of the people, and sometimes in another; and sometimes, and that for the most part, nowhere, as when the assembly is dissolved, it must rest in the air, or in the walls of the chamber where they were assembled.' See also, 'To be governed, is nothing else but to be obedient and subject to the will or command of another; it is the will in a man that governs' (*ibid.* p. 205). Filmer's use of Bodin was extensive. See *Patriarcha*, *passim*, and Constance I. Smith, 'Filmer and the Knolles Translation of Bodin', *Philosophical Quarterly*, XIII (1963).

[2] '...there is no such form of government as a tyranny' (*Patriarcha*, p. 229).

[3] '...it is not possible for the wit of man to search out the first grounds or principles of government (which necessarily depend upon the original of property) except he know that at the creation one man alone was made, to whom the dominion of all things was given, and from whom all men derive their title. This point can be learnt only from the scriptures' (*Patriarcha*, pp. 203–4); and '...the grounds of dominion and property, which are the main principles of government and justice' (*ibid.* p. 187).

[4] This seems to be a consequence of the Filmerian position: but cf. Laslett for what is an apparently contrary reading (*Patriarcha*, p. 13).

[5] John Locke, *Two Treatises*, I, §§ 41–3.

tion or consumption but only that it was a necessary condition for any such being justified).[1] More searchingly, it forced him to give an account of how it could be the case that the law of nature could at one point 'prescribe community' and at another 'prescribe propriety',[2] and of how the human race could have alienated irrevocably their entire freedom to political institutions which under any conceivable circumstances, and *a fortiori* under the British constitution, left them substantially unfree.[3] The abstract relationship which Locke employed to set out his answer, the state of nature, is the focus of the most startling of the myths and misconceptions which surround his thought. The tactics in each case were to substitute a more complicated set of relations for the unitary simplicity of Filmer's model. In place of the crude antithesis between everything belonging to everybody (with its logical incoherences so doggedly mocked by Filmer) or everything belonging to Adam or his heir, the world is presented as belonging to nobody but available for the appropriations of all.[4]

[1] But cf. C. B. Macpherson, *The Political Theory of Possessive Individualism* (Oxford, 1962), *passim*, esp. pp. 194–262.

[2] *Patriarcha*, pp. 262, 266, 274 (cited above, p. 60, n. 2). See also, 'If it were a thing so voluntary, and at the pleasure of men when they were free to put themselves under subjection, why may they not as voluntarily leave subjection when they please, and be free again? If they had a liberty to change their natural freedom, into a voluntary subjection, there is stronger reason that they may change their voluntary subjection into natural freedom, since it is lawful for men to alter their wills as their judgments. Certainly it was a rare felicity, that all the men in the world at one instant of time should agree together in one mind to change the natural community of all things into private dominion: for without such a unanimous consent it was not possible for community to be altered: for if but one man in the world had dissented, the alteration had been unjust, because that man by the law of nature had a right to the common use of all things in the world; so that to have given a propriety of any one thing to any other, had been to have robbed him of his right to the common use of all things' (*ibid.* p. 273).

[3] Filmer comments on the Lords and Commons: 'All these graces conferred upon the Peers, are so far from being derived from the law of nature that they are contradictory and destructive of that natural equality and freedom of mankind, which many conceive to be the foundation of the privileges and liberties of the House of Commons; there is so strong an opposition between the liberties of grace and nature, that it had never been possible for the two houses of Parliament to have stood together without mortal enmity, and eternal jarring, had they been raised upon such opposite foundations: but the truth is, the liberties and privileges of both houses have but one, and the self-same foundation, which is nothing else but the mere and sole grace of Kings' (*Patriarcha*, p. 157). See also pp. 118–19, 224–8, 287 and esp. pp. 69–70.

[4] The notable inadequacy of such a theory as a rationalization of the particular structure of property distribution in the late seventeenth century seems clear; but

The claim that the direct Old Testament revelation of God's bequest to Adam is an intelligible sample of divine positive law is subjected to the most withering (and interminable) criticism in the *First Treatise*. The intellectual tedium of this exercise was matched only by its ideological necessity; if a specific political doctrine could be extrapolated from the scripture, as Filmer's claimed to be, it clearly pre-empted any further form of political reflection. Where God had spoken, mere men must needs be silent. The ahistorical certitude of Filmer is replaced, not as he claimed by a sort of historicist supersession of divine orders,[1] but by a reading of the relevant divine injunctions within a continuing order of historical experience.[2] The state of nature is not of course in itself a specific historical stage; but it is intended to specify the continuing moral order within which human beings live and make their history. The notion that it must be an incompetent (and irrelevant) means of showing what men once were like or, still worse, *really* are like rests upon a failure to realize that for Locke, unlike Filmer, men *do make* history, that by their voluntary actions, however compulsive, they build the social world in which they live.

These are perhaps the elements of Locke's writing which are most liable to misunderstanding if they are not seen in confrontation with the thought of the man against whom he was writing. But they are not the only features of Filmer's ideas or strategies which help to make the specific character of the *Two Treatises* more readily intelligible. Both the type of general appeal which Filmer attempted to make to the English gentry and certain parts of his more specific arguments imposed certain demands upon a pro-

it should be noted that it is a highly successful resolution of the question which Locke states himself to be attempting to answer. See *Two Treatises*, II, §25, ll. 16–19.

1 See, for example, 'It were impiety...to imagine that the rules given in divers places in the gospel, by our blessed Saviour and his Apostles for obedience to Kings should now, like almanacs out of date, be of no use to us' (*Patriarcha*, p.278).

2 The enterprise of locating divine revelation within the order of human historical experience is one of the two key intellectual enterprises of Locke's life. In a sense a large part of the *Essay*, all of the *Reasonableness of Christianity* and the entire interpretative commentary upon St Paul's Epistles form a part of this enterprise. See also, for an illuminating example of how Locke employed the work of the most prominent contemporary European exponent of such an enterprise, the notebook MS Locke f 32, notes on Richard Simon. (For a helpful short account of Simon's work see Paul Hazard, *La Crise de la conscience européenne* (Paris, 1961), part 2, chapter 3, 'Richard Simon et l'Exégèse biblique', pp. 165–81.)

spective antagonist. It will be convenient to treat the latter first. Apart from the central issue of property, the most incisive demand that Filmer addressed to any prospective contractarian was that he should 'resolve the conscience, touching the manner of the peoples passing their consent; and what is sufficient, and what not, to make, or derive, a right or title from the people'.[1] Naturally, this was a demand which Locke himself noted in his preparatory workings for his reply,[2] though how far he did in fact conceive his reply in precisely such terms, as an effort to 'resolve the consciences' of his prospective audience, is controversial.[3] It seems likely that Locke himself felt that he had resolved the Filmerian difficulties through a combination of his theory of the origins of property right and his conception of tacit consent. It is clear that the problem which was critical in his mind was the problem of the legitimacy of contemporary societies, rather than the prehistoric origin of such a legitimate order. Even in terms of the conjectural history of government which he sketches in the *Second Treatise*, it is not clear that Filmer's criticism of contractarian accounts of consent or of majority rights were particularly damaging to his argument.[4]

Certain implications which Filmer claimed followed from the contractarian account of political obligation were accepted by Locke in his writing, though seldom in the precise form in which they were urged by Filmer. The contingency of the legitimacy of any government on the right of emigration which Locke's subsequent critics, especially Hume,[5] mocked so unmercifully can be seen as an acceptance within the contours of the Lockean analysis of property of Filmer's charge that natural freedom implied the permanent right of secession.[6] The issue of who should judge of

[1] *Patriarcha*, p. 226. See also p. 81, 82 ('No one man, nor a multitude, can give away the natural right of another'), 189, 211, 217–18, 224–6, 243–4, 273.

[2] MS Locke f 28, p. 119.

[3] Cf. Laslett in *Two Treatises*, p. 84 and p. 235 n.

[4] Cf. *Patriarcha*, p. 205 and references cited above, n. 1. For accounts of Locke's position on these two issues see below, chapter 10.

[5] David Hume, 'Of the Original Contract', *Essays, Moral, Political, and Literary* (London, 1903), pp. 461–2.

[6] 'Since nature hath not distinguished the habitable world into kingdoms, nor determined what part of a people shall belong to one kingdom, and what to another, it follows that the original freedom of mankind being supposed, every man is at liberty to be of what kingdom he please, and so every petty company hath a right to make a kingdom by itself; and not only every city, but every village, and

the degree of oppression which justifies popular resistance to the government is the question which, however ambiguously, the *Two Treatises* are largely concerned in answering.[1] The attempt to invoke the taboo against suicide as a basic axiom of the theory of political obligation[2] was precisely reversed by Locke. However, the obligation to preserve God's creatures, and *a fortiori* to preserve oneself, has implications in Filmer's thought which extend beyond this single example. God's intentions in creating government,[3] the grounds of the obedience which the populace owe to a

every family, nay, and every particular man, a liberty to choose himself to be his own King if he please; and he were a madman that being by nature free, would choose any man but himself to be his own governor. Thus to avoid the having but of one King of the whole world, we shall run into a liberty of having as many Kings as there be men in the world...' (*Patriarcha*, p. 286). The notion that men *could* have no rational motive for accepting subjection to political authority seems something of a qualification of Filmer's naturalism.

1 'If you would know who should be judge of the greatness and certainty of the danger, or how we may know it, Grotius hath not one word of it. So that for ought appears to the contrary, his mind may be that every private man may be judge of the danger, for other judge he appoints none' (*Patriarcha*, p. 67). On Hobbes: 'Page 68. Right of defending life and means of living can never be abandoned. These last doctrines are destructive to all government whatsoever, and even to the *Leviathan* itself...every man's goods being means of living, if a man cannot abandon them, no contract among men, be it never so just, can be observed' (*ibid.* p. 248). On Hunton: 'Now if you ask the author who shall be judge, whether the monarch transcend his bounds, and of the excesses of the sovereign power; his answer is, "There is an impossibility of constituting a judge to determine this last controversy"...I demand of him if there be a variance betwixt the monarch and any of the meanest persons of the community, who shall be the judge?...if the King be judge, then he is no limited monarch; if the people be judge, then he is no monarch at all. So farewell limited monarchy, nay farewell all government, if there be no judge' (*ibid.* pp. 294–5). See also p. 300. For an analysis of the extent to which Locke's doctrine provides an answer to the question of who should be judge, and of the ambiguities of this answer, see below, chapter 13.

2 On Hunton: '...if it be true that nature hath made all men free; though all mankind should concur in one vote, yet it cannot seem reasonable, that they should have power to alter the law of nature; for if no man have power to take away his own life without the guilt of being a murderer of himself, how can any people confer such a power as they have not themselves upon any one man, without being accessories to their own deaths, and every particular man become guilty of being *felo de se?*' (*Patriarcha*, p. 285). This move was a common one in authoritarian political theory. Cf., for example, Offspring Blackall, *The Divine Institution of Magistracy*...(London, 1708), pp. 5–6 and Benjamin Hoadly's embarrassed response, *Some Considerations humbly offered to the Right Reverend the Lord Bishop of Exeter*...(London, 1709), pp. 10–12.

3 'The right of fatherly government was ordained by God, for the preservation of mankind', (*Patriarcha*, p. 232). This, and the passages on pp. 233 and 234 (see p. 71, nn. 2 and 3, below) are all taken from the work *Directions for Obedience to Government*... which Filmer published in May 1652, three months after his *Observations on Mr*

usurper[1] (even the grounds for the legal fiction that the rightful monarch authorizes the commands of the usurper),[2] and the source of the duties of usurper himself[3] can all be expressed as instances of the duty to preserve life. However, this axiom of the law of nature does not imply either the natural hostility or the anarchic rights which Hobbes has ascribed to the human race.[4] Rather, it is

Hobbes's Leviathan...(*Patriarcha*, pp. 186, 238), in which the theme of the preservation of life as a duty first becomes prominent. This does not appear to be a result of pure accident—Filmer was clearly very impressed by Hobbes.

[1] 'Every man is to preserve his own life for the service of God, and of his King or Father, and is so far to obey a usurper, as may tend not only to the preservation of his King and Father, but sometimes even to the preservation of the usurper himself, when probably he may thereby be reserved to the correction, or mercy of his true superior' (*Patriarcha*, p. 232).

[2] 'The usurper may be so far obeyed, as may tend to the preservation of the subjects, who may thereby be enabled to perform their duty to their true and right sovereign, when time shall serve: in such cases to obey a usurper, is properly to obey the first and right governor, *who must be presumed to desire the safety of his subjects*' (*Patriarcha*, p. 232; my italics). Note that even at this point, no autonomous right of initiative is admitted to lie in the hands of the individual—it is only as executant of the presumed intention of the true ruler that he is authorized to act. However all the force of Filmer's own inquiries about who has the authority to judge of the legitimacy of public acts applies to this claim (see p. 70, n. 1, above). Subjectivity and the rational calculation of utility are intruded destructively into the Filmerian structure at this point. See also, 'It is to be presumed, that the superior desires the preservation of them that should be subject to him; and so likewise it may be presumed, that a usurper in general doth the will of his superior, by preserving the people by government, and it is not improper to say, that in obeying a usurper, we may obey primarily the true superior, so long as our obedience aims at the preservation of those in subjection' (*ibid.* p. 234).

[3] 'Every man hath a part or share in the preservation of mankind in general, he that usurps the power of a superior, thereby puts upon himself a necessity of acting the duty of a superior in the preservation of them over whom he hath usurped...Thus there may be a conditional duty, or right in a usurper to govern; that is to say, supposing him to be so wicked as to usurp, and not willing to surrender or forgo his usurpation, he is then bound to protect by government, or else he increaseth and multiplieth his sin' etc. (*Patriarcha*, pp. 233–4).

[4] *Patriarcha*, pp. 242 and 248. For Filmer (p. 242) as for Locke the presence of abundant resources of food is a precondition for human social existence. 'If such a multitude of men should be created as the earth could not well nourish, there might be cause for men to destroy one another rather than perish for want of food; but God was no such niggard in the creation, and there being plenty of sustenance and room for all men, there is no cause or use of war till men be hindered in the preservation of life...' (cf. *Two Treatises*, II, chapter V). But each man's right of self-preservation is one which he cannot have the power to enforce against the law of property: 'every man's goods being means of living, if a man cannot abandon them, no contract among men, be it never so just, can be observed' (*Patriarcha*, p. 248). (It is possible that Filmer would have regarded some contracts as void because of their 'injustice'; but he could not consistently allow any contractor, in any circumstances, to decide such an issue for himself.)

its direct sanction upon constituted human authority which is the basis of secure human social life,[1] which binds that authority more strongly than it does any private individual,[2] and which confers a specifically religious status on the judgement of the sovereign.[3]

Yet, whatever covert appeals to utilitarian considerations these elements of Filmer's thought introduce, the core of the argument remains in essence an argument from authority, as much as the force of its appeal rests upon existing structures of social authority. His most powerful arguments, those which gouged out of Locke the most explicit and central features of the Lockean doctrine, were all delivered from a dialectical emplacement very close to this structure of authority. The core of the Filmerian appeal was precisely the accusation that the contractarians denied

1 '...positive laws may be said to bind the King, not by being positive but as they are naturally the best or only means for the preservation of the commonwealth. By this means are all Kings, even tyrants and conquerors, bound to preserve the lands, goods, liberties and lives of all their subjects, not by any municipal law of the land, but by the natural law of a Father, which binds them to ratify the acts of their forefathers and predecessors in things necessary for the public good of their subjects' (*Patriarcha*, p. 103).

2 '...every Father is bound by the law of nature to do his best for the preservation of his family. But much more is a King always tied by the same law of nature to keep this general ground, that the safety of his kingdom be his chief law' (*Patriarcha*, p. 96); 'the prerogative of a King is to be above all laws, for the good only of them that are under the laws' (*ibid.* p. 105). See also the passage quoted from Bodin, 'the law of God, whereunto all princes are more straitly bound than their subjects' (*ibid.* p. 321). This insistence on the total responsibility of the ruler for his actions places him, in this respect, in a moral situation identical with that of an absolute monarch in the *Two Treatises*. In a sense, it is an indication of the limitation of Filmer's providentialism (hinted at above, p. 65, n. 1), when set against an unequivocal providentialist divine-right theory, such as that of William Sherlock (cf. the (misleadingly titled) article by Gerald M. Straka, 'The Final Phase of Divine Right Theory in England, 1688–1702', *English Historical Review*, LXXVII (1962), 638–58, and his *Anglican Reaction to the Revolution of 1688* (Madison, Wisconsin, 1962), and Quentin Skinner, 'History and Ideology in the English Revolution', *Historical Journal* VIII, 2 (1965), 171–6). The combination of providential glossing of all terrestrial events and of the restriction of morally autonomous and proper action to the ruler could lead to very far-reaching instances of the claim that the king could do no wrong in a moral and not merely legal sense. See, for a considerably later example, 'in the heyday of Lockean Liberalism', Edward Young's *An Apology for Princes*...(London, 1729), pp. 26–7: 'Princes not quite guilty of Faults they Commit'—because their actions must be seen as the judicial correction of the people by God, they cannot be considered as properly voluntary actions for which the rulers as physical agents are fully responsible.

3 '...natural equity...cannot fully be comprised in any laws, but is to be left to the *religious* arbitrament of those who know how to manage the affairs of state...' (*Patriarcha*, p. 96; my italics).

the very existence of this structure of authority—hence the clumsy alternation between simple incredulity that they could in fact mean what they appeared to be saying and the frightened, but often pungent, denunciation of them for the purposeful advocacy of anarchy. The assumption that there was a symmetry of authority relationships from top to bottom of the society gave to this argument a mordant controversial edge. However much a man might like to give free rein to his own desires on the political stage, it was inconceivable that he would abandon his own expectations of authority on the domestic stage. The most extreme radicals were all too likely, as Charles Leslie charged,[1] to be domestic tyrants. In the ritual, incantatory affirmation of the structure of authority in the society, in formal theology as in vulgar social practice, all power was rendered personal and intimate and the most intimate of relationships were asserted as structures of power. All kings were fathers and all fathers ruled. Just how great a purchase this muddled insistent formula may have had is hard to tell now. The nagging repetition may be as reliable an indicator of the precariousness of the moral plausibility of the society as of its crushing ideological weight. A sense of savage, inarticulate outrage is as possible a background to the persuasion as one of blithe moral acquiescence. If the relationships of authority are personal relationships, they are easier to charge with feeling than those we have towards the abstracted confusing bureaucracies of today—few love or hate a rural district council. And in a universe of gross deprivation, the feeling must often have

[1] 'These Men whose chief *Topick* is the *Liberty* of the *People*, and against *Arbitrary Power*, are the most *Absolute* of any other in their *Families*, and so Proportionably, as they rise *Higher*. If they Believ'd *Themselves*, or their own *Pretences*, they wou'd go *Home*, and call a *Council* of their *Wives*, *Children* and *Servants*, and tell them that the *Master* of a *Family* was ordain'd for the *Good* of those that were put under his *Government*, that it was not to be Suppos'd such a Number of *Persons*, equal to Him self in *Nature*, were all Created merely for his *Lusts* and *Pleasurers*; and that they must be the best *Judges* of what was for their own *Good*; And therefore, that they shou'd *Meet* and *Consult* together, as oft as they thought fit; and set him *Rules* for the *Government* of his *Family*: Which, if he *Broke*, or that they thought so, for they are the *Judges* of that; then that they shou'd *Abdicate* him; and Choose another *Master* for Themselves...can any Believe, that a *Tyrant* in a *Family* would not prove the same upon a *Throne*? It has ever prov'd so. And I desire no other *Test* for these Publick *Patrons* for *Liberty*, than to look into their *Conversation* and their *Families*' ([Charles Leslie], *The New Association of those Called Moderate-Church-Men*... (London, 1703), Part II, Appendix, pp. 6–7.)

been most immediately one of hate. Hence the need to weight the immediate aggression with a heavy sense of guilt, to train the most deprived in the endless responsibility to love their rulers.

Such a crude picture of the 'ideological' needs of such a society, of the form which political socialization had to take, makes it easier to understand how persuasive Filmer could be. When the children in the villages learnt from their parish priests, in those paradigms of Professor Oakeshott's 'cribs', the catechism books, that crude abridgement of their society's moral teaching, they learnt just that doctrine which Filmer claimed to explicate. All duties towards authority were specified in the fifth commandment —'Honour thy Father...', as they are still indeed specified today.[1] For Filmer, as for a more self-conscious intellectual like Bishop James Ussher,[2] as for the committee set up by the general court in distant Massachusetts to consider the misdeeds of selectman

[1] This does not, of course, indicate that this section was as emotionally meaningless in the seventeenth century as it is today. It is not its occurrence in the catechism books but the way in which it is constantly referred to in disputes concerning proper social attitudes that shows its emotional force in the life of the community. The importance of the text of the fifth commandment was emphasized by Laslett in his edition of Filmer (*Patriarcha*, p. 26) and more recently and extensively in Peter Laslett, *The World We Have Lost* (London, 1965), pp. 20, 176–8, etc. The universality of its occurrence in seventeenth-century English catechism books and something of the importance of this fact were first emphasized by Gordon Schochet of Rutgers University. The role of the family as an instrument of politico-religious discipline has been emphasized recently by many historians of Puritanism, especially by Michael Walzer.

[2] *Patriarcha*, pp. 62 and 188, and James Ussher, *A Body of Divinity*...(London, 1648), pp. 256–7: 'The meaning and scope of the fifth Commandment.' 'That the quality of mens persons and places, in whatsoever estate, Naturall, Civill, or Ecclesiasticall, and with whatsoever relation to us, be duely acknowledged and respected. For it requireth the performance of all such duties as one man oweth unto another, by some particular bond: in regard of special callings and differences, which God hath made between speciall persons.

Who are Superiours?

They be such as by *Gods* ordinance have any preeminence, preferment or excellency above others: and are here termed by the name of Parents...to whom the first and principall duties required in this Commandment do appettaine [*sic*]...

Why are all Superiours called here by the name of Parents?

1. For that the name of Parents being a most sweet and loving name, men might thereby be allured the rather to the duties they owe; whether they be duties that are to be performed to them, or which they should performe to their Inferiours. 2. For that at the first, and in the beginning of the world, Parents were also Magistrates, Pastours, School-Masters, &c...

Why is the Commandement [*sic*] *conceived in the name of Inferiours?*

Because their duties are hardest obeyed in all estates.'

John Ruddock of Sudbury[1] or indeed for the preachers of many of the election sermons in eighteenth-century Massachusetts, every instance of respect or responsibility or simple obedience which a man's place in his society imposed upon him was an instance of his duty to observe the fifth commandment. All this, of course, must be seen as an ideological enterprise, and not necessarily as an ideological achievement. We shall never know for sure what degree of surreptitious sniggering greeted the pious exhortations of the parish priest. It is difficult enough to reconstruct the consciousness of those who have left extensive written remains. In the case of those who could not write at all and whose words were never recorded it is almost, if not quite, impossible. The contrast between the literate articulate world of politics and the constricted, orally defined consciousness of the local community which Laslett stresses[2] is indeed critical for the understanding of the public life of the nation but it tells us necessarily only the *form* of political participation by the illiterate—it cannot tell us its *content*. And no depth of silence, no impotence to define their feelings in action can show the absence of the feelings. Even today, through the clumsy gropings of a Filmer, it is possible to sense the intense subjective fragility of the social order in the nervous urgency with which he attempts to swing the entire legitimacy of the social order on the pivot of each child's earliest learnt allegiances.

The strange, punning theory in which Filmer advanced these ideas gained force from the irrelevant appeals to English legalism and traditionalism and to the purer forms of social prejudice noted above. The Burkean doctrine of continuity,[3] the blunt appeal to the reality of English society or constitutional structure,[4] simple prescription,[5] simpler social snobbery,[6] the subversiveness of learning,[7] and the tyrannical practices of many popular governments,[8] all lent their weight. But the core of its persuasiveness lay in that ineffable incoherence in which God's power was paternal[9]

[1] Sumner Chilton Powell, *Puritan Village, The Formation of a New England Town* (paperback edition, Garden City, N.Y., 1965), pp. 168–9.

[2] Laslett, *The World We Have Lost*, esp. pp. 194–9.

[3] *Patriarcha*, pp. 226, 286.

[4] *Ibid.* pp. 118–19, 157, 227–8, 287.

[5] *Ibid.* pp. 69, 106.

[6] *Ibid.* pp. 89, 226.

[7] *Ibid.* p. 85.

[8] *Ibid.* p. 224.

[9] *Ibid.* p. 233.

and a king's power religious,[1] in which a family was a kingdom and a kingdom a family and all duties were one. The axioms of Filmer's thought, the legalism in which all change is seen as usurpatory, the stress on authority, prototypically paternal authority, as a social fact, made plausible his frenetic over-assimilation of differences to unity. But the plausibility was emotional and not intellectual. For Filmer men needed a concrete continuing authority in which they could be wrapped. Like crabs they could live only in a continuous God-given shell. But to Locke they were more like hermit crabs: the shells they needed, their instincts made available to them. It was God's world they lived in—but as difficult as it seemed.

[1] *Patriarcha*, p. 96.

7

LOCKE AND HOBBES

The worthy, if slightly bumbling Locke we all used to know (just as we knew that he wrote in defence of that worthy if slightly bumbling apotheosis of English constitutionalism, the Glorious Revolution) wrote to answer the terrible, if undeniably *clever* Hobbes. Both of these hallowed opinions were vigorously attacked by Mr Laslett in his edition of the *Two Treatises* and the attacks had an immediate impact. But, rather surprisingly, the complicated and difficult historical demonstration that the bulk of the work was written several years before the Revolution rapidly became the new orthodoxy, while the simple and wholly convincing dialectical demonstration that the shape of the *Two Treatises* was dictated by the attempt to answer Sir Robert Filmer's political tracts has never received a very enthusiastic response and its importance scarcely been sympathetically understood. One reason for this curious difference in the two responses, perhaps, is rather vulgar. The recognition that the *Two Treatises* was not the rationalization of a successful revolution in the past at most implied the abandonment of a particular historical doctrine about a single figure; brashly, it meant rewriting one lecture. But the historically supported argument that lining Locke up against Hobbes and comparing their various dimensions was not *the* way to approach the study of Locke (indeed, at its most disturbing, perhaps not even *a* way) had altogether more sinister implications. If it were correct, it did not just mean the rewriting of one lecture; it meant a significant revision of the entire way in which the history of political theory was conceived. It meant that the pedagogic experience of most people who teach the subject, the study of a historically selected series of accredited texts (in itself, perhaps the most crushing refutation ever of the empirical claims of Social Darwinism), barely meshed at all with the epistemological, empirical, and *hence* even the philosophical problems raised by the subject matter. In the face of this disturbing threat it is not altogether surprising that this particular claim should have received some sharp examination and we may no doubt expect it to continue to do so for some little time to come.

It would be wrong, however, to suggest, quite apart from the valuable historical light which any such dispute is likely to shed, that there are not admirable as well as rather unimpressive reasons for dissent. To put the point at its crudest: Hobbes was undoubtedly the most intelligent man to write about politics in England in the seventeenth century before Locke and he wrote about it in a specifically philosophical manner. Furthermore, his greatest book was devoted to the exposition of a political theory which at a pragmatic level espoused a set of imperatives directly antagonistic to those of the *Two Treatises*. Is it conceivable historically that a man with Locke's philosophical ambitions could have written such a work at the time when he did without his intellectual course being powerfully deflected by the magnetic pull, exercised by reason of its very existence, of that great mass of intellectual magma?[1] Thus it seems that, quite apart from the fact that what most interests us about the political theories of seventeenth-century England is the confrontation of these two intellectual giants (and this interest seems philosophically apt), there must be a definite sense in which the confrontation is also apt historically. The reasoning is not subtle but it has the force of its own crudity. In what sense, then, should it be unconvincing?

The problem arises, essentially, over the assimilation of the historical case to the philosophical. Because it is plausible to claim that there must have been some sense in which Locke felt himself in the intellectual presence of Hobbes in writing the book and because what is undoubtedly of supreme philosophical fascination to us, at least about Locke's work, is this confrontation of the two, we are prone to suppose that the confrontation must be the key to the meaning of the book, that, as it were, it enables us to crack the structural code of the work. But this is simply to pun on the word 'meaning'. All too irrefutable as an assessment at the level

[1] This is not something of which Mr Laslett is unaware. I make no attempt to give an account of his position because it is stated clearly in his introduction to John Locke, *Two Treatises of Government*, pp. 67–91. Rather, what I am attempting here is to follow the movement of thought which has led to the unsympathetic reception of these notions and to show that the undoubted force of this intellectual hesitancy does not have the implications which those who feel it sometimes suppose.

of our own autobiography, it simply begs the question of historical assessment and manages to beg it while ostensibly claiming support from historical evidence which does not bear at all on the issue. It is rather as though, possessing a heuristic device analogous to an X-ray which reproduced, however, only the nervous system of the human body, we should mistake its depictions for those of a conventional X-ray. Pictures of a skeleton are not inferior surrogates in physiology for pictures of the nervous system—though they may certainly seem to us more banal. The metaphor is loose but it brings out fairly the extreme oddity of the historical supposition.

In the concrete, this theme is delicate. The claim is that the disputed 'influence', negative or positive, of Hobbes upon the *Two Treatises* is irrelevant to the historical comprehension of that work. This is not because Locke did not care about Hobbes's arguments in *Leviathan*. Nor is it just vulgarly because the book was *addressed* to Filmer's position. It is rather because the problem which he needed to discuss in order to refute Filmer is not at all the same as Hobbes's problem.[1] Hobbes's problem is the construction of political society from an ethical vacuum. Locke never faced this problem in the *Two Treatises* because his central premise is precisely the absence of any such vacuum.[2] It was a premise which he emphatically shared with Filmer and this is why he could simply assume that part of his position which immediately controverts Hobbes. The reason why Hobbes confronted this problem was epistemological in essence;[3] and it was the demonstrative force of the conclusion of which he boasted.[4] Epistemologically, in the *Two Treatises* Locke is able to confront Filmer on a level of shared vulgar ideology, not because this represented the utmost refinement of which his own thought was capable but because his book was written to persuade those already irretrievably convinced of the truth of this premise. If we seek to discover

[1] All this is quite apart from Mr Laslett's argument that in a sense Locke and Hobbes were on the same side, as against Filmer, in their rejection of patriarchalism. Cf. *Two Treatises*, pp. 67–70, esp. p. 70.

[2] *Ibid.* II, §6.

[3] See, for example Stuart M. Brown, Jr., 'The Taylor Thesis: Some Objections', *Hobbes Studies*, ed. K. C. Brown (Oxford, 1965), pp. 57–71, esp. pp. 57–8; Quentin Skinner, 'Hobbes's Leviathan', *The Historical Journal*, VII (1964), 321–33.

[4] See, for example, *Leviathan*, ed. Michael Oakeshott (Oxford, 1946), pp. 6, 465–66, etc.

the point at which Locke does accept the Hobbesian challenge, does confront the demand to construe demonstratively from unchallengeable axioms the whole moral fabric of society, we shall find it most nakedly of all in that series of abortive sketches of a theologically based ethic which run from the *Essays on the Law of Nature* to the unfinished scraps of paper from the 1690s in the Lovelace Collection. And if we still demand the public locus of this confrontation, we find it readily enough, shifty though the form in which the challenge is accepted undoubtedly is, not in the cramped little anonymous octavo of the *Two Treatises*, but in the fine broad folio columns, sent proudly into the world under his own name and bearing his rank, of the *Essay concerning Human Understanding*. But because there too he accepted the challenge with such gingerly misgivings and brought it, even after the grand intellectual sweep of the *Essay*, to such an inconsequential and broken-backed conclusion, and because the sketches of the projected ethic *were* so persistently abortive, the final riposte came by necessity elsewhere. In the pages of the *Reasonableness of Christianity*, the psychological core of Locke's answer stands all too clear and its clarity reveals harshly how completely he failed to meet the epistemological challenge. Perhaps, to tease the traditional judgement, we may claim that his epistemological failure brought with it a greater sociological perception, that the dubious commitments of his theological conviction enabled him in compensation to sense the stolid dependability of a society in which reliable social control could be achieved with some assurance by educating the gentry[1] and refraining from sharply deflating the economy.[2] But this is to overstrain a paradox. We must surely allow that it was more the history of England, 1681 and 1688 instead of 1651, which permitted him this illumination while denying it to his terrible antagonist of the textbooks. Certainly Locke's own theory of individual psychology is no more felicitously linked to a social psychology than that of Hobbes, and his ethics in consequence far from sensitively articulated with his social assurance.

There is a sense in which this confrontation of the *œuvres* is apt—and apt not merely as a scholastic cliché. It is hard to believe that

[1] *Some Thoughts concerning Education*, Preface, side 2 (not paginated), *Works* (1768), IV.

[2] *Some Considerations of the Consequences of the Lowering of Interest...*, *Works*, II, 46.

when Locke transcribes a judgement upon Hobbes in his notebook in the 1680s[1] or when at an interval of more than ten years he twice identifies the secular authoritarian argument against the right of toleration as that of Hobbes,[2] there is no sense of the brooding presence of that challenge. The challenge, as Laslett insists, was certainly far from one of the confrontation of texts. But if the relationship was less by far than one of reflective intellectual communication, it was also in a sense more. *Leviathan* for Locke could never be merely an intellectual challenge, still less merely an intellectual seduction (though it was plausibly in some faint measure both). Rather it was an intellectual nightmare, a spectre which haunted Locke's thought. And not merely an *intellectual* nightmare and its hauntings not confined to the thought. For if, as I have tried to insist throughout, the life was a necessary condition for the thought, the thought was equally such for the life. *Leviathan* could never be a purely intellectual embarrassment, for inasmuch as its intellectual challenge was effective, it carried the power to destroy the entire psychological plausibility of Locke's life. Here we can see more clearly how savage was the irony of such occasions as Newton's paranoid brutality[3] or

1 'Bibliothèque 551 Hobbes tacha de mettre la Morale en un ordre geometrique et d'etablir l'hypothese d'Epicure qui pose pour principes des societez la conservation de soi meme et l'utilité. En effet le but principal de Hobbes etoit d'etendre le pouvoir des rois sur le temporel et sur le spirituel contre les seditieux et les fanatiques ce qui lui a fait dire des choses qui ne s'accordent pas avec le repos de la societe civile ni avec la religion Chretienne 493' (MS Locke c 33, fo. 29^{v}). The reference is to volume III of the *Bibliothèque universelle et historique*, see John Harrison and Peter Laslett, *The Library of John Locke*, Oxford Bibliographical Society Publications (1965), no. 332. For Locke's connection with this periodical in which both his first piece of signed publication in prose and the first (abridged) version of the *Essay concerning Human Understanding* appeared see M. Cranston, *John Locke, a Biography* (London, 1957), pp. 256, 289–91, 293 n. (corrected by Laslett in *Two Treatises*, p. 12). The journal was edited by Locke's close friend Jean Le Clerc. It also printed a lengthy abridgement of the *Two Treatises* in 1691, the year in which the French translation (of the *Second Treatise* only) was printed in Amsterdam by the publisher of the journal. (See *Two Treatises*, p. 126.) See also MS Locke c 33, fo. 35^{v}.

2 Cf. MS Locke c 39, p. 9 (quoted by Cranston, *John Locke*, p. 133) with MS Locke 34, p. 40.

3 See Newton's letter of 16 September 1693 to Locke: '...I beg your pardon for my having hard thoughts of you for it, and for representing that you struck at the root of morality, in a principle you laid down in your book of Ideas and designed to pursue in another book and that I took you for a Hobbist' (*The Correspondence of Isaac Newton*, ed. H. W. Turnbull (Cambridge, 1961), III, 280).

Tyrrell's all too needling questionnaire.[1] In the noise of the 'Drum Ecclesiastick',[2] beneath the vulgar hands of an Edwards,[3] the accusation of Hobbism may have meant to Locke largely the threat of real physical danger, his timorous sense of the social isolation of the heterodox intellectual. And when the charge was bandied about by his own friends, this anxiety was no doubt all the keener. But it is naïve to equate the anxiety simply with physical fear or intellectual embarrassment. It was no simple cowardice or pride that the charge evoked. The hysteria of Locke's letter to Covel, for instance,[4] is hardly just panic—indeed it suggests a considerable assurance about his rights as a member of the élite. The key tone in his complaint is outrage rather than fear.

What made the accusation of Hobbism intolerable was plainly the location of his intellectual embarrassment, the crude force with which it pressed upon the whole emotional structure of his life. No confrontation with the Hobbesian *œuvre* could be purely dialectical for Locke because in this confrontation any extended dialectical embarrassment threatened his entire identity. But if, in this way, there is a real historical illumination in pointing to the dialectical confrontation and if it carries indeed its own high drama, this lends no excuse to the determination to regard the *Two Treatises* as a gloss on *Leviathan*. Their epistemological glibness has been often noted and it is scarcely inadvertent. Hobbism comes in, it is true, for passing insult.[5] But it is the level of insult delivered by a man without the least anxiety as to the sympathies of his audience. The bitterness of his sneer is authentic enough. But that does not make a sneer into an argument. Hobbes himself and the dense and threatening mass of intellection which he represents make no appearance. It may be correct in a sense to see him as a ghostly adversary throughout the pages of the *Essay*

[1] MS Locke c 22, fols. 91, 93, etc. and, for how firmly Tyrrell saw Hobbes as Locke's proper antagonists, fols. 119^r, 128.

[2] Cf. *Two Treatises*, Preface, p. 156.

[3] John Edwards, *Some Thoughts Concerning the Several Causes and Occasions of Atheism*... (London, 1695) and *Socinianism Unmask'd*...(1697). Cf. the anonymous letter to John Churchill (MS Locke c 23, p. 200) reporting that Edwards had said that 'Mr Lock was Governour of the Seraglio at Oats with others of the like nature'.

[4] MS Locke c 24, p. 32. Cf. the anxiety of Covel's replies to Locke and to Damaris Masham, MS Locke c 7, pp. 161, 163, 176, 177.

[5] *Two Treatises*, II, §§19, 137. Perhaps also §93, but cf. Laslett's comment, §93n.

and the *Reasonableness of Christianity*, Locke's own evil angel with whom he wrestled throughout a lifetime and before whose malign strength he eventually collapsed in exhaustion.[1] But whether or not this is true is here of no significance. What concerns us is simply that it is not in the *Two Treatises* that the struggle is joined. In them, the Hobbesian *arguments* are not answered. They are merely and blandly ignored.

[1] This could at most be a psychological truth, a barely testable proposition about the shifting dimensions of semi-consciousness before which historical inquiry is almost paralysed. Whether it is true or not in any case (in any sense other than the metaphorical—and there indeed it is irrefutable because its truth depends upon our historical conditioning, not on how the past was), is of no relevance to my purpose here, which is to insist that however sympathetic one were to the picture of Locke's intellectual life as lived in a conscious tension with Hobbes, the focus of the tension cannot conceivably be located in the *Two Treatises of Government*.

PART III

Tyger, Tyger, burning bright
In the forest of the night,
What Immortal hand & eye
Dare frame thy fearful symmetry?

. . . .

When the stars threw down their spears,
And water'd heaven with their tears,
Did he smile his work to see?
Did he who made the lamb make thee?

William Blake ('The Tyger', in *The Complete Writings of William Blake*, ed. Geoffrey Keynes (London, 1966), p. 173, quoted from second draft in 1793 notebook)

8

THE PREMISES OF THE ARGUMENT

The entire cosmos is the work of God. He created every part of it for his own purposes and he created each part of it with a defined relationship to the purpose of the whole. It is an ordered hierarchy, a 'great chain of being', in which every species has its station, its rank. Almost the entire humanly apprehensible bulk of it obeys the laws, or may be thought to exhibit the sort of physical regularity, which Newton was shortly to demonstrate. It was a vast functionally integrated machine and all of its elements were to be construed in terms of this integrative picture. Yet, one element of this machine which could be apprehended by anyone did not seem very efficiently related to the rest and that element, embarrassingly enough, was the human species itself. Allotted a peculiarly exalted rank,[1] but a little lower than the angels (who, as Milton classically described, had also shown certain defects in their sense of cosmic responsibility), in this divine project, one which demanded self-conscious voluntary co-operation, men had by historical mischance lost many of the privileges initially attached to their role and consequently been forced to endure distinctly less attractive working conditions.

[1] This was only true in a terrestrial and humanly fully intelligible, not in any more metaphysical a sense. See, for example, '. . . when we consider the infinite power and wisdom of the Maker, we have reason to think that it is suitable to the magnificent harmony of the universe and the great design and infinite goodness of the Architect that the *species* of creatures should also, by gentle degrees, ascend upward from us toward his infinite perfection, as we see they gradually descend from us downwards; which if it be probable, we have reason then to be persuaded that there are far more *species* of creatures above us than there are beneath: we being, in degrees of perfection, much more remote from the infinite being of GOD than we are from the lowest state of being and that which approaches nearest to nothing. And yet of all those distinct *species*, for the reasons above said, we have no clear distinct *ideas*' (*An Essay concerning Human Understanding*, III, VI, 12). There are obvious epistemological difficulties about the precise placing of a species within an infinite scale and the rank accorded to men on the scale seems consequently to have been accorded largely in relation to the purely emotional attitudes of the writer. There was nothing very unconventional about Locke's rating. For the most convenient conspectus of the variations with which this set of notions was advanced and for a most perceptive account of the conceptual possibilities involved see

All this may seem the purest banality but its banality is precisely its crude relevance to the project of setting out 'the true original, extent, and end of civil government' in answer to Robert Filmer. It constitutes the common backcloth to the performances of the two men. Indeed their speeches are often incomprehensible without it. But though this is true and though they go so far as to mention it from time to time, neither ever troubles to describe it at any length. And this for the very simple reason that it is a rigidly *conventional* background, one which at this level of generality it would never occur to Locke or Filmer or anyone to whom Filmer might be persuasive or anyone to whom Locke would wish to appeal in public (or indeed perhaps at all) to question. Locke himself, of course, had in the past and would again in the future take on the prodigious epistemological enterprise of attempting to show the cognitive appropriateness of the conventional assumption. But in view of his difficulties in the attempt it hardly seems a foolish decision to have omitted it in this instance.[1]

The point at which the debate begins is the attempt to construe the question of how far a man can have power over another man in terms of the extent to which he has power over himself. The tactic is not unusual. One of the defining characteristics of political authority is that it has the right to put to death.[2] But one of the ten commandments, taken over by Christianity, is that men should not kill. Furthermore, since one of those whom a man is prohibited from killing is himself (suicide is conventionally considered under the sixth commandment),[3] it is obscure how political

Arthur O. Lovejoy's classic, *The Great Chain of Being* (paperback edition, New York, 1960).

[1] See above, however, chapter 7, for how simply impossible such a decision would have been, had his purpose been to confute Hobbes.

[2] John Locke, *Two Treatises of Government*, II, § 3. Cf. Jean Bodin (trans. R. Knolles), *The Six Bookes of a Commonweale*, London, 1606, reprinted Cambridge, Mass., 1962), bk. I, chapter X, pp. 159–63 (=162). William Paley, *Principles of Moral and Political Philosophy* (London, 1785), pp. 330–1. But cf. Thomas Hobbes, *Leviathan*, ed. Michael Oakeshott (Oxford, 1946), chapter XVIII, pp. 113–19, and chapter XXVIII, pp. 202–9.

[3] See, for example, James Ussher, *A Body of Divinity*...(London, 1648), p. 268: '*What is the summe and meaning of this Commandment?* That the life and person of man (as bearing the Image of *God*) be by man not impeached, but preserved: (*Gen.* 9.5) and therefore that we are not to hurt our own persons, or the person of our neighbour, but to procure the safety thereof; and to do those things that lye

power could be synthesized out of the jural impotences of individuals. For Filmer[1] or Bishop Blackall[2], as still for Paley[3] almost a century later, the compatibility of the suicide taboo with political authority indicates that the latter can only derive directly from God. But there is subtle incoherence in this argument, even if it was not one apparent to many of those who strove to show the meaning of the Great Chain of Being for man's political condition. The various ranks of creatures are disposed by God in such a fashion that the lower subserve the purposes of the higher. Not only has God given man jural authority over all animal nature, the right to appropriate it for his own subsistence; he has also given him physical power over it, the capacity to implement his rights. Of course, even at the level of animal nature the functional integration of the hierarchy is imperfect. Tigers, for instance, occasionally appropriate men for their consumption; and the convenient providentialist account of such a superficially unwelcome phenomenon, as immediate divine punishment for the sins of the consumed, does not harmonize with Locke's attitude to physics or theology.[4] Whatever he may have felt about this (and tigers were hardly a hazard in the life of seventeenth-century England),

in us, for the preservation of his and our life and health. 1. *Tim.* 5.23. *What is forbidden in this Commandement?* All kind of evill tending to the impeachment of the safety and health of mans person: with every hurt done, threatned, or intended, to the soul or body, either of our selves, or of our neighbours.'

[1] 'Nay, if it be true that nature hath made all men free; though all mankind should concur in one vote, yet it cannot seem reasonable, that they should have power to alter the law of nature; for if no man have power to take away his own life without the guilt of being a murderer of himself, how can any people confer such a power as they have not themselves upon any one man, without being accessories to their own deaths, and every particular man become guilty of being *felo de se*?' (*Patriarcha and other Political Works of Sir Robert Filmer*, p. 285).

[2] Offspring Blackall, *The Divine Institution of Magistracy* (London, 1708), p. 5.

[3] William Paley, *The Principles of Moral and Political Philosophy* (London, 1785), pp. 330–1.

[4] The only coherent rationale would have to be in such terms of the full abstract logic of the principle of plentitude as adopted directly by Averroës or less coherently by Archbishop King upon this subject. It could scarcely be met by the anthropomorphic blandness of St Thomas Aquinas's 'Non conservaretur vita leonis, nisi occideretur asinus'. (It is the tone of St Thomas's treatment rather than the structure of his explanation which has this distinctive blandness.) See on this issue Arthur O. Lovejoy, *The Great Chain of Being* (paperback edition, New York, 1960), pp. 82, 219–220, 77–78 respectively. It must always have seemed an emotionally bleak justification of a painful experience which one has suffered that it was *possible*.

or indeed even about the resolutely inanimate phenomena to which Thomas Burnet addressed himself,[1] there was here the risk of a disturbing opacity in the divine purposes. It was a conundrum to which the alert exponent of theodicy could only be acutely sensitive. If it was an accredited theological trope to extrapolate immanent divine purpose from the relative consumption patterns of different species and if in consequence the relationship between species was to be described not merely as one of practical manipulation but one of righteous authority, there were a number of embarrassing possible human applications. Could one not say—Hobbes, Filmer and later Sherlock[2] for example had seemed to do so with enthusiasm—that effective practical control *created* jural authority? The difficulties of this position in a highly legitimist society were readily apparent. But equally emotionally disturbing and never far away from the sense of social reality was the notion that recognized jural authority might carry the right of practical manipulation. If government was a right donated by God and if rights within a species were characteristically functional and subject to adjudication within that species—as, for instance, the rights of masters over servants or fathers over children were subject to the control of positive law—then the right of government would in one way be much closer in character to a right exercised by a member of one species over a member of another. With rare and theoretically embarrassing exceptions, the relationship between men and animals was one which men controlled. It was also one which was subject to the criterion of human and not of animal utility and it was one which, in the event of human misconduct within it, could be adjudicated only by God. A man might waste grouse, as it were, and might be punished in due course by the Deity for so doing, but the grouse had no jural standing in the affair.

But, whatever its plausibility in a relationship between species, within the human race no such separation of functional utility in

[1] *The Sacred Theory of the Earth* (London, 1684) *passim* (trans. and extended from Latin edition of 1681). On Burnet see Perry Miller, *Errand into the Wilderness* (paperback edition, New York, 1964), chapter IX, 'The End of the World', esp. pp. 223–39. Francis C. Haber, *The Age of the World: Moses to Darwin* (Baltimore, 1959), pp. 71–83. Basil Willey, *The Eighteenth-Century Background* (paperback edition, Harmondsworth, 1962), pp. 32–9.

[2] William Sherlock, *The Case of the Allegiance due to Soveraign Powers Stated*...(London, 1691).

the total order of creation from the cognitive capacity to judge this could be entirely plausible. Only an unflinching application of the principle of plentitude and a resolute refusal to project an anthropomorphic tenderness onto the Creation was entirely proof against the humanly disquieting appearance of much of that Creation. Consolation for how the world is must necessarily be energetically metaphysical in character (and even then the most profound argument for this being '*le meilleur des mondes possibles*' seems to imply that it is also the worst of all possible ones). Locke's own perspective on theodicy was always somewhat limply anthropomorphic. The goodness of God may be apprehended, faintly no doubt but unmistakably, in human relationships and moral notions.[1] It is a reasonable goodness and its rationality accessible to men. All this no doubt gives his work much of its authenticity and force but it also leaves it very exposed. If in the general relationship of one species to another God has combined jural authority with effective power to execute it and if the combination is intelligible as such to human beings, then there is much which is puzzling in the latitude which God has chosen to give to the consumption patterns of lions or tigers. And if it is asserted that God has given jural authority to all existing rulers, or to all monarchs, or even to a single monarch who abuses his effective power, is this not to reduce the derivation of political legitimacy and its relation to political control to that state of queasy moral obliquity and theological inscrutability held by the man-eating lion? Indeed, if one reflects on the grossly immoral way in which most political power is exercised in the world, do not the claims of divine right by implication subject the majority of mankind to their rulers as though these latter were of a different and higher species and one whose normal behaviour towards their subjects was correspondingly brutal? To attribute this disposition of authority to God seemed to argue that men *should* 'think it Safety, to be devoured by Lions'.[2]

We may say at this point that the need to confront Filmer forced Locke into a deeper confrontation of the implications for politics of his own profoundest religious and philosophical notions. The

[1] See esp. MS Locke f 3, pp. 201–2.

[2] *Two Treatises*, II, §93, ll. 30–2 and §137, ll. 15–18 (making themselves a prey).

biographical cause of his writing the work may be vulgar in the extreme but the reasons why the arguments take the form which they do have a direct relationship to the central dynamic of his intellectual ambition. And this indeed we might well expect. It would be odd if a philosopher were to produce a work on politics which was simply the logical implication for the field of politics of his previously elaborated epistemology. Hobbes perhaps came closer to doing so than any other philosopher and even there it would be an imaginative reader who could predict from the first fifty pages of *Leviathan* the precise character and content of the remainder. Where others have seemed to assert such a relationship, as perhaps with Plato or Hegel, the claim seems threadbare in the extreme. It would be even odder if an epistemological theory had determined the form of a response to such an adventitious polemical assignment as the *Two Treatises* seems to have been. But perhaps it would be at least equally odd if the work were untouched by the intense imaginative and intellectual effort already embodied in the drafts of the *Essay*. Conceivably, had the political work been a piece of pure hack work, we might suppose that Locke did not mean what it says. But, despite (or perhaps because of?) the clumsiness of the form, the very last impression which the work gives is one of disengagement and calm manipulation. There seems little reason to suppose that Locke did not believe both works (the *Two Treatises of Government* and the *Essay concerning Human Understanding*) to state the truth. Indeed those who have been readiest to accuse Locke of insincerity in the phrasing have also been often among the most insistent on the profound 'coherence' of philosophy and politics in his works. It is not intended here to claim that the works are fully consistent—both of them seem in so many ways patently inconsistent and absurd—but only to insist that there are reasons why Locke should have supposed them coherent and, more pointedly, reasons internal to the positions argued in the *Essay* which determined the particular shape of the response to the very specific polemical challenge of Filmer; not that the categories of the early drafts of the *Essay* determined a particular politics—they had previously been compatible with a very different theoretical structure[1]—but that when

[1] See above, p. 91, n. 1.

applied to the very specific positions of Filmer, they did determine the outlines of the reply which Locke made. It was a rational, not a causal, determination but, given the situation and the sincerity and energy which it elicited from Locke, the content of the rational transition exhibits its own causal determination. When what is being attempted is the causal explanation of an argument, it is never sufficient to show that one proposition logically implies another. The most brilliant of men talk nonsense, not to mention tell lies. But if a man of high intelligence confronts an argument with all the emotional energy and sincerity he can muster, he talks the best sense he can. And the best sense he can talk is causally determined just as much as it is rational in form.

We have seen before how readily Locke saw man's general political duty as simply one of conscientious subservience and the reasons for which he saw it in this way, its aptness for the fulfilment of God's purposes for man. All this is bland and pietistic enough. But its blandness looks less appealing when the duties of most men are construed as the rights of a few. Whatever the formal structure of Filmer's reasoning, in its application to human society it seemed to subject the majority of mankind to the purposes of a small number of other men. Cynically one might say that even this prospect was less disquieting when the small number included one's employer, Achitophel as philosopher prince. No doubt such convenience and its quotidian plausibility did distract attention from the moral enormity of the assumption. But it is perhaps not uncommon for political failure to elicit a sharper consciousness of the moral obliquities of past political conduct. The confrontation with Filmer at any rate *did* draw sharply to Locke's attention a possible practical bias in his earlier thought on politics and unsurprisingly his efforts to correct this commence with a re-examination of the theological premises of these earlier positions. Human political arrangements derive their sole legitimacy from their embodiment of the purposes of God. Most of their actual contours are grotesquely inadequate for this assignment. Hence the intellectual project for Locke in this book is to separate the moral (and thus legal) claims which their performance of these functions entitles them to make from those which their formal legal structure and their effective practical power enable them to make.

What rights, to take the limiting case, can a man have over himself? What are the ultimate criteria which must be satisfied for a right to exist at all? Here we recur to the great chain of being. All rights except those of God himself are circumscribed by the fact that they are exercised by one part of the created order over another part. All of them must serve (or at the very least be compatible with[1]) God's purpose in the creation of that order. There is, of course, an alarming problem over the question of how far God's purposes in the creation of this order are intelligible to human beings—'Our mindes are not made as large as truth nor suited to the whole extent of things.'[2] But it is the central axiom of Locke's thought, one which he no doubt supposed all his experience to support but one which for obvious reasons he never made any sustained effort to demonstrate explicitly that 'the candle that is set up in us shines bright enough for *all* our purposes'.[3] And one of the strongest beams which it casts is that which exhibits to the human race the existence of the creating deity.[4] The *a posteriori* reasons for believing in the existence of a deity are clumsily combined with *a priori* deductions as to his attributes and there can be no doubt that this part of Locke's thought, the unhappy marriage of naturalistic and ontological

[1] The ambiguity of the notion of the great chain of being becomes embarrassing here. Might not a consistent application of the principle of plenitude imply that anything which happened in the world was *ex hypothesi* demanded by God's purpose in the creation and would not this suggest most powerfully the force of antinomianism? However aesthetically appealing it might be as theodicy, was it not crudely incongruous with the project of expounding a morality? Locke escapes these embarrassments to some extent by his deployment of the more atavistically Hebraic persona of the deity. But plainly, had he not been conducting his normative examination of the implications of the great chain in the context of Filmer's overwhelmingly scripturalist arguments, he might have been acutely troubled by the problem of relating a structure of divine commands directed to human beings with an infinitely variegated set of power relationships which were all too perceptible in the actual world. Only the fact that the natural world was examined in a context of an overwhelmingly immediate and unhesitating acceptance of the biblically specified commands obscured their notable disharmony.

[2] Journal for 8 February 1677, in John Locke, *An Early Draft of the Essay*, ed. R. I. Aaron and Jocelyn Gibb (Oxford, 1936), p. 84.

[3] *Essay*, I, I, § 5 (my italics). See also 'Our business here is not to know all things, but those which concern our conduct' (§ 6).

[4] *Ibid.* II, XVII, § 17.

argument, is grossly incoherent.[1] But, however grotesque the intellectual tactic may now appear, it is of the last significance. For, given in this way the existence of a divine creator, we are supposedly entitled to assume both his benignity and his efficiency; that all that he created was created for some good purpose, that in creating he did nothing in vain, the principle of sufficient reason. And if God had created all of it for some good purpose, clearly none of it should be destroyed without good purpose. Hence that other central axiom of Lockean politics, the duty to maximize preservation and its curious consequence, the iniquity of waste. Everything which cannot be used must be preserved and no being may make use by right of another being of his own species. Furthermore, no man may make use of himself in a way which violates this divine order.

[1] The grounds adduced to establish the existence of a God go no way towards establishing the existence of a being with the attributes which Locke infers from the notion of God. My claim is that the combination of the two types of argument, in Locke's as in other theological writings, can only generate a series of puns on the word 'God'. It is only just, though, to point out that the attempt to use theistic language to say anything about the world which we do not already know anyway has not gained particularly in coherence since Locke's day and that there are as simple causes for men's continuance in it as there are reasons for their inevitable failure in it.

9

THE STATE OF NATURE

The human race belongs to the created order of nature. But it belongs to it in a highly distinctive way. Human beings have free will and they speak languages. Hence they not only live in a unitary history, the story of the created world; they also make their own history and are at least *capable* of knowing it. The societies in which they live have their own rules, formal and informal, and men can know these and recognize their historically distinctive character, can know that the laws and the constitution of England differ from those of France or Spain and have done so over long periods of time. Because these laws and values are historical artefacts, linguistically expressed and thus preserved through time from one generation to another, and because they represent the form in which men are educated morally, men are to some degree at the mercy of language and of history, perhaps at times even bewitched by them. Language, even though it can be employed with great care for the statement of the truth, is a conventional material—and normally not employed with any care at all. There is thus a problem over how men can learn to talk coherently about such values or laws and how they can escape the bewitchments of history, that fetishism of the existing moral vocabulary which *is* the moral consciousness of most men. In part, of course, the answer is purely linguistic; a necessary condition for talking coherently about anything is to *talk* coherently. Men must learn to use words with a consistent denotation and to use them in a formally consistent manner. Fortunately in the case of moral notions this is not an impossible ambition, because the entities denoted are human mental constructs and not alien essences. To know a human idea is axiomatically possible in various ways in which one cannot know an object in the external world.

But there is more to the project than such purely linguistic skills. Linguistic consistency at most makes fully available the resources of an existing moral and political vocabulary and this vocabulary which is in itself a historical product is still profoundly contaminated by history. It was not simply because of their misunderstanding of the grammar of the concept of property that the Spartans rewarded theft, or because they did not understand the notion of paternity that the Caribs used to geld, fatten and eat their children.[1] Societies and individuals are not simply deficient in their capacity to make sense of their moral inheritance. They also vary greatly in their good fortune as to its content. It is not merely the language of morals that history has infected, it is also the set of moral concepts. In order to rectify these defects it is necessary to find some criterion for human morality which is outside history. Hence the necessity for a law of nature.

The search for such a criterion from today's hindsight seems crudely anti-historicist. That was in fact, as we have seen, its *point*. It also appears likely to be discovered only by a resolute and rather reductivist naturalism. It is not difficult for instance to see why Hobbes's conception of human nature seemed a plausible starting place in such an attempt. Men as men could hardly have in common much more than their membership of the biological species. And Locke too, of course, begins conventionally from men in the state of nature, and from the 'law of nature' which governs this state. But the content of this law does not seem reductivist at all. Some other term has clearly intruded here and it does not take much investigation to determine that the intruding term is God. The state of nature, that state that 'all Men are naturally in',[2] is not an asocial condition but an ahistorical condition. It is that state in which men are set by God. The state of nature is a topic for theological reflection, not for anthropological research. There are two sorts of information that we have about God's purposes for men; what he has told us directly and what we can infer directly from the character of the created order—readings, in Bacon's classic phrase, in the book of God's word and the book of God's works.[3] The second possibility in this case looks a little like the anthropological naturalism previously mentioned—but somehow in practice the inferential resourcefulness of natural theology always proves to exceed that of descriptive

[1] See *Essays on the Law of Nature*, pp. 168, 170, 172. *An Essay concerning Human Understanding*, I, III, §9–12.

[2] *Two Treatises of Government*, II, §4, ll. 2–3.

[3] Francis Bacon, *The Dignity and Advancement of Learning*, in *The Physical and Metaphysical Works of Lord Bacon* (Bohn edition, London, 1860), p. 32.

anthropology. The reason why this is so is not exactly that *every* question is begged individually. The theological matrix functions rather as an interpretative axiom; it does not simply reduce to a set of factual claims (of however bizarre a character).[1] It is clear, however, that it is not merely the dubious inferential resources of this intellectual procedure which explain the content of Locke's theory but also that the procedure is the *second* of the two possibilities. It is not natural theology *tout pur* which explains the conclusions but natural theology undertaken by a mind saturated in the Christian revelation. Locke claims to be considering the human condition at large in terms of reason but what he perceives in it is what he already knows (from Christian revelation) to be there.

In itself this is a pretty banal perception but it is important to note it firmly because his explicit procedures in the *Two Treatises* do obscure it to a considerable degree. After the bland conventionality of his earliest political writings,[2] he never again attempted to extrapolate particular political precepts directly from God's positive law, the Christian revelation. Human society is dechristianized because it seemed in practice that the attempt to conceive it in Christian terms resulted simply in the sanctification of corrupt human purposes. The unequivocally providential role of society is restricted to the level at which it is a biological compulsion. That is to say: nothing about human society carries any transcendent status except that aspect which no large portion of men ever have occasion or motive for avoiding; and which, being common to any set of political purposes except those of genocide, can never be pleaded in favour of any particular purpose, namely the continuity of the urge to live in society with other men, in *any* form of society. The urge is not simply a conclusion of reason (though, like any biological datum, it is not conceivably in itself contrary to reason), it is rather a biologically specified disposition, an instinctual drive.[3]

1 See, helpfully, John Wisdom, 'Gods', in *Logic and Language*, ed. Antony Flew, first and second series (paperback edition, Garden City, N.Y., 1965), pp. 194–214. And, less sympathetically but brilliantly, David Hume, *Dialogues concerning Natural Religion*, ed. Norman Kemp Smith (2nd edition, London, 1947).

2 *Two Tracts on Government*, 198–9, 202–3, etc.

3 This is not Locke's terminology. But men are 'driven into Society', *Two Treatises*, II, § 127, l. 3. This exhibits not just a biological teleology. It was God who put man

But, though human society is in this manner formally de-christianized, the entire ratiocinative structure in which it is considered in the *Two Treatises* and from which the political conclusions follow is saturated with Christian assumptions—and those of a Christianity in which the New Testament counted *very* much more than the Old. The entire *First Treatise*, which is designed to discredit Filmer's extrapolations from the Old Testament, ends up by making the latter seem almost wholly irrelevant to issues of political right. Locke continues to use its exemplary resources as the accredited vocabulary for discussing political issues.[1] But the vocabulary becomes frictionless, devoid of external implication, conceptually inert. He handles the problem of combining a particularistic divine positive law and a universalistic natural theology by insulating the divine positive law from all possible practical implications for politics and proceeds by the exposition of a natural theology. But the insulation is far from perfect, and the terrain of nature is suffused with a distinctive form of light which escapes from this source and picks out in the world features which would not be discernible to those with a vision less privileged in its illumination. Jesus Christ (and Saint Paul) may not appear in person in the text of the *Two Treatises* but their presence can hardly be missed when we come upon the normative creaturely equality of all men in virtue of their shared species-membership. There is perhaps a hint of rather Western parochialism in Laslett's expository assimilation of the argument to contemporary assumptions that inequalities require justification.[2] In seventeenth-century England, if the gospel could only be forgotten (which it pretty readily was), there were no problems

'under strong Obligations of Necessity, Convenience, and Inclination to drive him into Society' (II, §77, ll. 1–4). Human sociality is not merely Aristotelian. It exhibits the purposes of an anthropomorphic God.

[1] See for instance the frequent appearance of Jephtha and his appeal to the judgement of heaven and the role of Genesis in the treatment of the basis of property rights (*Two Treatises*, II, §§21, 176, 241, but cf. Laslett's note to §21, and I, *passim*; II, §25, ll. 4–8, etc.).

[2] 'You do not have to accept a theology to agree that this is all a matter of common sense. All that happens if you wish to disagree is that you find the task of proving something different uncomfortably thrust upon you' (*Two Treatises*, Introduction, p. 93). For a clear presentation of the minimum form of the contemporary assumption see W. Von Leyden, 'On Justifying Inequality', *Political Studies*, XI, I (February 1963), 56–70.

at all about justifying inequality. You simply pointed. (As for giving reasons, our social structure will do that for us.) At the biological level the axiom of equality is wholly inert socially,[1] and in pre-industrial Western civilization it could hardly be a conclusion of sociological reason. Far from being extrinsic, the theology was the sole possible significant *locus* for equality. Here indeed it was true that the medium was the message.

Even if it is correct, though, to argue in this way that what is distinctive about Locke's politics is really a transposition of his theology, this must be the beginning rather than the end of the analysis. There are two great themes which men have perceived in the *Two Treatises*, the rights of property and the limitations of political authority. If this piece is more concerned with the second of these than the first, is indeed in a way preoccupied with assessing a dimension of the sociological hypothesis that the plausibility of the second ('constitutionalism') as it was expounded derived from the overwhelming social plausibility of the first ('bourgeois property rights'),[2] it is necessary at this point to bear both in mind. Men exercise claims over other men. They also exercise claims over non-human nature, both animate and inanimate. They have responsibilities, too, in the exercise of either of these—responsibilities to God in both cases and thus derivatively, in the case of claims over men, to other men and, in the case of claims over animals and things, to men and in practice also to animals. We have seen earlier how embarrassing he had found the combination of divine positive law and natural theology in interpreting the relationship between man and the non-human world. But in the case of relationships between human beings the historical ambiguities of divine positive law did not arise so acutely and the latter could thus be insulated with some effect.

The state of nature, that classically feeble expository cliché of the natural-law thinkers, could here be given an altogether sharper outline. In conceptual intention, though not of course in practical purpose, it was an outline which had much in common

[1] Cf. Hobbes. It was not that it had no rational implication for human duties; just that it lacked the mildest reformist implications for the structure of the social hierarchy.

[2] Cf. C. B. Macpherson, *The Political Theory of Possessive Individualism* (Oxford, 1962).

with that of Hobbes.[1] The project was to devise a criterion which was outside history, in terms of which to judge the moral status of the present political structure. Because political argument in all ex-feudal countries and most especially in England[2] revolved around history and particularly around early history, it was easy to suppose that what was wanted was the earliest history of all, an axiomatic pre-history which somehow pre-empts the most Ancient Constitution, an aboriginal condition which can be used to indict any objectionable portion of the historical story. Filmer's resolute insistence on the pages of Genesis is a peculiarly effective tactic in this style. Genesis was unchallengeably aboriginal and the only intruded sociological term used to construe it, the patriarchal family, looked as trans-historical and biologically defined as the seventeenth century could well wish. It is consequently not surprising that Locke in confronting Filmer should constantly have veered towards a historical interpretation of the state of nature in an effort not only to defuse the explosive potential of Filmer's procedures but to supplant them by others of the same logical type. The power of the dialectic of the Ancient Constitution argument is now widely familiar and there is nothing surprising in the fact that Locke should at times have argued on its terms, should have interpreted his assignment as the replacement of Genesis by comparative anthropology. But it seems important at this point to press the analysis further and in particular to make some effort to separate the structure of the argument from the cruder demands of polemic. If this is done, a rather different outline begins to emerge.

We have seen that certain aspects of Locke's thought offer him the oppportunity to escape from the conceptual morass of the Ancient Constitution. If what is required is a criterion outside history in terms of which to judge its moral notions, the earlier stages of historical development (let alone their surviving contemporary instances like the American Indians) hardly seem to exhibit the necessary purity. In the hands of Filmer

[1] This is in effect pointed out by Leo Strauss, though for very different purposes. See his *The Political Philosophy of Hobbes* (paperback edition, Chicago, 1963), esp. pp. 95–8.

[2] See, brilliantly, J. G. A. Pocock, *The Ancient Constitution and the Feudal Law* (Cambridge, 1957), *passim*.

the aboriginal condition draws its normative status from the fact that it displays divine positive law. But if revelation is removed it certainly is not clear why primitive human conditions, whether at (or most inconveniently before[1]) the dawn of history or in the woods of contemporary America should be normative for the sophisticated European societies of the seventeenth century with their 'Safety, Ease, and Plenty'. This point was put with great force (though not altogether consistently) both by Locke's pupil the third Earl of Shaftesbury[2] and by Vico[3] as a criticism of the form of the entire jusnaturalist enterprise. But the concept does not in fact operate in this fashion in Locke's work. Any stage of social development which was part of the historical story at all, any period within history, could not in itself be normative for any other period. It is true that one society at one time could be considerably more edifying than another at another time. But what makes it edifying must be some transitive attribute—it could not simply be its *date*. Or rather, there was only one dated epoch which could in any way be normative and this, the prelapsarian

[1] *Two Treatises*, II, §101, ll. 1–3. 'Government is every where antecedent to Records, and Letters seldome come in amongst a People, till a long continuation of Civil Society has, by other more necessary Arts provided for their Safety, Ease, and Plenty. And then they begin to look after the History of their *Founders*, and search into their *original*, when they have out-lived the memory of it' (*ibid.* ll. 11–16).

[2] Antony Ashley Cooper, Third Earl of Shaftesbury, *Characteristicks of Men, Manners, Opinions, Times* (5th edition, Birmingham, 1773), I, 104, 107–11; II, 308–9, 314, 316, 319. Shaftesbury appears to see the source of what he considered to be Locke's error in his rejection of innate ideas and his consequent dethronement of a normative account of human nature with a spuriously empirical one. See esp. his letter to Michael Ainsworth of 3 January 1709 in *The Life, Unpublished Letters, and Philosophical Regimen of Anthony, Earl of Shaftesbury, Author of the Characteristicks*, ed. Benjamin Rand (London, 1900), p. 403: 'Then comes the credulous Mr Locke with his Indian, barbarian stories of wild nations...' See also the letter to General Stanhope of 7 November 1709, *ibid.* p. 416. And for the general conceptual background to his position, see his *Second Characters of the Language of Forms*, ed. B. Rand Cambridge, 1914), pp. 173–8. There is a rather *simpliste* account of the relationship between Locke and Shaftesbury in Jason Aronson, 'Shaftesbury on Locke', *American Political Science Review*, LIII, 4 (December 1959), 1101–4.

[3] 'Né ci accusino di falso il primo i moderni viaggiatori, i quali narrano che popoli del Brasile, di Cafra ed altre nazioni del mondo nuovo (e Antonio Arnaldo crede lo stesso degli abitatori dell'isole chiamate Antille) vivano in societá senza alcuna cognizione di Dio...Queste sono novelle di viaggiatori, che proccurano smaltimento a' loro libri con mostruosi ragguagli' (Giambattista Vico, *La Scienza Nuova Seconda*, ed. Fausto Nicolini (3rd edition, Bari, 1942), §334, pp. 118–19). The whole purpose of Vico's extraordinary providentialist theodicy commits him to using history to show the absurdity of trying to make primitive societies normative for those of modern Europe.

condition, was separated from subsequent history by such a profound chasm that it could be simply ignored when attending to the problems of that history. Thus no portion of social history could serve as normative criterion for any other.

The state of nature, then, that 'State men are naturally in', is not asocial; nor is it psychologically or logically prior to society. It is neither a piece of philosophical anthropology nor a piece of conjectural history. Indeed it has literally no transitive empirical content whatsoever. For empirical specification, in Locke's conception, was in itself contamination by history and the analytical function of the concept lay precisely in its ahistoricity. In itself it is simply an axiom of theology. It sets human beings in the teleology of divine purposes. The story of how ineptly men have carried these out is the classic Christian story and the supposition that the way to discover the purposes is simply to extrapolate from the story of human performance could only seem slightly grotesque to a Christian philosopher of the seventeenth century who understood what was at stake. It is not surprising that the relationship of empirical evidence to Locke's notion should be strikingly different from that suggested by our still prevalent assumption that the state of nature must be a piece of conjectural sociology. We find indeed that the structure of Locke's theory, the movement of his mind, is mirrored in the shape of the book. The state of nature with all its normative trappings appears at the beginning of the *Second Treatise* as the premise of the subsequent arguments,[1] while its relationship to the world of fact appears subsequently only as a response to the crude (and now all too traditional) Filmerian challenge of when men had ever been in the state of nature,[2] or more sharply, when in *history*[3] they had ever

[1] *Two Treatises*, II, §§4–13. The *Second Treatise* was written first.

[2] ''Tis often asked as a mighty Objection, *Where are*, or ever were, there any *Men in such a State of Nature*?' (*Two Treatises*, II, §14, ll. 1–2).

[3] *Two Treatises*, II, §100, ll. 2–4 and cf. §101, ll. 1–3. Cf. Samuel von Pufendorf, *De Jure Naturae et Gentium* (Oxford, 1934), I, book II, chapter II, where the state of nature is not merely a jural condition but a sort of (rather fuzzy) sociological hypothesis, a counterfactual conditional concerned not solely with what duties men would have, abstracting from concrete social situations, but with what men would really be like, abstracting from concrete social situations. Locke of course *derived* the term and the analytical category from the tradition of political reflection of which Pufendorf was one of the most distinguished exponents but that did not prevent Locke from using it in an analytically much better-judged manner.

been so. Nothing about the world of nature (except presumably the epistemological basis of natural theology) is even relevant to the definition of the state of nature. But the accredited forms of argument in the political tradition and the broad previous meaning of the concept which Locke deployed made it polemically vulnerable in ways in which it was conceptually secure. Even this, though, is not a sufficiently sympathetic reading of the way in which the concept is employed. For the very fact that Locke wishes to insist on the concept in this way is a consequence of the precise purpose of the whole book, and this, as we have insisted before, is the destruction of the ideological purchase of Filmerian patriarchalism. In this perspective there is nothing adventitious about the polemical attention devoted to explaining the empirical status of the state of nature. It was not a matter of elucidating the character of this but rather of vindicating its relevance. So much of the force of the Filmerian position came from its insistence that men could *never* escape from the vast social clamp in which God had set them, from the origins of their species, throughout its history. Thus the need which Locke felt to write the *First Treatise*, a dialectical need probably made plain to him after he had completed the *Second*, by the publication of Filmer's complete system in *Patriarcha*, derived too from the difficulty of showing that the state of nature could ever be relevant. The whole argument of this work was already implicit when he reached the sixth paragraph of the *Second Treatise*. The rest of that *Treatise* is designed only to protect it from crude Filmerian rejection and to display its relevance to the central constitutional and political theme of the Exclusion controversy.

In itself this argument seems entirely self-contained and cogent. But this did not dispose of the need for the *First Treatise*. Locke put forward a rather precise and well-constructed variant of the Whig argument for the supremacy of the legislative. To do this convincingly he had to confront the most powerful ideology of prerogative power current in the society at the time and this was to be found in Filmer's incidental writings. However, the rather inconsequential series of publications in which Filmer's views were expressed, although their critical purchase was notably powerful, did not provide at all a convenient dialectical target.

Only with the publication of *Patriarcha* in 1680 was Locke presented with the opportunity for a systematic demolition of a systematic opposing position, the opportunity for which both his education and, one may feel, his disposition best fitted him. If this could be done in a decorous enough fashion without shocking the gentry, as Hobbes for example had done, it might be expected to exert the greatest political impact. And the full deployment of Filmer's system was not only pre-eminently qualified as a target. It also peculiarly demanded refutation since it claimed consistently, and with dramatic simplicity and blandness, to be indeed a *politique tirée des propres paroles de l'écriture sainte*. The vulgar social plausibility fused with an even more vulgar scripturalist appeal to form a reactionary ideology of insidious power.

We can see the burden of this Filmerian position lying behind even the point at which Locke begins to defend the relevance of the state of nature. For it is at the most abjectly incoherent point in Filmer's position, the point at which he must construe the unitary and indivisible authority of Adam as logically continuous with all subsequent plural authorities in the world, that the attack falls. Even Filmer could not avoid noticing that Adam's inheritance had become somewhat disseminated over the years, though he was far from explicit about what the implications of this unfortunate state of affairs might be for that unitary matrix of authority in which all men except the Adamic heir were divinely situated. All that Locke needed to establish the relevance of his axiom was that there could be a case in the world over which no *locus* of positive authority had jurisdiction. In the relationship between sovereigns in Filmer's system this situation classically obtained—and furthermore the only possible conceptual resource available to him in his own terms to handle this anomic relationship, the assertion of the real authority of Adam's unknown heir, must in principle subvert almost all constituted human authority. And any plausible tactic to escape this dilemma, such as an appeal to an available order of objective right or wrong in terms of which the relationship between sovereigns could be adjudicated, precisely destroys the coherence of his asserted amalgam of natural social authority and Bodinian sovereignty. Recognition of a law to judge sovereigns without a sovereign to validate it on earth would simply dissolve the entire Filmerian position. As a polemical riposte Locke's move is devastating.[1] The sole feature of history which Locke needs to validate the relevance of his axiom is one which the most besotted of authoritarians could not but concede to him, the plurality of territorially sovereign political authorities upon the face of the earth. This is not to say that he does not have a philosophy of history or a conjectural history of social and political development, nor that these do not appear at large in the text of the work. But it is to insist that their role in the argument[2] is expository and polemical, rather than logically essential. The history of society is material for expounding a theological argument. It can never be a substitute for the argument itself.

The state of nature, then, is a jural condition and the law which covers it is the theologically based law of nature. It is a state of equality and a state of freedom.[3] That is to say: men confront each other in their shared status as creatures of God without intrinsic authority over each other and without the right to restrict the (natural) law-abiding behaviour of others. But though it is a state of liberty it is not a state of licence; though apolitical, it is not amoral.[4] The reason why men are equal is their shared

[1] ''Tis often asked as a mighty Objection, *Where are*, or ever were, there any *Men in such a State of Nature*? To which it may suffice as an answer at present, That since all *Princes* and Rulers of *Independent* Governments all through the World, are in a State of Nature, 'tis plain the World never was, nor ever will be, without Numbers of Men in that State' (*Two Treatises*, II, §14, ll. 1–6). This position is quite unoriginal to Locke (cf. Laslett's note to this passage). But there is a certain distinctiveness to the use to which Locke puts it.

[2] Except at one particular point, that at which legitimate political communities are founded on consent.

[3] 'To understand Political Power right, and derive it from its Original, we must consider what State all Men are naturally in, and that is, a *State of perfect Freedom* to order their Actions, and dispose of their Possessions, and Persons as they think fit within the bounds of the Law of Nature, without asking leave, or depending upon the Will of any other Man.

A *State* also *of Equality*, wherein all the Power and Jurisdiction is reciprocal, no one having more than another: there being nothing more evident, than that Creatures of the same species and rank promiscuously born to all the same advantages of Nature, and the use of the same faculties, should also be equal one amongst another without Subordination or Subjection, unless the Lord and Master of them all, should by any manifest Declaration of his Will set one above another, and confer on him by an evident and clear appointment an undoubted Right to Dominion and Sovereignty' (*Two Treatises*, II, §4).

[4] *Two Treatises*, II, §6, 'But though this be a *State of Liberty*, yet it is *not a State of Licence*, though Man in that State have an uncontroleable Liberty, to dispose of his

position in a normative order, the order of creation. If they infringe the norms of that order, they forfeit their normative status of equality. Indeed they lower their status to that of lower members of this order—they become normatively beasts and may be treated accordingly by other men.[1] Those who by their aggression quit the law of reason do not of course by this behaviour cease to be voluntary agents responsible to God for their misdeeds. But they become liable to be treated by other men as though they were dangerous animals, *as though* they were no longer voluntary agents and hence had no rights against other men. This does not mean that men are obliged to kill them—indeed they are obliged not to do so, unless it serves some good purpose, both because the law of nature enjoins the preservation of all men 'as much as possible'[2] and also as an instance of the general prohibition on the waste of natural resources. The 'safety of the innocent is to be preferred'. But the preservation of even the wicked, provided it does not conflict with this, is not to be discounted.[3]

Person or Possessions, yet he has not Liberty to destroy himself, or so much as any Creature in his Possession, but where some nobler use, than its bare Preservation calls for it' (ll. 1–5).

[1] *Two Treatises*, II, §8, ll. 9–19; §10, ll. 1–4; §11, ll. 16–28; §16, ll. 9–18: 'For *by the Fundamental Law of Nature, Man being to be preserved*, as much as possible, when all cannot be preserv'd, the safety of the Innocent is to be preferred: And one may destroy a Man who makes War upon him, or has discovered an Enmity to his being, for the same Reason, that he may kill a *Wolf* or a *Lyon*; because such Men are not under the ties of the Common Law of Reason, have no other Rule, but that of Force and Violence, and so may be treated as Beasts of Prey, those dangerous and noxious Creatures, that will be sure to destroy him, whenever he falls into their Power'; §163, ll. 17–23; §172, ll. 5–19: '...Man not having such an Arbitrary power over his own Life, cannot give another Man such a Power over it; but it is *the effect only of Forfeiture*, which the Aggressor makes of his own Life, when he puts himself into the state of War with another. For having quitted Reason, which God hath given to be the Rule betwixt Man and Man, and the common bond whereby humane kind is united into one fellowship and societie; and having renounced the way of peace, which that teaches, and made use of the Force of War to compasse his unjust ends upon an other, where he has no right, and so revolting from his own kind to that of Beasts by making Force which is theirs, to be his rule of right, he renders himself liable to be destroied by the injur'd person and the rest of mankind, that will join with him in the execution of Justice, as any other wild beast, or noxious brute with whom Mankind can have neither Society nor Security'; §181, ll. 14–20; §182, ll. 18–21.

[2] *Ibid.* II, §16, ll. 9–10; §182, ll. 6–7.

[3] See above, chapter 8. See also *Two Treatises*, II, §6, ll. 20–2; §11, ll. 5–10; §16, ll. 9–11; §37, ll. 35–41; §46, ll. 7–30.

It is because such offenders become, in so far as they have no rights against other men, a part of sub-human nature, delivered over like mere animals to the enjoyments and benefits of men, that slavery can ever be an ethically justified condition—and then only in the case of those who have themselves forfeited their rights in this way and not in those of their wives and children.[1] Captives in a just war, that is, who have committed aggression, have by their actions abjured their rights to be treated as men according to the law of reason. They no longer have any *rights* at all against other men. They are incapable of ethical consent—though presumably capable of submission, which is a matter of mere behaviour and thus open to animals.[2] Those who punish them—and anyone may punish them as a representative of the species which they have assaulted[3]—may kill them or make use of them as they please;[4] and in so doing do them no 'injury'.[5] Because such captives have

[1] *Two Treatises*, II, §§23–4, 178, 179, 180, 182, 183 and 189.

[2] '...thus *Captives*, taken in a just and lawful War, and such only, are *subject to a Despotical Power*, which as it arises not from Compact, so neither is it capable of any, but is the state of War continued. For what Compact can be made with a Man that is not Master of his own Life? What Condition can he perform? And if he be once allowed to be Master of his own Life, the *Despotical*, *Arbitrary Power* of his Master ceases. He that is Master of himself, and his own Life, has a right too to the means of preserving it, so that *as soon as Compact enters*, *Slavery ceases*, and he so far quits his Absolute Power, and puts an end to the state of War, who enters into Conditions with his Captive' (*ibid.* II, §172, ll. 20–30). See also *ibid.* §24, ll. 1–8.

[3] *Ibid.* II, §7; §8, ll. 9–24, esp.: 'every man upon this score, by the Right he hath to preserve Mankind in general, may restrain, or where it is necessary, destroy things noxious to them' (ll. 17–19); §11, ll. 13–31.

[4] A captive transgressor of the law of nature who has entered the state of war against an innocent man comes under the absolute, arbitrary, or despotical power of his captor (*Two Treatises*, II, §23, ll. 9–13; §172, ll. 1–9, 19–22). The line of the argument is not very clear here. The key seems to be a separation between the structure of rights between man and man (which does not in these cases impose any obligation to preserve the guilty, if possible (II, §16, ll. 9–11)) and the structure of obligation between the individual human executor of the law of nature and his God (which does continue to do so). Presumably animals (or, *a fortiori*, acorns) do not have a 'right' not to be destroyed except for consumption or self-defence. To waste them is not to do *them* an 'injury' (II, §31; §46, ll. 14–24). The prohibition of waste here is set out as a prohibition of theft from the common human 'stock', an 'injury' to other human beings. The teleology at this point is strongly anthropomorphic. Only other men, and of course God himself, have 'rights' against men. The structure of rights between man and man is very far from specifying the full range of human duties in the world.

[5] '...having, by his fault, forfeited his own Life, by some Act that deserves Death; he, to whom he has forfeited it, may (when he has him in his Power) delay to take it, and make use of him to his own Service, and he does him no injury by it. For,

no right to their lives, they cannot engage in moral action at all. Not being 'masters of their own persons' they can only exhibit behaviour in the way that animals do. They are at liberty to terminate their slavery by death, not as a human moral right but as a behavioural option—in the same way as an animal, kept obedient by fear, could be said to be at liberty to 'choose' death by behaving in such a way as to get killed.[1] This is not to suggest that their thought processes had become empirically assimilated to those of an animal; but simply that the ethical frame of reference between them and other human beings is the same for both. Because it was logically impossible for slavery to be a consensual condition,[2] the slave was no longer fully human. His acts are no longer fully human acts; rather they were bestial. For him to behave in such a way as to procure his own death is no exercise of a human right, the right which the prohibition of suicide denies. It is merely the exploitation of an empirical opportunity. It is only

whenever he finds the hardship of his Slavery out-weigh the value of his Life, 'tis in his Power, by resisting the Will of his Master, to draw on himself the Death he desires' (*ibid.* II, §23, ll. 9–15). An 'injury' is the breach of a right, *injuria* being the antithesis of *jus* which Locke used in his Latin writings in accordance with convention to denote a right. It is important, particularly in view of the primacy of the suicide taboo in the structure of Locke's argument, that the slave, though he has the 'Power' to take his own life, does not have the 'right' to do so. Power is a descriptive category, not a normative one, in this context. Locke, being no Spinozist, did not suppose that a man has a right to do anything which he has a power to do. Indeed the entire *Two Treatises* is specifically concerned to refute such a position (though one maintained for very different reasons, of course, from those of Spinoza).

[1] See above, p. 108, n. 5. This is an interpretation of the jural category. We do not know what Locke thought about human suicide in any detail. The rather simple-minded jural perspective of the *Two Treatises* was far from exhausting the range of contemporary English discussion and much of this was considerably more rationalist in approach and empirically sensitive in tone (see S. E. Sprott, *The English Debate on Suicide from Donne to Hume* (La Salle, Ill., 1961), *passim*). It is not impossible that Locke may have believed that only human beings did have the power to procure their own deaths, since animals are incapable of sin. The position sketched in the text should be read as an account of what Locke should consistently have said had he been confronted by self-destructive behaviour on the part of sub-human nature, not as an argument that we know him ever to have been confronted by such evidence. The possibility that the significant *differentia* is simply the rationality of the slave need not be taken very seriously. Locke's conception of reason is very firmly teleological. In a man justly enslaved, its purpose has not, *ex hypothesi*, been achieved and the status correspondingly has been forfeited. No residual preferential status, based on some quasi-naturalistic ground, attaches to rationality as such.

[2] *Two Treatises*, II, §23, ll. 4–9; §24, ll. 1–8.

empirically that he is alive at all; jurally his life is already forfeit and he has no rights whatsoever in its disposal. He has no right to do one thing rather than another, no *right* at all. He is no longer 'capable of a law'. The fact that a slave-owner is not infringing the the rights of his slaves, though, does not mean that he is doing them no actual damage in enslaving them. No man is obliged to exact any specific degree of punishment and their captor can always terminate the state of war by making a compact with them. To do so is, in the capacity of competent judges, to recognize the captive as man and thus restore him to the ethical realm of human life.[1]

He has quitted this ethical realm by performing particular wrong actions and there will often be considerable incentive to perform such wrong actions in the state of nature. But the character of the state of nature itself cannot be defined in terms of the probability of the occurrence of wrong actions and it is in no sense in antithesis to this ethical realm. Indeed it is precisely a jural condition of equality and freedom *uncontaminated* by history, the history of human wickedness. But, simply because it is in this way an ahistorical abstraction, its jural essence is never to be found in a wholly uncontaminated form *within* human history. The state of nature, like the state of war or the legitimate polity, is never an exhaustive delineation of the set of rights and responsibilities existing among men at any point in time. Its very analytical function makes it impossible for it to be this. Rather than a graphic depiction of the actual moral situations of men, it represents the set of jural co-ordinates on which such situations must be placed if they are to be understood accurately. Although it may appear in history less often, in its purer forms, than do either the state of war or the legitimate polity, its logical status is prior to either of these. For both of these latter, though for obvious reasons trans-historical, cannot be, properly speaking, a-historical, for both of them are the product of particular human

[1] Slavery '*is* nothing else, but *the State of War continued, between a lawful Conquerour, and a Captive*. For, if once *Compact* enter between them, and make an agreement for a limited Power on the one side, and Obedience on the other, the State of War and *Slavery* ceases, as long as the Compact endures. For, as has been said, no Man can, by agreement, pass over to another that which he hath not in himself, a Power over his own Life' (*Two Treatises*, II, §24, ll. 1–8).

actions; the state of war, crudely, the history of human wickedness and the legitimate polity (though *not* human social existence as such), the historical response of human intelligence to the historical record of human wickedness.

What defines the state of nature is that it is neither the state of war nor a properly political condition.[1] It is *any* relationship between *any* men which is not modified by particular acts of direct aggression or by the particular explicit reciprocal normative understandings which institute a shared political society. It is also the rationale of the jural situation which exists between men in these conceptually deviant cases as a result of their invocation of its penalties or their evocation of its creative resources. Its a-historicity gives it a peculiar combination of creativity and abstraction. It seems natural to feel that any such category must be either socially and morally inert or else ruinously historical (and hence also normatively inert). That Locke's category does not appear to be so may be taken as simply a consequence of its being a natural-law category at all. But it seems less evasive to insist that it is a consequence of its place in a particular sort of natural law, one deriving from a highly theistically interventionist natural theology. It is perfectly correct to read it as a teleological account of men's moral resources derived from their performance in the most 'civilized' of contemporary societies.[2] If it was intended as a sociological fantasy, a conjectural pre-history or a hypothesis about behaviour, this might seem curious.[3] But in a conclusion drawn from natural theology it seems entirely intelligible.

1 'Men living together according to reason, without a common Superior on Earth, with Authority to judge between them, is *properly the State of Nature*. But force, or a declared design of force upon the Person of another, where there is no common Superior on Earth to appeal to for relief, *is the State of War*' (*Two Treatises*, II, §19, ll. 6–10). '. . . where there is an Authority, a Power on Earth, from which relief can be had by *appeal*, there the continuance of the State of War is excluded, and the Controversie is decided by that Power' (II, §21, ll. 5–8). '*Freedom of Men under Government*, is, to have a standing Rule to live by, common to every one of that Society, and made by the Legislative Power erected in it; A Liberty to follow my own Will in all things, where the Rule prescribes not; and not to be subject to the inconstant, uncertain, unknown, Arbitrary Will of another Man. As *Freedom of Nature* is to be under no other restraint but the Law of Nature' (II, §22, ll. 10–16).

2 See, for example, Macpherson, *Possessive Individualism*.

3 Curious, that is, at the level of rationality for Locke—not when it comes to our explanations of this rationality. *We* can see pretty quickly why poor Locke should have been *that* sort of a fool. Hence Professor Macpherson's book.

Its ahistoricity protects it too against the classic charge, made by Charles Leslie, following Filmer himself and by academic theorists from Bentham to Bertrand de Jouvenel,[1] that men are not born equal and never live for any period of time in a state of asocial freedom because all men are born into families in a condition of biological and psychological impotence. For the fact that it is an ahistorical concept does not mean that it denies the reality of history or altogether subsumes this. The set of moral obligations owed by an individual at any point in time is a function of his own particular life-history. In any instance of the state of nature at any point in history, the individuals who confront each other in this jural condition of equality do so not merely with hypothetical duties—it is as we have seen, not a 'state of licence'[2]—but with actual ones, and these latter those which they have specifically incurred in their individual lives. To understand the state of nature correctly it is necessary to think history away; but to apply it in discussing any concrete human issue, it is necessary to allow the return of history in the simple delineation of the issue to be discussed. The egalitarianism of the state of nature is more juridical than substantive,[3] ahistorical

[1] See Bentham in Elie Halévy, *La Formation du radicalisme philosophique* (Paris, 1901), I, Appendix III, 416–23, esp. 'Filmer's origin of government is exemplified every where: Locke's scheme of government has not ever, to the knowledge of any body, been exemplified any where. In every family there is government, in every family there is subjection, and subjection of the most absolute kind: the father, sovereign, the mother and the young, subjects. According to Locke's scheme, men knew nothing at all of government till they met together to make one. Locke had speculated so deeply, and reasoned so ingeniously, as to have forgot that he was not of age when he came into the world' (p. 418). Bertrand de Jouvenel, *The Pure Theory of Politics* (Cambridge, 1963). See esp. '"Social contract" theories are views of childless men who must have forgotten their own childhood' (p. 45). (This statement was not made specifically about Locke but it is clear that de Jouvenel would consider that it applies to him, see B. de Jouvenel, *Sovereignty* (Cambridge, 1957), p. 232). For Leslie's views see above, chapter 6.

[2] *Two Treatises*, II, §6.

[3] Cf. *ibid.* II, §4, ll. 7–16 with §54, ll. 1–12: 'Though I have said above, Chap. II, *That all Men by Nature are equal*, I cannot be supposed to understand all sorts of *Equality: Age* or *Virtue* may give men a just Precedency: *Excellency of Parts and Merit* may place others above the Common Level: *Birth* may subject some, and *Alliance* or *Benefits* others, to pay an Observance to those to whom Nature, Gratitude or other Respects may have made it due; and yet all this consists with the *Equality*, which all Men are in, in respect of Jurisdiction or Dominion one over another, which was the *Equality* I there spoke of, as proper to the Business in hand, being that *equal Right* that every Man hath, *to his Natural Freedom*, without being subjected to the Will or Authority of any other Man.' See also II, §70. This is all

rather than historical—and Locke was very much aware that it is history in which men have to live. The ascription of the state of nature is always merely the identification of a jural structure, never a moral inventory of an existing historical situation.

But even if the analysis of this concept given here is correct, it may still seem that Locke sets it in the context of a conjectural history of social development which is sociologically so ludicrous that the concept becomes gravely contaminated. To identify the the clear but limited sense in which this is true, it is necessary to give a brief outline of Locke's conjectural history of government.[1] It begins, classically, with the fact that men are inevitably born into families.[2] They are indeed biologically incapable of survival at first outside such units and can only become independent after a long period of prior nurture and protection.[3] Locke was so far from doubting these banal truths that his whole book is devoted to the proof that a certain set of conclusions does not follow from them. They are as much a datum for the *Two Treatises* as they are for Filmer's *Patriarcha*—and if Locke is to be censured

conventional enough, cf., for example, William Perkins, *The Whole Treatise of the Cases of Conscience*, *Works* (London, 1631), II, 150–2, on honouring one's superiors; Jeremy Taylor, *The Rule and Exercises of Holy Living* (London, 1907), chapter 3, 'Christian Justice', esp. section 1, for Puritan and Anglican versions of the same assumptions. Locke's analysis is perhaps slightly more functional and less insouciantly hierarchical than the versions of Perkins or Taylor if, that is, the observance that 'Nature' has made some to owe as a result of their 'Birth' is to their parents. If this is a correct reading, the force of the concessive 'may' here must refer not to the possibility of some men being *born* but to their owing observances to their parents in consequence. Such obligation can be voided by the misbehaviour of parents (see *Two Treatises*, II, §65, ll. 1–9). But it subsists, under normal conditions, without question (see *ibid.* §66, ll. 1–20). The obligation 'engages him in all actions of defence, relief, assistance and comfort of those, by whose means he entred into being, and has been made capable of any enjoyments of life. From this Obligation no State, no Freedom, can absolve Children' (ll. 17–20). Note that it is not a matter of any significance whether such obligations are *historically* posterior to the existence of political society or even *legitimate* political society. What Locke here insists on is that their obligation is entirely independent logically of any formal political obligations.

[1] As I have repeatedly insisted, Locke's argument does not turn at all upon this historical story. Even so, I should have felt it necessary to set out this account at rather greater length in order to avoid misunderstanding, were it not that Professor Gordon Schochet of Rutgers University has recently completed an article on this subject which states lucidly the position which I would hold myself. See *John Locke: Problems and Perspectives*, ed. J. W. Yolton (Cambridge, 1969).

[2] For what follows see esp. *Two Treatises*, II, §§55, 74–6. This is true of all men except Adam himself (*ibid.* §56).

[3] *Ibid.* I, §89, ll. 1–7, etc.

for his oblivion of them and Filmer commended for his grasp of them, this can only be because the adjudicator feels that the familial character of human life has something of the type of implication for problems of legitimacy that Filmer supposed it to have.[1] The force of sexual desire, for Locke, is the initial bond of the most basic social unit.[2] This is a voluntary union and its social, biological, and indeed theological function is precisely to provide the stable and protected environment needed by the child for its maturation.[3] It is within such an environment that men learn not only practical skills but also moral conduct. Children are naturally amoral, creatures of powerful and largely selfish desires. They strive for dominion over other human beings and attempt to appropriate such external objects as please them. Moral education requires the most subtle combination of physical and emotional sanctions.[4] It is at its most effective when it results in the establishment of *habits* of moral conduct. Men's desires, since the Fall at the least, would always be dangerously unruly without such a period of dependence.[5] But it is a strictly limited period. The

[1] But cf. Laslett's claim (*Two Treatises*, Introduction, p. 69) that Locke failed 'to share Filmer's vision of the emotional togetherness implied by all political relationships'; also its earlier rationale (*Patriarcha and other Political Writings of Sir Robert Filmer*, p. 42) that 'Locke's contractual government...assumed that the stuff of society was conscious ratiocination'. This seems to ignore the fact that Locke uses both 'reason' and 'society' as heavily normative concepts.

[2] 'The *first Society* was between Man and Wife, which gave beginning to that between Parents and Children' (*Two Treatises*, II, §77, ll. 5–7).

[3] *Ibid.* II, §§78–81.

[4] See esp. *Some Thoughts concerning Education*, *Works* (London, 1768) IV, 60–6, etc. Locke also persistently claimed that the moral opinions of most men were the result of unthinking orthodoxy. See *Two Treatises*, I, §58; *Essay*, II, XXVIII, §§10 and 12, and I, III, §§22–5; II, XXI, §69; II, XXVIII, §§6–14, etc.; *Conduct of the Understanding*, *Works*, IV, 156, 186–7. Since he considers in this way that men learn to be moral at all in a family and that their moral beliefs are in the main the effect of custom and differ enormously from nation to nation, it is hard to make sense of the criticism, most recently expressed by Professor Plamenatz (*Man and Society*, London, 1963, I, 221), that 'he does not trouble to inquire how their living together affects them psychologically and morally'. This seems to rest on a reading of Locke's remarks about the nature of moral truth as though they represented his opinions about the empirical psychology of morals. This is unfortunate since the major burden of Locke's moral thought is concerned with the fact of the gap between these and with the problem of narrowing it. See above, chapter 3, and below, chapter 14.

[5] Cf. *Some Thoughts concerning Education*, *Works*, IV, *passim* and esp. as cited in n. 4 above with: '...Education, the Parents Duty, seems to have most power, because the ignorance and infirmities of Childhood stand in need of restraint and correction; which is a visible exercise of Rule, and a kind of Dominion' (*Two Treatises*, II, §68, ll. 5–8); and *ibid.* §65, ll. 26–7, §67, ll. 11–17.

times of helpless physical dependence and of instinctual amorality come to an end and with them the right to moral paternalism.[1] As adults, men become free and independent individuals fully responsible for all their behaviour.

In this natural state, as at all stages of social development, men are forced into society with their fellows by the most elementary of compulsions. But it is not only the force of sexual desire or the affective enticements of the family which influence them to live in such groups. If we wish to understand the theoretical basis of the morphology of social development which Locke propounds, it is essential to grasp the role played in it by the Fall. For the sin of Adam not only originated human mortality,[2] it also originated that lesser punitive feature of the human condition, labour,[3] and the socio-moral category derived from labour in conditions of scarcity, private property.[4] It is this feature of the human condition that is responsible for the persistent insecurity and uncertainty which arise from the treatment which men meet at the hands of other sinful human beings. Hence, in a pre-political condition, they will naturally remain within the affective warmth of the family even after adulthood and will tend to accept the authority of their father to act as an appropriate leader in any relations with other men outside the family unit.[5] 'Thus 'twas easie, and almost

[1] 'The first part then of *Paternal* Power, or rather Duty, which is *Education*, belongs so to the Father that it terminates at a certain season; when the business of Education is over it ceases of it self, and is also alienable before. For a Man may put the Tuition of his Son in other hands; and he that has made his Son an *Apprentice* to another, has discharged him, during that time, of a great part of his Obedience both to himself and to his Mother' (*ibid.* II, §69, ll. 1–8).

[2] *The Reasonableness of Christianity*, *Works*, III, 3–6.

[3] 'Cursed is the ground for thy sake: in sorrow shalt thou eat of it all the days of thy life; in the sweat of thy face shalt thou eat bread, till thou return unto the ground: for out of it wast thou taken; dust thou art, and to dust shalt thou return' (Genesis III, 17–19), quoted in *ibid.* III, 5.

[4] 'When private posessions and labour, which now the curse on earth had made necessary, by degrees made a distinction of conditions it gave room for covetousness, pride and ambition which by fashion and example spread the corruption which has so prevailed over mankind. JL' ('Homo ante et post lapsum', MS Locke c 28, fo. 113v).

[5] *Two Treatises*, II, §74, ll. 10–37; §105, §107, esp. ll. 24–43. *Inside* the family unit at such a stage of social development covetousness was not a prominent emotion (*ibid.* §75, ll. 5–17, §107, ll. 28–37), because the ratio between economic temptation and fellow-feeling was more favourable on both axes than in large-scale societies of great wealth. But at any stage of social development those with whom they have no 'Acquaintance and Friendship' may threaten their security.

natural for Children by a tacit, and scarce avoidable consent to make way for the *Father's Authority and Government*.'[1] It was 'by an insensible change'[2] that fathers became rulers.

The problem which Locke confronts and which baffles him, somewhat as it later baffled Hume,[3] is the problem of explaining the development of legitimate society outside the given affective structure of the family; not of explaining the development of society at all—conquest would do that as well for Locke as for Hume himself—[4] but the development of legitimate society. In its rather rationalistic and abstract fashion, the ascription of this result to the human capacity to co-operate in pursuit of shared goals seems moderately well judged and, since the argument does not at all turn upon the issue, more or less harmless. If such issues of conjectural history are to be raised at all, it is not easy to improve on it—and Hume himself was obliged in effect to repeat it.[5]

Around this initial core of the blood relations there agglomerates a much more disparate group of men, bought servants and slaves who all form part of this family.[6] This group can number anything up to several hundreds without becoming a *political* community.[7] It may be augmented for specific exertions of power by the assistance of friends and companions, and even by the

[1] *Two Treatises*, II, §75, ll. 1–3.

[2] 'Thus the natural *Fathers of Families*, by an insensible change, became the *politick Monarchs* of them too: And as they chanced to live long, and leave able, and worthy Heirs, for several Successions, or otherwise; So they laid the Foundations of Hereditary, or Elective Kingdoms, under several Constitutions, and Manners, according as Chance, Contrivance, or Occasions happen'd to mould them' (*ibid.* II, §76, ll. 1–8).

[3] David Hume, *Treatise of Human Nature* (Everyman edition, London, 1911), II, 192–5.

[4] *Two Treatises*, II, §§175 and 211 (cf. David Hume, *Essays, Moral, Political and Literary* (London, 1903), 'Of the Original Contract', pp. 457–8). This was a continuing theme of Locke's; for example: 'All the entertainment of talk and history is of nothing almost but fighting and killing; and the honour and renown that is bestowed on conquerors, (who for the most part are but the great butchers of mankind) farther mislead growing youths, who by this means come to think slaughter the laudable business of mankind, and the most heroic of virtues' (*Some Thoughts concerning Education, Works*, IV, 73). He claims here that cruelty is not intrinsically pleasurable and that it is only this deleterious conditioning which makes it so.

[5] Cf. *Treatise of Human Nature*, II, 192–5, with the very late essay, 'Of the Origin of Government' (first published in 1777), *Essays*, pp. 35–9.

[6] *Two Treatises*, I, §§130 and 131; II, §§77, 86, 107–10.

[7] *Ibid.* I, §130, ll. 1–10 and §131, ll. 15–19.

hiring of soldiers specifically for the occasion. Such complexes of authority are built up, jurally speaking, entirely by consent (except in the case of slaves), and they do not necessarily give any power of life and death over their participants, unless these specifically surrender their freedom.[1] Their conceptual identity, being purely jural, a matter of the structure and character of rights within such a group, does not lie in any particular empirical characteristics and may be present at very different points of social, cultural and historical development, among the planters of the West Indies in the seventeenth century just as much as among the Hebrew patriarchs[2] and the Amerindian war bands. Since, too, these groupings combine apparent utility in the protection which they afford against the threat of external violence with a low degree of internal conflict, they tend to become stable and the institutionalized consent readily converts them into fully political societies.[3] These form the early golden age of government, an age in which kings are the 'nursing fathers'[4] of their kingdoms.[5] It is only disrupted by the new pattern of social relationships which results from the acceptance of money as a store of wealth and a means of exchange. This acceptance of the

1 See in general *Second Letter concerning Toleration*, *Works*, II, 423, *Third Letter for Toleration*, *Works*, II, 488, *Two Treatises*, I, §§130, 131; but cf. Laslett's note to §130 on the 'political character of the family under such circumstances'. This comment is perhaps misleading since Locke's point here is precisely that the existence of such a large group and the purposes to which its master devotes it do *not* make it necessarily into a political unit. Cf. I, §132.

2 *Ibid.* I, §§130, 133, 135, 137; II, §§24, 109 etc.

3 This is an exceedingly sympathetic reading of *Two Treatises*, II, §§105–10. Locke's own argument is much impaired, both in exposition and in conception, by the need to concentrate on the refutation of Filmer (see §§101–3).

4 This 'quasi-patriarchal' phrase (see *ibid.* II, §110n.) was not by any means always associated with the more authoritarian facet of the patriarchal arguments. Cf. the extremely restrictive interpretation given to it by [Charles Leslie,] *The Case of the Regale and of the Pontificat Stated*...(n.p., 1700), pp. 26–7; though it should be noted that in this work Leslie does not appear as convinced and explicit a Filmerian as he was afterwards to show himself (see *ibid.* 214–19).

5 *Two Treatises*, II, §111, ll. 1–9. It is clear that Lamprecht (*The Moral and Political Philosophy of John Locke* (New York, 1962), p. 127) is correct in seeing this as an instance of pre-commercial political society and not of the 'state of nature'. It contains 'Governours', 'prerogative', 'Privileges', 'magistrates', 'rulers', and a separate 'people'. These terms are used in a rather loose and, naturally, unhistorical fashion but they are clearly none of them relevant to the Master/Servant, Father/Child axis of authority which Locke insists to be the only type of authority present in the state of nature; in Aristotelian terms, the domestic rather than the political, the οἶκος rather than the πόλις.

role of money is necessarily consensual, a paradigm indeed of ἀνθρώπινη κτίσις,[1] because gold itself is of no great intrinsic value.[2] This leads to economic progress and betters the conditions of all members of the population,[3] though it restricts for many their opportunities for economic initiative, most particularly in the areas where they are born. Differentiation in wealth leads to greater social conflict and to a decline in the moral quality of social life under stress of the increasing motives for envy. This development might in principle take place outside any fully political society. But if it did so the intensity of conflict which it engenders would soon necessitate the creation of such a society. That is to say, political organization is not a logical precondition for the existence of advanced commercial society but it certainly is an empirical precondition for its continuance over any period of time.

External conflict, arising from the land hunger caused by economic development and population growth, combines with internal conflict to make government essential for the maintenance of internal order and the direction to best advantage of the external *protective* power of the society. Unfortunately the type of social organization produced by these needs, while perfectly

[1] Cf. *A Second Letter concerning Toleration, Works*, II, 423.

[2] See *Two Treatises*, Introduction, pp. 101, 104 and II, §45 n., on consent to the use of money as 'the consent of all mankind'. Laslett here glosses Locke's statement that there are parts of the world in which the inhabitants have not joined with the rest of mankind in the use of their common money with this statement. All that Locke meant by the phrase was that money was a very common institution and that it *was* an institution, a product of human contrivance and convention, not of natural necessity. He does not see any problem of justification in basing the value of money on consent since men can always register dissent by not using it. He could hardly *justify* differential property rights by the same tactic (though he could and did explain their emergence in this way) and he did not attempt to do so. The extent to which he did employ it to 'justify' differential property rights is peculiar, if the intention is hardly very clear (see below, chapters 15–17). The Italian translators of his monetary writings give a clear defence of his notion against a common misunderstanding. 'Non dee intendersi che il nostro Autore abbia voluto parlare di una convenzione propria, e secondo il vero significato di tal parola, ma più tosto di un uso, al quale insensibilmente, e tacitamente gli uomini si accordarono fra loro per il proprio commodo, e vantaggio' (*Ragionamenti sopra la moneta l'interesse del danaro le finanze e il commercio scritti e pubblicati in diverse occasioni dal signor Giovanni Locke*, Tradotti la prima volta dall'inglese con varie annotazioni [by Gio. Francesco Pagnini and Angelo Tavanti] (Firenze, 1751), I, 48 n., and see III, 22 n. (copy in Bibliothèque Nationale)).

[3] *Two Treatises*, II, §41.

adapted to the good ruler, leaves to the bad a power over his subjects which is almost without legal restriction. It remains the general interest of the ruler to enforce the law justly.[1] But economic prosperity provides much greater incentive to the abuse of power. And, since monarchs are just as much sinful men as are their subjects, this power is certain sooner or later to be abused.[2] This leads to revolutions and to the development of political forms which fetter the authority of the monarch. But these also cannot *solve* the problems of order and freedom among sinners. Nothing short of the Day of Judgement can achieve this. But in so far as society meets these problems at all it meets them as the historical response of human intelligence to the record of human wickedness. The development of a money economy may have increased the standard of consumption in this world which God has given to men 'richly to enjoy'. But it has also spread corruption at precisely the same time, the corruption of acquisitiveness. The gain in welfare might be more than balanced by the loss in moral quality were it not for two historical phenomena, the Christian revelation of divine positive law and the institutional experiments by which men had at least restrained the extent of those disasters which threatened their social orders. There does remain a sort of primitivism in Locke's politics but it is the primitivism of a man who knows that there is no return—and it is a primitivism which is altogether more effectively assuaged by the first of these historical recompenses than it is by the glories of English constitutionalism.

[1] *Third Letter for Toleration*, *Works*, II, 666–7.

[2] *Two Treatises*, II, §§91, 92.

10

THE CREATION OF THE LEGITIMATE POLITY

In order to discern the conditions which must be satisfied if a polity is to be judged legitimate, and in order to differentiate such a community from the broader set of human social arrangements which Filmer held to be so, it was necessary to perform two separate operations. The logical preconditions for the existence of a legitimate authority of one human being over another had to be elaborated and the sociological prerequisites for claiming that such a legitimate authority existed in a particular political society had to be analysed. In order to carry off the entire project for which his book was devised—the justification of revolutionary action or at least the threat of such action under certain circumstances—and in order to destroy the Filmerian position, Locke needed to pay much closer attention to the analysis of the logical preconditions than to the character of their embodiment in particular political societies. In the book as he finally published it what he provided in this latter respect were less accounts which analysed this issue with any philosophical adequacy than perfunctory sketches of the shapes which such arguments would take if anyone wished to elaborate them fully. This would have been a slightly peculiar procedure if his intention had been to write any sort of sufficient moral apologia for a particular political society, let alone a particular social structure. But, since the argument which he was conducting was with men who had not the faintest disposition to question the legitimacy of the English constitution or social structure from some more radical and subversive point of view, there was little need to pay attention to emergent moral implausibilities in his own analysis of the character of this structure. His problem was not any general moral precariousness sensed by his opponents in the political authority of the society but an all too obsessively plausible and over-homogenized conception of the scope of this political authority.

We have seen already how he set out his account of the logical preconditions by inference from his natural theology, in direct rebuttal of Filmer's assimilation of all relationships between men and other men and between men and natural objects to the single category of 'Dominion', the genetically (and exceedingly narrowly) distributed right to arbitrary and unchallengeable manipulation of God's entire created order by the wills of a handful of rulers. The crucial transition lies in his replacement of Filmer's account of God's providential provision for human moral education in eternal structures of social authority by his own account of God's imposition of individual religious duties on all men through their intellectual capacity to know the relevant moral truths.[1] All men are equal because the primary definition of their jural situation is the set of duties which they owe to God. The 'Jurisdiction or Dominion' under which they live[2] is that of God. The duties which they owe to God demand that they possess a certain sort of freedom and this demand is a logical demand, not a contingent fact about human psychology or social organization. The duties which religion demands from them require their autonomous choices before they can be executed. So men are equal 'in respect of Jurisdiction or Dominion one over another'[3] because they are put into the world 'by his order and about his business...whose Workmanship they are'.[4] This does not mean that they in fact exhibit any sort of substantive equality[5] or that it would be appropriate for them to do so. But it does mean that it must be possible to construe the legitimacy of any set of social arrangements in terms of the will of all adult participants in it, each individual counting for one.[6] This does not indicate that

[1] *Two Treatises of Government*, II, §57.

[2] *Ibid.* II, §54, l. 8.

[3] *Ibid.* II, §54, ll. 8–9.

[4] *Ibid.* II, §6, ll. 12–14.

[5] '*Age* or *Virtue* may give Men a just Precedency: *Excellency of Parts and Merit* may place others above the Common Level: Birth may subject some, and *Alliance* or *Benefits* others, to pay an Observance to those whom Nature, Gratitude or other Respects may have made it due; and yet all this consists with the *Equality*, which all Men are in, in respect of Jurisdiction or Dominion one over another' (*ibid.* II, §54, ll. 3–9).

[6] This statement is to be read as an account of the formal structure of Locke's theory, not of its application to the world. For instance Locke nowhere suggests that women have a status in political terms which is equal to that of men. He is prepared to be sharply naturalistic in his treatment of the relationships between men and

Locke felt any profound yearning to institute mass democracy, in Leslie's contemptuous phrase to 'poll the whole nation'.[1] It must be a series of relationships which could be hypothetically and accurately recognized by all the human beings concerned as necessary for their accomplishment of the assignment which God has allotted to each of them. This requirement imposes on the Lockean account of the nature of political society a peculiar balance of moral stringency and permissiveness. There are few formal standards which a political society must meet for it to be considered as hypothetically legitimate—a wide variety of highly inegalitarian and absolutist régimes might meet the standards in principle—but the legitimacy remains predicated on the services rendered to all members of the society. Whenever this legitimacy is claimed in order to bolster the interests of individual rulers its status is threatened gravely.

In a highly legitimist society like seventeenth-century England, and in the political theory which Filmer elaborated to sanction this society, the rights of the crown, even if they were ultimately attributed to its performance of some divinely appointed task, were seen very unequivocally as *rights* of its own, explicitly analogous in Filmer's own doctrine to property rights. For Locke, rulers did not in this sense have humanly indefeasible rights at all. Subjects had general duties of submission and because submission is always submission to individual men and not to abstract terms[2] these duties might in practice often be behaviourally identical with the Filmerian assessment of the rights of rulers. Of course, since Locke took the trouble to write and then to publish the

women when commenting on the status of Filmer's arguments for the power of fathers, reducing the residual force of paternal power to sexually egalitarian 'parental power' (*Two Treatises*, I, §§55, 60–7; II, §§52 and 65) or even when discussing the institution of marriage (II, §§78–83, esp. §81). But in the application to political relationships naturalism is not even specifically rejected. Convention is simply *assumed* to carry prescriptive weight. The 'representation' of women was as unexacting in institutional terms as that of the poor or of servants. The facile conventionalism of Locke's assumptions about the legitimacy of existing social subordination can be seen explicitly in p. 121, n. 5, above.

[1] [Charles Leslie,] *The New Association of those Called Moderate-Church-men*, Part II, Supplement (London, 1703), p. 10.

[2] MS Locke c 28, fo. 85v. Cf. fo. 84v: 'Allegiance is neither due nor paid to Right or to Government which are abstract notions but only to persons having right or government.' From notes on W. Sherlock's *The Case of the Allegiance Due to Soveraign Powers*...(London, 1691).

Two Treatises at all (as opposed to a formal work of general political theory), it is hardly surprising that he did not see them as behaviourally identical in all circumstances. But whenever the general duties of subjects were deployed to adorn the private purpose of the rulers—and rulers, being individual men, always possess private purposes—their moral quality evaporated. What gave normative status to human political communities were sociological necessities for the accomplishment of religious duty, assessed in the most rationalist fashion. The connection of these necessities with the actual purposes of rulers in the world is purely contingent and if the rulers manipulate these moral accoutrements to enhance the moral plausibility of their own wishes, they commit a sort of blasphemy. They conflate their own corrupt desires with the tender (if not operationally very deft) mercies of God. All the stringency of the Lockean account lies in its brusque dismissal of the complacent self-righteousness of human authority and the consequences which flow from it. The permissiveness extends to blanket a wider area of human life. There is no reason to believe that Locke ever enjoyed any authentic vision of a more libertarian and egalitarian political structure, still less social structure. But the defect here was perhaps more one of imagination than one of will.[1] And the permissiveness, not to say insensitivity, which he displays to the real constraints of individual life in a society as repressive as that of seventeenth-century England and to the social and political structures which protect these constraints, arise defensibly in his own terms from this conception of the role of society in human life. What society *has* to do for individuals, its essential function, is to make it possible for them to execute their religious duties in an environment of as widespread 'innocent delights' as economic progress can make

[1] I have tried to show something of the inertness of imagination which he displays in all his political writings by examining the feeble way in which he treats the concept of justice, the keynote of all pre-nineteenth-century critical social thought, throughout his writings in an article 'Justice and the Interpretation of Locke's Political Theory' in *Political Studies* (February 1968). To place the poverty of this response against the resources of the intellectual traditions to which I argue that he belonged, it would be necessary to set the analysis which I attempt in this book against the achievement of Thomas More's *Utopia*, as it has recently been so dazzlingly expounded by Professor Hexter: *Utopia*, ed. Edward Surtz, S. J. and J. H. Hexter (*The Complete Works of St. Thomas More*, New Haven, 1965, IV), xv–cxxiv.

available to all.[1] In consequence, many different styles of social injustice may be compatible with the fulfilment of this function. Locke's doctrine carries no direct and general charter for social revolution, but neither does it carry any such general charter for political repression. And whenever the purposes of God are claimed as sanctions for any individual's corrupt exercise of power the doctrine implies the rejection of that individual's claim.[2]

Hence any political society which derives its legitimacy formally from a set of rights of its sovereign which are not derivatives of the wills of his subjects violates the logical preconditions for a legitimate political society. This does not mean that every such society should be, or even, morally speaking, may appropriately be, subverted. But it means that such legitimacy as the society does enjoy must be extrapolated from features of it other than its official political creed or legal system. The most plausible bases for the limited legitimacy are the costs to others of promoting civil war within it and the degree to which it does in fact satisfy the need which all individuals experience for a social structure within which to undertake their religious duties. In contrast to the contingent and consequential legitimacy of such a social organization, based on the morally prudent calculations of the subjects, the intrinsic legitimacy of an authentic political society is fully symmetrical, the rights of rulers and the duties of the subjects being logically interdependent. The rights of the rulers derive from the wills of the subjects but, being properly derived in this way, they become genuinely rights *over* the subjects. A harmonious structure of mutual obligation has been created. Even when such a society has been instituted, its participants, remaining individual human sinners, are always liable to erase its legitimacy by the quality of their actions. But at least it does have a status to erase and this is attached to the formal political structure of the society. Only in such a society can genuinely *political* obligations exist.

The moral status of political societies derives from their capacity

[1] *Two Treatises*, II, §128, ll. 1–2 etc.

[2] This restriction appears to hold also of the concept of property which is the most classically 'bourgeois' element of Locke's thought. See below, chapters 15–17, and more generally my article cited on p. 123, n. 1.

to serve as instruments for men's struggle to discharge the religious assignments for which God created them. Hence the structure of political obligation is logically dependent on the structure of individual religious duty. Locke treats the suicide taboo, as we have seen above, as the first term in individual religious duty. He takes it categorically as a divine command without legitimate limitations[1] and does not argue for it, as for instance Aquinas did,[2] as an example of the general duty of charity. But there is nothing novel in his description of the duty itself.[3] God owns the lives of men because he made them—they are his 'workmanship'.[4]

1 Cf. More, *Utopia*, *Works*, IV, 186.

2 'Conclusio: Seipsum occidere, cum sit contra Dei. et sui, ac proximi charitatem, nullo modo cuiquam licet.' But cf. *ibid.* 'Tertio, quia vita est quoddam donum divinitus homini attributum, et ejus potestati subjectum, qui occidit et vivere facit. Et ideo qui seipsum vita privat, in Deum peccat. sicut qui alienum servum interficit, peccat in dominum cujus est servus (3); et sicut peccat ille qui usurpat sibi judicium mortis et vitae, secundum illud (Deuteronomy XXXII, 39): Ego occidam, et ego vivere faciam...homo constituitur dominus sui ipsius per liberum arbitrium: et ideo licite potest homo de seipso disponere quantum ad ea quae pertinent ad hanc vitam, quae hominis libero arbitrio regitur. Sed transitus (1) de hac vita ad aliam feliciorem non subjacet libero arbitrio hominis, sed potestati divinae; et ideo non licet homini seipsum interficere, ut ad feliciorem transeat vitam' (*Summa Theologiae*, II, 11. Quaest. 64, Art. 5).

3 See such conventional formulations as Jeremy Taylor, *Ductor Dubitantium* (London, 1660), II, 75–8, esp.: 'To put our selves to death without the Command of God or his lieutenant is impiety and rebellion against God; it is a desertion of our military station, and a violation of the proprieties and peculiar rights of God, who only hath power over our lives...' (p. 76) and St Thomas Aquinas in n. 2 above.

The most extensive treatment of the rights of human beings over their own bodies in the Catholic natural-law tradition was D. Balthassare Gomezio De Amescua, *Tractatus de Potestate in Seipsum* (2nd edition, Mediolani, 1609). See esp. Lib. 1. cap. 1. 1, 5 ('Nemo pacto se facit servum'), 8 ('Nemini licet se occidere'), 9 ('Homo non est dominus vitae suae'), 10 ('Sed solus Dominus'), 11 ('Ea, quorum quis est dominus, debet posse consumere'); cap. V, cap. VIII ('Nullam esse circumstantiam, praeter divinam jussionem, qua propricidium possit fieri licitum'); cap. XII ('Neminem consentire posse, ut occidatur, vel vulneretur'). For the central resemblance between such a traditional position and Locke himself as against Filmer see *ibid.* Lib. 1. cap. 1. 19 ('Aliud est jurisdictio, aliud dominium').

4 'Men being all the Workmanship of one Omnipotent, and infinitely wise Maker; All the Servants of one Sovereign Master, sent into the World by his order and about his business, they are his Property, whose Workmanship they are, made to last during his, not one anothers Pleasure' (*Two Treatises*, II, §6, ll. 10–15); 'Every one...is *bound to preserve himself*, and not to quit his Station wilfully' (ll. 19–20); 'For a Man, not having the Power of his own Life, *cannot*, by Compact, or his own Consent, *enslave himself* to any one nor put himself under the Absolute, Arbitrary Power of another, to take away his Life, when he pleases. No body can give more Power than he has himself; and he that cannot take away his own Life, cannot give another power over it' (§23, ll. 4–9); §56, ll. 11–13; §135, ll. 4–23; §137, l. 7;

No man can confer the right to take his life upon other men by his own will since he does not possess this right himself.[1]

But the belief that no individual has any authority over his own life raises acute problems. For if this claim holds, it is obscure how goverments can come to possess the attributes of Bodinian sovereignty and most notably the power of life and death over their subjects. Filmer resolves this dilemma by positing the direct and historically continuous divine provision of political communities as structures of social control within which all men live out their lives. Locke needed to dispose of this allegation, but in order to do so with impunity he needed a surrogate for the doctrine, with which to handle this theoretical problem. The surrogate was his 'strange Doctrine' that each man possessed the executive power of the law of nature.[2] Men confront each other without *a priori* authority over one another because their jural situation is extrapolated from God's purposes for each of them and these purposes are such that each must remain perpetually responsible for his execution of them. But because men are fallen, because they are sinners, they interfere with each other's performance of these divine assignments. Their relationships are governed by the law of nature and when they encroach on each other's jural space, violate each other's rights, they are liable to

§149, ll. 18–20; §168, ll. 25–30; §172, ll. 3–7. For the most deeply felt statement of the basis of this claim and the depth of its rejection of Filmer's argument for paternal power from the fact that fathers 'give Life and Being' to their children, see I, §§53 and 54, esp. 53, ll. 24–6: the fatherhood of God 'is such an one as utterly excludes all pretence of Title in Earthly Parents; for he is *King* because he is indeed Maker of us all, which no Parents can pretend to be of their Children'.

[1] Besides theological limitations on the scope of human authority over human lives, Locke also uses an axiom of rationality in his arguments for the necessary limits of political authority (*Two Treatises*, II, §137, ll. 1–23, esp.: 'It cannot be supposed that they should intend...' (ll. 6–7); 'since a Rational Creature cannot be supposed when free, to put himself into Subjection to another, for his own harm' (§164, ll. 1–2) It is important to insist that this derives its status in his argument from the theological context of human rationality, not from its empirical dominance in human psychology. It is perfectly true that Locke writes at times as though self-preservation were simply a peculiarly persistent human purpose, but it is not the persistence which gives it its normative status. Human beings persistently exhibit all sorts of purposes, many of them highly corrupt. It is not their frequency of occurrence but their compatibility with their religious duties which gives them their authority or indefeasibility. See below, chapter 14.

[2] *Two Treatises*, II, §9, ll. 1–2; §13, ll. 1–2. The basis of the power and its rationale are explained throughout §§7–13.

punishment according to this law.[1] The sufficient sanctions of this law are only exerted in the next world.[2] But for the law to constitute on earth more than a piece of sanctimonious divine wish-fulfilment (with belated and slightly spiteful compensations attached to it in the next world), there must be some mechanism for making it operational in the world.[3] It must be a mechanism which combines the indefeasible jural status of each member of the species with the potentiality for each to deploy effective sanctions against another. If a man is to judge another man and indeed to punish him in a way which he has no authority to employ in his own case, he can only do so by virtue of a derived authority. The power which individuals may exercise to frustrate the wrongful assaults of their fellows is the executive power of the law of nature and the executive power under all circumstances derives its authority from the legislative power. The legislative power of the law of nature rests with God. When men judge the offences of their fellows and execute sentences upon them for these offences, they judge them in the capacity of agents of God. This executive power of the law of nature is the basis of all legitimate power of one man over another man and every form in which it is redistributed among men throughout history retains this foundation. The foundation is not a historical origin but a logical prerequisite. There is no such category in Locke's political theory as authority which is both intrinsically human and legitimate. All legitimate authority everywhere and always exercised by one human being over another is an authority conferred upon him ultimately by God. And this authority does not extend beyond those actions of the authority which are correctly described as executions of the purposes of God.

All Locke's discussions about the normative standing of political structures have to be read with this rider firmly in mind. It will go far to explain the insouciance of much of his subsequent exposition on such points as the status of majorities and the merits

[1] *Ibid.* II, §7, ll. 1–7; §8.

[2] See below, chapter 14.

[3] 'For the *Law of Nature* would, as all other Laws that concern Men in this World, be in vain, if there were no body that in the State of Nature, had a *Power to Execute* that Law, and thereby preserve the innocent and restrain offenders, and if any one in the State of Nature may punish another, for any evil he has done, every one may do so' (*Two Treatises*, II, §7, ll. 7–12).

of different forms of government.[1] What differentiates a fully political society from any random aggregation of human beings for a particular purpose is that it possesses a determinate decision-procedure which is binding on all members of the society. Such a decision-procedure could take an infinite variety of forms. All of these forms are potentially capable of generating desirable results and all of them are liable (though not of course equally liable) to generate undesirable results. There is only one rule of social choice which can be extrapolated from the notion of a political society as such in this interpretation. It would apply in those (presumably rare) cases where there exist authentically political societies without set decision-procedures. The rule is that since it is a defining condition of a political society that it should possess *some* binding decision-procedure and since no man intrinsically possesses authority over any other man, where there is no set decision-procedure and the society is to make laws which bind all members, the procedure must take equal account of the choice of each. Hence the notion of a political society in the absence of any historically accredited decision-procedure prescribes majority voting on all legislative issues.[2] But of course nothing at all like such a situation existed in seventeenth-century England—or for that matter in any long-term political community which Locke ever mentions. And there is no doubt that he would have regarded majority voting on all issues by a whole population as a grotesquely dangerous and practically absurd political struc-

[1] There can be few more striking indications of the gap in intellectual purpose between the *Two Treatises* and academic studies like Pufendorf's *De Jure Naturae et Gentium* than those brought out by comparing Locke's extraordinarily perfunctory sketch in *Two Treatises*, II, chapter X with book VIII, chapter V of the *De Jure Naturae*.

[2] 'Whosoever therefore out of a state of Nature unite into a *Community*, must be understood to give up all the power, necessary to the ends for which they unite into Society, to the *majority* of the Community, unless they expressly agreed in any number greater than the majority. And this is done by barely agreeing to *unite into one Political Society* which is *all the Compact* that is, or needs be, between the Individuals, that enter into, or make up a *Common-wealth*' (*Two Treatises*, II, §99, ll. 1–8). The point stressed is that there must be *a* decision-procedure and that it must be binding on all inhabitants or the society will simply disintegrate on every occasion of disagreement (§§96, 98). Membership in society creates specifically political obligations (§97). The only alternative decision-procedure which has any *prima facie* status is simply unanimity. But requirement of unanimity would in practice make it impossible to preserve a political society in existence at all and it would remove the distinction between political and non-political relationships (§98).

ture. Because he is attempting to analyse only the logical prerequisites for political legitimacy he has no need to concern himself at this point in the argument with the problem in political choice posed by the merest glimmering of a sociological understanding of political relationships, still less with such sophisticated formal conundrums in the theory of social choice as 'Arrow problems'.[1] Locke did not 'ignore' the problems of majoritarian populism[2]—it simply never occurred to him that anyone could have reason to espouse such a peculiar theory. His comments on the status of majorities in political choice were a part of his formal analysis of the concept of political legitimacy. They were in no sense whatever a proposal for the appropriate form of social organization. Nor would he have supposed for a moment that any form of social organization could be *assumed* to generate just political acts.

But if the notion of majority consent is merely the minimum condition in the absence of any recognized political authority for the existence of a political society at all, the level of commitment to particular political arrangements which it implies must be demonstrable as obligatory for all citizens of legitimate political societies. To be a member of a legitimate political society is to have certain political *obligations*. These obligations are generated by the hypothetical agreement of the individual to be a member of the

They might insist on some larger majority (cf. §99, *loc. cit.*, §97, ll. 12–17), but at some stage in the logical construction, majority choice transmutes into the creation of the legislative and at this point the structure of historical societies appears (see, for example, §212, ll. 7–22). At this point men may agree on virtually any form of legislative authority. But the status of this authority whatever its social form must at some point in the historical past have flowed through the channels of majority will or it can have no legitimacy. At only one point in the development of his argument does Locke slip outside the boundaries of this formal argument. In §96, ll. 6–12, the rule is inferred from the necessity of preserving the society in existence, with the addition of a claim about the location of the preponderance of physical force in the society. The passage is ill considered and carelessly expressed. Even if pressed very hard, it seems as plausible to see the concept of force as moralized by the notion of consent as it is to see the notion of consent turned into a term of social coercion. The passage does maintain that members of the polity are *bound* by the consent. If all that this amounts to is the fact that they are socially coerced, it is not clear how §§97 and 98 could have any force at all.

1 Kenneth J. Arrow, *Social Choice and Individual Values* (2nd edition, New York, 1963).

2 Cf. Willmoore Kendall, *John Locke and the Doctrine of Majority-rule* (2nd edition, Urbana, Ill., 1959), *passim.*

society. This does not mean that the members of inadequately legitimate political societies have no obligations; they may indeed have direct obligations to obey the holders of power in the society. But they do not have authentically political obligations. For the defining characteristic of political obligations is that they reside in acknowledged formal structures of reciprocal rights and duties. The duties owed by subjects in imperfectly legitimate political communities are not rights of their rulers but constructs out of their duties to their fellow subjects in prevailing social conditions, as interpreted by the obligation to prudence. The duty of obedience in such a society is based solely upon the calculated consequences to others of disobedience, not on any authentic *authority* on the part of the rulers.

Equally, political obligations in the most elaborately and persistently legitimate of political societies are not indefeasible in all circumstances. But, where they do subsist, authentic political obligations are logically dependent on the prior consent of those subject to them. This is a somewhat opaque notion and its precise implications have greatly puzzled commentators on Locke.[1] There are thus two problems about the idea of a legitimate political community, the question of what behavioural criteria must be satisfied for a man to be held a member of a previously existing legitimate community and the prior question of what behaviour institutes a legitimate community. The latter question is easy to conflate with the causal and historical question of what circumstances did in fact lead to the creation of what Locke saw as legitimate political communities or, less temporally, the question of what the sociological prerequisites for the emergence and continuance of such communities were. But the question is not a causal question about the processes of human social development but a philosophical question about the logical preconditions for the existence of a certain type of human ethical obligation. We have treated briefly above Locke's conception of the mechanisms by which complex political societies develop out of family groups. It is not of any great significance in examining the general structure of Locke's theory to assess their sophistication, since no part

[1] See my article, 'Consent in the Political Theory of John Locke', *The Historical Journal* x, 2 (July 1967).

of the argument hangs upon them.[1] But since there are such profound differences in the theory between legitimate and illegitimate political societies and since the differences depend upon a historically delivered acknowledgement of the society's legitimacy by its members, the question of what constitutes such an acknowledgement is clearly central to the analysis of the theory. Unfortunately Locke's treatment of the point is notably perfunctory. Indeed he does not treat it directly at all. It is quite easy to give a causal explanation of this neglect in terms of the context of argument to which the book was addressed. Locke was arguing for a right of extra-constitutional resistance in a state, England, which both he and those against whom he was arguing agreed to be a model of a legitimate political society. The legitimacy of the English polity was one of the few shared premises of the argument and the dispute was over the nature of the English constitution, not over its obligatory status. Hence it is *assumed* throughout the *Two Treatises* that the English constitution simply meets the criteria of political legitimacy, whatever these may be.

This means that if we are to derive a clearer understanding of what Locke's view of these criteria amounts to in social terms, we must attempt to synthesize this from more incidental evidence. Perhaps the most enlightening approach is to begin by giving an analysis of the nature of consent within existing legitimate societies and then to relate this to instances where Locke expressly denies the legitimacy of a particular political society. There are two sorts of consent which subject an individual to the laws of a legitimate political society. Tacit consent is incurred by anyone who voluntarily takes any advantage of the resources of the country. Simple voluntary presence in the territory of the country is a sufficient condition for being held in this way to have consented tacitly, though the persons of whom the category is predicated at all specifically appear mostly to be resident or

[1] It should be noted, though, that they are based on extremely wide reading in the travel literature which formed the only large body of anthropological information accessible to a seventeenth-century intellectual (see my article cited above, *The Historical Journal* x, 2, p. 173, n. 77). And cf. a forthcoming article by Hans Aarsleff, 'The State of Nature and the Nature of Man in Locke', *John Locke: Problems and Perspectives*, ed. J. W. Yolton (Cambridge, 1969).

transient aliens.[1] In any case the power in the hands of the sovereign to exercise the executive power of the law of nature on behalf of all members of the society against all those in a state of nature with it would appear to be coextensive in effect with the scope of legitimate authority derivable from tacit consent over these same people.[2] This is appropriate since the sovereign's power inside the society as well as outside its ranks is derived from the transferred power to execute the law of nature possessed by each member of it.[3] The existence of a territorial sovereignty and of a formal legal system which applied throughout it merely gave a more concrete specification to this power.

But plainly this concept could hardly provide an acceptable account of the means by which membership could be acquired in the political community itself. Tacit consent might provide an elegant exposition of how itinerant aliens could be obliged to obey the laws of England. But it could only provide the same service for Englishmen at large if their civil status in their own community could be assimilated to that of resident aliens. Even Professor Macpherson's jaundiced interpretation of Locke's intentions at this point claimed only that Locke consigned the propertyless to this role.[4] So it is an unsurprising acceptance of the logic of his own argument that Locke should have supplemented

[1] *Two Treatises*, II. §122 and §119, ll. 19–22. This is an exceedingly sympathetic reading of Locke's text. Here, as in many other parts of the work, a sterner reading can easily convert the argument into complete incoherence, without doing the author the least formal injustice.

[2] *Ibid.* II, §9, ll. 1–17, esp.: '. . . if by the Law of Nature, every Man hath not a Power to punish Offences against it, as he soberly judges the Case to require, I see not how the Magistrates of any Community, can *punish an Alien* of another Country, since in reference to him, they can have no more Power, than what every Man naturally may have over another' (ll. 12–17). Cf. §122, ll. 1–6, esp.: 'This is only a local Protection and Homage due to, and from all those, who, not being in a state of War, come within the Territories belonging to any Government, to all parts whereof the force of its Law extends' (ll. 3–6); and §119, ll. 13–22.

[3] *Ibid.* II, §89, ll. 1–19, esp.: 'Where-ever therefore any number of Men are so united into one Society, as to quit every one his Executive Power of the Law of Nature, and to resign it to the publick, there and there only is a *Political, or Civil Society*. And this is done where-ever any number of Men, in the state of Nature enter into Society to make one People, one Body Politick under one Supreme Government, or else when any one joyns himself to, and incorporates with any Government already made' (ll. 1–8); and §11, ll. 1–10, §87, ll. 1–16, §135, ll. 4–12.

[4] C. B. Macpherson, *The Political Theory of Possessive Individualism* (Oxford, 1962), pp. 249–50, and cf. my article 'Consent in the Political Theory of John Locke', *The Historical Journal*, X, 2 (July 1967), 153–82.

the notion of 'tacit consent' by that of 'express consent'. Express consent demands the making of some overt sign of agreement by the consenting party to the legitimacy of the existing political structure which he himself intends to be taken as a promise to obey the rules in the future.[1] An oath of allegiance taken to a king is an obvious example of such an undertaking and, given Locke's definition of membership in a political society, it is easy to see why such an undertaking should be regarded by him as binding in perpetuity. Emigration is a right which in terms of his theory every adult should enjoy at any moment unless he has previously violated the laws of the society and hence become liable to punishment by it or unless he has formally committed himself to it in perpetuity.[2] Oaths of Allegiance are not retractable at will. Full membership of a legitimate political society is indefinite membership, although it would not necessarily be morally appropriate for a sovereign to refuse to subjects permission to emigrate if they had good reason to do so—as perhaps the Huguenots in France might have been thought to have had even if Locke had not thought France to be illegitimate as a political society and even if he had not believed Catholicism mistaken as a set of religious beliefs. But for full members of a legitimate polity the power to emigrate could only be a permission appropriately granted to them by the legal sovereign. It could not be intrinsically a right, a title, which they could justly claim in their own person against that sovereign.[3]

[1] 'No body doubts but an *express Consent*, of any Man, entring into any Society, makes him a perfect Member of that Society, a Subject of that Government' (*Two Treatises*, II, §119, ll. 7–9). '...he, that has once, by actual Agreement, and any *express* Declaration, given his *Consent* to be of any Commonweal, is perpetually and indispensably obliged to be and remain unalterably a Subject to it, and can never be again in the liberty of the state of Nature...' (§121, ll. 11–15). '...*Foreigners*, by living all their Lives under another Government, and enjoying the Priviledges and Protection of it, though they are bound, even in Conscience, to submit to its Administration, as far forth as any Denison; yet do not thereby come to be *Subjects or Members of that Commonwealth*. Nothing can make any Man so, but his actually entering into it by positive Engagement, and express Promise and Compact' (§122, ll. 12–18).

[2] *Two Treatises*, II, §§115, 116; and §121, ll. 4–11.

[3] M. Seliger ('Locke's Theory of Revolutionary Action', *Western Political Quarterly*, XVI, 3 (September 1963), 566, n. 91) takes *Two Treatises*, II, §191, as a statement that a *member* of the society has the right to emigrate. But this reading has no textual warrant whatever.

But if what distinguishes express from tacit consent consequentially is the unequivocal nature of the commitment to obey the legitimate political authority within the society, what distinguishes it in essence is the explicit and self-conscious character of the occasion on which it is incurred. The requirement certainly enhances the moral plausibility of the very stringent nature of the commitment which express consent is held to imply. But it makes the issue of just who is believed to have given such express consent a little baffling. I have commented elsewhere[1] on the inadequacy of Professor Macpherson's vigorous solution of this problem; but no alternative *solution* appears to be available. There is an indubitable lacuna in Locke's theory at this point. There may not, as I have suggested before, be much of a problem in the causal explanation of this conceptual insouciance. But perhaps a little more light can be thrown on the conceptual resources which made such evasive and incoherent formulations seem plausible to Locke himself. The key to Locke's treatment of the issue lies in the fact that although he stresses, as he was bound in consistency to do, the voluntary and explicit character of the commitment which alone can make a man a full member of a political society, when he discusses the reasons for which such a commitment might be made he treats them as the acceptance by the individual of 'terms' imposed upon him by society as a condition for his drawing benefits from it.[2] Because the inheritance of property is an inheritance of legal rights within a legal order men may not normally enjoy it without accepting the legal duties implied in that order. Macpherson sees the significance of the passage as lying in the fact that it treats the inheritance of property (presumably in Locke's unextended sense) as the sole potential motive (and consequently the sole potential opportunity?) for entry into political society.[3] But this is a little partial. All that the passage says is that

[1] 'Consent in the Political Theory of John Locke', *The Historical Journal*, x, 2.

[2] 'Commonwealths not permitting any part of their Dominions to be dismembred, nor to be enjoyed by any but those of their Community, the Son cannot ordinarily enjoy the Possessions of his Father, but under the same terms his Father did; by becoming a member of the Society: whereby he puts himself presently under the Government, he finds there established, as much as any other Subject of that Commonwealth' (*Two Treatises*, II, §117, ll. 2–7). See also §120.

[3] '...the only men who are assumed to incorporate themselves in any commonwealth by express compact are those who have some property, or the expectation of some

since governments do not normally permit their territories to be dismembered, inheritance of land in a given country normally commits the filial inheritor to the political obligations of his father simply because the government requires such a commitment in return for its recognition of the inheritance. There is no reason to take it as an exhaustive account of the possible reasons for becoming a member of an existing political society and to take it as such has several peculiar consequences. First, the example is based upon the idea of the indivisibility of established territorial sovereignties and the argument is confined to landed property. Except in so far as they have inherited landed property from their fathers, the great merchant capitalists of the City of London, the magnates of the Joint Stock Companies and the future Bank of England will not on this interpretation be members of the 'Body Politick' of England. Such a temporary obliviousness of his ideological duties to the rising bourgeoisie may of course have reflected only a momentary carelessness on Locke's part. But there is a more remarkable implication than this in the passage if one accepts Macpherson's interpretation, for it is not merely the status of 'Member of the Society' which is at stake—it is also that of 'Subject of that Commonwealth'.[1]

We may find it odd if the inheritance of property is all that is at stake that it is coming of age which is the occasion of men's 'separately in their turns'[2] giving the consent which makes them

property, in land' (*Possessive Individualism*, p. 249). (The second part of this sentence is not supported by Macpherson's reading of the text. Either the passage is intended as an exhaustive repertory of those who are full members of the society (in which case, there is no textual sanction for presuming anyone who does not actually himself own land to be a member) or it is intended merely as an example in which case there is no internal warrant for restricting it as narrowly as Macpherson does himself.) See also: 'every full member is assumed to be a proprietor of land' (*ibid.* p. 250). Assumed by whom?

[1] '...the Son cannot ordinarily enjoy the Possessions of his Father, but under the same terms his Father did; by becoming a Member of the Society: whereby he puts himself presently under the Government, he finds there established, as much as any other Subject of that Commonwealth' (*Two Treatises*, II, §117, ll. 4–8); see also §118, ll. 3–5, 13, 19; §119, ll. 2, 5, 8–9 ('a perfect Member of that Society, a Subject of that Government'); §120, ll. 10–11; §121, ll. 13–14; §122, ll. 2–3, 7–8 ('*a Member of that Society*, a perpetual Subject of that Commonwealth'), 16 ('Subjects or Members of that Commonwealth'), 20.

[2] '...*the Consent of Free-men, born under Government*, which only *makes them Members of it*, being given separately in their turns, as each comes to be of Age, and not in a multitude together; People take no notice of it...' (*ibid.* II, §117, ll. 9–12).

members of the society—not of course that minors can exercise full control over their own property but surely not all English property-holders can have inherited by the time that they became adults. Coming of age has more extensive social significance than its status as the point at which a minor acquires the right to dispose of his own property. One significance which it has at least symbolically is that it represents the occasion at which men could in principle become fully liable to political responsibilities, fully 'Subjects of the Commonwealth'.[1] It is perhaps harder to suppose that Locke denied to the propertyless mass the status of 'Subject' than that of 'Member of the Society'.

The whole tactic seems somewhat misconceived. If we consider the positions which Locke was attempting to rebut, the rationale of his presentation should appear more obvious. He wished firstly to dispose of an interpretation of allegiance as a purely natural relationship, based upon Filmer's argument that fathers had a direct right to impose political duties upon their children and that these duties would continue to bind them throughout their adult lives. He wished also to dispose of an even more peculiar argument that political obligation derives from the contingency of being born in a particular geographical area, an inference perhaps from Filmer's equivocal concept of 'Dominion' which treated both land and subjects as equally the property of the monarch. Embarrassingly both of these principles, the personal tie[2]

[1] The common law principle of allegiance held that it was owed to the crown from the age of fourteen (J. R. Tanner, *Tudor Constitutional Documents* (Cambridge, 1922), p. 375). But most statutory specifications of the duty (for example, the Acts against recusancy in the reign of James I, 3 & 4 Jac. I, cap. iv and 7 & 8 Jac. I, cap. vi) held it to apply from the age of eighteen. (See *The Political Works of James I*, ed. C. H. McIlwain (Cambridge, Mass., 1918), Introduction, pp. li–lii.) See *Two Treatises*, II, §61, ll. 26–8: 'If any body should ask me, When my Son is *of Age to be free*? I shall answer, Just when his Monarch is of Age to govern'; and §62, ll. 1–5: 'Common-wealths themselves take notice of, and allow that there is *a time when Men* are to *begin to act like Free Men*, and therefore till that time require not Oaths of Fealty, or Allegiance, or other publick owning of, or Submission to the Government of their Countreys.'

[2] Sir W. S. Holdsworth states, *A History of English Law* (3rd edition, London, 1923), IX, 77, 78: 'The personal tie of faith between king and subject, which had once attached by birth or otherwise, was independent of boundaries. And so we find that no one has ever supposed that mere departure from the king's dominions can cause the loss of the status of a subject. This is assumed in the debates in Parliament in 1343, and in the debates which led up to the passing of the statute of 1351. No question is raised as to the status of parents; the only doubt is as to the status of the

and the territorial principle,[1] had a basis, though a basis not identical with that given them in Filmer's argument, in the English common law of allegiance and its statutory extensions. It is these concepts of natural subjection deriving from paternal power and from geographical accident which he attempts to dispose of in order to vindicate his analysis of the contractual character of legitimacy. He has already drawn the teeth of the first argument in his massive critique of Filmer's conception of paternal power,[2] and his treatment of the inheritance of property at this point is an expository convenience rather than the vehicle for further substantive development in the argument. It is largely with the second argument that his perfunctory treatment of naturalization is concerned.[3] Between them the two arguments contrive to throw effective doubt on the idea that either the biological accident of paternity[4] or the geographical contingency of place of birth constitutes any unequivocal basis for a natural duty of allegiance. But they do not do so in order to dissolve political legitimacy into the anarchic play of individual caprice. The legal order of legitimate political societies is not forever trembling at the faintest breath of individual moral disapproval. Still less do individual men in such societies gain by their own moral dissent from the existing order the right to carry with them throughout its territories a little private enclave of legal immunity. The reason why the heirs of the landed gentry make their professions of political commitment is because society 'sets these terms' to them. But such terms might in principle be set to any adult

children born abroad, as between whom and the king there is, by reason of their foreign birth, no personal tie.' The statute of 1351 settled the point that those born abroad of English parents share the status of English subjects (*ibid.* pp. 75–6). Holdsworth's whole treatment of the development of the law of allegiance from the Conquest to the seventeenth century is extremely helpful (*ibid.* III, 56, 288, 461; IX, 72–88).

1 '. . . all persons born on English soil, no matter what their parentage, owed allegiance to, and were therefore subjects of the king. It is not surprising, therefore, that at the beginning of the fourteenth century the lawyers were beginning to think that birth within the king's allegiance signified birth within a defined "geographical tract"' (*ibid.* IX, 75). The decision in Calvin's Case (1609) established the principle that 'generally anyone born in England was an English subject' (*ibid.* pp. 80–1) and that this status of subject was indelible (*ibid.* p. 84).

2 *Two Treatises*, I, chapters II, VI, and VII; II, chapters VI and later XV.

3 *Ibid.* II, §118 and §118n.

4 *Ibid.* I, §§53–4.

member of the society.[1] All political rights are conditional on the acceptance of political duties. Even itinerant aliens owed certain duties because they exploited the resources of the society in some fashion[2] and the society had the right to insist on any conditions compatible with the law of nature in return for permitting this exploitation. In the case of natural free-born Englishmen they insisted potentially if not always in practice on the making of an explicit formal promise to observe allegiance to the sovereign. It is the duty of allegiance owed by the subject to the crown which differentiates the subject from the alien[3] and every man born an Englishman owes this duty to the crown. All members of the Anglican church who attended church prayed for the divine blessing on their monarch and all of them who were catechized were taught to love, honour and obey him. And those Englishmen who dissented from this church stimulated the anxiety of their fellow-countrymen in few ways with as much urgency as they did simply by their consequent failure to participate in this prescribed and shared ritual of political subservience. Any subject of the crown was held to owe him allegiance and accordingly could be called on at will to proclaim this allegiance in a public oath if there was cause to doubt his loyalty.[4] Allegiance was held to be a natural obligation[5] and it was held by James I to derive from an imputed promise 'closely sworne, by their birth in their naturall Allegiance'.[6] The first oath of allegiance, for example, which he prescribed in 1606 could be imposed upon any non-noble subject over the age of eighteen who was suspected of recusancy, by the authority of a bishop or of two Justices of the

[1] '...an English king could insist upon an oath of allegiance from all his subjects, whosoever['s?] men they were' (Holdsworth, *History of English Law*, III, 461). Every male of the age of twelve was liable to take an oath of fealty to him and his heirs, the oath of 'ligeantia' (Sir F. Pollock and F. W. Maitland, *The History of English Law* (Cambridge, 1895), I, 279–80). Cf. above, p. 136 n. 1.

[2] *Two Treatises*, II, §119, ll. 13–22; §121, ll. 1–11.

[3] Holdsworth, *History of English Law*, IX, 72.

[4] See J. R. Western, *The English Militia in the Eighteenth Century* (London, 1965), pp. 33–4, for an example from the aftermath of the Venner rising. Generally, see *ibid.* p. 83; K. Feiling, *A History of the Tory Party 1640–1714* (Oxford, 1924), pp. 262–6, 284–5, 319–21.

[5] James I, *Triplici Nodo, Triplex Cuneus, or an Apologie for the Oath of Allegiance...*, *Works*, p. 71.

[6] *Ibid.* pp. 81–2.

Peace.[1] The older oaths of Allegiance and Supremacy of 1559[2] and the later oaths under the Test Acts were under most circumstances applied only to potential office-holders under the crown and efforts to impose more specific oaths even on these, such as the suggested Non-resistance Test oath of 1675[3] or the more anti-Tory of the oaths suggested in the aftermath of the Revolution of 1688[4] always aroused great hostility. But the hostility, apart from its personal political motivation, was directed at the potential injustice of imposing such strict requirements when those at whom they were most urgently aimed would in all probability be wholly unconstrained by them and the least dangerous and most painfully conscientious would alone be harmed by them.[5] No one expressed such hostility on the grounds that subjects were not believed in principle to owe allegiance or to be liable to give expressions of their allegiance if such were required. It is scarcely surprising that Locke should have found himself obliged to take such strenuous examples from the law of nationality in order to deny the truth of King James's analysis.[6] It would hardly have been an effective rhetorical device to have pointed to native-born Englishmen and asked if they were naturally subjects of the commonwealth. And it is hardly accidental that the example which he takes of men who remain in the society for long periods of time without becoming members of the society (and hence subjects of the commonwealth) is of resident *aliens*.[7] There is no reason to suppose that Locke can ever have thought native-born

[1] *Ibid.* Introduction, pp. li–lii.

[2] *The Tudor Constitution*, ed. G. R. Elton (Cambridge, 1960), p. 366, but cf. p. 367.

[3] David Ogg, *England in the Reign of Charles II* (paperback edition, Oxford, 1963), II, 532–3. H. C. Foxcroft, *The Life and Letters of Sir George Savile, Bart., First Marquis of Halifax*...(London, 1898), I, 118–21.

[4] Feiling, *History of the Tory Party*, pp. 284–5. Foxcroft, *George Savile*, II, 125–7, esp. on the projected 'Oath of Abjuration of the late King James and his Title', pp. 126–7, and cf. the comparative restraint of the earlier oaths imposed in 1689 (David Ogg, *England in the Reigns of James II and William III* (Oxford, 1955), p. 230).

[5] See, for example, Halifax's argument (*Life of William Lord Russell*, quoted from Foxcroft, *George Savile*, I, 120), 'that as there really was no security to any state by oaths, so also no private person, much less statesman, would ever order his affairs as relying on it; no man would ever sleep with open doors, or unlocked-up treasure or plate, should all the town be sworn not to rob: so that the use of multiplying oaths had been most commonly to exclude or disturb some honest, conscientious men, who would never have prejudiced the government'.

[6] *Two Treatises*, II, §118. Cf. above, p. 138 n. 5.

[7] *Ibid.*, II, §122, ll. 12–20.

Englishmen were not 'subjects of the commonwealth'. But if he did regard the English Body Politick as having the same membership as one might today presume that it had at the time, he could not accept the adequacy of King James's analysis of the basis of this allegiance. It was not the fact of birth or indeed any pre-adult behaviour which could constitute such a promise. But at the time at which a man comes of age, the political society in which he has been reared sets certain terms to him which he must accept if he is to attain adult membership in it. As an incipient member of the society he does not have a right to reject such membership and remain within the society. The terms are terms of residence for a member of the society. Only by emigrating could he escape from membership and evade the context of duties which history has prepared for him. It is not a matter of choice whether native-born Englishmen who remain in England are members of English society, though they may choose to emigrate to escape such membership[1] and if they are not permitted to emigrate they can hardly be said to have consented,[2] hence the logical necessity (scarcely matched by the textual explicitness) of the right of emigration to the viability of the entire theory. The thought in Locke's argument at this point is crude and the exposition scruffy, perhaps largely because of the incompatibility of his argument with the English law of allegiance, but it is not difficult to follow the drift of his mind. Any express declaration is sufficient to commit a man to membership of the society and if some may be required to make such declarations on more ceremonial

[1] As we have seen above (Holdsworth, *History of English Law*, IX, 84), this right does not exist in English law. It was implicitly rejected by the decision in Calvin's Case (1609) that the status of a subject is indelible.

[2] In Locke's usage consent is not a notion which demands the removal of causality—it is fully compatible with any degree of psychologically compulsive behaviour. It is not the absence of humanly available alternatives which erases consent but only the coercive removal of such alternatives by the actions of other human beings: 'He that has his chains knocked off and the prison doors set open to him is perfectly at *liberty*, because he may either go or stay as he best likes, though his preference be determined to stay by the darkness of the night or illness of the weather or want of other lodging. He ceases not to be free, though the desire of some convenience to be had there absolutely determines his preference and makes him stay in his prison' (*Essay*, II, XXI, §50). Cf. Hobbes's resolute refusal to make any such distinction. For a simple account of his rationale see Howard Warrender, 'Hobbes's Conception of Morality', *Rivista Critica di Storia della Filosofia*, XVII, 4 (October–December 1962), 436.

occasions and others may never be required to make them at all, there are enough occasions in any man's life in which he uses verbal formulae which imply a recognition of his membership in the national society to which he belongs for any adult to be held to have made some express declaration of such membership. Since so little of the argument turns upon the precise type of occasion in question at this point, Locke may perhaps be to some extent excused for his hapless and clumsy treatment of it.

In effect, the context of political duties which awaits each member of the community as he comes of age[1] is in some ways extremely demanding. Even quite heedless acceptance of a man's historical identity could be construed as a promise to obey the laws. And promises were no light commitment. Promises and oaths were the bonds of society.[2] They bound even God himself.[3] Locke shared in the growing seventeenth-century sense that an excessive multiplication of oaths was eroding the moral significance which men attached to the most powerful of contemporary taboos and he felt profoundly the rationale of this uneasiness.[4] Language was the symbolic distinguishing characteristic of the human race and it was the actual bond which made specifically human existence possible.[5] Promises and oaths were the most formal and the most important linguistic performances which

1 'Common-wealths themselves take notice of, and allow that there is *a time when Men* are to *begin to act like Free Men*, and therefore till that time require not Oaths of Fealty, or Allegiance, or other publick owning of, or Submission to the Government of their Countreys' (*Two Treatises*, II, §62).

2 'Athei enim nec fides, nec pactum, nec jus jurandum aliquod stabile et sanctum esse potest, quae sunt societatis humanae vincula; adeo ut Deo vel ipsa opinione sublato haec omnia corruant': John Locke, *A Letter concerning Toleration*, ed. M. Montuori (The Hague, 1963), Latin Text, p. 92.

3 '...Promises and Oaths, which tye the infinite Deity' (*Two Treatises*, I, § 6, l. 6). Cf. below, chapter 14.

4 Cf. Christopher Hill, *Society and Puritanism in Pre-Revolutionary England* (London, 1964), pp. 411–14. Hill's entire chapter, 'From Oaths to Interest' (pp. 382–419), is the most learned and interesting discussion yet of the place of oaths in seventeenth-century English society. It is a matter of some interest that the arch bourgeois Locke should fail so dimly to follow the historicist line of the chapter in substituting rational interest for religious taboo as a basis for the sanction of oaths, indeed that he should suppose the bonds of society to be dissolved by the very adoption of atheism as a theory (see n. 2 above).

5 'God, having designed man for a sociable creature, made him not only with an inclination and under a necessity to have a fellowship with those of his own kind, but furnished him also with language, which was to be the great instrument and common tie of society' (*Essay*, III, I).

men enacted towards one another.[1] They formed the primary tissue of human mutual obligation and their binding force was sustained directly by the will of God. In no component of Locke's view of human experience is the intimate sense of human moral obligation set in more direct dependence upon the provisions of religious sentiment. Political obligations derive from promises, and promises are held to be given tacitly or expressly by all members or inhabitants of legitimate political communities. The metaphors have certainly become pretty slack here and their slackness has not only given justifiable grounds for disapproval to critics of the philosophical coherence of Locke's argument. It has also seemed to them to fail him in the execution of his political purposes.[2] Locke advocates government by consent as a means for realizing freedom and yet his concept of tacit consent removes all behavioural specification from the notion of consent. If, as we have suggested, even the notion of express consent is somewhat lacking in stringency as a criterion, does this imply that Locke has simply surrendered his putative objective in writing the book at all? The criticism mistakes the portions of Locke's theory which can be brought to bear upon actual political situations. The most consensually based and legitimate polity is not protected by its formal legitimacy from political challenge where it has been guilty of morally vicious behaviour,[3] and the most formally illegitimate

[1] Cf. 'societatis humanae vincula' (p. 141, n. 2) with 'common tie of society' (p. 141, n. 5).

[2] See, for example, John Plamenatz, *Consent, Freedom, and Political Obligation* (Oxford, 1938), p. 8. I have commented more generally on this style of criticism in 'Consent in the Political Theory of John Locke, *The Historical Journal*, x, 2. Cf. *Two Treatises*, II, §151, esp.: '...yet it is to be observed, that though *Oaths of Allegiance* and Fealty are taken to him, 'tis not to him as Supream Legislator, but as *Supream Executor* of the Law, made by a joint Power of him with others; *Allegiance* being nothing but an *Obedience according to Law*, which when he violates, he has no right to Obedience, nor can claim it otherwise than as the publick Person vested with the Power of the Law, and so is to be consider'd as the Image, Phantom, or Representative of the Common-wealth, acted by the will of the Society, declared in its Laws; and thus he has no Will, no Power, but that of the Law. But when he quits this Representation, this publick Will, and acts by his own private Will, he degrades himself, and is but a single private Person without Power, and without Will, that has any Right to *Obedience*; the Members owing no *Obedience* but to the publick Will of the Society' (ll. 12–26).

[3] 'For it is not Names, that Constitute Governments, but the use and exercise of those Powers that were intended to accompany them' (*Two Treatises*, II, §215, ll. 9–11; and see chapter XIX, '*Of the Dissolution of Government*', *passim*).

political society may only be justly resisted where the consequences of such resistance may be judged likely to benefit rather than harm others. The role of the notion of consent is not to discriminate between governments which may be resisted and governments which should not be resisted. It is merely to explain why any government is in principle subject to just resistance, if it behaves wickedly. The *Two Treatises* is an attempt to argue for limitations on the possible scope of political obligation. The notion of consent is a key term in the expository structure of this argument but it is not a term which exerts any very precise control over the application of the argument to particular cases in the world. Its role is as a formal component of the logical structure of the argument, not as a practical criterion of its applicability in particular cases. Consent is a necessary condition for the legitimacy of a political society, but the consent which creates such legitimacy is not a sufficient condition for the obligatory force of any particular act of authority in such a society.

But even if it is correct to assert in this way that the scope of application of the concept is not of great significance, it is still difficult to know just what Locke envisaged as the creation of a legitimate political society. One possible evasion of this issue, which had a lengthy and influential ancestry in English political debate, was the claim that although its historical origins were literally immemorial the English constitution, as visible throughout English history, was transparently an example of such legitimacy. One might be able to recognize a legitimate polity when one confronted it even if one did not know exactly how it had come to attain this enviable condition.[1] We know that Locke himself wrote in a private letter in 1689 as though he accepted unequivocally the obligatory status of the 'ancient constitution'.[2] And certainly that

[1] This account of Locke's attitude to the role of consent suggests that his doctrine, correctly understood, would place him much closer to the position held by Burke in his interpretation of the legitimacy of the Revolution of 1688 than has normally been supposed. (For a beautifully lucid placing of Burke in this tradition of argument see J. G. A. Pocock, 'Burke and the Ancient Constitution: A Problem in the History of Ideas', *The Historical Journal*, III, 2 (1960), 125–43.)

[2] '. . . the settlement of the nation upon the sure grounds of peace and security is put into their hands, which can no way so well be done as by restoring our ancient government; the best possible that ever was, if taken and put together all of a piece in its original constitution. If this has not been invaded men have done very ill to complain, and if it has men must certainly be so wise by feeling as to know

constitution as the Whigs broadly interpreted it could be readily presented as remedying the inconveniences of the state of nature which it was the putative purpose of political society to rectify.[1] The most embarrassing thematic hiatus in this hallowed historical story had always been the Norman Conquest, and the chapter on 'Conquest' in the Second Treatise[2] may be seen as the insulation of any possible historical interpretation of this event against the risk of its having damaging theoretical consequences. The Whig interpretation of the constitution as embodying a historically continuous consensual relationship between government and society, being fully compatible with Locke's own criteria for political legitimacy, could be protected against any theoretical damage resulting from an apparent historical détour by showing that the criteria for legitimacy which would be implied by conceding a normative status to the détour were not compatible with the logical preconditions for legitimacy. Locke's conception of legitimacy was quite compatible with a recognition of the wavering character of the historical trajectory of English society, its persistent deviations from true legitimacy and the unsteady and unreliable quality of its returns to this condition. Its application to English political society thus presented few problems. But since it was the application of it to this case which was the purpose that Locke had in mind in writing the book, it is, not surprisingly, more obscure how it applies to societies which lack even this patched-up historical continuity. There are only two points which throw any light on this problem. First, absolute monarchy cannot meet the criteria because the form of its claims to legitimacy

where the frame has been put out of order, or is amiss; and for that now they have an opportunity offered to find remedies, and set up a constitution, that may be lasting, for the security of civil rights and the liberty and property of all the subjects of the nation' (Locke to Edward Clarke, 8 February 1689, printed in *The Correspondence of John Locke and Edward Clarke*, ed. B. Rand (London, 1927), p. 289). For the background of political argument from which this notion comes see J. G. A. Pocock, *The Ancient Constitution and the Feudal Law* (Cambridge, 1957). Also J. W. Gough, *Fundamental Law in English Constitutional History* (Oxford, 1955); David Douglas, *English Scholars 1660–1730* (London, 1939); S. Kliger, *The Goths in England* (Cambridge, Mass., 1952); Christopher Hill, 'The Norman Yoke', *Puritanism and Revolution* (London, 1958), chapter 3; and a valuable article by Quentin Skinner, 'History and Ideology in the English Revolution', *The Historical Journal*, VIII, 2 (1965), 151–78.

1 *Two Treatises*, II, §13, ll. 10–11; §90, ll. 4–10 etc.

2 *Ibid.* II, XVI.

is incompatible with the logical preconditions for the existence of legitimacy.[1] Absolute monarchy could be causally based upon consent, that is, normative acceptance on the part of its subjects, but its legitimacy would then be consensual in basis too and this is what the theory of absolute monarchy specifically denies. In so far as it has the courage of its own ideological pretensions, its historical continuity, which in France compared quite favourably with that of England, cannot be deployed to defend it and it lacks any normative status at all. Secondly, though conquest may well be the historical origin of many, or even of most[2], political societies, it cannot be the basis of the *legitimacy* of any. The Turkish conquest of Greece was not a recent historical event, but its antiquity had in no way increased its moral respectability.[3] For the régime of a conqueror to acquire legitimacy it required the voluntary and formally conveyed acceptance of its subjects, a general consent.[4] And a general submission is not the same as a general consent.[5]

[1] 'Hence it is evident, that *Absolute Monarchy*, which by some Men is counted the only Government in the World, is indeed *inconsistent with Civil Society*, and so can be no Form of Civil Government at all. For the *end of Civil Society*, being to avoid, and remedy those inconveniencies of the State of Nature, which necessarily follow from every Man's being Judge in his own Case, by setting up a known Authority, to which every one of that Society may Appeal upon any Injury received, or Controversie that may arise, and which every one of the Society ought to obey; where-ever any persons are, who have not such an Authority to Appeal to, for the decision of any difference between them, there those persons are still *in the state of Nature*. And so is every *Absolute Prince* in respect of those who are under his *Dominion*' (*Two Treatises*, II, §90). See also *ibid.* §137, ll. 1–3; §174, ll. 4–6.

[2] '... such has been the Disorders Ambition has fill'd the World with, that in the noise of War, which makes so great a part of the history of Mankind, this *Consent* is little taken notice of' (*Two Treatises*, II, §175, ll. 3–6). This is a continuing theme of Locke's.

[3] 'Who doubts but the Grecian Christians descendants of the ancient possessors of that Country may justly cast off the Turkish yoke which they have so long groaned under when ever they have a power to do it' (*ibid.* II, §192, ll. 14–17). The honorific use of the word 'ancient' should be linked with its role in English political rhetoric (cf. above, p. 143, n. 2). The uneasy relationship between the resonances of this rhetoric and the structure of Locke's theory comes out in this passage, where Locke in arguing against the relevance of the simple passage of time as a source of right, prescription, manages to extract a rhetorical gain from the fact of the greater antiquity of the Greek occupation of the territory in question. 'Ancient' in Greece too seems to be construed as immemorial.

[4] *Two Treatises*, II, §192, ll. 7–14.

[5] MS Locke c 28, fo. 96^{r} (from notes on Sherlock's *The Case of Allegiance*). Commenting on Sherlock's claim that the 'settlement' of a government gave it political authority: 'How long a month a year. or an hundred & by what rule

Men must accept it as appropriate, not merely submit to it as inevitable. Only free mutual agreement on a set of common rules can terminate the state of war between a conqueror and those whom he has conquered. But there are no clear criteria for what behaviour is necessary to constitute this free mutual agreement. Certainly Locke was prepared to consider the agreement as being made on behalf of the subject population by their 'representatives'.[1] The selection of these representatives would no doubt have been carried out on at least as inegalitarian a basis as the English franchise of 1680, and it is not clear that any process of formal social choice at all was a necessary condition for their being considered as representatives. Locke's picture of social structure is one in which hierarchy is as unthinkingly accepted by most men as it is morally appropriate for it to be so. It is the incompetence of the élite or the dissensions within it which alone are likely to make most men 'forget respect'.[2]

Whatever distribution of power and authority men accept as legitimate may be presumed so and it is this acceptance which creates the legitimacy. The authority of the Turks in Greece is a practical authority, a fact of social experience, derived from their military power. But only its acceptance as just, as the rightful distribution of power in the community, could make it morally obligatory on their Greek subjects. And such a legitimacy, devoid of formal institutional recognition and resting merely upon the psychological condition of the subject population, would not survive a change in this psychological condition. Only the

what law of God. Long and short in such cases unless defined have no meaning people submit where they do not resist so that where there is no resistance there is a general submission, but there may be a general submission without a general consent which is an other thing.' The Greek Christians (above, p. 145, n. 3) had no doubt submitted generally. But their right of resistance did not need the enhancement of a continuing tradition of guerrilla resistance to the Turkish conquerors.

1 'For no Government can have a right to obedience from a people who have not freely consented to it: which they can never be supposed to do, till either they are put in a full state of Liberty to chuse their Government and Governors, or at least till they have such standing Laws, to which they have by themselves or their Representatives, given their free consent, and also till they are allowed their due property, which is so to be Proprietors of what they have, that no body can take away any part of it without their own consent, without which, Men under any Government are not in the state of Free-men, but are direct Slaves under the Force of War' (*Two Treatises*, II, §192, ll. 17–27).

2 *Some Considerations of the Consequences of the Lowering of Interest...*, *Works*, II, 46.

existence of a framework of recognized institutions for articulating the will of the people made the moral status of the sovereign's will more resistant to the corrosion of popular hostility. And even here it is not clear that the status of this constitution, for all the painfully achieved value of its institutional resources, could survive the loss of moral legitimacy in the eyes of its subjects.

11

PREROGATIVE

Two sorts of legitimacy can be predicated of political authority. The first (and for the purposes of Locke's dispute with Filmer the paradigmatic) is that which attaches to the prescriptions of a consensually based legislative. The laws of a morally acceptable polity have a right to demand the obedience of the occupants of the territory of that polity. But this is to state merely the jural relationship, not to describe the actual human situation. Positive laws, just as much as the law of nature itself,[1] can only become operational in the world through the acts of executors. Jurally the acts of such men are judicial as well as executive. They constitute decisions as to what action a general rule prescribes in a particular instance. The private judicial decisions of individuals are simply ordinary moral life, in so far as this is not immediately affected by positive law. The public judicial decisions of a legitimate political authority are simply enforcements of positive law by an executive, a judiciary or even a legislative. The authority of a legislative sovereign derives from the consent of its subjects, a complicated legal fiction, though one which purports to have a determinate sociological component. He executes what are, jurally speaking, their rights to execute the law of nature, to decide the applications of its prescriptions and to enforce these.[2] The form in which he is unequivocally entitled to exercise these rights is determined by the set of constitutionally proper positive laws of the community. But there is a more extensive power of execution, a reservoir of

[1] '...the *Law of Nature* would, as all other Laws that concern Men in this World, be in vain, if there were no body that in the State of Nature, had a *Power to Execute* that Law, and thereby preserve the innocent and restrain offenders, and if any one in the State of Nature may punish another, for any evil he has done, every one may do so' (*Two Treatises of Government*, II, §7, ll. 7–12). See also the critical comment on William Sherlock's *The Case of Allegiance* (London, 1691) in his notes on that work: 'Allegiance is neither due nor paid to Right or to Government which are abstract notions but only to persons having right or government' (MS Locke c 28, fo. 85^r). The whole of his objections to Sherlock's book, written to justify the Glorious Revolution, revolves around this simple observation.

[2] *Two Treatises*, II, §§87–9.

authority, which is imputed to him, by sociological necessity, because legislative activity is inherently incapable of providing for the full complexity of actual social circumstance.

This reservoir of authority is known as prerogative. The term is, of course, central to the tradition of political ratiocination on which Locke draws most heavily[1] and it is of pivotal importance in the political situation to which he addresses himself and in the dialectical problems which this presents to him. But all this is not here to the point. What concerns us here is the logical standing of this power and the criteria for its use and abuse. Its basis, plainly, is the same individual executive power of the law of nature on which the binding force of positive law itself ultimately rests. But the criterion for the proper exercise of the latter is located solidly enough in a tradition of constitutional practice. Not only is it rule-bound (a characteristic which logically must hold if a practice is to be subject to a criterion) but the rules are specified in a set of written documents.[2] These rules are highly definite in character and their prescriptions in any concrete instance have to satisfy dual criteria. To be fully binding they have to represent correct interpretations of the duly enacted positive laws and they have to be compatible with the purposes which the laws are properly intended to serve. The second criterion is regulative, the first constitutive. What the law is must always be what the law is; but what the law is does not always bind.[3] But in the English polity prerogative is as much a legal category as is

[1] The availability of this category gives Locke's analysis of the relationship between law and power a much more lucid quality than is to be found in Pufendorf's treatment in his *De Jure Naturae et Gentium* (1672), though for a more sympathetic view of Pufendorf's incoherence on this point see Friedrich Meinecke, *Machiavellism* (London, 1957), chapter 9, esp. p. 230. For a sophisticated explanation and account of the general incoherence of Pufendorf's thought see Leonard Krieger, *The Politics of Discretion* (Chicago, 1965).

[2] Statutes, judicial decisions, etc. This seems pretty evasive as a view of the English constitution but the abstraction is simple to defend. The law of England is what the law of England is. The issue of how it is to be determined in any particular instance is a technical matter. But technical matters are not of any overwhelming inconvenience because technical accuracy cannot be claimed in defence of social damage. Locke does not discuss constitutionalist issues at all adequately because his own thought specifically evades their purchase. It is in essence wholly opposed to the legalistic perspective.

[3] *Two Treatises*, I, §58, ll. 11–18; II, §12, ll. 8–19, esp.: '... the Phansies and intricate Contrivances of Men, following contrary and hidden interests put into Words... truly are a great part of the *Municipal Laws* of Countries...' (ll. 14–17).

statute and, as Filmer had argued powerfully, there was much reason to view it as historically and hence logically prior to statute. Furthermore the control of prerogative power was precisely the political assignment which Locke faced. The dialectical problem here, the dilemma of how to relate the functional necessity of binding prerogative power, power which is by definition in some measure legally indeterminate in its exercise,[1] with the social and legal control of this power, is critical to Locke's enterprise. Hence an examination of his tactics at this point should highlight some structural features of his approach. The most important facet to emphasize is simply what he *does* attempt at this point. His argument does not revolve around the logically forlorn enterprise of determining what is by definition indeterminate. More astutely, it begins from this functional necessity and elicits from the reasons for the essential character of the prerogative the criteria which are to restrict its exercise.

The reason why the prerogative must exist is not a matter merely of the empirical complexity of political activity. The fact that there are many cases to which the rules do not apply would not in itself necessitate a special form of treatment for such cases. It is because the sorts of political action which cannot be adequately prescribed by general rules may be, indeed characteristically *are*,[2] those in which the ends of political society are most at risk, those which most demand the deployment of force, that there *has* to be a special power of this sort. The criteria for its deployment are thus, and without the least historical mediation, the ends of political society itself.[3]

But while this displays the essence of the power it does not determine its actual form in any particular polity. Though one of its defining characteristics is its legally unregulated character, what is totally unregulated is only the mode of its exercise, not the

[1] '*Prerogative* can be nothing, but the Peoples permitting their Rulers, to do several things of their own free choice, where the Law was silent, and sometimes too against the direct Letter of the Law, for the publick good; and their acquiescing in it when so done' (*Two Treatises*, II, §164, ll. 5–9). See also §159, ll. 15–19; §160, ll. 1–3; §165, ll. 9–12.

[2] *Ibid.* II, §153, ll. 1–11, and esp. §§145–8.

[3] *Ibid.* II, §159, ll. 8 ('by the common Law of Nature'), 15–19, 26–8, §161, ll. 1–3, 9–10, §164, ll. 8–9; §165, ll. 14–15, §166, ll. 20–1 ('*Prerogative is nothing but the Power of doing publick good without a Rule*').

limits within which this exercise may take place, nor for obvious reasons the identity of the man who exercises it. The extent of its legal authority is determined by the constitution, that is, by the 'original contract' as modified through time by legitimate acts of the legislature.[1] What the constitution determines is what it may not do, not what it may do. It *is* a residuary power. But even this is too tidy. The constitution contains a legal description of the area within which prerogative power may be exercised. But it is also an attribute of the prerogative, as we have seen already, that it may in principle be exercised against the law. Just prerogative action may even be specifically illegal. Because in this way prerogative has to be seen as a reserved power which cannot finally be subject to a purely constitutionalist criterion and because its application, by sociological necessity, is a matter of private judgement on the part of its bearer, it eludes that careful tissue of legal restraints which men have devised over the centuries for their protection against their rulers. The entire history of political development and its variations leaves the individual, from this point of view, in an unchanged situation.[2] Precisely because prerogative power is frequently and legitimately exercised against the law at the judgement of an individual the discrimination of the acceptability or unacceptability of its exercise cannot be consigned with a high degree of reliability (as Locke seems for instance to be happy enough to consign taxation) to a fairly determinate social and political process. In the exercise of prerogative, at every point, sovereign and individual confront each other directly. In any prospective dispute there could be no terrestrial judge of the rights of the issue.[3] The conventional royalist assumption that the king himself must be the judge, despite its legalistic force, begged the question in dispute just as much as the conventional Whig assumption that the English parliament had the right to judge his exercise of the prerogative. The bland assumption that there must be a legal criterion is simply rejected by Locke. Prerogative power is exercised by a sovereign over his subjects in the most sophisticated political society in western Europe in precisely the same

[1] *Ibid.* II, §§165, 166.

[2] That this is a jural rather than a sociological point of view barely needs emphasis. Locke was perfectly aware that 'all the world is not Mile-end' (*Third Letter for Toleration*, *Works* (London, 1768), II, 488).

[3] *Two Treatises*, II, §168.

jural mode as it is exercised in the primeval political community of the family. Empirically, Locke believes that its exercise when this appears in general to its subjects to be for their own good will elicit from them just such a 'tacit and scarce avoidable consent'[1] as the patriarch secures from his progeny. In the hands of the wise and moral ruler (or even those subject only to the normal level of human frailty)[2] the conduct of politics tends constantly to revert to this warm and unthinking familial relationship, this sense of security and emotional participation touched by awe which is picked out in the (faintly bizarre) twin metaphors of 'nursing fathers' and 'mortal gods'.[3] Both as moral norm[4] and as sociological possibility this picture of the human political condition was every bit as real to Locke as it was to Filmer. We can hardly suppose that either ever imagined that political relationships are always much like this. But that it served for both as key image of that ideal political relationship which could at times become actual in the world is evident enough. What separates Locke so sharply from Filmer at this point is not the latter's preference for a settled, stable, traditionalist[5] and massively paternalistic political

[1] *Two Treatises*, II, §75, ll. 1–5, §107; cf. with §§162, 165, 166.

[2] *Ibid.* II, §165, ll. 5–9.

[3] *Ibid.* II, §110, l. 22, §42, l. 24, §166, l. 1. Locke himself firmly uses the adjective 'godlike' rather than the substantive.

[4] It is important to be clear how it could be a norm for a man who in effect made each individual responsible for the behaviour of the political society in which he lived. The principles, later so readily seen as committing to political activism, were not seen so by Locke because he simply accepted the hierarchical character of the society that he lived in and because he saw government as being only very tangentially relevant to the achievement of the majority of important human purposes. In a less firmly hierarchical society or to someone who thought of human purposes as necessarily to be achieved in this world or not at all, this peculiar equilibrium unsurprisingly broke down. The sneer which he perhaps cannot quite escape is that he seems quite prepared to restrict his substantive demands for social change by political means to making the world safe for prosperous intellectuals to engage in the pursuit of knowledge. I do not wish to suggest that there is no corruption of moral consciousness in seeing the moral demands of Christianity upon the social structure of seventeenth-century England as restricted to this assignment. But it is important to be clear just where the corruption lies. It does not lie in the blanket commendation of the society. For this simply is not to be found in the works. The entire conceptual point of the *Two Treatises* is the insistence on how very limited the rights which one human being may claim over another necessarily are. Locke may have been an obsequious and morally insensitive lackey of a corrupt aristocrat but it is certainly not his theories which commit him to being so.

[5] Cf. his letter to Edward Clarke of 8 February 1689, in *Correspondence of John Locke and Edward Clarke*, ed. B. Rand (Oxford, 1927), p. 289.

order, a preference which his antagonist in many ways shared, but rather the fact that Locke realized the sheer impossibility of any *permanent* return to this sociological womb and the crude inadequacy of such an attractive fantasy to resolve political problems which had become active in the world. Weirdly, the two protagonists, arch traditionalist and classic liberal, dreamed in one sense the same dreams.[1] But only one of them supposed that to recite the dream was to dispose of the reality.

To Locke, by contrast, no such *simpliste* strategy could be persuasive. Lacking Filmer's naïvely providentialist assumptions, he never wholly contrived to overlook in his theory the gap between the desirable and the actual and never pretended that the problems of the actual could be resolved by pretending that the gap was not there. In a complex and intricate sense men had made their social world and could not, however fervidly they proclaimed their own guilt, transfer the responsibility for dilemmas which arose within it from their own shoulders to the Deity. Social life was the mode for the fulfilment of the purposes of God. But its concrete configuration at any point in time was a function of the sins and virtues of individuals, not a constant and strenuous divine response to the particular recalcitrances of his creatures. God made Human Nature, the potentialities inherent in the species, the framework within which human life takes place. But men make human history.

Thus, precisely because they have created social problems as a result of their actions and because these *are* problems and not merely vehicles of the divine wrath, to be borne with patience, it is men who must grapple with these problems. There is no one else to grapple with the difficulties on their behalf. The social world, product of men's historically heterogeneous purposes, carries no legitimacy but its adaptation to these purposes. Itself the consequence of myriad clumsy manipulations, it is perpetually open morally and practically to further manipulation in the interest of these purposes. It is true that these purposes themselves are

[1] Though in fact the weirdness is more apparent than real. Locke as much as Filmer had every reason to desire the stability of the hierarchical society of seventeenth-century England. Having been closer than Filmer to the conduct of central administration, he also had a clearer sense of the advantages which could in principle flow from the sophisticated use of unrestricted governmental power.

subject to a criterion, namely the purposes of God; but it is a criterion which is outside society because it is outside history. Filmer attempted to use a particular picture of society as a criterion by means of which to place the significance of historical change. Whatever his antiquarian felicities, his picture of the human situation is wholly ahistorical. It is not that he simply did not know that there are many differences between one part of the world and another, one time and another. But his conceptual framework was quite incapable of seeing any relevance in this fact. For Locke, in contrast, the social world is totally historical and hence it can never in principle furnish an abstract criterion with which to judge history. To accept the reality of history is to accept the possibility of real social dilemmas, dilemmas of which there *is* no complete resolution.

Prerogative is the point in English constitutional law and in Locke's theoretical analysis in which this ineluctable possibility is most sharply posed. Lurking behind the legitimacy of the most settled legislative, there remains the perpetual judicial authority of every subject, capable in principle of appealing against the misdeeds of the legislative, outside all social order, to an eternal authority; and, with this appeal, the possibility of reducing such a polity to a condition of jural (though probably not, of course, social) anarchy. But this shattering possibility, even if it was precisely that which Locke wished to affirm in writing the book at all, is normally kept at a very decorous distance in the world by the complex of political and social institutions drawing their legitimacy from the long past consent of the ancestors of those subject to them, given because these evidently served their interests and not since annihilated because no gross impairment of this utility had since resulted. Men have consigned their social fate to be determined by a set of rules and its custodians. In so doing they have both conferred on their environment a greatly enhanced predictability and order and avoided the naked confrontation of self-righteous wills. But in some measure men could not escape entrusting their fate also to a power which cannot be regulated. The formal legitimacy of this power lies in its use for the general good.[1] But this formulation neatly avoids specifying

[1] *Two Treatises*, II, §166, ll. 20–1. Cf.: '*Salus Populi Suprema Lex*, is certainly so just and fundamental a Rule, that he, who sincerely follows it, cannot dangerously err'

the social *locus* of the legitimacy. Institutionally, it has a certain legal specification but this too cannot act as a stable criterion, as we have already seen. The sole final criterion is the consent of the subjects; and not the constitutionally mediated and prescriptively committing consent of a legislative but the continuing consciousness of each individual member of the society. No convenient analytical device like tacit consent intervenes here to blur this relationship. The authority of the prerogative over the individual subject is precisely and exclusively what the individual recognizes it to be.[1] That is to say, prerogative, the paradigm and guarantee of all human authority to a royalist like Filmer, has in fact no *authority* over the individual whatever. In this particular political context there is no obligation on an individual which is not recognized as such. This is not to suggest that Locke did not recognize the actuality of social authority—indeed a central axis of his account of political change is the dialectic between the powerful urge to accept authority on the part of the appreciative subjects of benign monarchs and the equally powerful disposition of their less edifying successors to abuse the authority thus inherited.[2] Nor, of course, does it mean that Locke thought of actual confrontations between the prerogative and populace as being at all like this. What is being emphasized here is a point about the structure of his theory, not a point about how he expected the world to be. But that the theory does bear this aspect is not in doubt; and the perspective makes it easy to understand how a

(*ibid.* §158, ll. 1–3). It is not totally clear what the force of 'cannot' is here; whether it is logical (acting with proper intentions is what acting well is) or empirical (people who act with good intentions usually act well). The point is plainly of great importance. See for a (still somewhat inconclusive) discussion below, chapter 12.

[1] The fact that the individual's recognition of the moral state of affairs is not infrequently apt to be imperfect was not a point that Locke failed to take but he did not suppose that the intensity of men's anxiety could come to enhance their moral authority. The world he lived with was a more alarming one than Filmer permitted himself to recognize.

[2] *Two Treatises*, II, §§162–6. The recognition of the inescapable character of this dilemma is one of the enduring strengths of Locke's thought and, however much more sophisticated we may be in our empirical notions of the nature of this tension, it is highly dubious whether we have got any more coherent notion of the moral issues at stake. Cf., at the theoretical level, an inquiry like Bertrand de Jouvenel's *Sovereignty* (Cambridge, 1957) or, more vulgarly, the fantastic mixture of banality and implausibility with which the question of the standing of one-party states and military dictatorships in underdeveloped countries has been discussed.

Kantian outline could come to be extrapolated from the vehicle of the political obliquities of a Frondeur like Shaftesbury[1] and an imperative for individual political activism in the backwoods of Connecticut in the days of the Great Awakening from a work published to commend the decorous achievements of 1688.[2] Even more plainly, the blandness of Locke's statement of this position explains the horror which drove the non-juror Charles Leslie into his hysterical and brilliant ten-year polemic against the mixture of gross hypocrisy, subversion and blasphemy which he saw in it.[3]

1 Cf. Raymond Polin, *La Politique Morale de John Locke* (Paris, 1960).

2 'Philalethes' [Elisha Williams], *The essential Rights and Liberties of Protestants. a seasonable Plea for The Liberty of Conscience, and The Right of private Judgement, In Matters of Religion, without any control from Human Authority* (Boston, 1744), pp. 1–11. For attribution see Alice M. Baldwin, *The New England Clergy and the American Revolution* (reprint, New York, 1958), p. 65. Also marked on the Rev. Andrew Eliot's copy in the Houghton Library at Harvard. The best sketch of Williams is characteristically contained in Clifford K. Shipton's treatment in *Sibley's Harvard Graduates* (Boston, Mass., 1937) v.

3 From *The New Association*, Part III, Appendix, 'A Short account of the Original of Government' dated 25 March 1703 (London, 1703), to *The Finishing Stroke* and *A Battle Royal between Three Cocks of the Game* (London, 1711), etc. These two works contain the best summaries of his doctrine and the others do not greatly extend them. For a convenient short list of many of the pamphlets and a useful survey of Leslie's life see the article in the *D.N.B.* For an example of Leslie at his most hysterical see above, chapter 6. The arguments which he used were in the main those of Filmer but he expounded them in a more theoretically systematic form and with even greater force and it was from his writings rather than those of his predecessor that they descended to the Tory Ultras in the 1790s.

12

PUBLIC GOOD AND REASON OF STATE

It is one of the most platitudinous axioms of contemporary moral consciousness that there is a crude asymmetry between political morality and personal morality. Indeed we are so sharply conscious of the discontinuities between them that we are often incapable of discerning any continuities at all, still more so of giving a coherent account of the precise nature of whatever continuity there is. We are all too familiar with the tendency to consider the conduct of states of which we happen to disapprove in a legalistic fashion and that of those of which we approve in a 'realistic' fashion, or for a judgement which seems moralistic in the mouth of others to become simply moral in our own. There is nothing very obscure in the abstract about how this conceptual chaos has arisen—the transition from judging the intrinsic quality of acts in terms of a highly definite legal system, enforced by divine sanctions, to assessing their returns in terms of the free-floating calculation of interests. This converts the practice of moral judgement from a predominantly judicial activity, casuistry, to a predominantly empirical one, prediction. Instead of being a self-evident moral enormity to do evil that good may come of it,[1] it is precisely what comes of it which determines whether it *is* good or bad.[2] This transition seems to produce its most pressing difficulties in the analysis of the relation of intention to moral responsibility.[3] Even

[1] 'to Argue for our *Complyance* with them, is to do *Evil*, that *Good* may come of it: And to make it *Right* to *Comply* with *Wrong*. That is indeed Destroying all Notion of *Right* and *Wrong*' ([Charles Leslie,] *The Case of the Regale and of the Pontificat Stated*...(n.p., 1700), p. 87).

[2] 'Ce n'est rien de bien partir si l'on ne fournit la carriere: le prix est au bout de la lice, & la fin regle toujours le commencement' (Gabriel Naudé, *Considerations Politiques sur les Coups d'Estat* (n.p., 1667), p. 172).

[3] See Jonathan Bennett, 'Whatever the Consequences', *Analysis*, XXVI, 3 (January 1966), 83–102; G. E. M. Anscombe, 'A Note on Mr. Bennett', *Analysis*, XXVI, 6 (June 1966), 208. And for the background to this dispute see G. E. M. Anscombe, 'Modern Moral Philosophy', *Philosophy*, XXXIII, 124 (January 1958), 1–19; G. E. M.

today there seems something rather startling about the attempt in effect to make all other virtues subsidiary to that of prudence. But if the proposal still seems drastically revisionist to many today, it would certainly have seemed more so to most people in the seventeenth century.

It is largely Locke's partnership with Hobbes in promoting this alleged drastic deterioration of the European natural-law tradition which Leo Strauss has been concerned to expose in his treatment of Locke, and a former pupil of his, Richard H. Cox, has analysed exhaustively its implications for the conception of international relations embodied in the *Two Treatises*. Cox's treatment is undeniably vigorous and it certainly leaves Locke with a clear and coherent theory.[1] The only question is whether it is a theory which Locke held. But this is in some respects a harder question to answer than might at first sight be supposed. For Cox's intellectual tactics are exceedingly diverse and it is a complicated matter to assess their relative degree of success. At their least impressive they seem almost to descend to the level of numbering the Beast.[2] The argument *ex silentio*, which necessarily depends upon a psychological assumption about the author for whatever force it has, is deployed on the basis of a crude and question-begging biographical hypothesis and in a fashion which repeatedly ignores the characters of the texts analysed.[3] No doubt it also explains the odd logic of some of the arguments, the occasional instances of what might perhaps be called *a debiliori*

Anscombe, 'War and Murder', in *Nuclear Weapons: A Catholic Response*, ed. Walter Stein (paperback edition, London, 1963), pp. 45–62; and for the philosophical psychology assumed G. E. M. Anscombe, *Intention* (Oxford, 1957); Anthony Kenny, *Action, Emotion and Will* (London, 1963).

[1] Richard H. Cox, *Locke on War and Peace* (Oxford, 1960). Cf. Leo Strauss, *Natural Right and History* (Chicago, 1953), pp. 202–51.

[2] 'It is interesting that not only are these three chapters linked by the fact that Locke treats the problem of self-preservation in them, but each of the chapters also contains exactly twenty-three sections, and these are the only chapters in the whole of the *Treatises* to contain that number' (*Locke on War and Peace*, p. 85, n. 2).

[3] 'As to why he did not then advocate a world-state or world-commonwealth, no categorical answer is possible' (*ibid.* p. 190). Why did Locke not advocate world government? Why indeed, rationalist that he was, did he not advocate votes for women, the dismemberment of the Austro-Hungarian empire or the revival of Erse as the national language of Ireland? As a historical problem Cox's puzzle is roughly on a par with that of explaining why the Greeks did not have an industrial revolution.

reasoning.[1] But the defects of the procedures employed do not necessarily vitiate the conclusions.

Cox argues that the essential characteristic of Locke's notion of the ends of political society is their limitation to the preservation of human security and that in social life as it existed in Locke's time this characteristic can be seen most clearly in the field of international relations. Locke's individual psychology and his ethics are based upon the primacy of the human propensity to self-preservation and upon his assertion of this propensity as a right which is logically prior to any human duty.[2] His theory of international relations, the endless quest for the maximization of the wealth and power of the state in order best to secure the preservation of the individual, is merely the logical extension of this initial premise.[3] Cox's analysis of this conception of international relations is in the main descriptively convincing: Locke clearly did see the relationships between states as predominantly conflicts for wealth and power, and the justification for enthusiastic

[1] *Ibid.* pp. 170–1, where, from the fact that Locke argues that a conqueror does not have a right to exact full reparations from a conquered country if this would threaten the preservation of the innocent inhabitants of the country (because where one group has more than it needs to maintain life and another does not, it is the duty of the first to give to the second), Cox concludes that the conqueror has a specific and unequivocal right to let the innocent starve rather than risk his own preservation. This reasoning is peculiar in several ways. First, because Locke takes a simple case of a moral duty to establish an unconventionally humane moral notion, why should it follow that the duty simply ceases to exist in a more complicated case? Secondly, why should one take the specification of a simple case of a right or duty as restrictive unless the context clearly implies it to be so?; i.e. why should 'A man does not have *X* right, if not *Y*' imply 'If *Y*, he does have *X* right'? This is simply not a valid form of inference—it involves reading 'A man does not have *X* right, if not *Y*' as though it were identical with '*Only* if not *Y*, does a man not have *X* right'. Cf. Cox, *loc. cit.*, with *Two Treatises of Government*, II, §§183–4, which Cox there claims to analyse. The pedantic insistence on the defective quality of the argument is necessary to make clear how much is going wrong here. Not only is the general reading of the works so very inconsequential both from the biographical and the literary point of view but the interpretative hypothesis employed is so strong that it actually alters the content of parts of the text which are specifically cited to support it. (N.B. Because one might say that a man has no right to criticize Cox's book unless he has read it, it does not follow that if he has read it, he therefore has *every* right to criticize it. Having read it is a necessary condition for having *any* right to criticize it. But only the (true) belief that the criticism is correct constitutes a sufficient condition for having *every* right to criticize it.)

[2] Cox, *Locke on War and Peace*, pp. 85–8, 159, 169, 170, etc.

[3] *Ibid.* pp. 136–54, esp. pp. 149–54.

participation in the pursuit of wealth and power as to some extent the attempt to guarantee public security. (It was scarcely a remarkable perception for a seventeenth-century Englishman.) But the fact that the maximization of wealth maximized security (which is at best a very strenuous inference from what Locke said) does not necessarily imply that whatever behaviour would maximize wealth was therefore legitimate. Furthermore, the fact that the endless accretion of power might not in itself be illegitimate did not mean that any particular use of it must be legitimate, or even that many of them were likely to be so.[1]

There are two major points at which Cox misrepresents Locke's position. The first is his assertion of the primacy of right over duty and the second is the meaning which he gives to the primacy of security over consumption. Both of these can be qualified by re-examining Locke's texts (sometimes even portions of them printed by Cox himself) and removing the commentator's italics. The fact that Locke sometimes refers to self-preservation as a right, rationally accessible to man, in the course of discussing the legitimacy of eating animals, hardly elides the much larger number of passages in which he insists upon it as a duty to God which is also rationally accessible to man.[2] Similarly the fact that Locke asserts wealth and the growth of population to be likely to promote security, that he asserts men's earliest political intentions as protection against external attack,[3] does not dispose of the fact that he asserts that wealth is desirable *because* it makes available the conveniences of life, that God gave the world to mankind richly to enjoy, that mankind consequently has a *right* to these conveniences, other things being equal, and that it was God who commanded mankind to be fruitful and multiply,[4] the duty of the maximization of preservation and hence the persistent increase in numbers of the human race both being corollaries of the principle

[1] Cf. esp. MS Film. 77, pp. 310–11.

[2] Cf. *Two Treatises*, I, §§86 and 92, with II, §6, etc.

[3] The fallacy here is to equate temporal with logical priority, a fallacy for which Locke himself is customarily attacked but of which it is not at all clear that he was in fact guilty. Cf. *Two Treatises*, II, §107.

[4] Cox, *Locke on War and Peace*, pp. 175–83 (esp. p. 177 and pp. 180–1), and p. 172. Cf. the passages cited by Cox himself at p. 172 (*Two Treatises*, II, §107) and p. 177 (*Considerations on Money*, *Works of John Locke* (London, 1768), II, 9); *Two Treatises*, I, §40; §41, l. 13; etc.

of plenitude. Here, as elsewhere, Cox takes a portion of Locke's position, claims it to be his *real* position and uses it to show the disingenuousness of his belief in the rest of his position as stated. Cox also uses the notion of 'primacy' in a highly elastic way to mean (1) temporally earlier; (2) logically prior; (3) legally superior; (4) empirically dominant. Of these, his claims about temporal priority are entirely acceptable but have no further significance for Locke's theory.[1] Claims 2 and 3 are ambiguous and 4 is greatly overstated. To be concrete, it is clearly correct to say that Locke believed that states threaten each other and it is equally clearly correct to say that their purpose is partly to protect their inhabitants against external attack and that they are more likely to be successful in this assignment if they are militarily strong. But from this it does not follow that their only or predominant purpose is to provide such protection and their dominant duty to maximize their military strength, nor that *whatever* maximizes their military strength is obligatory for them nor that whatever is obligatory for them for this reason is obligatory for them for this reason alone.

But even if it is not a defensible analysis of Locke's work to turn it in this fashion into an apology for the *machtstaat*, there is still some little opacity to just what the ethical limitations on the exercise of political power *are* held to be by Locke.[2] Cox notes correctly in this context Locke's reading of the *raison d'état* theorist Gabriel Naudé and suggests a broad harmony of approach, the new prudence.[3] An elaborate interpretation is clearly needed to sustain this claim since the *Two Treatises* for obvious reasons does not look much like a mirror for princes and since its for the most part pietistic and conventional tones do not sound much like those of the Florentine diplomat or the librarian of

[1] Cox, *Locke on War and Peace*, pp. 63–105, 172, etc. Cf. above, chapter 9, for an account of the categorical error which makes Cox's claim possible.

[2] See, for example, Carl J. Friedrich, *Constitutional Reason of State* (Providence, R.I., 1957), pp. 82–4 (and, less happily, p. 90). Cf. Cox, *Locke on War and Peace*, pp. 190–5.

[3] *Ibid.* p. 194, etc. and see the references, not cited by Cox but dating from 1681, in MS Locke d 10, esp. pp. 111, 137, 139. Locke owned the 1667 (Paris) edition of Naudé's *Considerations Politiques sur les Coups d'Estat* (see John Harrison and Peter Laslett, *The Library of John Locke*, Oxford Bibliographical Society Publications, N.S. XIII (1965), 2074a), from which these references were taken.

Mazarin.[1] We have seen that the suggested interpretation cannot be fully maintained. Is there an alternative which could be? The most hopeful areas of the text appear to be the discussions of prerogative and of the federative power.[2] In the former it becomes clear that the law can be disregarded, if its purposes can be better served by so doing, and that the decision whether this is so is necessarily left to the executive. But it is important to note some qualifications to this picture. First, it derives from the analysis of what makes it obligatory for the executive to enforce the law in ordinary circumstances[3]—since the basic justification for rule-following must be extrinsic to the practice itself, it is not surprising in principle that there can be extra-legal reasons for departing from the rules. Here it is enormously important that Locke does not see the relationship between government and people as a contract, a *promise*. The reason why government is a trust is precisely because discretion is intrinsic to the proper exercise of government whereas it is not even compatible with the observance of promises. Human laws are merely crude social devices for controlling the exercise of governmental power, and normatively coercive on their executor only when they do serve this purpose. But promises in Locke's scheme are not intrinsically human social devices—they are the elementary human moral bonds and, once they have been made, their obligatoriness is almost a logical truth—so much so that they even bind the Almighty.[4] Their

[1] For an intellectually over-sympathetic account of Naudé's rather perfunctory work see Friedrich Meinecke, *Machiavellism* (London, 1957), pp. 196–204.

[2] *Two Treatises*, II, chapters XII–XIV. See above, chapter 11 and cf. Cox, *Locke on War and Peace*, pp. 123–30, Friedrich, *Reason of State*, pp. 82–4. The status of the federative power must depend directly and solely on the jural situation of any individual in the state of nature. Cox's arguments on its character are flawed drastically by his misunderstanding of this situation. Laslett too sees it as being of peculiar importance in the development of Locke's theory (*Two Treatises*, Introduction, p. 118, and 'John Locke, the Great Recoinage and the Board of Trade, 1695–1698', *William and Mary Quarterly*, 3rd ser. XIV, 3 (July 1957), p. 396). But his position here is difficult to follow. If the British colonies in North America were subject to the British crown under the federative power, then either at the level of the colonial governor or at that of the British crown itself there would be a jurally schizophrenic relationship within an individual who was the federative power of one community at the same time as he was the executive power of another community, and this incoherence would be mirrored in the specific legal relationship between the two communities. This does not seem an adequately charitable reading on such an insecure textual basis.

[3] *Two Treatises*, II, §164, ll. 1–9.

[4] 'Promises and Oaths, which tye the infinite Deity...' (*ibid.* I, §6, l. 6).

obligatory status is one of the few ethical propositions which remain stable amid the general incoherence of Locke's ethical thought from the early 1670s onwards, and any denial of it elicits from him the peculiarly shrill and rigid response, compounded of moral outrage and intellectual embarrassment, received by all those who pressed him forcefully in this very tender area.

By contrast, this stress on the status of promises is one of the taboos which the exponents of *raison d'état* regarded with the greatest contempt, as the merest superstition.[1] Naudé, for instance, used the *salus populi* axiom to justify doing virtually any sort of evil in order that public good might come of it.[2] What then are we to make of Locke himself when he says that whoever sincerely follows the Rule *Salus Populi Suprema Lex* 'cannot dangerously err',[3] and when we note for instance that Locke was taking notes from Naudé's book at a time which must have been quite close to his writing of parts of the *Two Treatises*?[4] One possibility is to point severely to the context in which he uses this particular expression, note that it refers to the exercise of executive discretion to carry out the axiomatic purposes of the society,[5] insist that it does not at any rate involve any breach of a promise or oath, and urge that the discretion is being exercised *ex hypothesi* in the interests of those upon whom it is being exercised. One could then go on to point out that this last condition does not obtain in the case of the federative power, that promises and oaths are customarily the guarantees of treaties, the sole socially effective regulators of international society, and that if Locke wished to exempt princes from their obligations he would be in the odd

[1] Cf. the justification of the massacre of Saint Bartholomew in Gabriel Naudé, *Considerations Politiques sur les Coups d'Estat* ([Paris], 1667), esp.: 'Je ne craindray point toutefois de dire que ce fut une action tres-juste, & tres-remarquable, & dont la cause estoit plus que legitime...' (p. 170). The identification of the Catholic religion with the (in effect Machiavellian) maxim that faith need not be kept with heretics, a commonplace of Protestant polemic since the French wars of religion, is of great importance in understanding Locke's attitude to the toleration of Catholicism. Its crude contemporary relevance became clear once again with the Revocation of the Edict of Nantes in 1685. Cf., for instance [M. Claude], *Les Plaintes des Protestans, cruellement opprimez dans le Royaume de France* (Cologne, 1686), pp. 106, 113–14, 145, 152, 181.

[2] Naudé, *Considerations*, pp. 121–2.

[3] *Two Treatises*, II, §158, ll. 1–3.

[4] MS Locke d 10, pp. 111, 137, 139 (dated 1681).

[5] *Two Treatises*, II, §158, cf. §3, ll. 5–6.

position of supposing Charles II (or, later, William III) not to be bound by a practice which bound God himself. He would also on Cox's reading find some difficulty in giving an account of how a soldier can be unequivocally obliged to obey orders when to do so is to risk his life,[1] or even to explain why an individual's political obligation does not cease *whenever* his own preservation comes into conflict with it, as classically where he is threatened directly with death for wrongdoing. But all this is rather too glib—indeed it falls into just the error which Cox himself makes—it assumes a real coherence where there appears to be merely muddle.

It seems preferable to say that where the action in question is technically illegal, not *prima facie* immoral and believed sincerely by the executive to be in the interest of the subjects, Locke regards it as being transparently justified; but that it simply is not clear at all whether he would regard the deliberate breach of a sworn public agreement with another state, which had not in effect already been violated by that state, in the interest of his own state as ever simply right. It should, though, also be insisted that the fact that rule-breaking for the benefit of those covered by the rules is defended morally could hardly show that promise-breaking against the interests of those to whom one has made the promise is legitimate. That the normative status of an intrinsically unconstitutional act can be changed by the end for which it is performed does not imply that an intrinsically immoral act can be sanctioned in the same way. And Cox's maxim of the primacy of self-preservation, quite apart from its erroneous formulation, could only show in terms of objective natural law that it overbore other moral considerations when there were adequate reasons to suppose that self-preservation was *directly* at stake. To maintain his interpretation he needs to establish both that the moral quality of an act lies in its subjectively seen purpose and that the end of human actions is basically the project of biological self-maintenance. It is easy to see how he contrives to extrapolate both of these from Locke's incoherent and carelessly written work but it is equally easy to see what a very partial and question-begging reading of the work as a whole they represent.

[1] Cf. *Two Treatises*, II, §139.

13

THE CONDITIONS FOR LEGITIMATE RESISTANCE

The right of resistance within Locke's theory is based upon a concept logically antithetical either to the state of nature or to the legitimate polity. It derives from the notion of the state of war. The state of war is the historical product of particular human actions and it can be created by these actions whether they are performed in the state of nature or within a legitimate political society. In order to place the right of resistance which Locke affirms, it is necessary to trace the development of this conception of the state of war and its application to the cases of conquest, usurpation, and tyranny. The cumulative movement of the exposition follows the movement of Locke's own argument.

The state of war is initiated by the use of force.[1] Force and violence are the terms which appear throughout the book as the vehicles of disruption to the peace of the state of nature and as solvents of the legitimacy of political society.[2] Force is the way of beasts and it reduces all human beings who perpetrate it to the jural status of beasts. We have seen above the incoherent

[1] '. . . force, or a declared design of force upon the person of another, where there is no common Superior on Earth to appeal to for relief, *is the State of War*' (*Two Treatises of Government*, II, §19, ll. 8–10).

[2] *Ibid.* II, §16, l. 16; §17, l. 10; §18, ll. 3, 5; §19, ll. 5, 8–9, 17, 23–4; §20, ll. 14, 16–17; §172, ll. 13, 15; §176, l. 7; §179, ll. 3, 7, 9, 18; §181, ll. 4–9 ('. . . 'tis the use of Force only, that puts a Man into the State of War. For whether by force he begins the injury, or else having quietly, and by fraud, done the injury, he refuses to make reparation, and by force maintains it, (which is the same thing as at first to have done it by force) 'tis the unjust use of force that makes the War.'), 9–11, 14–15, 17–19; §182, ll. 4, 12, 19, 25; §183, l. 10; §184, ll. 38–9; §186, ll. 1, 8, 10, 11, 13, 20; §187, l. 2; §189, l. 11; §192, l. 3; §196, l. 22; §202, ll. 2–7 ('And whosoever in Authority exceeds the Power given him by the Law, and makes use of the Force he has under his Command, to compass that upon the Subject, which the Law allows not, ceases in that to be a Magistrate, and acting without Authority, may be opposed, as any other Man, who by force invades the Right of another.'); §204, ll. 1–2; §206, ll. 2–3; §207, ll. 8–11, 21; §208, ll. 7–8; §209, l. 7; §211, l. 9; §212, l. 28; §222, ll. 15–16; §226, ll. 9–15; §227, ll. 4, 14, 22; §228, ll. 5, 14, 16; §230, l. 29; §231, ll. 1–2; §232, ll. 1–3; §233, ll. 7–8 (Locke's translation from Barclay); §235, ll. 28–30; §242, ll. 12–14.

theoretical structure from which this notion acquires its meaning and derives its resonances, the metaphors of the predator and the cannibal.[1] These beasts are noxious. They are no pleasantly available, perhaps even domestic, animals, convenience and food supply for their human masters, epitome of God's beneficent provision for the needs of the human race,[2] but the wild, the savage, the threatening, beasts of prey, the creatures, almost, of nightmare.[3] They are not the placid, complaisant animals with which man can live at ease or which he can safely pursue and at length ingest in the crudest proprietorial act of all.[4] They are those

[1] '...by supposing they have given up themselves to the *absolute Arbitrary Power* and will of a Legislator, they have disarmed themselves, and armed him, to make a prey of them when he pleases' (*ibid.* II, §137, ll. 15–18). 'Who would not think it an admirable Peace betwixt the Mighty and the Mean, when the Lamb, without resistance, yielded his Throat to be torn by the imperious Wolf? *Polyphemus*'s Den gives us a perfect Pattern of such a Peace, and such a Government, wherein *Ulysses* and his Companions had nothing to do, but quietly to suffer themselves to be devour'd' (§228, ll. 17–23). See also §181, ll. 16–20, and 'As if when Men quitting the State of Nature entered into Society, they agreed that all of them but one, should be under the restraint of Laws, but that he should still retain all the Liberty of the State of Nature, increased with Power, and made licentious by Impunity. This is to think that Men are so foolish that they take care to avoid what Mischiefs may be done them by *Pole-Cats*, or *Foxes*, but are content, nay think it Safety, to be devoured by *Lions*' (§93, ll. 26–32). The absolute ruler is in a state of licence and not merely one of liberty (cf. §6, ll. 1–2), because he is unrestrained, in his own ideological understanding, by anyone in the world with the effective power to execute the law to which he is alone subject and the law is consequently 'in vain' (cf. §7, ll. 7–10).

[2] *Two Treatises*, I, §86, ll. 21–8; §87, ll. 5–12; §92, ll. 1–3; §97, ll. 1–3. And cf. II, §163, ll. 21–3.

[3] '...a Criminal, who having renounced Reason, the common Rule and Measure, God hath given to Mankind, hath by the unjust Violence and Slaughter he hath committed upon one, declared War against all Mankind, and therefore may be destroyed as a *Lyon* or a *Tyger*, one of those wild Savage Beasts, with whom Men can have no Society nor Security' (*ibid.* II, §11, ll. 21–6). 'And one may destroy a Man who makes War upon him, or has discovered a Enmity to his being, for the same Reason, that he may kill a *Wolf* or a *Lyon*; because such Men are not under the ties of the Common Law of Reason, have no other Rule, but that of Force and Violence, and so may be treated as Beasts of Prey, those dangerous and noxious Creatures, that will be sure to destroy him, whenever he falls into their Power' (§16, ll. 12–18). Having 'made use of the Force of War to compasse his unjust ends upon an other, where he has no right, and so revolting from his own kind to that of Beasts by making Force which is theirs, to be his rule of right, he renders himself liable to be destroied by the injur'd person and the rest of mankind, that will joyn with him in the execution of Justice, as any other wild beast, or noxious brute with whom Mankind can have neither Society nor Security' (§172, ll. 12–19). See also §181, ll. 16–20; §182, ll. 18–21.

[4] See *ibid.* II, §26, on the means by which a man can create property in the fruits of the earth by appropriating them: 'The Fruit, or Venison, which nourishes the

members of the animal kingdom with whom men can have no society at all.[1] Their power is immense and it is, by their own ideological proclamation, the explicit official theory of absolutism, unharnessed. Their way is the way of force, of physical violence; and between them and the rest of the human race the only relationship can be that of war. The formal language of legitimacy in seventeenth-century England which gilded with such precision each level of the elaborately stepped pyramid of social hierarchy is here wrenched violently away from the structure which it shelters. The gentle flattery of the language, the power and sacredness of the crown, dominion, the noble, the great, shifts to a brutal ambivalence.[2] Power is potential force and the more elevated the power, the greater the force. It was because Locke so readily felt the structures of social control in the society in which he lived to be legitimate that he rejected their abuse with such intensity. They were so stable, so sheltering, so reassuring; but if the spell was broken, their menace was lethal. The withdrawal of security was unendurable not only because men had come to depend so completely upon its existence, but because their dependence had itself conferred such deadly power upon their rulers. To employ Locke's own metaphor, the trust which men instinctively feel towards the good ruler is so complete[3] that the force which they consign to him (which is in its physical composition

wild *Indian*, who knows no Inclosure, and is still a Tenant in common, must be his, and so his, i.e., a part of him, that another can no longer have any right to it, before it can do him any good for the support of his Life' (ll. 12–16). This is held to be a nobler use than its 'bare Preservation' (II, §6, ll. 3–5).

[1] *Ibid.* II, §11, ll. 25–6; §172, ll. 18–19.

[2] The point which I wish to make here is similar in style to one recently made by J. H. Hexter in a brilliant article, 'The Loom of Language and the Fabric of Imperatives: The Case of *Il Principe* and *Utopia*', *American Historical Review*, LXIX, 4 (July 1964), 945–68, and more extensively in his introduction to *Utopia, Complete Works of St. Thomas More* (New Haven, 1965), IV. Hexter shows how More systematically destroys the honorific connotations of the language of nobiliar status in sixteenth-century Europe by setting it against the crude militarist rationale of the lives of the men who enjoyed it. In the same way Locke takes the authoritarian language of royal absolutism and sets its delicate and deferential cadences against the crude physical realities which it is often called upon to shield.

[3] 'It being as impossible for a Governor, if he really means the good of his People, and the preservation of them and their Laws together, not to make them see and feel it; as it is for the Father of a Family, not to let his Children see he loves, and takes care of them' (*Two Treatises*, II, §209, ll. 13–17).

and its moral status their own force) comes to be overwhelming. The trust which they feel derives from the peace which he provides for them. The 'trust' with which he is 'entrusted' is the preservation of this peace. Law is the barricade which protects this peace and confers this assurance. Law, consequently, is the antithesis of force. It represents ease as against anxiety, liberty as against subjection. It is the guarantor of all the elements of a fully human life in the complex societies of Locke's day. If the guarantee is reneged on, the betrayal is total.

When force without right disrupts the proper peace of the state of nature[1] every man's hand is justly against the aggressor, not because of the universality of the threat in natural terms but because the aggressor has violated the Hebraic unity of the tribal family[2] and bears in consequence the brand of Cain.[3] It is not a

[1] 'And here we have the plain *difference between the State of Nature, and the State of War*, which however some Men have confounded, are as far distant, as a State of Peace, Good Will, Mutual Assistance, and Preservation, and a State of Enmity, Malice, Violence, and Mutual Destruction are one from another. Men living together according to reason, without a common Superior on Earth, with Authority to judge between them, is *properly the State of Nature*. But force, or a declared design of force upon the Person of another, where there is no common Superior on Earth to appeal to for relief, *is the State of War*' (*ibid.* II, § 19, ll. 1–10). The difference remains plainer to some men than others.

[2] Cf. chapters 8 and 9 above on Locke's problems in identifying a universalistic natural theology with the prescriptions to be found in the Judaeo-Christian tradition.

[3] 'And thus it is, that every Man in the State of Nature, has a Power to kill a Murderer, both to deter others from doing the like Injury which no Reparation can compensate, by the Example of the punishment that attends it from every body, and also *to secure* Men from the attempts of a Criminal, who having renounced Reason, the common Rule and Measure, God hath given to Mankind, hath by the unjust Violence and Slaughter he hath committed upon one, declared War against all Mankind, and therefore may be destroyed as a *Lyon* or a *Tyger*, one of those wild Savage Beasts, with whom Men can have no Society nor Security: And upon this is grounded the great Law of Nature, *Who so sheddeth Mans Blood, by Man shall his Blood be shed.* And *Cain* was so fully convinced, that every one had a Right to destroy such a Criminal, that after the Murther of his Brother, he cries out, *Every one that findeth me, shall slay me*; so plain was it writ in the Hearts of all Mankind' (*Two Treatises*, II, § 11, ll. 16–31). It is profoundly significant that it is at the point where Locke makes the central claim of his entire argument and makes it in words which constitute the most explicit flouting of the epistemological criteria which he had adopted ever since the *Essays on the Law of Nature*, that he should desert a plausible naturalism so bluntly for the record of divine positive law (cf. *Two Treatises*, II, § 11, ll. 30–31 n.). The message might indeed be difficult to decipher in the 'hearts of all mankind' (cf. Christoph Von Fürer-Haimendorf, *Morals and Merit* (London, 1967), pp. 72–3 on the Daflas). But it was easy enough to find in the book of Genesis (see E. E. Urbach, 'The Laws regarding Slavery as a source for social history...', *Annual of Jewish Studies*, I (1963), 93).

naturalistic individualism which gives to all men the executive power of the law of nature in others' cases, but the Hebraic simplicity of what Benjamin Nelson called 'tribal brotherhood' as opposed to 'universal otherhood'.[1] The state of nature is an order of law which, if it is observed, preserves men in peace, in 'security'.[2] Wherever human misdemeanours encroach on this order it is open to all men to take measures to restore its integrity.[3] It is open to *all* of them because of the duties of justice and charity which they owe to one another as jural equals.[4] It is the primary type of occasion on which a man can come to acquire a power over another, a power defined by the categories of reparation and restraint, whose purpose is the re-establishment of order and its subsequent protection.[5] The law of reason and equity is the tie which God has given men to secure them from injury and violence. To break it is to transgress against the whole species by infringing its peace and safety.[6] The right of restraint is a form of

[1] See Benjamin Nelson, *The Idea of Usury: From Tribal Brotherhood to Universal Otherhood* (Princeton, 1949), *passim*. [2] *Two Treatises*, II, §8, ll. 9–13, etc.

[3] 'And that all Men may be restrained from invading others Rights, and from doing hurt to one another, and the Law of Nature be observed, which willeth the Peace and *Preservation of all Mankind*, the *Execution* of the Law of Nature is in that State, put into every Mans hands, whereby every one has a right to punish the transgressors of that Law to such a Degree, as may hinder its Violation' (*ibid.* II, §7, ll. 1–7).

[4] 'This *equality* of Men by Nature, the Judicious *Hooker* looks upon as so evident in it self, and beyond all question, that he makes it the Foundation of that Obligation to mutual Love amongst Men, on which he Builds the Duties they owe one another, and from whence he derives the great Maxims of *Justice* and *Charity*' (*ibid.* II, §5, ll. 1–5), and the lengthy passage from book I of the *Lawes of Ecclesiasticall Politie* which follows. Locke uses the passage to some degree as a claim to respectability for one of the propositions which he treats axiomatically. But it is worth noting that Hooker's derivation of justice and charity from human equality is considerably more naturalistic than Locke's own construction of them out of the will of an anthropomorphic creator (cf. MS Locke f 3, pp. 201–2; *Two Treatises*, II, §6, ll. 10–25, etc.). It is an attractive irony in the face of the Straussian interpretation of Locke's writing habits that the first quotation from Hooker which he included in his work should have been closer to the position of Hobbes than the main outline of Locke's own theory.

[5] *Two Treatises*, II, §8, ll. 1–24, esp.: 'And thus in the State of Nature, *one Man comes by a Power over another*; but yet no Absolute or Arbitrary Power, to use a Criminal when he has got him in his hands, according to the passionate heats, or boundless extravagancy of his own Will, but only to retribute to him, so far as calm reason and conscience dictates, what is proportionate to his Transgression, which is so much as may serve for *Reparation* and *Restraint*' (ll. 1–7).

[6] 'In transgressing the Law of Nature, the Offender declares himself to live by another Rule, than that of *reason* and common Equity, which is that measure God

punishment open to all but the right of reparation belongs only to the injured party, though if he chooses to assert it any other men who consider his claim to be just are at liberty to assist him.[1] We have seen before that it is the transfer of these jural resources to the magistrate which creates the legitimate polity. Its dual character survives in political society in a difference in the extent to which the magistrate can remit the punishment.[2] In the case of less serious breaches of the law of nature the permissible punishments are reduced in degree, but the criterion of their scale remains the same.[3] Because the administration of this law is, by definition, totally individualist in the state of nature, because men are for the most part judges in their own case and because the

has set to the actions of Men, for their mutual security: and so he becomes dangerous to Mankind, the tye, which is to secure them from injury and violence, being slighted and broken by him. Which being a trespass against the whole Species, and the Peace and Safety of it, provided for by the Law of Nature, every man upon this score, by the Right he hath to preserve Mankind in general, may restrain, or where it is necessary, destroy things noxious to them, and so may bring such evil on any one, who hath transgressed that Law, as may make him repent the doing of it, and thereby deter him, and by his Example others, from doing the like mischief' (*Two Treatises*, II, § 8, ll. 9–22).

[1] '... he who hath received any damage has besides the right of punishment common to him with other Men, a particular Right to seek *Reparation* from him that has done it. And any other Person who finds it just, may also joyn with him that is injur'd, and assist him in recovering from the Offender, so much as may make satisfaction for the harm he has suffer'd' (*ibid.* II, § 10, ll. 6–12). See also § 11, ll. 3–4, 8–16.

[2] '... the Magistrate, who by being Magistrate, hath the common right of punishing put into his hands, can often, where the publick good demands not the execution of the Law, *remit* the punishment of Criminal Offences by his own Authority, but yet cannot *remit* the satisfaction due to any private Man, for the damage he has received. That, he who has suffered the damage has a Right to demand in his own name, and he alone can *remit*: The damnified Person has this Power of appropriating to himself, the Goods or Service of the Offender, by *Right of Self-preservation*, as every Man has a Power to punish the Crime, to prevent its being committed again, *by the Right he has of Preserving all Mankind*, and doing all reasonable things he can in order to that end' (*Two Treatises*, II, § 11, ll. 4–16). Since this is one of the most unequivocal of Locke's presentations of the 'right of self-preservation' it is worth emphasizing that it appears as a peer of the 'right of preserving all mankind', which hardly makes sense except in terms of his general natural theology.

[3] 'By the same reason, may a Man in the State of Nature *punish the lesser breaches* of that Law. It will perhaps be demanded, with death? I answer, Each Transgression may be punished to that *degree*, and with so much *Severity* as will suffice to make it an ill bargain to the Offender, give him cause to repent, and terrifie others from doing the like. Every Offence that can be committed in the State of Nature, may in the State of Nature be also punished, equally, and as far forth as it may, in a Common-wealth' (*ibid.* II, § 12, ll. 1–8).

measures of it are complex, the legal order is all too likely at any point of dispute to degenerate into the state of war.[1]

The state of war is created by a 'sedate setled Design, upon another Mans Life'[2] and in this state, by the principle of equity, the injured man, or anyone acting on his behalf,[3] has the right to destroy the life of his aggressor. For although the law of nature wills the maximization of preservation, if there are internal conflicts in the application of this principle, as there necessarily are in the state of war, the preservation of the innocent is to be preferred.[4] A claim to absolute power over individual or community, a claim to control other human beings against their will, is tantamount to the claim to make them slaves.[5] In fact the whole purpose of absolute power is precisely to prise away from the

[1] 'To avoid this State of War (wherein there is no appeal but to Heaven, and wherein every the least difference is apt to end, where there is no Authority to decide between the Contenders) is one great *reason of Mens putting themselves into Society*, and quitting the State of Nature. For where there is an Authority, a Power on Earth, from which relief can be had by *appeal*, there the continuance of the State of War is excluded, and the Controversie is decided by that Power' (*ibid.* II, §21, ll. 1–8). See also §13, ll. 10–14.

[2] *Two Treatises*, II, §16, l. 3.

[3] 'Any one that joyns with him in his Defence, and espouses his Quarrel' (*ibid.* §16, ll. 6–7). See also ll. 7–9 and §8, ll. 11–18.

[4] 'For *by the Fundamental Law of Nature, Man being to be preserved*, as much as possible, when all cannot be preserv'd, the safety of the Innocent is to be preferred: And one may destroy a Man who makes War upon him, or has discovered an Enmity to his being, for the same Reason, that he may kill a *Wolf* or a *Lyon*; because such Men are not under the ties of the Common Law of Reason, have no other Rule, but that of Force and Violence, and so may be treated as Beasts of Prey, those dangerous and noxious Creatures, that will be sure to destroy him, whenever he falls into their Power' (*ibid.* II, §16, ll. 9–18). See also §159, ll. 26–8. Note that the law of nature prescribes 'Man to be preserved', not merely that man may preserve himself. All creatures are to be preserved unless they can be put to some nobler use (§6, ll. 3–5). Locke makes effective use in the passage quoted here of the etymological derivation of the word 'innocent' by contrasting it with 'noxious' to bring out its root sense of harmless in supplement to its normal meaning of guiltless. The assimilation of physical threat to law-breaking is an effective rhetorical device, though, as stressed earlier, it presents acute theological problems. Human beings present threats because they are corrupt (have broken divine laws) but tigers present threats of the same crudely physical sort because God made them that way.

[5] 'And hence it is, that he who attempts to get another Man into his Absolute Power, does thereby *put himself into a State of War* with him; It being to be understood as a Declaration of a Design upon his Life. For I have reason to conclude, that he who would get me into his Power without my consent, would use me as he pleased, when he had got me there, and destroy me too when he had a fancy to it: for no body can desire to *have me in his Absolute Power*, unless it be to compel me by force to that, which is against the Right of my Freedom, *i.e.* make me a Slave' (*ibid.* II, §17, ll. 1–9).

individual his own freedom and open him to unlimited and immediate exploitation. So the effort to acquire (or presumably to assert the existence of) arbitrary power can be construed as the threat of force.[1] And the threat of force, as before, destroys the only security for human preservation.[2] The freedom which is the 'fence' to this preservation is freedom from the threat of the use of force or at worst of violent death itself. It is a legal, not a practical freedom; and it is his legal rights, not his physical strength, which a man is losing when he acknowledges the legitimacy of absolute power over him either in the state of nature or in a political society.[3] The use of force to create such dependence, irrespective of the actual intentions of its user, and simply in virtue of the fact that it is a rejection of the law of nature, may be construed as the utmost possible exploitation of this power.[4] Even in political society, the proper remedy for the inconveniences of the state of nature,[5] such a use of force, in the absence of an available tribunal to which the victim of aggression can effectively make his appeal for relief, leaves the right of war against an aggressor perpetually open to all men.[6] In political society only the

[1] *Two Treatises*, II, §17, ll. 10–21, esp.: 'To be free from such force is the only security of my Preservation: and reason bids me look on him, as an Enemy to my my Preservation, who would take away that *Freedom*, which is the Fence to it: so that he who makes an *attempt to enslave* me, thereby puts himself into a State of War with me' (ll. 10–14).

[2] 'This makes it Lawful for a Man to *kill a Thief*, who has not in the least hurt him, nor declared any design upon his Life, any farther then [*sic*] by the use of Force, so to get him in his Power, as to take away his Money, or what he pleases from him: because using force, where he has no Right, to get me into his Power, let his pretence be what it will, I have no reason to suppose, that he, who would *take away my Liberty*, would not when he had me in his Power, take away every thing else' (*Two Treatises*, II, §18, ll. 1–8). The axiom of presumed unlimited malevolence which Locke employs here is the most 'Hobbesian' component of his political theory.

[3] But, of course, where absolute power is acknowledged in political societies the monarch disposes of the force of 'a multitude' in his confrontation with his subject (see *Two Treatises*, II, §13, ll. 15–29, esp. l. 21. Also §93, ll. 26–30). The acknowledgement by his other subjects of his legal status greatly enhances his physical force in this encounter.

[4] *Ibid.* II, §18, esp. ll. 1–2, 6.

[5] *Ibid.* II, §13, ll. 9–11.

[6] *Ibid.* II, §18, §19, ll. 13–22, §20, ll. 11–23, esp.: 'For wherever violence is used, and injury done, though by hands appointed to administer Justice, it is still violence and injury, however colour'd with the Name, Pretences, or Forms of Law, the end whereof being to protect and redress the innocent, by an unbiassed application of it, to all who are under it; wherever that is not *bona fide* done, *War is made* upon the Sufferers...' (ll. 16–21).

continued exercise of force maintains the state of war, because when force ceases, appeal can be made among the subjects to adequate legal arbitration.[1] But in the state of nature where no such machinery for enforcing an impartial settlement is available, the state of war continues until the aggressor is destroyed or desires reconciliation on terms which restore the integrity of the legal order.[2] The creation of fixed arbitration procedures is an institutional service which provides one of the most powerful reasons for accepting the legitimacy of political society.[3] In its absence, once the state of war has commenced, as it is apt to do on the least dispute in the state of nature, the only judge between the contending parties is God himself,[4] and each individual must decide whether another man has 'put himself in a state of war' with him by his aggression.[5] The rights which an innocent victim of aggression possesses in the state of war are those appropriate to a 'State of Enmity, Malice, Violence, and Mutual Destruction'.[6]

Human freedom inside or outside society is a jural status, a relationship between the individual and a body of law. The status cannot be abjured voluntarily; it can only be forfeited as a result of actions which in themselves deserve death.[7] It is this forfeiture

1 'But when the actual force is over, the *State of War ceases* between those that are in Society, and are equally on both sides Subjected to the fair determination of the Law; because then there lies open the remedy of appeal for the past injury, and to prevent future harm' (*ibid.* II, §20, ll. 1–5). This situation of course does not obtain if the dispute is between the holders of power in the society and their subjects. See p. 172, n. 6, above.

2 '...but where no such appeal is, as in the State of Nature, for want of positive Laws, and Judges with Authority to appeal to, *the State of War once begun, continues*, with a right to the innocent Party, to destroy the other whenever he can, until the aggressor offers Peace, and desires reconciliation on such Terms, as may repair any wrongs he has already done, and secure the innocent for the future' (*Two Treatises*, II, §20, ll. 5–11), and cf. §24, ll. 3–8.

3 'To avoid this State of War (wherein there is no appeal but to Heaven, and wherein every the least difference is apt to end, where there is no Authority to decide between the Contenders) is one great *reason of Mens putting themselves into Society*, and quitting the State of Nature' (*ibid.* II, §21, ll. 1–5). (N.B. *one* great reason, not the sole ground.) See §101, ll. 3–6.

4 *Ibid.* II, §20, ll. 21–3, §21, §168, §176, etc.

5 *Ibid.* II, §7, §9, esp.: 'as he soberly judges the Case to require' (l. 14).

6 *Ibid.* II, §19, ll. 4–5. The key right is the right to destroy.

7 '*Despotical Power* is an Absolute, Arbitrary Power one Man has over another, to take away his Life, whenever he pleases. This is a Power, which neither Nature gives, for it has made no such distinction between one Man and another; nor Compact can convey, for Man not having such an Arbitrary Power over his own Life, cannot give another Man such a Power over it; but it is *the effect only of*

which alone gives rise to the condition of slavery, the only jural condition in which a man can have absolute power over another man.[1] It is a status the essence of which is to be unconditional; it implies the loss of all rights whatsoever, including the right to one's own life.

The nature and limitations of slavery are further explored in the discussion of conquest, the sector of the argument in which it has the greatest potential political significance. Locke has noted before that the making of any form of agreement with a slave which the latter is presumed capable of executing is implicitly a recognition of him as a free agent, a responsible human being, 'capable of a law',[2] capable of being obliged. Liberty is defined as the capacity to be obliged, the essence of human nature being

Forfeiture, which the Aggressor makes of his own Life, when he puts himself into the state of War with another' (*Two Treatises*, II, §172, ll. 1–9).

[1] *Ibid.* II, §23, ll. 4–13. Locke treats the embarrassing scriptural evidence for voluntary slavery firmly as evidence for the existence of a particular sort of system of indentured labour with fixed terminal dates and with severe legal restraints on the masters' power to harm the bondsmen. The evidence of Exodus XXI which he cites (§24, ll. 9–17) does lend some superficial support to his position but the correct interpretation of this passage remains highly controversial today (see David Brion Davis, *The Problem of Slavery in Western Culture* (Ithaca, N.Y., 1966), p. 48, n. 34) and it is quite clear that Locke's account of the legal basis of slavery could not be made congruent with the system of holding heathen foreigners as chattel slaves prescribed in Leviticus XXV, 44–6, however compatible it might be with the arrangements in the case of debt-bondage or slavery to avoid destitution inside the tribal community. The respective statuses of 'Jewish' and 'foreign' slaves remain obscure and changed over time—for a very helpful general discussion see E. E. Urbach, 'The Laws regarding Slavery as a source for social history...', *Annual of Jewish Studies*, I, 1–94. Urbach emphasizes that the rules governing the treatment of non-Jewish slaves are concerned with their assimilation into Jewish ritual practice (pp. 31–50) and notes that all slaves enjoy an equal protection of their lives (p. 93). The relationships do not fit Locke's concepts at all happily. (Dr M. I. Finley very kindly called this reference to my attention.)

[2] '...if once *Compact* enter between them, and make an agreement for a limited Power on the one side, and Obedience on the other, the State of War and *Slavery* ceases, as long as the Compact endures. For, as has been said, no Man can, by agreement, pass over to another that which he hath not in himself, a Power over his own Life' (*Two Treatises*, II, §24, ll. 3–8), and see §61, l. 30. Also: 'For what Compact can be made with a Man that is not Master of his own Life? What Condition can he perform? And if he be once allowed to be Master of his own Life, the *Despotical*, *Arbitrary Power* of his Master ceases. He that is Master of himself, and his own Life, has a right too to the means of preserving it, so that *as soon as Compact enters*, *Slavery ceases*, and he so far quits his Absolute Power, and puts an end to the state of War, who enters into Conditions with his Captive' (§172, ll. 23–30). Freedom is defined as the possibility of making contracts but this indicates the logical preconditions for the making of an agreement, not the teleology of human freedom.

its jural status.[1] In the same way as just execution of the rights of war against an aggressor initiates the condition of slavery for an individual, the same execution provides the basis for the just conquest of a political society by another political society.[2] But the limits of the power in the one case remain in the other. Furthermore, their continuance has powerful implications for political theory. Because, as Locke later put it, 'every one's sin is charged upon himself only',[3] only those who were directly implicated in the unjust use of force can under any circumstances come to be slaves.[4] Neither male non-combatants nor wives, nor children, can hence become enslaved under any circumstances.[5]

[1] 'The *Freedom* then of Man and Liberty of acting according to his own Will, is *grounded on* his having *Reason*, which is able to instruct him in that Law he is to govern himself by, and make him know how far he is left to the freedom of his own will. To turn him loose to an unrestrain'd Liberty, before he has Reason to guide him, is not the allowing him the priviledge of his Nature, to be free; but to thrust him out amongst Brutes, and abandon him to a state as wretched, and as much beneath that of a Man, as theirs' (*ibid.* II, §63, ll. 1–9).

[2] *Two Treatises*, II, §178, ll. 3–6; §180, ll. 1–4; §196, ll. 1–5.

[3] *The Reasonableness of Christianity*, *Works* (1768), III, 5.

[4] *Two Treatises*, II, §196, ll. 1–8, etc. But cf. Laslett's note (§24, ll. 1–8 n.), for the reading of Chapter IV as Locke's justification of 'the slave-raiding forays of the Royal Africa Company'. The biographical assumption here seems bold. The notion that a chapter in his book called 'Slavery' is to be read as a moral rationalization of an activity in which he was implicated is precisely parallel to Professor Macpherson's assumption that the succeeding chapter, called 'Property', must be intended as a moral rationalization of the social order in which he lived. We simply do not know if there exists such an intellectual contrivance as 'Locke's justification of slavery' as a continuing social institution. The point is not merely that the justification 'may seem unnecessary, and inconsistent with his principles' but that, as subsequently expounded in the section which explains its presence in the book at all and reveals its role in the argument, the category of legitimate slavery developed here could not be the basis of any *continuing* system of slavery at all. The whole analytic point of the category is that it cannot persist beyond one generation (§§182, 188, 189, 196). Whatever Locke may have believed about the slave-raiding forays of the Royal Africa Company, he can hardly have believed that they did not ever capture female slaves or indeed children (cf. §183). What we confront here is not an example of bland but deliberate moral rationalization on Locke's part but merely one of immoral evasion.

[5] 'I say then the *Conquerour* gets no Power but only over those, who have actually assisted, concurr'd, or consented to that unjust force, that is used against him. For the People having given to their Governours no Power to do an unjust thing, such as is to make an unjust War, (for they never had such a Power in themselves:) They ought not to be charged, as guilty of the Violence and Unjustice that is committed in an Unjust War, any farther than they actually abet it' (*ibid.* II, §179, ll. 1–8). 'But because the miscarriages of the Father are no faults of the Children, and they may be rational and peaceable, notwithstanding the brutishness and injustice of the Father; the Father, by his miscarriages and violence, can forfeit

Nor can an unjust conqueror ever acquire dominion over anyone by his conquest.[1] Nor does any conqueror, just or unjust, acquire a title to the property, more especially the land, of the conquered, except to the extent of adequate reparations for the particular economic damage done to him by the conquered.[2] It is not possible in principle for the value of reparations to amount to the value of the lands of the conquered because these have a capital value as a source of continuing wealth which is beyond the damage that any country could conceivably inflict on another.[3] But even if the value of reparations justly due was such as to justify the permanent expropriation of large parts of the lands of the conquered, there would be other claims upon them which have priority over those of the conqueror. This is because the lands of the conquered are in some sense the property of their families.[4] The just conqueror may repay his expenses by appropriating revenue from their estates and by employing their labour,[5] provided that he does not infringe the rights of any others, most particularly by endangering their physical survival. The status of slave, which from the point of view of the slave is incurred by his own iniquity, is preserved for the justly victorious slave-owner by his duty to execute the law of nature to the degree at which it becomes an effective deterrent to other potential sinners[6] and by

but his own Life, but involves not his Children in his guilt or destruction' (§182, ll. 1–5). 'I am Conquered: My Life, 'tis true, as forfeit, is at mercy, but not my Wives and Childrens. They made not the War, nor assisted in it. I could not forfeit their Lives, they were not mine to forfeit' (§183, ll. 11–14). See also §§189 and 196.

[1] *Two Treatises*, II, §176.

[2] *Ibid.* II, §182, ll. 5–31, §§183, 184, 192, 194.

[3] *Ibid.* II, §184, ll. 1–36, esp. ll. 6–23.

[4] '...the Father, by his miscarriages and violence, can forfeit but his own Life, but involves not his Children in his guilt or destruction. His goods, which Nature, that willeth the preservation of all Mankind as much as is possible, hath made to belong to the Children to keep them from perishing, do still continue to belong to his Children. For supposing them not to have joyn'd in the War, either through Infancy, absence, or choice, they have done nothing to forfeit them: nor *has the Conqueror any right* to take them away, by the bare title of having subdued him, that by force attempted his destruction' (*ibid.* II, §182, ll. 3–13; see also §183, ll. 5–7, ll. 14–28; §194, etc). This suggests that if men are legally incapable of alienating their property completely by their vice, they are under fairly strong obligations not to alienate it merely by their wills (but cf. §116, ll. 22–4, for a formally incompatible assertion). Property even in goods is defined more exhaustively in moral terms (that no one has a right to remove it from the owner without his consent) than by a right on his part, untrammelled by obligations towards others, to employ it as he wills.

[5] *Two Treatises*, II, §183, ll. 3–4, and the whole discussion on slavery.

[6] 'And thus in the State of Nature, *one Man comes by a Power over another*; but yet no

his right to exploit the degenerate human 'beast' who has assaulted, until he has received adequate reparations for the damage done to him by it. Only when security has been re-established and his own debts paid does a justly victorious slave-owner have any sort of moral obligation to recognize the slave as a full human being—and even in this case the obligation is not analysable as a right of the slave.

We have seen above that Locke's analysis of legitimacy makes it impossible for this to originate from foreign conquest. Usurpation, which Filmer had held to be one of the possible sources of legitimacy,[1] is held by Locke to be of essentially the same jural status as conquest, the seizure of the rights of one person by another, a kind of domestic conquest.[2] Where a dynasty of rulers owes its historical origin to usurpation, it must derive elsewhere any legitimacy which it is to possess, must derive it in fact like any other legitimate holders of political power, from the free consent of the subjects.[3] The rules of succession to office in a legitimate political society are a part of the 'constitution' and authority in a political society derives solely from the 'constitution'.[4]

The unjust use of force against men by other men who have no

Absolute or Arbitrary Power, to use a Criminal when he has got him in his hands, according to the passionate heats, or boundless extravagancy of his own Will, but only to retribute to him, so far as calm reason and conscience dictates, what is proportionate to his Transgression, which is so much as may serve for *Reparation* and *Restraint*. For these two are the only reasons, why one Man may lawfully do harm to another, which is what we call *punishment*' (*ibid.* II, § 8, ll. 1–9).

[1] Cf. above, chapter 6, for the nature of Filmer's argument and *Two Treatises*, Preface (pp. 155–6); I, § 121 and n. The treatment as it stands is a perfectly adequate critique of Filmer's position on this issue and it is difficult to regret the omission of the more extended treatment mentioned.

[2] 'As Conquest may be called a Foreign Usurpation, so *Usurpation* is a kind of Domestick Conquest, with this difference, that an Usurper can never have Right on his side, it being no *Usurpation* but where one *is* got into *the Possession of what another has Right to*' (*ibid.* II, § 197, ll. 1–5).

[3] 'Whoever gets into the exercise of any part of the Power, by other ways, than what the Laws of the Community have prescribed, hath no Right to be obeyed, though the Form of the Commonwealth be still preserved; since he is not the Person the Laws have appointed, and consequently not the Person the People have consented to. Nor can such an *Usurper*, or any deriving from him, ever have a Title, till the People are both at liberty to consent, and have actually consented to allow, and confirm in him, the Power he hath till then Usurped' (*ibid.* II, § 198, ll. 11–19).

[4] 'In all lawful Governments the designation of the Persons, who are to bear Rule, is as natural and necessary a part, as the Form of the Government it self, and is that which had its Establishment originally from the People' (*ibid.* II, § 198, ll. 1–4).

authority over them cannot be the basis of an authority of the first over the second. Nor can the unjust or illegitimate use of force even by the rightful authorities of a 'Just Government'[1] carry any intrinsic authority over the subjects of that government.[2] For all legitimacy resides in the legal order and the powers granted to terrestrial authorities within the legal order are logically dependent on their being exercised to serve the ends of that order, the ends, that is, of those subject to it. Any use of the powers of the state to further the private and corrupt purposes of the rulers by the threat of force shatters the structure of authority and initiates the state of war between the ruler and the subject whom he has wronged.[3] In practice this will not lead to the dissolution of the government unless the ruler behaves in this way with some persistence, because subjects are in general highly subservient.[4] Equally, it does not mean that the wronged subject would be morally entitled, however well or ill advised from a prudential viewpoint this may be, to claim his revenge in action.[5] The title which

[1] For this phrase see *Two Treatises*, II, §230, l. 32.

[2] *Ibid.* II, §199, §201. Also '*Where-ever Law ends, Tyranny begins,* if the Law be transgressed to another's harm. And whosoever in Authority exceeds the Power given him by the Law, and makes use of the Force he has under his Command, to compass that upon the Subject, which the Law allows not, ceases in that to be a Magistrate, and acting without Authority, may be opposed, as any other Man, who by force invades the Right of another' (§202, ll. 1–7).

[3] *Ibid.* II, §208, ll. 6–8 and: 'Whosoever uses *force without Right*, as every one does in Society, who does it without Law, puts himself into a *state of War* with those, against whom he so uses it, and in that state all former Ties are cancelled, all other Rights cease, and every one has a *Right* to defend himself, and *to resist the Aggressor*' (§232, ll. 1–5).

[4] *Two Treatises*, II, §208, ll. 3–14; §223, esp.: 'People are not so easily got out of their old Forms, as some are apt to suggest. They are hardly to be prevailed with to amend the acknowledg'd Faults in the Frame they have been accustom'd to' (ll. 7–10); '... such *Revolutions happen* not upon every little mismanagement in publick affairs. *Great mistakes* in the ruling part, many wrong and inconvenient Laws, and all the *slips* of humane frailty will be *born by the People*, without mutiny or murmur' (§225, ll. 1–5); §230, ll. 1–5. And see above, chapter 11.

[5] '... yet the *Right of resisting*, even in such manifest Acts of Tyranny, *will not* suddenly, or on slight occasions, *disturb the Government*. For if it reach no farther than some private Mens Cases, though they have a right to defend themselves, and to recover by force, what by unlawful force is taken from them; yet the Right to do so, will not easily ingage them in a Contest, wherein they are sure to perish; it being as impossible for one or a few oppressed Men to *disturb the Government*, where the Body of the People do not think themselves concerned in it, as for a raving mad Man, or heady Malecontent to overturn a well-settled State; the People being as little apt to follow the one as the other' (*ibid.* II, §208, ll. 3–14).

he has to punish the ruler is one which he may only exercise if to do so is unlikely to damage the interests of others.[1] But where the ruler has established in the minds of his subjects by even a small number of such actions an acute anxiety about the malignity of his future intentions, they are entitled to go to the aid of his previous victims and resist his abusive actions.[2] The appropriate form of resistance varies to some extent with the constitution of the society—in England for instance it appears not to be legitimate to attack the monarch himself.[3] But its rationale is the same anywhere in the world and at any point in human history. The ruler has deserted the way of 'reason' and its law for force and violence. He has destroyed the security which the law of reason guarantees, has poisoned 'the very Fountain of public Security',[4] and removed the conditions which make human relationships possible inside or outside political society. In so doing he has reverted from his own kind to that of beasts and so may be destroyed like any other noxious creature. The sons of 'Charles Stuart, that Man of Blood', are relegated to an even lower place in the order of creation than that to which Cromwell had consigned their father. The relegation, too, was not merely performed in the heat of a brief period of angry political struggle. Its emotional intensity is confirmed

[1] 'He that troubles his Neighbour without a Cause, is punished for it by the Justice of the Court he appeals to. And he that *appeals to Heaven*, must be sure he has Right on his side; and a Right too that is worth the Trouble and Cost of the Appeal, as he will answer at a Tribunal, that cannot be deceived, and will be sure to retribute to every one according to the Mischiefs he hath created to his Fellow-Subjects; that is, any part of Mankind' (*ibid.* II, §176, ll. 34–40). Cf. Locke's judgement: 'the Inconveniency of some particular mischiefs, that may happen sometimes, when a heady Prince comes to the Throne, are well recompenced, by the peace of the Publick, and security of the Government, in the Person of the Chief Magistrate, thus set out of the reach of danger: It being safer for the Body, that some few private Men should be sometimes in danger to suffer, than that the head of the Republick should be easily, and upon slight occasions exposed' (§205, ll. 19–26). The right is not cancelled but its use is restricted on grounds of moral responsibility and the consequent (unjust) individual suffering is sanctioned by social expediency.

[2] 'But if either these illegal Acts have extended to the Majority of the People; or if the Mischief and Oppression has light only on some few, but in such Cases, as the Precedent, and Consequences seem to threaten all, and they are perswaded in their Consciences, that their Laws, and with them their Estates, Liberties, and Lives are in danger, and perhaps their Religion too, how they will be hindered from resisting illegal force, used against them, I cannot tell' (*Two Treatises*, II, §209, ll. 1–8), and §220, *a fortiori*, 'a long train of Actings' or more systematic oppression also gives them a right to resistance (see §§210, 212, 214–19, 221, 222, etc.).

[3] *Ibid.* II, §§ 205–6; but cf. §§213–19.

[4] *Ibid.* II, §222, l. 40.

in an addition which Locke made to the flyleaf of the copy of the book which contained his final amendments for posterity.[1]

In the face of this jural degeneracy, the individual wronged subject has no terrestrial court of appeal open to him but the judgement of his fellow subjects, the people,[2] and the people has no court of appeal open to it but the judgement of God.[3] Vicious actions on the part of the ruler do not destroy the moral standing of the entire political community nor erase the full set of obligations which a man has incurred through his membership of it, they merely destroy the legal status which the ruler derives from his

[1] 'ego ad Deos vindices humanae superbiae confugiam: et precabor ut iras suas vertant in eos, quibus non suae res, non alienae satis sint quorum saevitiam non mors noxiorum exatiet: placari nequeant, nisi hauriendum sanguinem laniandaque viscera nostra praebuerimus. Liv. Lib. ix.c.i.' The copy is in the Library of Christ's College, Cambridge (see *Two Treatises*, p. 154n.).

[2] *Ibid.* II, §243, ll. 1–20, esp.: '...The *Power that every individual gave the Society*, when he entered into it, can never revert to the Individuals again, as long as the Society lasts, but will always remain in the Community; because without this, there can be no Community, no Common-wealth, which is contrary to the original Agreement: So also when the Society hath placed the Legislative in any Assembly of Men, to continue in them and their Successors, with Direction and Authority for providing such Successors, *the Legislative can never revert to the People* whilst that Government lasts: Because having provided a Legislative with Power to continue for ever, they have given up their Political Power to the Legislative, and cannot resume it' (ll. 1–12); §240, ll. 1–9; §242, ll. 1–10 ('If a Controversie arise betwixt a Prince and some of the People, in a matter where the Law is silent, or doubtful, and the thing be of great Consequence, I should think the proper *Umpire*, in such a Case, should be the Body of the *People*. For in Cases where the Prince hath a Trust reposed in him, and is dispensed from the common ordinary Rules of the Law; there, if any Men find themselves aggrieved, and think the Prince acts contrary to, or beyond that Trust, who so proper to *Judge* as the Body of the *People*, (who, at first, lodg'd that Trust in him) how far they meant it should extend?').

[3] *Ibid.* II, §168, ll. 1–37, esp.: 'tho' the *People* cannot be *Judge*, so as to have by the Constitution of that Society any Superiour power, to determine and give effective Sentence in the case; yet they have, by a Law antecedent and paramount to all positive Laws of men, reserv'd that ultimate Determination to themselves, which belongs to all Mankind, where there lies no Appeal on Earth, *viz.* to judge whether they have just Cause to make their Appeal to Heaven. And this Judgement they cannot part with, it being out of a Man's power so to submit himself to another, as to give him a liberty to destroy him' (ll. 18–27); §241; §242, ll. 10–17; §243, ll. 12–20; §21, esp.: 'And therefore in such Controversies, where the question is put, *who shall be Judge*? It cannot be meant, who shall decide the Controversie; every one knows what *Jephtha* here tells us, that *the Lord the Judge*, shall judge. Where there is no Judge on Earth, the *Appeal* lies to God in Heaven. That Question then cannot mean, who shall judge? whether another hath put himself in a State of War with me, and whether I may as *Jephtha* did, appeal to Heaven in it? Of that I my self can only be Judge in my own Conscience, as I will answer it at the great Day, to the Supream Judge of all Men' (ll. 15–24).

legal role within it.[1] Only the systematic destruction caused by a foreign conquest is likely to dissolve the nexus of persisting relationships of mutual obligation which make men members of a single Body Politick.[2] The right of resistance is an individual right of initiative in the making of an appeal. But neither in practical effect nor in legal determination has an individual the right to conduct the prosecution[3] or execute the appropriate

[1] '*Where-ever Law ends, Tyranny begins*, if the Law be transgressed to another's harm. And whosoever in Authority exceeds the Power given him by the Law, and makes use of the Force he has under his Command, to compass that upon the Subject, which the Law allows not, ceases in that to be a Magistrate, and acting without Authority, may be opposed, as any other Man, who by force invades the Right of another' (*ibid.* II, §202, ll. 1–7). See also §206 for the assimilation of this principle to English constitutional proprieties.

[2] *Ibid.* II, §211, ll. 1–27, esp.: 'That which makes the Community, and brings Men out of the loose State of Nature, into *one Politick Society*, is the Agreement which every one has with the rest to incorporate, and act as one Body, and so be one distinct Commonwealth. The usual, and almost only way whereby *this Union is dissolved*, is the Inroad of Foreign Force making a Conquest upon them. For in that Case, (not being able to maintain and support themselves, as *one intire* and *independent Body*) the Union belonging to that Body which consisted therein, must necessarily cease, and so every one return to the state he was in before, with a liberty to shift for himself, and provide for his own Safety as he thinks fit in some other Society. Whenever the *Society is dissolved*, 'tis certain the Government of that Society cannot remain' (ll. 4–16). Another type of social event which has such an effect is 'open and visible Rebellion', 'which when it prevails, produces Effects very little different from Foreign Conquest' (§218, ll. 11–14). But cf. §§219 and 220 and Laslett's reading, *ibid.* p. 114. There does not seem to be a real problem here. §211 states that the dissolution of a society is a sufficient condition for the dissolution of government. It does not claim, nor did Locke believe (§§212–19), that it was a necessary condition. §219 maintains that the physical removal of the source of executive power from a society 'dissolves' the government of the society, which is what maintains political order in the society (ll. 7–10). It is political order and connection which disappears, the 'Government' which ceases (ll. 1–2, 4–6, 9, 14–17, §220, l. 1). Those who have the right to 'provide for themselves' are 'the People' or 'the Society' still, not the individual members of it (§220, ll. 2, 5). The state of nature which is created by the dissolution of government, if such is created, exists between the members of the society, not between them and the sovereign who has entered into a state of war with them. Laslett reads §219 as a causal statement in sociology, whereas it should be read as a logical statement in legal theory. It is logically impossible for the state of nature to be a state of war. Locke's writing here is confused but it is certainly less confused than that of his commentators; cf. Martin Seliger, 'Locke's Theory of Revolutionary Action', *Western Political Quarterly*, XVI, 3 (September 1963), 548–68, 557, n. 48 ('In Sec. 218, internal arbitrariness and foreign conquest are put on the same level, as they must be, because both cause the dissolution of government and bring about a state of nature, in the sense of a state of war').

[3] Because of the individually unappetizing and morally prohibitive consequences—see above, n. 2, and below, p. 182, n. 1.

sentence. The creative human resources embodied in the political community serve to restrain the vicious intentions of the ruler. In highly developed political societies, with their sophisticated institutional representation of the will of the people, it is easy to see what might be meant by appealing to the people. Where better to appeal to the people, for instance, than to the two Houses of Parliament?[1] But naturally such resources are not available in the same way in an absolute monarchy and there the conditions for just resistance are more individualist, direct and starkly physical. They are neither mediated nor moralized by being consigned to the judgement of accredited and impartial representatives of the people's will. It is thus partly the intellectual resources, as well as the conventional pieties,[2] of English constitutionalism which enable Locke to combine his theological individualism with an articulated and differentiated theory of the right to resistance, and to make this a theory of the restoration of an existing degree of legality rather than a conceptually primitive doctrine of tyrannicide, that emotionally injured corollary of the 'Mirror for Princes' vision of politics. The tension between the individualism, a logical precondition for individual obligation, and the constitutionalism provides, too, a less flaccid and superstitious account than either that of Calvin himself or that developed by later and more radical Calvinist theorists of resistance.

For the religiously guaranteed framework for action, on which the right of resistance depended for Locke, was an order of intelligible truths accessible in principle to all men, not a structure of social authority under the effective control of the few.[3] It is not an organized society and its authoritatively articulated power which is acclaimed as the repository of the divine will,[4] but a set

[1] *Two Treatises*, II, §242, cf. esp.: 'But if the Prince, or whoever they may be in the Administration, decline that way of Determination, the Appeal then lies nowhere but to Heaven' (ll. 10–12). This suggests that Locke did have some notion of an appropriate 'way of Determination' which it made sense to talk of 'declining'. It is difficult to see what could be meant by this, if not the judgement of the Houses of Parliament, perhaps even, as Shaftesbury's propaganda in the Exclusion controversy advocated, the results of an election to the House of Commons.

[2] *Ibid.* II, §§205, 206, 'Don't kill the King', etc.

[3] Cf. Jean Calvin, *Institution de la Religion Chrestienne*, IV, XX, 31, ed. Jean-Daniel Benoit (Paris, 1957–63), IV, 535–6.

[4] I have in mind here the interpretation of Calvinist resistance theory set out by Michael Walzer, *The Revolution of the Saints* (London, 1966), pp. 57–65.

of rationally intelligible prescriptions accessible to all men. It was this which gave its vast social plasticity to the Lockean doctrine. It did not, as John Knox did, consign the right of revolutionary initiative to the religious 'enthusiast'.[1] There was nothing esoteric about the judgement of the appropriate occasion for revolution.[2] If the protective integument of trust towards authority in which the community is swathed so intimately is ripped apart, it can only be because the normal recipients of this trust have grossly betrayed it.[3] The yearning which men feel for security creates a psychological dependence upon their rulers which gives these enormous freedom of action. Errors and incidental injustices which they may perpetrate will be accepted placidly by their subjects. Only the destruction of the climate of trust will threaten their effective control and this destruction can only be caused by their gross misconduct. If, however, it is destroyed, the people will sooner or later resist.[4] How often such resistance takes place depends upon the moral quality of the behaviour of the rulers.[5]

[1] Walzer, *Revolution of the Saints*, pp. 106–9.

[2] '...how can a Man any more hinder himself from being perswaded in his own Mind, which way things are going?' (*Two Treatises*, II, §210, ll. 14–15); §225, ll. 5–8; also 'For till the mischief be grown general, and the ill designs of the Rulers become visible, or their attempts sensible to the greater part, the People, who are more disposed to suffer, than right themselves by Resistance, are not apt to stir. The examples of particular Injustice, or Oppression of here and there an unfortunate Man, moves them not. But if they universally have a perswasion, grounded upon manifest evidence, that designs are carrying on against their Liberties, and the general course and tendency of things cannot but give them strong suspicions of the evil intention of their Governors, who is to be blamed for it? Who can help it, if they, who might avoid it, bring themselves into this suspicion? Are the People to be blamed, if they have the sence of rational Creatures, and can think of things no otherwise than as they find and feel them?' (§230, ll. 5–18). The metaphors throughout assimilate cognitive and sensory experience—the key to their veridical consciousness is that they have 'the sence of rational Creatures' which leads them both to 'find' and to 'feel' the betrayal of trust by their leaders.

[3] *Ibid.* II, §209, ll. 8–17.

[4] *Ibid.* II, §224, ll. 3–16. The incidence of revolutions is here claimed to be independent of the political theory espoused in the societies in question.

[5] Seliger ('Locke's Theory of Revolutionary Action', *Western Political Quarterly*, XVI, 3, 548–68) is concerned to argue that it will not happen very frequently. This conclusion might be expected to be correct in the case of a country like England which Locke regarded as a legitimate political society. There is no reason to suppose that Locke would have believed it to hold in France or any absolute monarchy. Locke does not 'advocate frequent (or indeed occasional) revolutions'. He claims that revolutions are only likely to occur in legitimate polities when the rulers have destroyed the legitimacy of these, an empirical claim about the frequency of occurrence of revolutions, and that where this has occurred, it is wholly appro-

Locke himself is only interested in discussing its prospective frequency at all in order to calm the readers' fears of possible social chaos promoted by accepting the normative theory which he is espousing. How often legitimate resistance will occur depends only upon how often and how effectively the governors convey their malign intentions to their subjects.[1] When it does occur, the form of resistance will depend upon the form of social organization characteristic of the society and the degree of disorganization caused by the misbehaviour of the rulers. Rebellion, descent to the state of war, is a sin and as such it is to be attributed to the men who initiate it,[2] to unjust Princes who break their trust and not to resisting populations 'exposed to the boundless will of Tyranny'.[3] Where resistance takes place in legitimate political societies, even where it cannot be conducted through appropriate constitutional institutions,[4] there is no reason to suppose that it will take the form of the *jacquerie*. When the people become 'a confused Multitude',[5] because the judicial system of the country has disintegrated, they cease to have 'order or connexion' derived from the formal political system of the country[6] but there is no reason to suppose that social hierarchy would disappear and the populace be reduced to a state of war with each other. The order which can be erased through such a desertion by the executive is the formal

priate that revolutions should occur, a normative claim. It is the latter claim in which he is interested and he is even prepared at one point to leave the first question as an open issue (§230, ll. 18–35), because it does not in fact bear upon the issue which he *is* concerned to argue (§230, ll. 29–37). Seliger's anxiety about the 'many Revolutions' which have characterized English history (pp. 565, 567, cf. *Two Treatises*, II, §223, ll. 7–20) is thus slightly gratuitous. It cannot be the case that Locke is here talking about prerogative (cf. ll. 18–20). He is merely arguing that despite the many vicissitudes of English constitutional history, including various changes of occupancy of the crown, the continuity of the Ancient Constitution has remained unbroken. (Cf. Locke to Edward Clarke, 8 February 1689, *The Correspondence of John Locke and Edward Clarke*, ed. Benjamin Rand (London, 1927), pp. 288–9.)

1 *Two Treatises*, II, §§209, 210, 224, 225.

2 *Ibid.* II, §226, esp.: 'For Rebellion being an Opposition, not to Persons, but Authority, which is founded only in the Constitutions and Laws of the Government; those, whoever they be, who by force break through, and by force justifie their violation of them, are truly and properly *Rebels*' (ll. 5–9), 'those who set up force again in opposition to the Laws, do *Rebellare*, that is, bring back again the state of War, and are properly Rebels' (ll. 12–14); §227, *passim*; §228; §232, ll. 1–12, esp.: 'all resisting of *Princes* is not Rebellion' (l. 12).

3 *Ibid.* II, §229, ll. 2–3.

4 Cf. above, p. 181, n. 2; p. 182, n. 1.

5 *Ibid.* II, §219, ll. 1–10.

6 Cf. above, p. 181, n. 2.

legal order of the English Body Politick, not the substantive social order of the village or even perhaps of the county. But if Locke expected resistance to be contrived and controlled by the existing holders of social authority and if the legitimacy of the resistance was to be judged rationally in terms of the conscientious individual judgement of these representative figures, this did not mean that its legitimacy depended upon its being confined to this social stratum. The axiomatically superior rationality which Seliger attributes to these figures in Locke's theory, however plausible as an assessment of Locke's own assumption about social order, enjoys no textual sanction and is difficult to reconcile with the comments which Locke does in fact make about the achieved rationality of the gentry.[1] It is not the category of

[1] Seliger, 'Locke's Theory of Revolutionary Action', *Western Political Quarterly*, XVI, 3, 551 (and see his article 'Locke's Natural Law and the Foundation of Politics', *Journal of the History of Ideas*, XXIV, 3 (July-September 1963), 337–54, esp. pp. 351–2). Seliger's reading of the *Second Treatise*, §34, l. 5, as an account of the moral rationale of the power of the English gentry should be contrasted with Locke's own explicit comments on their level of achieved rationality. Cf. 'How men, whose plentiful fortunes allow them leisure to improve their understandings, can satisfy themselves with a lazy ignorance, I cannot tell; but methinks they have a low opinion of their souls, who lay out all their incomes in provisions for their body and employ none of it to procure the means and helps of knowledge; who take great care to appear always in a neat and splendid outside, and would think themselves miserable in coarse clothes or a patched coat, and yet contentedly suffer their minds to appear abroad in a piebald livery of coarse patches and borrowed shreds, such as it has pleased chance or their country tailor (I mean the common opinion of those they have conversed with) to clothe them in. I will not here mention how unreasonable this is for men that ever think of a future state and their concernment in it, which no rational man can avoid to do sometimes; nor shall I take notice what a shame and confusion it is, to the greatest contemners of knowledge, to be found ignorant in things they are concerned to know. *But this at least is worth the consideration of those who call themselves gentlemen, that, however they may think credit, respect, power, and authority the concomitants of their birth and fortune, yet they will find all these still carried away from them by men of lower condition, who surpass them in knowledge.* They who are blind will always be led by those that see, or else fall into the ditch; and he is certainly the most subjected, the most enslaved, who is so in his understanding' (*Essay*, IV, XX, 6; my italics). It is perfectly true that Locke supposed that there was a connection between an elevated social situation and the acquisition of knowledge but it was one of moral responsibility to acquire it, not of practical achievement in having done so. (See *Conduct of the Understanding*, *Works*, IV, 153: 'Those methinks, who, by the industry and parts of their ancestors, have been set free from a constant drudgery to their backs and their bellies, should bestow some of their spare time on their heads, and open their minds, by some trials and essays in all the sorts and matters of reasoning.') And for the connection between the possibilities for acquiring knowledge in different 'callings' and the responsibility to acquire it see *ibid.* pp. 154–5, and for

office,[1] either in the formal political system or in the hierarchy of social authority, which sanctions resistance but the conformity of the decision to resist with rationally assessed normative criteria. Anyone, in some circumstances, had the right to act on his judgement of the application of these criteria and God would be the judge of the justice of his appeal.[2]

the degree to which the responsibility for the ignorance of all should be attributed to the 'policies of Courts' see the note *Labour* of 1693 (MS Film. 77, pp. 310–11).

[1] Cf. again Walzer, *Revolution of the Saints*, pp. 57–65.

[2] Seliger's argument that Locke bases his exclusion of revolution in the case of threats to particular individuals on *raison d'état* is misleading. The passage at which Locke states that if 'a busy head, or a turbulent spirit' desires the alteration of the government as often as pleases them, it 'will be only to their own just ruin and perdition' (*Two Treatises*, II, §230, ll. 1–5, cf. Seliger, 'Locke's Theory of Revolutionary Action', *Western Political Quarterly*, XVI, 3, p. 567) is part of his argument that his affirmation of the right to resistance will not have subversive consequences. Busy heads and turbulent spirits are not to be read as men who have been unjustly assaulted but as men who aspire to overturn the social order merely because they *want* to do so (cf. 'whenever they please'). Their perdition is just because they do not have a right to engage in subversion. Where Locke does proclaim the desirability from the point of view of the society as a whole of securing the executive even at some risk to individual citizens, he does not say and did not believe that the sufferings of these private men would therefore be 'just' (§205). *Raison d'état* in Locke's usage never makes oppressive action *just* (cf. Locke's comments in 1693 on the threat to civil order presented by 'aspiring and turbulent men', 'designing or discontented Grandees' (MS Film. 77, p. 311)). It would be perfectly appropriate for an individual to revolt, if the assault upon him by the government precluded any appeal to an impartial tribunal and if he believed that the threat to others implied by this assault justified the prospective cost to them which would be caused by his revolt. The limitation on his right to revolt implied in this account is simply a combination of the obligation to which he has committed himself by membership in the political community and of his own duty of charity towards all men. It has nothing to do with the arcane obligation of the sovereign to take account of reason of state, merely a matter of the universal human duties of keeping a promise and taking account of the consequences of one's actions.

14

THE LAW OF NATURE

The law of nature appears as a premise of the argument of the *Two Treatises of Government*. We know, too, that Locke intended it to appear as the conclusion to the *Essay concerning Human Understanding*, but that he broke off the attempt to establish it and suppressed the chapter in which the attempt was announced.[1] We also know that he never completed any such demonstration of its contents, although he seems to have tried frequently enough, and that he rejected with some asperity the urgings of several friends, most especially James Tyrrell and William Molyneux, to complete and publish such a demonstration.[2] We may also suspect that he wrote the *Reasonableness of Christianity* at least in part to fill the gap which this failure had left in his intellectual bequest to his contemporaries and to posterity. At a more intellectual level, we have an effective explanation of why Locke never completed such a demonstration in the fact that such a demonstration is not in principle possible and that the development of Locke's ideas had drawn the difficulties of such an effort sharply to his attention.[3] There is, however, little agreement among interpreters of Locke's thought on the significance which should be attached to these facts. Not only interpretations with as extensive *a priori* components as those of Strauss and Macpherson which I have treated elsewhere,[4] but even more cautious and sensitively documented treatments like those of Von Leyden and Abrams are in sharp conflict.

It is not always easy to see just what is at issue in the disputes or

[1] See 'Of Ethick in General', MS Locke c 28, pp. 146–52 (printed in Peter King, *The Life of John Locke* (London, 1830), II, 122–33). For its relationship to the *Essay* see Von Leyden's note, *Essays on the Law of Nature* (Oxford, 1954), p. 69.

[2] I have not felt it necessary to repeat the documentation for biographical points of this type where they have been widely noted by recent commentators.

[3] This has been shown with great clarity and force by Von Leyden in his seminal introduction to the *Essays on the Law of Nature* and his article 'John Locke and Natural Law', *Philosophy*, XXXI (1956), 23–35.

[4] See my article, 'Justice and the Interpretation of Locke's Political Theory', *Political Studies* (February 1968), and below, chapters 15–17.

what sort of evidence would be appropriate to resolve them and this is not the place to attempt to do justice to the complexity of a controversy to which there have been so many contributors.[1] All that is attempted here is a crude outline of the nature of the problem and a brief statement of the position implied in the reading of the *Two Treatises* set out above.[2] It is normal to see the issue as one of how far Locke should be assimilated to the voluntaristic (Ockhamite) or the rationalist traditions in the analysis of the nature of moral obligation. The position implied in most of his directly epistemological writings, in the *Essays on the Law of Nature*, the drafts of the *Essay concerning Human Understanding* to the *Essay* itself, suggests a persistent attempt to establish a rationalist position, worked out in close relationship with a natural theology which was necessary to make it operational among the human race. But the final position developed in the *Reasonableness of Christianity* reverts to a sort of fideist voluntarism. It is easy, too, to see why Locke should have been tempted to assume this last position. His analysis of the character of human motivation, his theory of the will, as developed from the 1676 notes onwards,[3] being in a broad sense hedonist, was not directly compatible with

[1] Valuable contributions are made by Sterling Power Lamprecht, *The Moral and Political Philosophy of John Locke* (1918) (reprinted, New York, 1962); Åke Petzäll, 'Ethics and Epistemology in John Locke's Essay concerning Human Understanding', *Göteborgs Högskolas Årsskrift*, XLII, 2 (1937); John W. Yolton, 'Locke on the Law of Nature', *Philosophical Review*, LVII, 4 (October 1958), 477–98; Philip Abrams in his edition of *Two Tracts on Government*; in addition to the work of Von Leyden cited above, p. 187, n. 3. See also Richard I. Aaron, *John Locke* (2nd edition, Oxford, 1955), pp. 256–69; J. W. Gough, *John Locke's Political Philosophy* reprint, Oxford, 1956), pp. 1–23; Leo Strauss, *Natural Right and History* (Chicago, 1953), pp. 202–51, and 'Locke's Doctrine of Natural Law', *American Political Science Review*, LII, 2 (June 1958), 490–501; Charles H. Monson, Jr., 'Locke and his Interpreters', *Political Studies*, VI, 2 (1958), 120–33; Richard H. Cox, *Locke on War and Peace* (Oxford, 1960); R. Polin, *La Politique Morale de John Locke* (Paris, 1960); A. P. Brogan, 'John Locke and Utilitarianism', *Ethics*, LXIX, 2 (January 1959), 79–93; Raghuveer Singh, 'John Locke and the Theory of Natural Law', *Political Studies*, IX, 2 (1961), 105–18; M. Seliger, 'Locke's Natural Law and the Foundation of Politics', *Journal of the History of Ideas*, XXIV, 3 (July-September 1963), 337–54; for less convincing readings.

[2] I have tried to bring out the type of inference involved within the book itself above in chapter 8. The question at issue here is what sort of a defence Locke would have been able to make of the natural law premise of the argument had he chosen to attempt a full formal academic defence of it.

[3] See *Essays on the Law of Nature*, pp. 265–72, printed from MS Locke f 1, pp. 325–47 (=Journal for 16 July 1676).

a rationalist theory of the nature of the Good. But it is noteworthy, in contrast to this resolution, that the aim which he announced in the suppressed late chapter of the *Essay* was the natural theological demonstration of all men's access to knowledge of their moral duties.[1] It is abundantly clear that the provisions of the *Reasonableness of Christianity* are distinctly more limited than this. Indeed it is not too drastic to say that that work restricts reasonableness, effective access to knowledge of the obligatory force of *recta ratio*, to those privileged to receive the Christian revelation.[2] It may be true that Locke makes no very abrupt disjunction between revelation and reason, that reason is 'natural revelation',[3] that all knowledge is ultimately based upon intuition[4] and that what is revealed by the incarnation is indeed

[1] 'To establish morality therefore upon its proper basis and such foundations as may carry an obligation with them we must first prove a law which always supposes a law maker one that has a superiority and right to ordain and also a power to reward and punish according to the tenor of the law established by him. This Sovereign Law Maker who has set rules and bounds to the actions of men is god their maker whose existence we have already proved. The next thing then to show is that there are certain rules certain dictates which it is his will all men should conform their actions to, and that this will of his is *sufficiently promulgated and made known to all man kind*' (MS Locke c 28, p. 152, printed in King, *Life of Locke*, II, 133; my italics).

[2] Men may often *act* in fact in conformity with right reason for a variety of prudential reasons without any clear grasp of its obligatory status. See, for example: 'If law-makers in making of laws, did not direct them against the irregular humours, prejudices and passions of men, which are apt to mislead them: if they did not endeavour with their best judgement, to bring men from their humours and passions, to *the obedience and practice of right reason*; the society could not subsist, and so they themselves would be in danger to lose their station in it, and be exposed to the unrestrained humours, passions, and violence of others. And hence it comes, that *be men as humoursome, passionate, and prejudiced as they will*, they are still by their own interest obliged to make use of their best skill, and with their most unprejudiced and sedatest thoughts, take care of the governments, and endeavour to preserve the commonwealth' (*A Third Letter for Toleration*, *Works* (1768), II, 667; my italics).

[3] '*Reason* is natural *revelation*, whereby the eternal Father of light and fountain of all knowledge communicates to mankind that portion of truth which he has laid within the reach of their natural faculties; *revelation* is natural *reason* enlarged by a new set of discoveries communicated by God immediately, which *reason* vouches the truth of, by the testimony and proofs it gives that they come from God' (*Essay*, IV, XIX, §4).

[4] On Locke's theory of knowledge see in general James Gibson, *Locke's Theory of Knowledge and its Historical Relations* (reprint, Cambridge, 1960), and Richard I. Aaron, *John Locke* (Oxford, 1955). I should not wish to go quite as far as Professor Lovejoy and maintain (see Arthur O. Lovejoy, *The Great Chain of Being* (paperback edition, New York, 1960), p. 360, n. 2) that Locke in his epistemology was

'reasonable'.[1] But if natural revelation had remained ineffectual throughout the period before the birth of Christ[2] and no doubt even in his own day among the Chinese, Japanese, Hurons and all those other unfortunate heathens on whose religious practices Locke took such conscientious notes, the classic belief that *gratia non tollit naturam sed perficit* took on a quality of heavy irony. Furthermore, if Locke had begun by believing the demonstration of their duties to all mankind (a rationalist performance) either impossible or unnecessary, it is difficult to see why he should have troubled to compose at all the *Essay concerning Human Understanding* with its persisting concern with the nature and accessibility of moral knowledge.[3] It is essential at this point not to conflate statements about Locke's literary intentions and statements about our own interpretations of his theoretical dilemma into a claim about his own perception of his theoretical position.

His analysis of morality throughout the workings of the *Essay* and thereafter combines a deductive formal system of appropriate norms naturally intelligible by rational inquiry on the basis of sensory data, a demonstrative ethics based on natural theology, with a series of substantive sanctions backing the commands of a God with infinite powers of enforcement. Rightness is a formal relationship between a rule and an action. Obligatoriness is a substantive relationship between an authority with a power to enforce its commands and an individual subject to that authority.[4] In the case of the commands of God there was a perfect symmetry between the formal order of rectitude and the substantive order of power. Locke's analysis of the empirical psychology of morals in the *Essay*[5] starts off from the fact that most men do *not* derive their moral notions from the only law which does necessarily combine rectitude and authority, the law of God. But its analysis

'essentially a Platonist'. But it remains important to stress the limited character of his 'empiricism'.

1 Cf. *The Reasonableness of Christianity as delivered in the Scriptures.*

2 *Reasonableness, Works*, III, 87–94.

3 See esp. Petzäll, 'Ethics and Epistemology', *Göteborgs Högskolas Årsskrift*, XLII, 2 and Von Leyden, *Essays on the Law of Nature*, Introduction, pp. 73–6.

4 See, for example, the note 'Voluntas', MS Locke c 28, fo. 114^{v}, on the distinction between moral good and evil (hedonic) and moral rectitude and pravity (printed in *Essays*, Introduction, pp. 72–3).

5 *Essay*, II, XXVIII, §§6–16.

of moral ideas, mixed modes and moral language is concerned not with the exposition of effective obligation but with the possibility of constructing a coherent moral language which men could employ consistently to order their comprehension of moral rectitude and pravity. The point at which he breaks off in the *Essay* is where he is attempting to demonstrate a similar clarity in the structure of obligations. His purpose in investigating the human understanding and the human moral understanding in particular had always been a practical one. The intention of the entire epistemological venture was to provide a theoretical account of the development of truth and falsehood in the human mind, one which could be employed to restrain the encroaching flood of partiality. The corruption of men's all too educated perceptions was to be purged by a stern epistemological self-consciousness. In a sense, the whole *Essay* is predominantly a study in the morals of thinking, an extended casuistry of the duty of 'regulating' one's assent.[1]

But the availability of the materials for carrying out this purification was in itself clearly insufficient to impel men to perform it. The conceptual confusion which had been generated by their moral corruption could hardly be removed by the injunction to act morally by thinking clearly. The conceptual confusion had largely arisen from a defect in the human will and this could only be amended by an agent which could act directly upon the will. Hence most of the discussions of ethics which Locke himself did not publish in the later versions of the *Essay* are concerned directly with the problem of how men can be brought to *practise* the moral

[1] 'He that believes without having any reason for believing may be in love with his own fancies; but neither seeks truth as he ought, *nor pays the obedience due to his Maker*, who would have him use those discerning faculties he has given him, to keep him out of mistake and error. He that does not this *to the best of his power*, however he sometimes lights on truth, is in the right but by chance; and I know not whether the luckiness of the accident will *excuse* the irregularity of his proceeding. This at least is certain, that he must be *accountable* for whatever mistakes he runs into; whereas he that makes use of the light and faculties God has given him, and seeks *sincerely* to discover truth by those helps and abilities he has, may have this satisfaction in doing his duty as a rational creature: that, though he should miss truth, he will not *miss the reward* of it' (*Essay*, IV, XVII, § 24, my italics). Cf. IV, XIII, esp. 'Our *knowledge*, as in other things, so in this, has a great conformity with our sight that it is *neither wholly necessary, nor wholly voluntary*' (§ 1), Locke's italics. See also the repeated stress on the necessity of avoiding 'laziness' in regulating one's assent.

principles which they could perceive as rational.[1] The coercive instrument which he employed to bring home these obligations to his own society was his own interpretation of the Christian revelation, the *Reasonableness of Christianity*. The problem of reconciling human ignorance and vice with divine power and benevolence was a theological problem and the categories with which it is handled in the Christian religion, the doctrines of original sin and of the atonement, are the starting point of the *Reasonableness of Christianity*. The *Essay* breaks off at the point at which Locke is confronted by his inability to present morality as a system of universally intelligible obligatory truths, and the *Reasonableness of Christianity* provides both a moral rationalization of human 'partiality' and moral incomprehension and a practical strategy for amending it.

Clearly there is a sharp problem about the relationship between the two works. Clearly, too, since Locke wrote the *Reasonableness* at least in part after two editions of the *Essay* had been published and proceeded to complete two further editions of the *Essay* in his own lifetime, he must have regarded the implications of the two works as compatible at some level. But compatibility is not the same as overt logical implication and it is historically inept to see the *Essay* as *implying* the *Reasonableness of Christianity* or indeed the *Reasonableness* implying the *Essay*. Or, at least, if such an

[1] 'Of Ethick in General' (cited above, p. 187, n. 1); 'Voluntas' (cited above, p. 190, n. 4); 'Morality' (MS Locke c 28, p. 139, and esp. MS Locke c 28, fo. 113[r], *c*. 1693; cf. resemblance of language on 113[v]). 'Ethica': 'There be two parts of Ethics, the one is the rule which men are generally in the right in though perhaps they have not deduced them as they should from their true principles. The other is the true motives to practice them and the ways to bring men to observe them and these are generally either not well known or not rightly applied. Without this labour moral discourses are such as men hear with pleasure and approve of. The mind being generally delighted with truth especially if handsomely expressed. But all this is but the delight of speculation. Something else is required to practice, which will never be till men are made alive to virtue and can taste it. To do this one must consider what is each man's particular disease, what is the pleasure that possesses him. Over that general discourses will never get a mastery. But by all the prevalencies of friendship all the arts of persuasion he is to be brought to try the contrary course. You must bring him to practice in particular instances and so by habits establish a contrary pleasure and then when Conscience, Reason and pleasure go together they are sure to prevail. Which is the way to do this in particular cases will be easier for a prudent man to find when the case offers than for any one to foresee and determine before the case happens and the person be known. J.L.'

allegation is to be supported, it must be purely an allegation about Locke's psychology and not at all one about the logic of his ideas. The conviction of their compatibility should be set against his conviction, as proclaimed to Molyneux, that human free will and divine omniscience were compatible, though he could not see *how* they were.[1] The highly attenuated form of the category of original sin which he sets out in the *Reasonableness*, after several years of anxious and not very coherent reflection on the issue,[2] provides a certain feeble theological rationalization for the fact that those men who have not been vouchsafed the Christian revelation have in fact been created by the deity in a condition in which they do not have the effective *moral* resources to discern and practise the full law of reason.[3] But the resolution which it achieved was merely a fideist compatibility between two items of belief, not a demonstration of their logical interdependence. The conviction of coherence which Locke displayed over this point is similar in style to his initial assurance of the existence of a perfect parallel between the calculus of rationally apprehended moral truths and the divinely furnished system of hedonic sanctions. God is determined by what is best[4] and tied by promises and

[1] 26 January 1693: '...I own freely to you the weakness of my understanding, that though it be unquestionable, that there is omnipotence and omniscience in God, our maker, and I cannot have a clearer perception of anything, than that I am free; yet I cannot make freedom in man consistent with omnipotence and omniscience in God, though I am as fully persuaded of both, as of any truths I most firmly assent to. And, therefore, I have long since given off the consideration of that question, resolving all into this short conclusion; that if it be possible for God to make a free agent, then man is free, though I see not the way of it' (*Some Familiar Letters*, *Works*, IV, 278).

[2] See MS Locke c 28, fo. 113v ('Homo ante et post lapsum'), and the fragments from the composition of the *Reasonableness* in MS Locke c 27, pp. 101–3, 111–12, 116–19, 129–30, etc. See esp. fo. 101r for an important change of mind. Cf. MS Film. 77, pp. 294–5, and MS Locke c 43, pp. 36, 38, etc. In contrast see the more hysterical formulations of his first work, *Two Tracts on Government*, p. 155.

[3] For Locke's adoption of the conventional evasion of the problem, see *Reasonableness*, *Works*, III, 83 and MS Locke c 27, p. 112. But there are traces in his work of a sort of primitivism which might blur the harsh lines of this position by making human cognitive incompetence a result of secular social development and hence more intimately a *consequence* of human actions and not merely a result of genetic deficiency. (See, for example, *Two Treatises of Government*, I, §58.) Leo Strauss ('Locke's Doctrine of Natural Law', *American Political Science Review*, LII, 2 (June 1958), 497–8) notes forcefully the importance of this lacuna in Locke's thought.

[4] '...I think we might say that God himself cannot choose what is not good: the freedom of the Almighty hinders not his being determined by what is best' (*Essay*, II, XXI, §49).

oaths[1] because his essence is Reason.[2] Because he is rational, the order of sanctions which his omnipotence enables him to deploy is at all points symmetrical with the order of rationally intelligible moral truths. God is actually reasonable because he is himself pure Reason. Human beings are only potentially and intermittently rational, because although their will is determined by what they perceive to be best in the sense of most hedonically fulfilling, their rational apprehension and their skill at hedonic calculation are clouded by the corrupt passions released by the Fall.[3] Reason and instinct cease to go together.[4] The *Essay* proclaims the possibility of yoking them together again by sustained, skilful and morally serious reflection. The *Reasonableness* offers an immediate and effective psychological instrument for performing the conjunction for that vast majority of human beings who do not find the requisite semantic and philosophical inquiry autonomously rewarding. The psychological link for Locke between the convictions embodied in the two works was undoubtedly intimate. None of his purported natural demonstrations of the existence of God provided any ground for attributing to Him such unequivocally and humanly 'rational' attributes. But it becomes repeatedly clear in his investigations of these issues that he feels it necessary only to demonstrate the existence of a God to feel that he has established the existence of a substantially Christian God.[5] The degree

[1] '...Promises and Oaths, which tye the infinite Deity' (*Two Treatises*, I, §6, l. 6); 'the Obligations of that Eternal Law...are so great, and so strong, in the case of *Promises*, that Omnipotency it self can be tyed by them. *Grants*, *Promises* and *Oaths* are Bonds that *hold the Almighty*' (II, §195, ll. 4–7).

[2] But cf. Lamprecht, *Moral and Political Philosophy of Locke*, esp. pp. 107–8, for a forceful assertion of Locke's theoretical incoherence at this point. It is not clear that Lamprecht's assumption—that the relationship of reason to God's motivation must be parallel to its relationship to human motivation—is well judged.

[3] In terms of psychology they fail to take advantage of the 'hinge on which turns the *liberty* of intellectual beings, in their constant endeavours after and a steady prosecution of true felicity, that they can *suspend* this prosecution in particular cases, till they have looked before them and informed themselves whether that particular thing which is then proposed or desired lies in the way to their main end, and make a real part of that which is their greatest good' (*Essay*, II, XXI, §52). Cf. 'Thus I thinke' (MS Locke c 28, pp. 143–4, printed in King, *Life of Locke*, II, 120–2).

[4] MS Locke c 28, fo. 113^v, and cf. fo. 113^r.

[5] This does not mean that he accepts all arguments for the existence of God as valid. (See, for example, his rejection of Descartes' proof from the idea of necessary existence written in 1696, the year after the publication of the *Reasonableness*, MS Locke c 28, pp. 119–20, printed in King, *Life of Locke*, II, 133–9.) But, given the

of religious assurance repeatedly seeps into the results of the rational demonstrations. The voluntarism and the rationalism remain very intimately linked throughout Locke's later intellectual life. But there can be no doubt that they were 'yoked by violence together' and that the yoke which kept them together was a religious faith rather than an achieved philosophical position.[1]

It is not necessary to develop this analysis further here, but two incidental points need additional emphasis. Although it is true that Locke held a broadly hedonistic theory of the will from 1676 on and that this led him to analyse human obligation as the rationally calculated maximization of individual utility, it is essential to note that he believed that rational men would spend a considerable portion of their time contemplating the rewards and punishments of a future state. It is true that he analyses the obligations to temperance or charity as instances of prudently delayed gratification, investments made in search of greater eventual profits. Indeed he seems even to imply at one point that the *only* way in which children can be trained not to be greedy and hoard their possessions is by bribing them heavily to be 'generous', providing them, that is, with heavy short-term profits in return for their elicited 'liberality'.[2] But, except in the artificial and insulated

existence of a God, inferred from human self-consciousness (MS Locke c 24, p. 163; MS Locke c 28, fo. 120v; *Essay*, IV, III, §27), 'the most obvious truth that reason discovers', its evidence 'equal to mathematical certainty' (*Essay*, IV, X, §1), very energetic inferences about his attributes then appear to become legitimate in Locke's eyes. (See *Essay*, IV, III, §18; MS Locke f 3, pp. 201–2; *Two Treatises*, II, §6, etc.)

[1] Locke's religious rationalism took some of its assurance and some of its vocabulary from the writings of the Cambridge Platonists. (See conveniently for presentations of some of their major positions, John Passmore, *Ralph Cudworth. An Interpretation* (Cambridge, 1951) and Ernst Cassirer, *The Platonic Renaissance in England*, trans. James P. Pettegrove (London, 1953).) Locke's religious ideas are discussed briefly in H. McLachlan, *The Religious Opinions of Milton, Locke and Newton* (Manchester, 1941), and G. R. Cragg, *From Puritanism to the Age of Reason* (paperback edition, 1966), pp. 114–35. And there are helpful incidental observations in Lamprecht, Von Leyden, Viano, Polin and Abrams. But there has yet to be a serious synthetic study which re-examines Locke's intellectual life from the perspective of his religious concerns. It is an astonishing lacuna.

[2] '...let them find by experience, that the most liberal has always most plenty, with esteem and commendation to boot...' 'This should be encouraged by great commendation and credit, and constantly taking care, that he loses nothing by his liberality. Let all the instances he gives of such freeness be always repaid, and with interest; and let him sensibly perceive, that the kindness he shews to others is no ill husbandry for himself; but that it brings a return for kindness, both from those

process of child-rearing, the profits of virtue are not only exceedingly long-term, they are mostly not of this world.[1] The utility which is advocated is not the utility of terrestrial sensual gratification or the long-term rewards of capital accumulation, but the spiritual and eventually heavenly utility of labouring industriously in the calling. Locke did not regard this world as providing the possibility of an autonomously rewarding existence and he believed that a heady indulgence in its immediate pleasures was necessarily bought at the price of everlasting death.[2]

Although all men, or at least all adults who were not 'idiots', were rational and hence capable in principle of making these calculations correctly,[3] they were also all liable to sin, driven by their passions, and hence likely to misapprehend the prudential obligations to which they were subject. Some men were more sinful than others, more lethargic in seeking to discern their moral obligations and more readily enticed by their corrupt passions. Hence Locke does accept the reality of differential rationality. But the differential is not a class differential nor a purely intellectual differential, but rather a moral differential. If Locke's title to revolution is not such as to make it quite a Revolution of the Saints, it does make it a revolution of the good, or, more accurately, of men acting well.[4] The transposition unfortunately transforms Seliger's analysis from interesting support for Locke's theory of class differentials in rationality to the near tautology that for a revolution to be made appropriately it must be made by men who are promoting revolution at a time at which it is appropriate to do so. It is not the rationality of the individuals, presumably a dispositional characteristic, but the rightness of their

that receive it, and those who look on' (*Some Thoughts concerning Education*, *Works*, IV, 64–5).

[1] 'The portion of the righteous has been in all ages taken notice of, to be pretty scanty in this world' (*Reasonableness*, *Works*, III, 93).

[2] See below, chapter 18.

[3] But cf.: 'You may as soon hope to have all the day-labourers and tradesmen, the spinsters and dairy-maids, perfect mathematicians, as to have them perfect in ethicks this way' (*Reasonableness*, III, 91). This is because they not only lack leisure but also 'capacity in demonstration'. The latter sounds embarrassingly like a genetic deficiency.

[4] Cf. Seliger, 'Locke's Natural Law and the Foundation of Politics', *Journal of the History of Ideas*, XXIV, 3 (July-September 1963), 337–54, and 'Locke's Theory of Revolutionary Action', *Western Political Quarterly*, XVI, 3 (September 1963), 548–68.

actions which determines the status of the revolution—and this latter observation is scarcely analytically revealing.

The existence of differential rationality does, however, make more intelligible Locke's vacillations over strategies for convincing others, his hesitation between academic and propagandist expositions of his ideas. To appeal to the 'industrious and rational' all that is necessary is to expound the truth coherently, and natural revelation can be trusted to complete the task. But if you wish to convince the lazy and licentious some more immediate and aggressive purchase over their minds is required to achieve this. All moral errors are implicitly misapprehensions about the moral truth as well as imprudent items of behaviour. All men inherit a moral vocabulary and are trained in a set of moral notions which embody misapprehensions of the moral truth generated by the laziness and viciousness of their forebears. It is a logically necessary condition for full knowledge of the moral truth that a man be able to give a coherent account of its basis and content in a language of fixed denotation. All men are educated in historical societies and are thus trained in particular moral errors merely by learning their duties in the language of their society.[1] Those who are prepared to think hard and carefully can dissolve the mystifications transferred to them in this way. But the 'idle and licentious' being disinclined to think their way through any set of ideas for themselves can only be brought to obedience to their duties by much more readily intelligible sanctions. The promise of a demonstrative morality is a promise of clarity and assurance in moral knowledge, but it is a promise which only the industrious and rational have the moral stamina to take up. The idle and licentious need a cruder clarity and a more intrusive assurance. For those with limited moral talents, *Principia Ethica* was as pointless a substitute for a catechism book as *Principia Mathematica* would be to the mathematically incompetent for a calculating machine.[2] Furthermore, only the simplest and

[1] Cf. II, XXII, §7, and II, XVIII, §§10–12 (but N.B. the stress, §12, that 'even in the corruption of manners, the true boundaries of the law of nature, which ought to be the rule of virtue and vice, were pretty well preserved'). And for the psychology which lies behind this interpretation see *Some Thoughts concerning Education*, *Works*, IV, 92, §146; *Two Treatises*, I, §58, etc. See in general 'Of Ethick in General', King, *Life of Locke*, II, 122–30 (MS Locke c 28, pp. 146–52), esp. 125–6.

[2] Cf. *Reasonableness*, *Works*, III, 91 (quoted above, p. 196, n. 3).

clearest exposition of the content of duties would be at all likely to influence these morally shiftless figures to emend their conduct. It is thus correct to see the practical intentions of the *Essay* and the *Reasonableness* as convergent, the analysis of the nature of moral knowledge and the provision of effective opportunity to live according to this knowledge. A similar balance will be found elsewhere in Locke's works in his insistence on the formal proprieties of debate and the definition of terms[1] coupled with crude polemical manoeuvres against his intellectual adversaries. Where Locke is attacking the argument of another and this man fails to define his terms and uses them ambiguously, this indicates his corrupt confusion. But if the same man misinterprets what Locke himself meant in making some claim (even when Locke had scarcely defined his terms at all), the assailant exhibits his own bad faith. The moral duty to eschew laziness in regulating one's assent readily becomes the moral duty to agree with Locke. The *Two Treatises*, like his other polemical works, is an argument developed from the core of theoretical confidence which he had attempted to define in the *Essay*. Its exposition of why the political theory of absolutism, in its Filmerian form above all, is morally mistaken is premised on the ambition of the *Essay*, though its phrasing may occasionally diverge from the canons set out in that work.[2] But the ambition on which it was premised was one which, as we have seen, was never achieved. And if we read the achievement of the *Essay* with the eyes of nineteenth-century historians of philosophy, its splendid contribution to the great line of English empiricism,[3]

[1] On the degree of verbal self-consciousness appropriate to different human activities see *Essay*, III, IX, esp. §§3, 15; III, XI, §§9, 10. There is no reason to suppose that Locke would have considered any of his works as samples of 'vulgar discourses', such as those of 'merchants and lovers, cooks and tailors'. Laslett's correction of Strauss is clearly apt (see *Two Treatises*, Introduction, p. 85n., and cf. Strauss, *Natural Right and History*, pp. 220–1). For Locke's insistence on the intellectual propriety of his own manoeuvres and the impropriety of those of his opponents, particularly from the point of view of verbal accuracy, see, for example, *Two Treatises*, Preface, ll. 23–6; I, §6, ll. 14–23, §7, ll. 1–10, §11, 2–12, §12, §16, ll. 8–11, 17–18, 25–8, §17, ll. 1–5, §19, l. 1, §20 (esp.), §21, ll. 2–4, §22, ll. 3–5, etc. And see the notes on William Sherlock's *The Case of Allegiance*, MS Locke c 28, pp. 83–96, esp. the headings, 'Termes', 'Mistakes', 'Self-contraditions', 'Jargon', 'Positions', 'Propositions', etc.

[2] Cf. *Two Treatises*, II, §11, l. 31 with *Essay*, I, III, *passim*.

[3] Or even perhaps with more modern interpreters of the tradition: cf. Robert L. Armstrong, 'John Locke's Doctrine of Signs', *Journal of the History of Ideas*, XXVI,

and then continue to attribute this to Locke as his own ambition, then it does become extremely difficult to elicit the form of the *Two Treatises* from *this* as a premise.[1] It is certainly obscure just what sort of political theory it is appropriate to expect to 'follow' from the *Essay concerning Human Understanding*. But there have been widely held interpretations of the meaning of the *Essay*, mostly extrapolations from the notion of the *tabula rasa*, with which the *Two Treatises* are scarcely even compatible. In the perspective which it has here been attempted to recapture, the relationship of the two works may seem less surprising.

3 (July-September 1965), 369–82: 'Berkeley's metaphysics then, may be regarded as a development of an idea suggested by Locke. Or we may regard Locke's theory as an anticipation of Berkeley's metaphysics' (p. 382).

[1] This seems to be the allegation which Laslett is concerned to counter with his distinction between a 'Lockeian attitude' and a 'Lockeian philosophy', *Two Treatises*, Introduction, pp. 79–91. Perhaps the distinction between a philosophy (a closed deductive system) and a 'work of policy' which Laslett here maintains is not the most helpful contrast for bringing out the distinctive features of the book. The notion of philosophy as necessarily a closed system seems to take the intention of the philosopher as a statement of his achievement. Equally, the *Two Treatises* does appear to be a work about the nature and limits of political rights, rather than a work of advice on how men should behave. It does not appear very like the works of the *raison d'état* tradition. Locke was certainly interested in this genre of writing but that scarcely makes the *Two Treatises* into an example of the genre.

PART IV

15

THE COHERENCE OF A MIND 1

Some men are shrewd guessers, and others would be thought to be so: but he must be carried far by his forward inclination, who does not take notice, that the world is apt to think him a diviner, for any thing rather than for the sake of truth, who sets up his own suspicions against the direct evidence of things; and pretends to know other mens thoughts and reasons, better than they themselves.

John Locke (*A Vindication of the Reasonableness of Christianity from Mr Edwards' Reflections*, *Works* (1768), III, 107)

There are always a number of different historical arcs on which it is appropriate to place any complex intellectual performance in the effort to disclose its 'meaning'. The choice of the appropriate arc is neither a simple nor an arbitrary matter but it plainly does depend to a considerable extent on the purposes of the historian. The set of possible contexts which would be needed to exhibit the full meaning of Locke's intellectual life is so vast that there is no significant possibility that anyone will ever be competent to grasp them all and, should such a paragon of learning and imagination exist, it is a little difficult to believe that he would choose to devote his talents to the elucidation of the intellectual achievement of John Locke. The histories of theology and epistemology, of ethics and scriptural analysis, of psychology and political theory, of economics and medicine, of liberal constitutionalism, the spirit of capitalism, comparative anthropology[1] and English toilet-training,[2] education and the decline of the West[3]—the list

[1] *Two Treatises of Government*, Introduction, p. 98n.

[2] *Some Thoughts concerning Education*, *Works*, IV, 12–14, §§23–8. The advice did not go unheeded. See, for example, *Boswell in Holland*, *1763–64*, ed. Frederick A. Pottle (London, 1962): 'Tuesday 11 October. From this day follow Mr. Locke's prescription of going to stool every day regularly after breakfast' (p. 43).

[3] See, for example, W. B. Yeats: 'Locke sank into a swoon; / The Garden died; / God took the spinning-jenny / Out of his side' (*The Collected Poems* (New York, 1956), p. 211). The tradition was given its fiercest imprint by reactionaries and Utopian radicals at the time of the French Revolution. See esp. William Blake (*The Complete Writings of William Blake*, ed. Geoffrey Keynes (London, 1966), pp. 246, 385, 476–7, 483 533, 661, 685, 702, 708, 772).

is certainly distressingly lengthy and all of the items cast some light on the nature of the Lockean achievement, or at least of the Lockean ambition. It might seem that the problem would be drastically simplified by confining attention to a single work, as in this case to the *Two Treatises*. But a case of sorts has been or could be made for the crucial place of any of these developments in assessing the meaning of the book.

Since the book appears in the history of political thought in two separable, if not separate, guises, as a classic document in the ideological self-realization of constitutionalist politics and as 'the classical expression of bourgeois society's ideas of right as against feudal society',[1] a certain polarization of interpretative attention is scarcely remarkable. The basis for the 'liberal' interpretation of Locke has been provided by the creation of a predictable legal order and the physical security which goes with this, and the central role of popular approval in contriving this notable human achievement ('government by consent'), the constitutionalist theme.[2] The mildly fortuitous relationship of the book to the American Revolution has confirmed its status from this perspective. To those who have seen its main significance in its discussion of property, the moral rationalization of an effective structure of exploitation, its flavour is correspondingly more acrid.[3] Where the key to the book is believed to be its advocacy of constitutionalist politics, the tone in which it is discussed is usually fairly disengaged emotionally and the focus of the discussion is often narrow. But those who emphasize the centrality of property rights are inclined to see in it the reflection of a more comprehensive vision, a new metaphysical conception of the place of man in the world, appropriate to the new bourgeois order. There is much plausibility to this expectation; a sturdy confrontation of the moral challenge of property relations does demand a more profound and intimate grappling with the realities of most men's

[1] Karl Marx, *Theories of Surplus Value* (Moscow, n.d.), I, 356.

[2] See esp. J. W. Gough, *John Locke's Political Philosophy* (reprint, Oxford, 1956), and from a different viewpoint W. Kendall, *John Locke and the Doctrine of Majority-rule* (2nd edition, Urbana, Ill., 1959). It is accepted broadly by Cranston, Polin and Viano, in so far as they take a position on the issue.

[3] See esp. C. B. Macpherson, *The Political Theory of Possessive Individualism* (Oxford, 1962), and his analysis of the interpretative situation, pp. 194–7. See also Leo Strauss, *Natural Right and History* (Chicago, 1953), pp. 202–51.

existence than one can well imagine to be generated by the sanctification of a few genteel political pieties. The Marxist and Straussian pictures of Locke do at least see him as having the courage, tempered though it may have been in public pretty thoroughly by the better part of valour, of his own filthy morality. Their firm assurance as to what was historically significant lends him at any rate the dramaturgical glory of appearing as protagonist of one of the great forces in the historical process. There may be a certain cardboard quality to the representation, but the accusation that a man reduces rationality to appropriation concedes him the status of a *persona*, if not perhaps quite that of a person. It is hard, in contrast, for the traditional liberal reading to present him on the basis of the resources of the text alone as much more than the pedlar of a few tired and jejune political nostrums, a very Polonius of the theory of politics. The capitalist interpretation, too, whatever its general adequacy, does have a certain analytical force. It explains how a man could have cared to write such a book—though, perhaps, only a man one greatly disliked. It is difficult to see in contrast that the liberal reading offers much more than taxonomic facilities; it merely tells you what chapter in your history of political thought to put the man in.

The liberal claim that the central meaning of the book lies in a specifically political doctrine can be interpreted in two ways. One might claim that Locke, a great philosopher, had the capacity and inclination to write a work of political theory and just *happened* to choose the Exclusion crisis as the occasion for its composition and the Glorious Revolution as the occasion for its publication. Alternatively it might be seen as a political doctrine in which (given the book's inordinate length) one must suppose Locke to have believed but which he took the trouble to write out at such length to sanction two particular political projects. If one reads it in this way, one must take the purpose of the book to be in these situations at least, if perhaps only *faute de mieux*, the consecration of the political purposes of the Whig political élite. And from this perception it is simple, if hardly legitimate, to proceed to the conclusion that the historical meaning of the book is that it 'expressed' the political ideology of the Whig oligarchy.[1] One might

[1] See, e.g., Harold J. Laski, *The Rise of European Liberalism* (London, 1962), pp. 77, etc.

even use the contaminating quality of the second interpretation as an explanation of the inadequacies of the doctrine in terms of the criteria appropriate to the first: Locke tried to be a political philosopher, but failed deservedly.

By contrast the Marxist interpretation, while fully recognizing the political reference of the work, sees the meaning of its political doctrines as a logical consequence of the more profound economic and social values to which its author was committed.[1] This interpretation too is in some measure equivocal. It might be a re-interpretation of the nature of the political commitment itself rather than a re-interpretation of the relationship between Locke's ethical and social values and the political commitment. One might wish to assert the priority of the social and economic values over the purely political because one wished to insist for moral reasons on the greater human significance of an order of systematic social repression as against a set of decorously presented juristic niceties. Locke's politics, it is alleged, may *sound* like a respectable defence of the rule of law but what they should really be *understood* to be about is whipping vagrants. And this simply because in the England of the late seventeenth century it was in the name of legality, stability, and security that such draconic penalties were imposed. Vagrant-whipping was the essence of the law which ruled. All this might be true, and if true would clearly be sharply significant for an assessment of the character of the political theory contained in the book, without in any way altering the interpretation of the relationship between the political group on whose behalf Locke wrote it and the content of the book itself. It merely transposes this group from its political role in the development of the English constitution, the growth of freedom under law, to its social role in the consolidation of the new economic order, the intermittent burning of vagrants through the gristle of their ears.[2]

But there is a perhaps more interesting possibility which would stress how far the Shaftesbury entourage and the Lords of the

[1] Cf. Macpherson, *Possessive Individualism*, p. 196.

[2] Cf. Michael Walzer, *The Revolution of the Saints* (London, 1966), p. 227. For Macpherson's emphasis on Locke's attitude to the idle poor see *Possessive Individualism*, pp. 222–6, and cf. H. R. Fox Bourne, *The Life of John Locke* (London, 1876), II, 377–91.

Convention were in fact *faute de mieux* as political embodiments of Locke's social doctrine. For if Locke's social doctrine *was*, as Marx put it, 'the classical expression of bourgeois society's ideas of right as against feudal society', he had perhaps chosen mildly refractory figures for its political protagonists on the two occasions. It would have been odd, should one accept the aptness of this description, if Locke did not at times sense a sharp tension between the demands of his social and economic doctrine and the performance of its political representatives. The doctrine indeed could in this perspective become a critical theory of some power, not the moralization of an already fully existing series of economic and social relationships but the moral manifesto of an as yet only incipient order and, consequently, an indictment of much of the society contemporary with its composition. This restores to it a degree of intellectual integrity and autonomy but it does so at the price of removing some of its intelligibility as a human action. There is a simple transparency to the notion of a man providing an ideological sanction for an existing social régime which cannot be extended to that of a man writing a charter for a social régime which had never been fully realized anywhere. It is precisely the gain in attributed intellectual integrity which causes the loss in intelligibility. The ascription of an autonomous intellectual purpose requires, if it is to be intelligible, the indication of what resources in the writer's social experience could make it possible to conceive such a purpose. Precisely the same problem arises over the first interpretation of Locke's theory considered above, that it was an autonomous philosophical exposition of the great truths of liberal constitutionalism and, precisely because it was such, it was appropriate to note gently those occasions on which it fails to rise to the heights of our own surpassing insights.[1] Indeed in this case the explanatory problem becomes a little oppressive: what in God's name *would* Locke have been up to, wrestling away to sanction Professor Plamenatz's political prejudices? But even in the case of the proclamation of the coming bourgeois order the difficulty persists. This may well be the significance of Locke's writings for us but it can hardly be an

[1] Cf., for example, John Plamenatz, *Consent, Freedom and Political Obligation* (Oxford, 1938), pp. 7–8.

adequate causal account of how he himself came to conceive his theme.

There is a genuine dilemma here and it is one which goes far to explain the rather dialectical progress of studies of the major political theorists, Plato, Hobbes, Locke, even Marx. To present a complex argument from the past in terms of its significance for us may often seem mendacious and to present it with the greatest concern for historical specificity but without exploring its 'significance' is likely to seem trivial. Its description as an individual historical act and its description as a philosophical argument jostle uneasily against one another. The appropriate form of analysis tends to be more simply a function of what has been said most recently by other analysts and of the sympathies of the present analyst than it is a function of the contours of the work itself. The polar antithesis between the two styles lies between the determination to use the philosophical work to illuminate social history and the determination to use social history only (if indeed at all) to illuminate the philosophical work. Clearly both strategies are legitimate in principle. I have indeed argued elsewhere[1] that however casually one of the two may be performed on any occasion, they are in fact not alternatives to one another but logically indispensable complements. Every philosophical argument is a moment in social history but it is also *ex hypothesi* a philosophical argument. The tension between the ambitions of identifying each of these is severe and it is not surprising that both historians and philosophers should be irked by the claim that until historians become philosophers or philosophers become historians, these matters will remain confused.

The question which needs elucidation here is just how it is appropriate to use a work of complex intellection to illuminate social history. And here the central notion is surely 'illumination' and the notion which is to be contrasted with it and against which it is necessary to exercise some little vigilance is that of 'reflection' or 'repetition'. For this latter notion is exceedingly easy to turn into a crude tautology. If one alleges that an intellectual performance mirrors the social structure of a society, it is simple to take the conception of the social structure at a crude level, identify

[1] 'The Identity of the History of Ideas', *Philosophy* (April 1968), pp. 85–104.

a similarly crude structure in the argument of the work and allege a causal or perhaps merely functional relationship. But what this indicates is not that the particular instances of the causal relationship or the general sociological theory are confirmed (though, if made sufficiently crude, they might occasionally be falsified) but merely that if you clasp the telescope firmly to your eye and gaze fixedly at the flagstaff, you stand an excellent chance of seeing the signal. But the causal explanation of this may not be that a communication has been despatched but rather that you already know what the message must be. The dramaturgical metaphors bring out the danger here very well. The knowledge that the bourgeoisie are waiting in the wings readily gives way to the historical mirage of their already being on stage. If one knows that the seventeenth century was plagued by problems of labour discipline and that the rise of capitalist industry demands a new and effective form of labour discipline, it is simple to read all injunctions to 'industry' which one finds in that century as moral commitments to the strenuous task of generating the capitalist ethic. The danger of this is that it risks making all things new, and all things probably include many old things. If pursued consistently over time it may involve turning into moral champions for capitalism men who must be supposed to have had about as much sympathy for unlimited capitalist appropriation as Mao Tse-tung has.[1] There is always the prospect that the assimilation of dozens of instances of praise of industriousness, extricated from their contexts, to the rise of the new capitalist ethic of work may reveal less about social change in seventeenth-century England than about the hallucinatory propensities of historians. In this guise intellectual history and in particular the study of great works of political philosophy may come to seem a deliciously sophisticated and spiritually inexpensive surrogate for doing social history.

One may wonder too whether conducting the inquiry in this manner does not, in addition to generating historically dubious conclusions, rather deftly ablate the conceptual point of entering upon the inquiry in the first place. For, if we already know the

[1] The most startling example of this transformation is perhaps the *embourgeoisement* of Thomas More. Cf. J. H. Hexter's brilliant commentary in, *Utopia*, *The Complete Works of St. Thomas More*, ed. E. Surtz and J. H. Hexter (New Haven, 1965) IV, l–lvii.

social history anyway, it is not clear what is gained simply by noting that Locke can be kneaded into assenting to the truth of what we already know. It seems that not only is the method of inference exceedingly perilous but little further insight is provided by the attempt to infer at all. The urge to produce a neatly and conclusively tied and packaged demonstration is inimical to the whole enterprise of learning from the character of the connection. For it is precisely what eludes such neat *a priori* categorization that enables us to extend our comprehension both of the intellectual project and of the social matrix out of which this emerged. It is only the fullest recognition of the particularity, emotional ambivalence and conceptual disorganization of the intellectual project which will disclose its full explanatory potential and will clarify just why a man should have come to think in this way. From the intersections between these accounts of the thinking of individuals, it becomes possible to distinguish sociology from psychology and indeed from conceptual analysis. Only when this distinction has been made does it become possible to employ complex intellectual performances as a clue to the elucidation of a social structure. Even here they are potentially as misleading as they are revealing except in one crucial respect. Where what is to be analysed is specifically the changes in a social structure and what is puzzling is how men conceived of the transitory stage, the conceptual definition and explicitness characteristic of such works can disclose the unravelling of logical relationships between concepts[1] in a way that no other type of evidence could possibly do. Where what one is attempting to investigate is the rational working out of a way of life in a conceptual[2] rather than a banausic[3] sense, it is to the effort of conceptual analysis that it is appropriate to attend. It is not, then, in any way absurd to look in a slightly Weberian mood at the writings of Locke in an effort to discern the birth of a role, the authentic spirit of capitalism, even if one may feel that the misdescription of its features at the

[1] Cf. Alasdair MacIntyre's analysis of Weber's argument in *The Protestant Ethic and the Spirit of Capitalism*, 'A Mistake about Causality in Social Science', *Philosophy, Politics and Society*, ed. P. Laslett and W. G. Runciman, 2nd series (Oxford, 1962), pp. 48–70.

[2] He is working out the problem.

[3] He is working out his own salvation.

point of its nativity has led so far to some misunderstanding of the circumstances of its conception.

Our concern here, however, is not in the first place with how Locke's work can be used to elucidate the genetics of the spirit of capitalism, but with how Locke himself could have come to be possessed by this particular familiar. It is at this point that the resources of the Marxist interpretation are most parsimonious. The liberal interpretation, if it does not explain anything, records accurately that Locke defended political liberty, religious toleration, the right to the fruits of one's labours and the liberty of the press. The Marxist interpretation explains why a man with these demure values should be prepared to contemplate unlimited capitalist appropriation and the whipping of beggars, by noting that these legalistic benefactions were prerequisites for the populace to be given a sufficient length of rope to get its head firmly into the noose of the new capitalist order. There is a clear explanatory gain here. But it does not disclose why *Locke* should have chosen to cast himself as the ideological hangman of the new régime. One plausible biographical explanation has been given. It is that Locke derived his insight into the nature of capitalism from the view from Thanet House and his sympathy for its aspirations from his experience of the ebullient emotional commitment to it of the Shaftesbury family. This is certainly an advance on the notion that it might have been his own position in the relations of production which lent him such insight. The minor absentee landlord, the stockholder in the slave-trading Royal Africa Company, the beneficiary of an annuity arranged in reward for his equivocal personal services to an 'ambitious Grandee'[1]—Locke's own roles in the economy would hardly in themselves have been sufficient to drive him to base property on 'the labour of a man's body and the work of his hands'. I have suggested elsewhere—and the absence of any sustained treatment of the problem earlier or later in his work tends to confirm this—that what in fact drove him to these straits was a polemical crux inflicted upon him by Filmer. But it is certainly persuasive to see this as the occasion of his using the notion at all, rather than the

[1] The phrase is Locke's own of 1693, though naturally not applied to his deceased master (MS Film. 77, p. 311).

cause of his embracing it with such enthusiasm and such retrospective smugness.[1] At the last point even the account of Locke as the perfectly heteronymous intellectual, hired brain of the Shaftesbury ménage, falters. He presumably drew no pay for remarking privately on the excellence of his own analysis of property. He may, of course, simply have succumbed to his own propaganda. But this imputation is perhaps closer to being an insult, or at least an incisive withdrawal of moral tolerance, than it is to being a causal explanation.

The materials for deriving a greater illumination on this issue can be found in a point noted for rather different purposes elsewhere by Macpherson, that Locke lived in a 'transitional' society.[2] Macpherson employs this notion to explain (record? excuse? remove the credit for?) the presence in Locke's arguments of remnants of traditional medieval social values, like the condemnation of covetousness.[3] The force of the explanation used in this way is chronological and not rational or Freudian. Locke wrote as he did because he made his entry before the Third Act (the Industrial Revolution or other prerequisite for the final triumph of capitalism), not because his own distinctive intellectual biography made him speak this way or caused him to forget his lines at that point.[4] But it suggests a possible explanation of a different type, a rationale of the transitional stage. This explanation has by

[1] See the famous letter to his cousin the Rev Richard King, 25 August 1703, on the appropriate reading for a young gentleman to understand 'the real interest of his country', where he notes that the young man will need to grasp 'true notions of laws in general; and property, the subject-matter about which laws are made', and comments, 'And property, I have no where found more clearly explained than in a book intitled, "Two Treatises of Government"' (*Works*, IV, 640).

[2] 'His confusion about the definition of property, sometimes including life and liberty and sometimes not, may be ascribed to the confusion in his mind between the remnant of traditional values and the new bourgeois values' (Macpherson, *Possessive Individualism*, p. 220). See also the controversy between Macpherson and Jacob Viner in the *Canadian Journal of Economics and Political Science*, XXIX, 4 (November 1963), 548–66.

[3] '...retaining in some measure the traditional moral principles' (*Possessive Individualism*, p. 237).

[4] It is worth noting that when a Marxist philosopher is attempting to provide an account of the thought of *Marx* at a particular point in time, the vulgar Marxist teleological framework provokes the most bitter response from him simply because it turns any question about the structure of Marx's thought into a question about how far through the plot he had got on a given date. (When did he reach the final Act, 1844, 1846, 1848?) See, brilliantly, Louis Althusser, *Pour Marx* (Paris, 1966), pp. 51–8.

now become more than a little shop-soiled by its touted appearance as a Humean necessary condition for the emergence of capitalism.[1] But however infelicitously conceived at times in the past, the Protestant ethic retains an explanatory potential at the level of individual rationality. I propose to demonstrate this in two stages. First, I shall take the most effective Marxist reading of the work, that of Professor Macpherson, note a number of inferences which he feels able to make on the basis of the text, compare these with Locke's explicit opinions on these issues stated elsewhere, and demonstrate that, while Locke's statements cannot be rendered coherent inside Macpherson's reading, they make a simple enough sense in terms of the doctrine of the calling. Secondly, I shall present Locke's own social theory as an exploration of this Puritan doctrine and its social meaning, once the social framework of the theocratic community has been removed. In conclusion I shall attempt a biographical sketch of how this nexus of ideas could have come to seem cogent to Locke and of the meaning which it conferred on his life.

[1] The Weber thesis was read this way most of the time by Max Weber himself and it has certainly been so interpreted by subsequent sociologists and historians. Cf. MacIntyre, 'A Mistake about Causality', *Philosophy, Politics and Society*.

16

THE COHERENCE OF A MIND 2

Macpherson's analysis of Locke's discussion of property sees its key intention as the removal of the sufficiency limitation on private accumulation and the consequent sanctioning of unlimited appropriation.[1] At the individual level the effect of this is to make property a pure private right, excised from the context of social responsibility implied by the medieval understanding of the duty of charity.[2] It reduces rationality to appropriation[3] and sets out as the apt project for each individual life an endless traverse of accumulation directed not to consumption, ease, or happiness but to its own relentless perpetuation.[4] The poor are consigned to a convenient ignorance,[5] made palatable by their compulsive credulity in the Christian faith,[6] and the ends of the rich are embellished by their proclaimed superior rationality. In the internal politics of the country the propertyless are expelled from the political community and turned into a vast labour gang under the discipline of the rich and bereft of any protection against the most

[1] C. B. Macpherson, *The Political Theory of Possessive Individualism* (Oxford, 1962), pp. 203–21, 235–6, etc. esp. 'any property right less than this would have been useless to Locke' (p. 219); 'In short, Locke has done what he set out to do. Starting from the traditional assumption...he has turned the table on all who derived from this assumption theories which were restrictive of capitalist appropriation. He has erased the moral disability with which unlimited capitalist appropriation had hitherto been handicapped....He also justifies, as natural, a class differential in rights and rationality, and by doing so provide a positive moral basis for capitalist society' (p. 221).

[2] 'The traditional view that property and labour were social functions, and that ownership of property involved social obligations, is thereby undermined' (*ibid.* p. 221). Cf. Leo Strauss, *Natural Right and History* (Chicago, 1953), p. 243 ('Unlimited appropriation without concern for the need of others is true charity') and *ibid.* pp. 247–8. I have commented at length on the relationship between justice and charity in Locke's ethics and on the misconstruction of this in Macpherson and Strauss's writings in an article 'Justice and the Interpretation of Locke's Political Thought', *Political Studies* (February 1968).

[3] 'Locke's denunciation of covetousness is a consequence, not a contradiction, of his assumption that unlimited accumulation is the essence of rationality' (Macpherson, *Possessive Individualism*, p. 237); and, generally, see *ibid.* pp. 221–38.

[4] *Ibid.* pp. 204–5, 207.

[5] *Ibid.* pp. 221–38.

[6] *Ibid.* pp. 224–6.

brutal exploitation except for the obligation of the replete not to permit human beings actually to starve to death.[1] In foreign politics, its effect is to consign the political community to a career of self-conscious and unceasing territorial expansion and population growth in the classic mercantilist tradition,[2] in the effort to protect national security, as Cox urges,[3] and to maximize accumulation, as Macpherson himself prefers to emphasize.[4] The doctrine which Macpherson thus reveals in the depths of Locke's thought[5] is a moral charter for capitalism every bit as brutal as any that Marx alleged and its occasional verbal tremors of disquiet are to be read as merely faint historical after-images, or conceived as traces left floating in the moral language after the vision which gave them meaning has faded away.[6]

My whole treatment of Locke's work so far has been designed to suggest the oddity of such an account[7] as a summary of Locke's intentions in writing the work as a whole. But despite occasional waverings in the phrasing it seems unlikely that Macpherson's purpose was simply to analyse Locke's intentions in writing the work.[8] Clearly, too, it is in no way illegitimate for a commentator to feel a very far-reaching lack of interest in Locke's enterprise in writing most of the book. There is no reason why Macpherson should not ignore Locke's performance over most of the course and instead concentrate severely on how he takes the most taxing hurdles on it. As a treatment of some of these issues Macpherson's account is extremely penetrating.[9] But it suffers from a misleading identification of just what these issues are for *Locke*. To Locke they are a matter of how to combine a doctrine of a basis for property right which is not reducible to positive law and

[1] *Ibid.* pp. 225–9, 247–51, cf. Strauss, *Natural Right and History*, p. 248.

[2] Macpherson, *Possessive Individualism*, pp. 207, 228–9.

[3] Richard H. Cox, *Locke on War and Peace* (Oxford, 1960), pp. 136–54, esp. pp 149–54.

[4] Macpherson, *Possessive Individualism*, pp. 207, 256–7.

[5] Cf.: 'But to say that Locke had to show a natural individual right to possessions or estate *is not to see very far into* what he was doing in the chapter, "Of Property"' (*ibid.*, p. 198, my italics).

[6] *Ibid.* pp. 220, 237, etc.

[7] The superiority of Macpherson's account is held by him to reside in its capacity to solve a pair of what I trust I have shown to be pseudo-problems. Cf. *ibid.* pp. 196–7 with chapters 9 and 14 above.

[8] But cf. Macpherson, *Possessive Individualism*, pp. 219–21.

[9] The section, 'The Theory of Property Right', *ibid.* pp. 197–221, is probably the most brilliant piece of analysis of any part of Locke's text yet produced.

a substantive doctrine which protects instances of property held under positive law against the arbitrary encroachments of political authorities. Macpherson takes Locke's exposition of the development of differential property rights as the theoretical link unifying these two enterprises. In doing so he perhaps succumbs to some extent to an illusion generated by perspective, an effect of conceptual foreshortening. Seeing so clearly the challenge which confronts Locke, he implicitly attributes to Locke himself a comparable clarity of vision and in consequence sees the latter rising to meet a challenge which there is no evidence that he ever sensed in this form. There is every reason to believe that Locke supposed that a man in a non-political situation had a right to the whole produce of his labour or to the price which it would bring on a market. There is every reason to suppose that he believed that the relations of capitalist production and monetary exchange provided the basis for the emergence of vast but altogether just differentials in the ownership of property. There is also every reason to suppose that he wished to commend constitutional guarantees for the security of property held under English law. But there is no sufficient reason to suppose that he wished to claim an individual natural-law sanction for all or even for most instances of property held under English law.[1] Nor is there any reason to suppose that he believed the life of unlimited capitalist appropriation to exemplify a greater level of moral rationality than the life of the devout peasant. It is essential to recollect the challenge which the property rights which he wished to defend were *in fact* undergoing. The spectre which haunted the English property-owner in 1680 or between 1685 and 1688 was the threat of non-parliamentary taxation and the confiscation of freeholds in order to consolidate executive authority. It was not a determined policy of redistributive social justice. Macpherson in a sense in this context does Locke too much intellectual honour in foisting upon him such an intractable moral assignment. In doing so he fails to recapture the shifty and devious strategy which Locke in fact pursued at this point.

I have commented elsewhere on the misleading character of

[1] Cf. 'the Phansies and intricate Contrivances of Men, following contrary and hidden interests put into Words... truly are a great part of the *Municipal Laws* of Countries' (*Two Treatises of Government*, II, §12, ll. 14–17).

Macpherson's analysis of the relation of Locke's notions of property right to the social responsibilities of the rich. In this matter the researches of Professor Jordan and the analysis of Mr Hill[1] have surely shown that whatever the mutations which notions of bourgeois property right were to undergo in later centuries, they certainly did not lead to the *disappearance* of the eleemosynary duty of charity in seventeenth-century England. It is apt enough to note that Locke makes property a pure private right, but that in no way impairs the social responsibilities which emanate from it. The individualization of the right is matched symmetrically by an individualization of the duty. It is theoretically illegitimate—and it has in fact been substantively misleading—to attempt to extrapolate from the *Two Treatises* a casuistry of the private economic life, either in the sphere of production or in that of the disposition of wealth. Locke's attitude to 'capitalist appropriation' as such was in some ways extravagantly permissive. The claim that the just price was the market price in actual markets is as bland an approbation as could well be contrived.[2] In other ways it was exceedingly restrictive. Such a balance should not be surprising. Puritan ethics was overwhelmingly an ethics of intention rather than one of taboo. It was not a precise set of behavioural rules which was imposed on individual Christians, but the duty of endless aspiration. Unlimited capitalist appropriation and intensive agricultural labour were equally apt vessels for this aspiration. It was not *what* was done (unless this directly damaged other people) but *why* it was done which mattered. But this did not mean that the two roles were equally likely in practice to elicit a reliable supply of the appropriate emotions. And here Macpherson's construction of differential rationality has surely led him astray.[3] So far from the rich being rational and the poor merely amoral beasts, in Locke's eyes the rich are mostly corrupt and those who are virtuous are likely to stay poor.[4]

[1] See esp. W. K. Jordan, *Philanthropy in England, 1480–1660* (London, 1959), and Christopher Hill, *Society and Puritanism in Pre-Revolutionary England* (London, 1964), pp. 264–97.

[2] See the note Venditio of 1695, MS Film. 77, pp. 268–9 (printed in Dunn, 'Justice and the Interpretation of Locke's Political Thought', *Political Studies*, February 1968).

[3] Macpherson, *Possessive Individualism*, pp. 222–47.

[4] See below, chapter 18, and *The Reasonableness of Christianity*, *Works* III: 'The portion of the righteous has been in all ages taken notice of, to be pretty scanty in

The location of the tension implied here between Locke's theory and Macpherson's construction out of it may be identified more accurately by taking a number of Locke's treatments of labour and exploring their implications. There are several different contexts in his writings in which he comments on the part played by labour in human existence, the essay on recreation written for his friend Denis Grenville in 1677, his analysis of the relationship of knowledge to the ends of human existence in the same year, the note on labour which he wrote in 1693, the discussion of cognitive effort as a duty in the *Conduct of the Understanding*, as well as the celebrated fifth chapter of the *Second Treatise*.[1] The last two in time of the discussions are slightly more pietistic in flavour and the note on labour of 1693 is both more Utopian and more obsessively concerned with physical health than the others but there is a simple and stolid continuity from first to last. What defines human life is a set of duties and the right to promote happiness in any way compatible with these duties. It is a mistake to see man's right to promote his happiness, wide though it may be,[2] as having a priority over his duty.[3] Indeed the scope of this right is defined by the limits of its compatibility with 'our main duty which is in sincerity to do our duties in our calling as far as the frailty of our bodies or minds will allow us'.[4] So far from the right of self-preservation being a sufficient basis for the derivation of the content of this duty, 'an Hobbist with his principle of self-preservation whereof him self is to be judge, will not easily admit

this world. Virtue and prosperity do not often accompany one another; and therefore virtue seldom had many followers' (p. 93).

[1] 'An Essay concerning Recreation, in answer to D. G.'s desire', MS Locke f 3 (1677), pp. 351–7 (printed in Peter King, *The Life of John Locke* (London, 1830), II, 165–9). Cf. the piece 'Study', MS Locke f 2, pp. 87–140 (March-May 1677), *ibid.* I, 171–200. *An Early Draft of Locke's Essay*, ed. R. I. Aaron and Jocelyn Gibb, pp. 84–90 (8 February 1677). 'Labour', MS Film. 77, pp. 310–11. *Some Thoughts on the Conduct of the Understanding in the search of Truth*, *Works*, IV, 153–5. (See also by inference in the *Essay concerning Human Understanding*, *passim*.) *Two Treatises*, II, v. See also *Reasonableness*, *Works*, III, 5. MS Locke c 28 'Morality', p. 139, 'Homo ante et post lapsum', fo. 113v, etc.

[2] 'there is the liberty of great choice, great variety, within the bounds of innocence' (MS Locke f 3, 353, printed in King, *Life of Locke*, II, 166). Cf. *Two Treatises*, II, §128, ll. 1–2.

[3] 'Recreations supposes labour and weariness and therefore that he that labours not hath no title to it' (MS Locke f 3, 353–4, printed in King, *Life of Locke*, II, 167).

[4] MS Locke f 3, pp. 354–5 (King, *Life of Locke*, II, 167).

a great many plain duties of morality'.[1] And so far from terrestrial utility providing an adequate rule of life under all circumstances, it cannot even generate happiness on earth,[2] let alone in the world to come. If, as Strauss and his followers insist, Locke was in fact of Hobbes's party, he was surely of Hobbes's party without knowing it. In fact, the party membership ascribed in this way appears more as a piece of twentieth-century taxonomy than an observation on seventeenth-century experience, however cautious or incautious in expression this latter may have been.

If labour, then, is an obligation which must be analysed as a component of the calling, a certain tension with Macpherson's reading begins to emerge. For Locke, like other sixteenth- or seventeenth-century Protestant thinkers, conceived the calling as that station in life to which it had pleased *God* to call a man. It might have been possible in a primitive society to ascribe differences in wealth to individual differences in rationality or industriousness. But however corrupt Macpherson may suppose (and surely suppose correctly, at some level) Locke's social perception to have been, he cannot suppose that Locke believed rationality and industry to be necessary conditions for the inheritance of great wealth or sufficient conditions for the *inheritance* of anything at all. Because Macpherson sees very well that Locke moralizes social roles, he infers that Locke must be moralizing the social structure as a whole (or perhaps the authentically capitalist segments of it?). This, however, is a mistake. Locke treats the set of social roles as a datum. It is a consequence of human history, to be sure, of what men have done in the past, but its moral status does not derive from this naturalistic perspective, but from its being a result of *Gesta Dei per Anglos*, the actions of corrupt men being controlled by the purposes of God. The chaos which men have made of their history is ordered into a set of possible moral assignments for individuals in each generation by the continuing providence of God. The fantasticated array of social forms washed up by history, the vast patchwork of 'laws of

[1] MS Locke f 2, p. 128 (*ibid.* I, 191). Cf. Leo Strauss, *Natural Right and History* (Chicago, 1953), Richard H. Cox, *Locke on War and Peace* (Oxford, 1960), etc.

[2] 'We are so far from true and satisfying happyness in this world that we know not wherein it consists...' ('Happynesse', MS Locke f 1, p. 446 (26 September 1676)).

reputation and fashion' which sanction men's lives[1] and the corrupt legal orders which guarantee to them the limited physical security which they enjoy,[2] do not in themselves suffice to confer emotional ease or intelligible pattern on human existence. In every human pleasure 'there is naturally a deficiency, a dark side...'.[3] Only a belief in the fact of a future life and the steady, simple summons to moral effort which this, in the most literal of senses, *made* rational, could provide such ease and order. All men had their calling and the voice of God could reach out into the most physically abandoned niches and morally foetid recesses of human social organization and disorganization. But when it did so, it did not do so in order to acclaim the moral splendour of that social fabric, but to make the call audible to those who had been assigned by history to be the victims of the crimes which men had committed in the past, as much as to those who were the beneficiaries of past human achievements. The key to the notion of the calling in Puritan thought remains the same in Locke's reworking of it, a Christian egalitarianism, and the *locus* of this equality was the shared exposure to the most strenuous emotional demands. It is not difficult to grasp the place of labour in this complex of ideas. The almost unlimited character of the demands created a pervasive sense of guilt, and Calvinist theology tended to equate a persistent sense of guilt with prospective damnation. The abandonment of the old law with its simple taboos for this ethic of unlimited aspiration created an oppressive need for the rediscovery of some palpable index of salvation. The strains of physical labour came to have an apodictic quality. The sweat of their brows in which men were compelled to eat their bread until they returned under the ground[4] could serve as a baptismal guarantee of the authenticity of their efforts, a sacrament for their struggle. The concreteness of its testimony to the force of this struggle gave to it the power to allay their anxieties.

It is unnecessary to emphasize how convenient this emotional state would be to those with projects for extensive accumulation on hand. The more richly rewarding the emotional pilgrimage on

[1] *Essay* II, XXVIII, §§6–13; 'Virtus', MS Film. 77, p. 10.
[2] See above, p. 216, n. 1; and cf. the phrasing of *Two Treatises*, II, §157, ll. 7–8, 13.
[3] 'Happynesse', MS Locke f 1, p. 446 (cf. entire note, pp. 445–7).
[4] Genesis, III, 17–19. Cf. esp. *Reasonableness*, *Works*, III, 5.

which these devout labourers should feel that they were progressing, the more docile and attentive labour-gang they would furnish to the 'enterprising' employer. There is no question that this ideological complex was capable of doing the class some service. But it is grotesque to suppose that Locke spent year after year wrestling to rescue the intelligibility of the Christian faith because he was anxious to preserve or promote the docility of the labour force. Macpherson's reading of the *Reasonableness of Christianity* is wholly gratuitous.[1] It implies that Locke looked upon seventeenth-century England and 'saw that it was good'. But noticing a hole in the ideological dike he knocked up the *Reasonableness of Christianity* as a makeshift plug to fill this. Even if Locke had sensed the labouring masses as seething with revolt (which it is perfectly clear that he did not),[2] this interpretation would have been supererogatory.

It was the meaning of most men's lives for which Locke was fighting his epistemological and theological battles, 'the heart', perhaps, 'of a heartless world'. The Marxist interpretation is searching and delicate here but it must be taken *au pied de la lettre* and not skimped. When Locke looked upon the England of his day, there was much in the society to make him uneasy and as much in his own personality to accentuate the feeling. In viewing his own life as an individual project and his theories of society as an ideological project, it is pertinent enough to say that he used Christianity as a balm to soothe the pain which these elicited. But it is neither perceptive nor just, having said this, to proceed to forget that the balm in question was Christianity. Confronted by such a disturbing balance of terrestrial enjoyment and distress, there is little surprising in the fact that Locke should have struggled to construct a rationale for human existence which transcended these obliquities. We may certainly feel that he failed shatteringly. But, if he looked upon seventeenth-century England and could not see how to 'make' it good, which according to the

[1] Macpherson, *Possessive Individualism*, pp. 224–7, esp.: 'But the ability of his fundamental Christian doctrine to satisfy men of higher capacities Locke regards as only a secondary advantage. His repeated emphasis on the necessity of the labouring class being brought to obedience by believing in divine rewards and punishments leaves no doubt about his main concern' (p. 226).

[2] *Considerations of the Lowering of Interest...*, *Works*, II, 46, cited by Macpherson himself, *Possessive Individualism*, p. 223.

Marxist scenario would have been an apt enough performance in the role and which seems to have been true enough in mere fact, an effort to use the next world to transcend this irrationality cannot legitimately be read as an embracing of its existing moral adequacy. To describe his intellectual life as though it had all been a conceptually desperate and morally placid effort to rescue the seedy appearances is indefensible. There is a tendency in the writings of both Strauss and Macpherson to describe Locke's theories as though they were packaged in a sort of theological 'Polythene' which has only to be torn off to lay bare the comfortable secular contours beneath and which is so exquisitely fitted and so morally transparent that Locke's contemporaries and still more we ourselves can gauge its corrupt availability without disturbing the packaging at all. But this image is only so tempting because the future of Locke's doctrine was to be such a grimly secular future. To read the doctrine, as Locke handled it, as though the future had already happened is to visit the sins of the children or even great-grandchildren upon the father. In the sophisticated endeavour to tug aside Locke's mask, what such interpreters succeed in doing is to rip the skin off the living face. Doing so, they remove his humanity and transform him from one of those 'real living men who make history' into a lifeless but sinister effigy fit to adorn a crude morality play.

In order to improve on the historical specificity of this level of analysis and to identify the precise character of Locke's development of the Protestant ethic, it is necessary to explore briefly the structure of this set of ideas.[1] The central theme is the doctrine of the calling. Men are put into the world in particular social situations and with particular individual talents. They are called by God to fill a particular role,[2] and they can discern what this role

[1] The construction which follows is historically crude in that it is not an attempt at the full historical reconstruction of the ideas of any particular individual or even small sect but an exploration of the resources of a set of concepts employed by many different individuals over a considerable period of time. There is nothing original in my presentation of it, which relies heavily on the writings of William Haller and Christopher Hill and on Michael Walzer's *The Revolution of the Saints* (London, 1966) and Charles H. and Katherine George, *The Protestant Mind of the English Reformation 1570–1640* (Princeton, 1961).

[2] Cf. Robert Sanderson, *XXXVI Sermons* (London, 1689), 'that is every man's *Proper* and right *Calling*, whereunto God calleth him' (p. 215). The whole of the fourth sermon (pp. 203–31) is an illuminating analysis of the calling.

is to be by conscientious reflection on the relationship between their genetic endowment and the social situation into which they are born. When they have construed this divine provision correctly, they will have identified their 'particular calling'. The calling is thus a summons from God, but it is a summons for the interpretation of which each adult individual is fully responsible. Chronic indecision over the choice of an appropriate calling was morally suspicious and the stubborn refusal to settle down to any particular calling was morally outrageous.[1] God had summoned each man and any deafness to the call arose not from the indistinctness of the divine vocal articulation but from the corrupt inattentiveness or immoral obduracy of his auditors.[2] Once a man had recognized and adopted his calling, his responsibility was to discharge it with energy. The problem of the world is the problem of its enticements,[3] of its deflections of energy from religious aspiration to self-satisfied consumption. 'You may use the World; but as there is a libertie, so there is a danger, you may, but you may goe too farre...' 'Use it as a servant all thy dayes, and not as a Master...'[4] Natural goods are God's provision and are to be accepted and enjoyed as such.[5] There is a liberty of innocent

[1] George and George, *Protestant Mind*, pp. 126–31, 134–5; Walzer, *Revolution of the Saints*, p. 216.

[2] This is a slightly Arminian version of the doctrine. In the brutally consistent determinism of classical Calvinism, the deafness of an individual auditor is a simple causal product of the deity's not having intervened directly in order to make the message fully audible. Because of Adam's sin, natural obligations are in practice unintelligible as obligations to all men unless God bestows his particular grace upon them. All men are justly damned but God mercifully rescues one or two. Locke found this version of the doctrine of original sin morally revolting and theoretically incoherent.

[3] George and George, *Protestant Mind*, p. 126. Cf. Locke, 'being immersed in the body and beset with material objects, when they are continually importuning us' (MS Locke f 1, p. 338, *Essays on the Law of Nature*, p. 269). See also 'Happynesse', MS Locke f 1, pp. 445–7 (=16 July and 26 September 1676). See also *The Conduct of the Understanding*, *Works*, IV, 'Outward corporeal objects, that constantly importune our senses and captivate our appetites' (p. 155).

[4] Richard Sibbes, *The Spiritual Man's Aime* (1637), *The Saints Cordials* (1637) quoted from George and George, *Protestant Mind*, p. 125.

[5] *The Works of that Famous and Worthy Minister of Christ... William Perkins...*, III, *A Commentarie upon the eleventh Chap. to the Hebrewes* (London, 1631), '*temporall blessings*, as money, lands, wealth, sustenance, and such like outward things, as concerne the necessary or convenient maintenance of this naturall life. And in this sense, the world is not to be contemned, for, in themselves, these earthly things are the good gifts of God, which no man can simply contemne, without injury to Gods disposing hand and providence, who hath ordained them for naturall life' (p. 102).

delights.[1] Recreation and rest are permissible and indeed indispensable adjuncts to the calling. But they are permissible only in so far as they are genuinely subsidiary to the fulfilment of the central religious purpose of the individual's life. The emotional tone is very precarious here. A rigid and unrelenting asceticism does at least make unambiguous demands. The calling, by rejecting such unequivocal behavioural norms,[2] forced men to nerve themselves to the most unrelenting moral exertion. Because there was no 'sufficiency limitation' in the moral demands placed on men, they needed desperately some unambiguous touchstone for the grace of their actions. The only available touchstone within the structure of the theory must be their own sense of their authentic and total subjection to the demands of their religious role. They had to discipline their entire lives so that these felt totally subordinated to the fulfilments of this purpose. Any sense of emerging insouciance in their attitudes had to be met by undertaking some unambiguously taxing practical duty.[3] Physical labour for any man, theological and moral study for those capable of it,[4] could serve as such concrete tokens of dutifulness. There

[1] Presumably a tautology. Cf. Perkins, *Works*, II, 140–3, esp. 'by Christian libertie, we are allowed to use the creatures of God, not onely for our necessitie, but also for meet and convenient delight...' and cf. his rebuke to Saint Ambrose and Saint Chrysostom, 'be not too righteous, be not too wise' (p. 140). See in general George and George, *Protestant Mind*, pp. 141–2. Cf. *Two Treatises*, II, §128, ll. 1–2.

[2] The rejection of the idea that salvation could be attained by the observance of a set of rigid rules of behaviour was part of the general Puritan critique of 'Popish idolatry and superstition', the use of forms as a substitute for feelings. Cf., for example, Perkins's attack on monasticism as a vehicle for the duty of chastity and on 'Popish vows' in general as 'a meere will-worship', the substitution of factitious duties which are often beyond the power of individuals to discharge and which interfere with their execution of the duties of their actual social situation, for these latter duties (*Works*, II, 99–101). And 'it is a meere devise of a mans braine, and hath no warrant in Gods word' (III, 102).

[3] But it had to be a duty which they could see as naturally assigned to them within the order of nature, not an arbitrary assignment which impaired this natural order. Cf. Perkins as cited in n. 2 above.

[4] In this matter Locke was perhaps a good deal more socially radical than most of his Protestant precedessors. Cf. his claims for the advantages to human happiness which would derive from every labourer spending three hours a day on 'knowledge' and his tart emphasis that it was only the derelictions of the ruling class ('the industrious and rational', no doubt?) which had prevented this ('Labour', MS Film. 77, pp. 310–11). But the development is implicit in the whole dynamic of Protestant thought, the spread of literacy being a pre-requisite for each individual taking on the burden of an autonomous scripturally based religion. Cf. James Ussher, *A Body of Divinity*...(London, 1648), 'Object. 4. *There be many poor*

were few other types of action in which the requisite sense of strain could be felt with such reassuring immediacy and moral tensions be resolved in the acceptance of physical or intellectual exhaustion. The innocent delights of recreation were *rendered* innocent, purged of their potential 'concupiscence', by the physical exhaustion on which they ensued.

Recreation thus was to be distinguished rigidly from idleness. Idleness afforded opportunity for sin[1] and it carried no intrinsic psychic rewards. In itself it represented a perilous break in the continuous ritual of purification and it could not be sanctioned for its contribution to the replenishing of exhausted energies. In effect it was itself a sin, a desertion of the purposes of God for a listless and potentially perilous human inanition. The distinction between recreation or rest and idleness was a distinction of motive as much as one of behaviour. The degree of relaxation commended was one which must in no way threaten the dedicated order of the life.[2] The goals for which men were permitted to indulge themselves in this fashion were the preservation of health and the restoration of energy. They must be authentically re-creative, not intrinsically destructive.

In social terms the dominant characteristic of the calling was its egalitarianism. This was not, it is true, a *secular* egalitarianism. It involved no proposals for the destruction of terrestrial hierarchy.[3] But it did explicitly reject the medieval conception of, in

Country-men, as Plough-men and Shepherds, which never learned to read; which yet are saved, though they never read Scripture. / They ought to have learned to read: and being not able to read, yet they might heare the Scriptures read by others. / Object. 5. *If all ought to read Scripture, then should they understand Hebrew and Greek, wherein Scripture was written.* / It were happy if they could understand the Hebrew and Greek: but howsoever, they may read Translations' (p. 27). Note that what is desirable is universal access to the texts and what stands in its way is social possibility, an attitude which is mirrored in Locke's *published* comments on the issue and which makes his private social fantasy all the more significant. For insights into the significance of this point in Protestant thought in England see William Haller, *The Rise of Puritanism* (paperback edition, New York, 1957): 'The end toward which the whole movement was tending was the reorganization of society on the basis of a Bible-reading populace' (p. 178). Cf. with Laud's attitude, *ibid.* p. 234. And see also George and George, *Protestant Mind*, pp. 334–5.

[1] *Ibid.* pp. 132–3; Walzer, *Revolution of the Saints*, p. 216.

[2] For some valuable insights into Puritan recognition of the type of social change necessary to ensure this goal see Hill, *Society and Puritanism*, chapter v, 'The Uses of Sabbatarianism'.

[3] See esp. Walzer, *Revolution of the Saints*, pp. 148–98.

Troeltsch's terms, a 'cosmos of callings'.[1] Men were equal as Christians, however unequal they might be as members of societies. They were all born unto trouble and called to labour,[2] though the forms of labour appropriate varied, naturally, with their social situation. But if the appropriate forms of labour varied, the level of energy and commitment which it was proper for each to display did not vary at all.[3] There was no role in God's world for a leisure class.[4] God gave the world to all men richly to enjoy; but to none, however richly born, did he give it *merely* to enjoy. Here the socially subversive potential of the doctrine becomes more evident and the resources on which the Levellers and Winstanley were able to draw begin to appear. It is not only the pastoral imagery of the Scriptures themselves which explains the obsessive extent to which the Puritan metaphors for the duties of a Christian are taken from manual labour. The insistently physical reference of the language—sweat, toil, ploughing, sowing, reaping—brings out the unequivocal injunction to strain and effort.[5] But the summons carries with it its own ambivalence. It was convenient enough to be able to exhort the labourers in such accents: 'People Goe to your callings, that you may eate the

1 Ernst Troeltsch, *The Social Teaching of the Christian Churches* (paperback edition, New York, 1960), I, 293–6 and II, 561–2 (Lutheranism) with II, esp. 620–1 (Calvinism). On the axiomatic spiritual equality between callings see George and George, *Protestant Mind*, pp. 131–2, 138–9, 78–87, and Walzer, *Revolution of the Saints*, p. 214. For the theological basis see Haller, *Rise of Puritanism*, p. 153.

2 Robert Bolton, *Works*, IV, 'God hath made man to labour as the sparks to flie upward...' (p. 628, quoted in George and George, *Protestant Mind*, p. 136).

3 See Joseph Hall, *Works*, I (London, 1628): 'The homeliest service that we doe in an honest calling, though it be but to plow, or digge, if done in obedience, and conscience of God's Commandement, is crowned with an ample reward; whereas the best workes for their kinde (preaching, praying, offering Evangelicall sacrifices) if without respect of God's injunction and glory, are loaded with curses. God loveth adverbs; and cares not how good, but how well' (p. 137, quoted in George and George, *Protestant Mind*, p. 139n.); and Perkins, *Works*, I, 'The meanenesse of the calling, doth not abase the goodnesse of the worke: for God looketh not at the excellency of the worke, but at the heart of the worker. And the action of a sheepheard in keeping sheepe, performed as I have said, in his kind, is as good a worke before God, as is the action of a Judge, in giving sentence; or of a Magistrate in ruling, or a Minister in preaching' (p. 758).

4 Dod and Cleaver, *Proverbs XVII–XX*: 'Every man, of every degree, as well rich as poor, as well mighty as mean, as well noble as base, must know that he is born for some employment to the good of his brethren, if he will acknowledge himself to be a member, and not an ulcer, in the body of mankind' (p. 11, quoted in Hill, *Society and Puritanism*, p. 140, and see *ibid.* pp. 138–44).

5 See, for example, George and George, *Protestant Mind*, pp. 131–2.

labours of your owne hands.'[1] But it was not conceptually difficult for the labourers or their self-appointed spokesmen, with a neat inversion of the injunction, to denounce the existing social distribution of foodstuffs and its relationship to productive activity. Not only had the poorest in England lives to live as the greatest[2] but some of them certainly appeared to be living their lives in a style more responsive to these norms of production than that displayed by their betters. Even when these disturbing possibilities remained latent, the customary snobberies over styles of work suffered a sharp jolt. The quality of a human life was judged by the effort embodied in it, not by some ascriptive criterion of social status. 'God loveth adverbs and cares not how good, but how well.'[3]

However, this axiomatic human equality certainly had its harsh side. Because all men's callings, the meanest as much as the proudest, were equal, their responsibilities were equal too. There was little complaisant in the way that the Saints looked upon the sinner. Human weakness in the face of temptation won little sympathy from them. They bestowed on all those who failed to heed their calling, and most particularly on the more riotous and disturbing idleness of the poor, the most virulent and pitiless denunciation.[4] Beggars commit a sort of sacrilege in cloaking their idleness with the name of Christ[5] and no man *owes* them any

1 Thomas Adams, *Works* (1629), p. 419 (quoted in George and George, *Protestant Mind*, p. 131).

2 See Colonel Rainborough in the Putney Debates, ed. A. S. P. Woodhouse, *Puritanism and Liberty* (London, 1938), p. 53, etc.

3 Joseph Hall, as quoted above, p. 226, n. 3.

4 See especially the writings of Christopher Hill, *Puritanism and Revolution* (paperback edition, London, 1962), chapter VII 'William Perkins and the Poor'; *Society and Puritanism*, esp. pp. 259–97. Walzer, *Revolution of the Saints*, pp. 210–31. George and George, *Protestant Mind*, pp. 157–9. Cf. with Brian Tierney, *Medieval Poor Law* (Berkeley and Los Angeles, 1959), pp. 44–67.

5 Cf. Henry Bullinger, *The Decades*, II (Cambridge, 1850), 'beggars commit sacrilege who abuse the name of Christ, and make their poverty a cloak to keep them idel still' (quoted by George and George, *Protestant Mind*, p. 158), and cf. Perkins' acute embarrassment in the course of his attack on monasticism (*Works*, II, 101), over the possibility that Christ and the disciples might have looked like 'vagabonds' to the Roman authorities: 'They say Christ himself was a begger, and therefore why may not wee also be beggers? *Ans.* Though Christ was poore, yet he was no begger. For he kept a family, and had a treasure: Judas was the steward of his family, and bare the bagge, *John* 13.29. Againe, there is mention made of 200. pence, *John* 6.7. which in likelihood was in the bag that *Judas* kept: yea, of the money which he had, the Disciples are said to buy meat, *John* 4.8.'

charity.[1] The ferocious moralism of the Puritan social vision was often brutal in its implications. But in the seventeenth century and in the works of Locke, as I shall argue, it was still a consistent moralism. The denunciations of covetousness, or greed, or envy, or ambition were seriously intended, even if they have a hypocritical ring to our ears today. Furthermore it is simply not true that those of a Puritan persuasion believed that social differentials in wealth were symmetrical with those in virtue. The rich were not necessarily credited with virtue and the devout poor enjoyed the traditional Christian homage.[2] Clearly if Locke's ideas were closely linked with this complex of notions, Macpherson's analysis must at times do him a certain injustice. It should be easier now to judge the closeness of the fit between his doctrine and Macpherson's interpretation of it.

[1] Cf. Dod and Cleaver, *The Ten Commandments*, 'so the Apostle speaketh, *He that will not work, let him not eat.* And what more dishonest thing can be in a Christian commonweal than that such men should be permitted? which fill the land with sin, making their life nothing else but a continual practice of filthiness, theft and idleness (which are sins of Sodom), that live without a calling, without magistracy, without ministry, without God in the world; that neither glorify God, nor serve the prince, nor profit the commonweal: but are an unprofitable burthen to the earth or blot to the state, and (as drones) live on other men's labours, and on the sweat of other men's brows' (quoted by Hill, *Society and Puritanism*, p. 284). See also Perkins, *Works*, III, 102.

[2] Walzer, *Revolution of the Saints*, p. 216; George and George, *Protestant Mind*, pp. 161, 162 (citing Sibbes' *The Saints Cordials* (1637), 'There is a pit digging for the wicked; he flourisheth and bears out all impudently under hope of success, but his grave is a making, and his present prosperity will but aggravate his future misery' (p. 168)); Hill, *Society and Puritanism*, pp. 139–43.

17

THE COHERENCE OF A MIND 3

Considering 'man bearly as an animal of three or four score years duration and then to end his condition and state requires no other knowledg then what may furnish him with these things which may help him to passe out to the end of that time with ease safety and delight which is all the happynesse he is capeable of...'[1] Yet, 'when he hath all that this world can afford', 'he is still unsatisfied uneasy and far from happyness'.[2] But, with the probability of the existence of a future state in which the actions of men will be judged by God, a probability which only those with the most corrupt intentions have any good reason to deny,[3] '...here comes in another and that the main concernment of mankinde and that is to know what those actions are that he is to doe what those are he is to avoid what the law is he is to live by here and shall be judg'd by hereafter...'.[4] God makes accessible to all men the knowledge which is necessary to improve their physical situation and to instruct them in their duties. 'I thinke one may safely say that amidst the great ignorance that is soe justly complaind of amongst man kinde, where any one endeavourd to know his duty sincerly with a designe to doe it scarce ever any one miscaried for want of knowledg.'[5]

The discussion places Macpherson's reading with some accuracy. The first role assigned to knowledge is its capacity to promote economic growth by technological innovation.[6] Economic growth is required to procure for man

[1] MS Locke f 2, p. 48 (8 February 1677) (printed in *An Early Draft of Locke's Essay* ed. R. I. Aaron and Jocelyn Gibb (Oxford, 1936), pp. 86–7).

[2] MS Locke f 2, p. 49 (*ibid.* p. 87). And see MS Locke f 1 (1676), pp. 445–7.

[3] MS Locke f 2, p. 50 (*ibid.* p. 87).

[4] MS Locke f 2, p. 51 (*ibid.* p. 88).

[5] MS Locke f 2, pp. 51–2 (*ibid.* p. 88).

[6] MS Locke f 2, pp. 43–5 (*ibid.* pp. 84–5) esp.: 'If we consider our selves in the condition we are in this world we cannot but observe that we are in an estate the necessitys whereof call for a constant supply of meat drinke cloathing and defence from the weather and very often physick; and our conveniences demand yet a great deal more. To provide these things nature furnish us only with the materials

the happynesse which this world is capeable of which certainly is noe thing else but plenty of all sorts of those things which can with most ease pleasure and variety preserve him longest in it, soe that had man kinde noe concernments but in this world noe apprehension of any being after this life they need trouble their heads with noe thing but the history of nature and an enquiry into the qualitys of the things in this mansion of the universe which hath fallen to their lott, and being well skild in the knowledg of materiall causes and effects of things in their power directing their thoughts to the improvement of such arts and inventions, engins and utinsils as might best contribute to their continuation in it with conveniency and delight.[1]

'The businesse of men being to be happy in this world by the enjoyment of the things of nature subservient to life health ease and pleasure,'[2] the Englishman of any class can appreciate the blessing of knowledge by contrasting his situation with that of an inhabitant of the West Indies, a situation which but for the grace of technology, the capacity to work iron, he would share himself.[3] But the glowing panegyric to economic advance and the bland rejection of theoretical knowledge, Science, for technology do not stand alone. 'Besides a plenty of the good things of this world and with life health and peace to enjoy them we can thinke of noe other concernment man kinde hath that leads him not out of it, and places him not beyond the confines of this earth...'[4] The main concernment of mankind is its destiny in the next world. The ineffable quality of Locke's own emotional response is caught fairly in his phrasing, 'the comfortable hopes of a future life when this is ended',[5] and in the baldness of the argument that terrestrial

for the most part rough and unfitted to our uses it requires labour art and thought to suit them to our occasions, and if the knowledg of men had not found out ways to shorten the labour and improve severall things which seeme not at first sight to be of any use to us we should spend all our time to make a scanty provision for a poore and miserable life...'

[1] MS Locke f 2, pp. 46–7 (*An Early Draft*, pp. 85–6).

[2] MS Locke f 2, pp. 52 (*ibid.* p. 88).

[3] '...the inhabitants of that large and firtill part of the world the west Indies, who lived a poore uncomfortable laborious life with all their industry scarce able to subsist and that perhaps only for want of knowing the use of that stone out of which the inhabitants of the old world had the skill to draw Iron...' (MS Locke f 2, p. 44, *ibid.* p. 85). Cf. with the analysis in *Two Treatises of Government*, II, §41, which appears to reduce the differential standards of living solely to differentials in labour expended, esp. 'for want of improving it by labour' (ll. 6–7).

[4] MS Locke f 2, p. 49 (*An Early Draft*, p. 87).

[5] MS Locke f 2, p. 52 (*ibid.* p. 88).

discomfort makes probable the existence of 'some better state some where else'.[1] The Pascalian vein which he was self-consciously working at this date[2] has certainly degenerated in moral urgency. But no distaste for Locke's own spiritual complacency can elide the fact that he conceived human duties as 'the ordering of our selves in our actions in this time of our probationership here'.[3] The dominant end of human action is necessarily the realization of these 'comfortable hopes'.

The end of knowledge is seen as practice, directed to the attainment of worldly or other-worldly ends.[4] In many of the pieces Locke is concerned with the casuistry of cognitive effort, perhaps initially predominantly with the casuistry of the intellectual life. The later published reflections, the *Essay concerning Human Understanding, The Conduct of the Understanding in the Pursuit of Truth, The Reasonableness of Christianity*, are concerned more broadly with the cognitive responsibilities of all human beings. The main burden of the thought is to impose the duty of systematic reflection on all men.[5] Appropriately, the most Utopian of the pieces suggests a complete social equality of opportunity for cognitive effort (six hours a day for all),[6] before shifting away in alarm at the egalitarian *social* implications of the proposal and substituting a distribution which preserved the opportunities of the poor, while respecting existing status differences.[7] One of the dominant motifs of

[1] MS Locke f 2, p. 49 (*ibid.* p. 87).

[2] See, for example, MS Locke f 1, pp. 368–70 (29 July 1676), *ibid.* pp. 81–2, and for his interest in the *Pensées* and his ownership of the work see MS Locke f 2, p. 86 (24 March 1677), p. 109 (April 1677). Noted in John Lough, 'Locke's Reading during his Stay in France (1675–79)', *The Library* (December 1953), pp. 236, 237. For an account of his interest in Pascalian themes whilst in France see Gabriel Bonno, *Les Relations Intellectuelles de Locke avec la France* (University of California Publications in Modern Philology, XXXVIII, 2, 37–264 (1955)), pp. 60–2, 244–7.

[3] MS Locke f 2, p. 49 (*An Early Draft*, p. 87).

[4] 'Study' (from Locke's Journal for 6 March 1677: 'The end of Study is knowledge and the end of knowledge practice or communication', MS Locke f 2, p. 87 (printed in Peter King, *The Life of John Locke* (London, 1830), I, 171)).

[5] Cf. 'the moral foundation, that the labouring class does not and cannot live a rational life' (C. B. Macpherson, *The Political Theory of Possessive Individualism* (Oxford, 1962), p. 229).

[6] 'Six hours thus allowed to the mind the other 6 might be employed in the provisions for the body and the preservation of health. Six hours labour everyday in some honest calling would at once provide necessaries for the body and secure the health of it in the use of them' ('Labour', MS Film. 77, p. 310).

[7] 'If this distribution of twelve hours seem not fair nor sufficiently to keep up the distinction that ought to be in the ranks of men let us change it a little. Let the

each man's calling is the duty of self-education. The calling becomes in part for all men a cognitive assignment.

It is a characteristically Lockean fact that the most Utopian presentation of this perspective should apparently have been elicited from him by his unremitting reflection on the state of his own physical health,[1] perhaps by the bronchial trauma inflicted by the London atmosphere. The scheme which consigns the aristocracy to a minimum of three hours' manual labour per day, in a determined, almost Maoist, assault on the distinction between life and labour, is to be read in part as a delicate retrospective self-reproach for the imprudent single-mindedness of his own past intellectual activity. But with Locke physical anxiety is often close to shame and, in his shame, the rationale of seventeenth-century social structure is subjected to the most corrosive scepticism. Labour may be a divine imposition, but it is one which those men who avoid it are likely to regret escaping. Physical labour is a necessary condition for maintaining physical health.[2] God's bounty turns even the most intractable element of man's fate to his advantage.[3] And those who escape the pains of labour by their social situation also justly lose the physical benefits which it provides.[4]

Gentleman and Scholar employ nine of the twelve on his mind in thought and reading and the other three in some honest labour. And the man of manual labour nine in work and three in knowledge. By which all man kind might be supplied with what the real necessities and conveniences of life demand in a greater plenty then they have now and be delivered from that horrid ignorance and brutality to which the bulk of them is now everywhere given up' (MS Film. 77, pp. 310–11).

1 MS Film. 77, p. 310, *passim*. The Straussian stress on the extraordinary physicality of Locke's imagination is apt here. Besides his professional interest in medicine he showed a neurasthenic absorption in his own ill health.

2 Cf. Charles H. and Katherine George, *The Protestant Mind of the English Reformation 1570–1640* (Princeton, 1961), pp. 131–3, esp. Joseph Hall, 'Paradise served not onely to feed his [Adam's] senses, but to exercise his hands. If happinesse consisted in doing nothing, man had not beene employed; all his delights could not have made him happy in an idle life. Man therefore is no sooner made, then he is set to worke: neither greatnesse, nor perfection can priviledge a folded hand; he must labor, because he was happy', cited pp. 132–3.

3 'We ought to look on it as a mark of goodness in god that he has put us in this life under a necessity of labour not only to keep mankind from the mischiefs that ill men at leisure are very apt to do. But it is a benefit even to the good and the vertuous which are thereby preserved from the ills of Idleness or the diseases that attend constant study in a sedentary life' (MS Film. 77, p. 310).

4 'Had not the luxury of Courts and by their example inferior Grandees found out idle and useless employments for themselves and others subservient to their pride

We may use this perspective to inspect the cogency of Macpherson's construction of differential rationality as the moral basis of Locke's class state.[1] Macpherson has three main pieces of evidence for his construction. The first, Locke's observation that the labouring classes are not well placed to form an economic pressure group in conditions of slump, because the level of their consciousness of economic structure is not sufficiently high to tell them how to act as a body,[2] is clear enough. But in itself it suggests neither enthusiasm for nor revulsion against the class structure of seventeenth-century England, merely knowledge of it. As Macpherson says, 'however confused Locke may have been, he was not confused about the class structure of his own England'.[3] The second piece of evidence is the comment in chapter v of the *Second Treatise* that God gave the world 'to the use of the Industrious and Rational, (and *Labour* was to be *his Title* to it;) not to the Fancy or Covetousness of the Quarrelsom and Contentious'.[4] This also cannot greatly enhance Macpherson's position since Locke's repeated insistence on the empirical dominance of force in human history makes it clear that God's gift is a normative rather than descriptive transaction. The industrious and rational are the rightful heirs, but neither human genetics nor the property laws nor the social structures of historical societies have been particularly finicky about respecting such a title. The description can hardly be turned into an ascriptive status, a glow stored in the property and reflected back from it onto all who subsequently own it. Locke must certainly have seen in his society some measure of differential opportunity for achieved rationality, but it is bizarre indeed to assume that because the rich have greater

and vanity. and so brought honest labour in useful and mechanical arts wholly into disgrace whereby the studious and sedentary part of mankind as well as the rich and the noble have been deprived of that natural and true preservative against diseases' (MS Film. 77, p. 310). It is the 'Lazily voluptuous', those who 'sit still' at 'their pleasure', rather than the 'busily studious', who suffer altogether justly in this way. Excessive devotion to scholarship is to be seen as imprudent rather than vicious. But Locke seems to attribute the emergence of the role of the 'sedentary scholar' to the corrupt division of labour created by the 'pride and vanity' of the rulers.

1 Macpherson, *Possessive Individualism*, pp. 221–38.

2 See *Considerations*, *Works* (1768), II, 46; Macpherson, *Possessive Individualism*, p. 224–5.

3 Macpherson, *Possessive Individualism*, p. 216.

4 *Two Treatises*, II, §34, ll. 5–6; Macpherson, *Possessive Individualism*, pp. 233–6.

opportunity to exercise their rationality, they must all therefore display greater *industry*[1] than those who never have time to raise their eyes from their labour.[2] The third piece of evidence which Macpherson adduces is by far the most impressive,[3] the section of the *Reasonableness of Christianity* in which Locke expatiates on the convenience of the Christian revelation as a disciplinary instrument over those who 'cannot know and therefore must believe'.[4] Two initial qualifications of Macpherson's enthusiastic gloss need to be made. The discipline and obedience which the greater part are liable otherwise to escape are not those requisite to maintain civil order[5] but those necessary to ensure their own salvation. The great blessing brought by the Christian revelation was not in Locke's allegation any enhancement of the effective control of the political rulers or the preservation of civil order[6] but a greater clarity and adequacy to individuals' possible apprehension of the full range of moral duties whose performance was necessary to guarantee their eventual salvation. Furthermore, it is essential to note just what it is that the greater part 'cannot know'. For it is not the knowledge of the moral values prevalent in their community, the law of 'reputation or fashion', which they are excluded from knowing, but the full deductive system of the obligatory law of nature. In this ignorance they are joined by every pre-

1 Cf. 'the industrious and rational' (*Two Treatises*, II, §34, ll. 5–6).

2 Cf. *Considerations*, *Works*, II, 46.

3 Macpherson, *Possessive Individualism*, pp. 224–9.

4 *Reasonableness of Christianity*, *Works*, III, 92.

5 'Those just measures of right and wrong, which necessity had any where introduced, the civil laws prescribed, or philosophy recommended, stood not on their true foundations. They were looked on as bonds of society, and conveniences of common life, and laudable practices' (*ibid.* p. 90). And: 'So much virtue as was necessary to hold societies together, and to contribute to the quiet of governments, the civil laws of common-wealths taught, and forced upon men that lived under magistrates. But these laws being for the most part made by such, who had no other aims but their own power, reached no farther than those things that would serve to tie men together in subjection; or at most, were directly to conduce to the prosperity and temporal happiness of any people' (*ibid.* p. 87). Cf. Locke's insistence in *A Paraphrase and Notes on the Epistle to the Romans*, *Works*, III, 546n., that the Christian revelation had made no difference whatever to the scope of human political rights and duties.

6 Indeed Locke claimed as early as his Gibbonian additions to the 1667 *Essay on Toleration* (MS Film. 77, p. 270, printed as *Sacerdos* note in King, *Life of John Locke*, II, 87), that the exclusive pretensions of the Christian priesthood have caused dramatic damage to the peace of mankind, indeed have 'been the cause of more disorders tumults and bloodshed than all other causes put together'.

Christian human being, by Plato and Confucius and Zeno,[1] and conceivably even by every Christian moral philosopher up to the year 1695.[2] Most notably of all they are joined as Von Leyden's analysis implies and as Abrams has emphasized so illuminatingly, by Locke himself.[3] There is a more than seventeenth-century force to Locke's observations on the implausibility of the majority of the population contriving to grasp a complete deductive system of ethical obligation by rational reflection. Certainly no community in the world today has come within intelligible distance of contriving such a feat and if this is what we are offered with the arrival of the Socialist millennium, we may well wonder whether it quite, in the immortal words of the Michelin guide, 'vaut le voyage'.

But these cavils do not go to the heart of the matter. For Macpherson's purpose in adducing the context is to demonstrate Locke's realization that only such crude and conceptually perfunctory indoctrination could be relied upon to preserve political order in seventeenth-century England.[4] At this point it becomes clear that either Macpherson or Locke *must* in fact have been confused about seventeenth-century class structure. Two years before Locke published the *Reasonableness of Christianity* we find him arguing that it was precisely the brutish ignorance of the majority of the population which makes it possible for ambitious and discontented Grandees to rouse revolts, that if the members of all classes were to spend six hours a day in study (or in deference to the demands of the status system, if labourers were to spend only three hours a day), the result would be greater social stability and more widespread happiness.[5] The loss in essential production

[1] *Reasonableness*, *Works*, III, 85, 88, 89, 90.

[2] 'It is true, there is a law of nature: but who is there that ever did, or undertook to give it us all entire, as a law; no more, nor no less, than what was contained in, and had the obligation of that law? Who ever made out all the parts of it, put them together, and shewed the world their obligation?' (*ibid.* p. 89). Locke intends this charge to relate to the period before the Christian revelation. But it is also a challenge which he never found it possible to meet himself.

[3] *Essays on the Law of Nature*, pp. 70–7; *Two Tracts on Government*, esp. pp. 93–8.

[4] 'His repeated emphasis on the necessity of the labouring class being brought to obedience by believing in divine rewards and punishments leaves no doubt about his main concern' (*Possessive Individualism*, p. 226).

[5] '...the Governments of the world...wholly intent upon the care of aggrandizing them selves at the same time neglect the happiness of the people and with it their own peace and security. Would they suppress the arts and instruments of Luxury

would be trivial and the benefits from every human point of view enormous.[1] Furthermore the reason why this desirable state of affairs is not realized is the corruption, idleness, vice and luxury of courts, the betrayal of its responsibilities by the ruling class.[2] Macpherson is entirely correct in seeing effective political power, most particularly the power of effective initiative, as confined according to Locke's political sociology within a tiny group of people. But he does not grasp the ambivalence in Locke's attitudes towards this fact. He reads the *Two Treatises of Government* as an unequivocal moral charter for this group, whereas it should be read apologetically at most as a moral brief for two particular projects of members of it, in 1680–1 and 1688. Like any moral brief, it contains implicit terms which constitute a hypothetical moral rationale for a social structure. But it is a moral rationale of the duties of the tenants of the various roles, not a rationale of the relationships between the roles themselves. Macpherson misunderstands the extent to which Locke treats the social structures in which men live as data, as social facts, which cannot be explained as the immediate products of intentional actions and which cannot be effectively manipulated by individuals, which constitute in fact the context of their lives. Throughout his work Locke is concerned with the legitimacy of the claims which men levy on each other in terms of the moral resources of these social structures. His central assumption is what I have called elsewhere 'the ideological viability of hierarchy'.[3] There could be no more effective demonstration of the force of this assumption than his confidence that removing the labouring force from labour for three or even six hours a day and consigning it to

and Vanity. And bring those of honest and useful industry into fashion, There would be neither that temptation to Ambition where the possession of power could not display it self in the distinctions and shows of pride and vanity Nor the well instructed minds of the people suffer them to be the instruments of Aspiring and turbulent men. The populace well instructed in their duty and removed from the implicit faith their ignorance submits them in to others would not be so easy to be blown into tumults and popular commotions by the breath and artifice of designing or discontented Grandees' (MS Film. 77, p. 311).

1 '...this is certain that if the labour of the world were rightly directed distributed there would be more knowledge peace health and plenty in it than now there is. And mankind be much more happy than now it is' (*ibid.*).

2 (The industrious and rational?) See MS Film. 77, pp. 310–11, *passim*.

3 See my article in *The Historical Journal*, x, 2 (July 1967), 181, n. 116.

study instead would greatly enhance the prospects for social order.[1]

The sources of this confidence at the social level are religious as well as sociological. There is no reason to suppose that he sensed any particular fragility in the English social structure at any date subsequent to the beginnings of his association with Shaftesbury and it seems an apt enough observation on the English social order of the 1680s or 1690s that it displayed this dependability. It may seem curious that Locke should have been able to forget so completely his sense of imminent social disintegration recorded in the earliest *Tracts on Government*. But there is every reason to believe that he *was* able to forget it. In any case the social psychology which he had elaborated with increasing confidence over the course of his epistemological inquiries portrayed most men's consciousness as so firmly and powerfully conventional[2] that only the most cursory governmental attention was necessary to ensure that any social structure in which men lived over time was cemented together by their profoundest expectations and emotional inclinations. Education and their own aspiration to attract the sympathy and secure the co-operation of their fellows drilled all men into an acute attentiveness to the 'law of reputation or fashion'. There were rich and extensive resources in human psychology for giving the most reassuring solidity to any intrinsically viable social or political structure.

Indeed it was this very solidity, this all too excessive plausibility of existing social moralities, this confused conventionality of human moral attitudes which formed the real target of his most powerful political works. In different ways both the *Letter on Toleration* and the *Two Treatises of Government* are attempts to derive criteria for restricting the range of legitimate claims which can be levied in terms of any society's conventional moral understanding. The apparatus of moral indoctrination available to any society was so crushing in its effectiveness and so crude in its

[1] See also *Two Treatises*, II, §208, ll. 9–14, on the stability of a 'well-settled State', §223, ll. 7–20, and the comments on the social efficacy of educating the gentry, *Some Thoughts concerning Education*, *Works*, IV, Epistle Dedicatory, side 2.

[2] '...when Fashion hath once Established, what Folly or craft began, Custom makes it Sacred, and 'twill be thought impudence or madness, to contradict or question it' (*Two Treatises*, I, §58, ll. 11–13). Cf. *Reasonableness*, *Works*, III, 85, 'what dread or craft once began, devotion soon made sacred, and religion immutable', etc.

incidence that the rulers could be left to fend ideologically for themselves. They might damage social order by their own administrative incompetence in the field of economic policy,[1] by their oppressive intentions in political affairs,[2] or by their persecutory enthusiasms in religious matters. But if they did so, they would have only themselves to blame. Furthermore, since the initiative in any dangerous disruption of the social order is thus confined in practice to the behaviour of the rulers, the most effective service which an intellectual can supply for preserving this order is to make the rulers more sensitive to their duties and to the risks which they will run if they ignore these. The social duty of an intellectual who grasped this point thus became precisely to hollow out and shore up a certain moral and social space for each individual member of the subject population, to preserve the vestiges of individual autonomy against the crushing and undifferentiated mass of the social structure.

It is at this point in the reconstruction of Locke's intellectual purposes that misunderstanding is most likely to ensue. One can search through the works uncovering instance after instance of Locke's unsurprised recognition of the grossly oppressive features of seventeenth-century English society and one can comment tartly that he was 'prepared to contemplate' a rich repertoire of types of unfreedom. In doing this one records firmly the fact that it was the seventeenth century in which he lived. Alternatively one collects an equally impressive repertoire of items which record his strenuous championship of many different forms of liberty, most particularly liberty of conscience, and he becomes a doughty protagonist of 'liberalism'. It is quite easy in pursuit of one of these intimations to lose sight entirely of the other. But the commoner course is to subsume one perspective under the other, so that Locke becomes as good a liberal as the seventeenth century could turn out, the John Stuart Mill *de ses jours*, but of course thus of an inferior *set* of days. Alternatively he becomes the moral embellishment of the new order of economic oppression, not because he was a peculiarly vicious man[3] but because this

[1] *Considerations*, *Works*, II, 46.

[2] See above, chapter 13.

[3] Cf. Macpherson, 'Locke could not have been conscious that the individuality he championed was at the same time a denial of individuality. Such consciousness was not to be found in men who were just beginning to grasp the great possibilities of

economic system furnished all its participants with those particular blinkers. Neither of these strategies provides a genuine resolution of the tension between the two readings.

We can see the conceptual bridge on which the tension is held when we apply the 'ideological' language to this analysis of just what Locke was trying to achieve. 'He was prepared to contemplate' the continuance of a crushingly oppressive social structure, though he did find some examples of the incidence of this upon religious behaviour and indeed upon religious consciousness a trifle disturbing. This might mean several different things. It might mean that he perceived the social structure to be oppressive in this sense and applauded it for being so. It might mean that he simply couldn't *see* that it was oppressive in this way[1] or in any case never actually noticed that it was. Or it might mean that he perceived the social structure to be oppressive and it simply did not occur to him that any social structure might be anything other than oppressive. All of these responses may properly be taken as examples of ideological contamination, but they are clearly distinct and indeed incompatible allegations. In the latter case the psychological stance involved in preparedness to contemplate the oppressiveness of the social structure might be fairly close to the preparedness to contemplate the fact of mortality. In itself the prospect might elicit little enthusiasm. But no great energy would be devoted to elaborating the desirability of an alternative precluded by it, simply because there did not appear to *be* any real and possible alternative.

The type of enlargement of human freedom which Locke

individual freedom that lay in the advancement of capitalist society. The contradiction was there, but it was impossible for them to recognize it, let alone to resolve it' (*Possessive Individualism*, pp. 261–2).

[1] See above, p. 238, n. 3. But there is a problem of intelligibility in the case of such ascriptions of social invisibility. How could one have adequate evidence for the claim that a man did not perceive an oppressive social structure to be such? Disagreements about how oppressive particular features of a society really are are more often disagreements about how to describe them or about how remediable they are than they are simply disagreements about what is the case. The fact that a man, in discussing political societies, does not dwell on certain oppressive features of them does not necessarily mean that he doesn't think the features oppressive, any more than the fact that a secular moralist does not dwell on the fact of human mortality means that he cannot perceive that men die. Both may simply reflect judgement about what can in practice be done about these in some ways deplorable states of affairs.

wished to promote was certainly not one which demanded egalitarian social revolution. But this was not because the liberty of unlimited capitalist appropriation was liberty enough for the whole human race, as much as men could desire, still less because it was the most essential form of human liberty, the form to which all other forms must appropriately be sacrificed. In the first instance the reason why Locke fails even to consider the moral challenge of such a revolution was that nothing in his experience made credible the *possibility* of an achieved and stable egalitarian social structure in an economically advanced society. We have seen already that some of Locke's social ideas were startlingly egalitarian in substance. The reason why he never constructed these ideals into a programme of politically revolutionary social change was that he had every reason to believe that the social world in which he lived was simply not open to the possibility of such drastic and directed change. No doubt, too, egalitarian social democracy as a moral ideal would have offended against many of his deepest social and moral assumptions, and had he been confronted by the reality of such a social revolution these assumptions would probably have placed him among the defenders of the Ancien Régime. But it seems essential to insist that the profoundest structures of seventeenth-century English society made the prospect of any such revolution succeeding altogether impossible and that it was a correct assessment of his own social experience which in this way formed Locke's sense of the socially accessible dimensions of human freedom. To confront him with the possibility of such a successful revolution is to confront him with a possibility which he had every reason to know could not happen. It is to add a variable illicitly to one side of the equation linking the man to his society without adding it to the other. A Locke confronted by the possibility of achieved social revolution is no longer the Locke on whose attitudes we have the evidence to pronounce. To transfer the Locke we know, intact, to a context in which he could not have been the same man and then to comment on the quality of his performance (pretty blinkered) is to desert historical truth for a self-congratulatory mendacity about the past.

We may find the more radical denunciations of seventeenth-century English society morally more appealing in the feelings expressed than Locke's own more conventional apologetic. But there are crude moral dangers involved in elevating the expression of edifying feelings over the evincing of a sense of social reality. It is easy enough to write moral charters for socially impossible institutions. But it is scarcely *morally* less appropriate to explore the moral dimensions of effectively possible social arrangements. Against the morality of those for whom changing the world is such a pressing necessity that the consequences of attempts to change it, however forlorn the efforts or ghastly their results, become wholly trivial, there must be set the morality of those whose moral interpretation of the world is restricted by an accurate sense of the limited possibilities for changing it. The exploration of the moral potentialities of authentically possible social change cannot be assimilated to the reactionary claim that social improvement is impossible. What matters is whether the change commended is derived from the exploration in fantasy of what is desirable but only logically possible or the investigation of what is desirable and sociologically possible. Willing the millennium is not a substitute for exploring the moral potentialities of the possibly available orders of repression. Still less is it a moral improvement on the latter enterprise. There should be no moral prizes for insecurity of grasp on the 'reality principle'.

PART V

'...if there be nothing else worth notice in him, accept of his good intention'

John Locke (Note to the Reader, *Paraphrase of the Epistle of St Paul to the Galatians*, *Works*, III, 290)

18

THE CALLING: TRADITION AND CHANGE

It is in the traditional concept of the calling that the key to Locke's moral vision lies. In examining his treatment of this notion it is possible to grasp the scope and limitations of his moral thought, that precarious balance of conservatism and innovation which gives it its distinctive quality. It is also perhaps possible to understand why the historical individual, John Locke, came to think in this way. His analysis of the calling takes as a datum the intractability and oppressive ideological sanction of existing social structures. The liberties which he struggles to vindicate are not the socially unavailable and in his eyes morally perilous liberties of unrestricted physical indulgence, but those freedoms which are necessary for executing the responsibilities of the calling. Prevailing social moralities might often be strikingly corrupt in detail and the legal structures of societies might reflect this corruption with some accuracy.[1] That was how the human world was due to be ever since the Fall of Man.[2] Men are above all else proud. In their cradles they cry for dominion,[3] and throughout their life

[1] *Two Treatises of Government*, II, §12, ll. 14–17.

[2] 'When private possessions and labour which now the curse on earth had made necessary, by degrees made a distinction of conditions it gave room for covetousness, pride and ambition which by fashion and example spread the corruption which has so prevailed over man kind. JL' ('Homo ante et post lapsum', MS Locke c 28, fo. 113v). Before a distinction of conditions had been established in this way by the results of the Fall, 'instinct and reason carried him the same way and being neither capable of covetousness or ambition when he had already the free use of all things he could scarce sin' (*loc. cit*). This note dates from 1693.

[3] 'Children love dominion; and this is the first original of most vicious habits, that are ordinary and natural. This love of power and dominion shews itself very early, and that in these two things. / We see children (as soon almost as they are born, I am sure long before they can speak) cry, grow peevish, sullen, and out of humour, for nothing but to have their wills. They would have their desires submitted to by others; they contend for a ready compliance from all about them... / Another thing, wherein they shew their love of dominion is their desire to have things to be theirs; they would have propriety and possession, pleasing themselves with the power which that seems to give, and the right that they thereby have to dispose of them as they please. He that has not observed these two humours working very

ambition and covetousness,[1] 'amor sceleratus habendi',[2] drive them towards the 'bogs and precipices' of sin.[3] The passions of corrupt human nature demand restraint[4] and social existence does at times provide such restraints, though it also and perhaps equally often creates its own distinctive temptations. There are few circumstances in which it is appropriate for a man to invest his energies in assaulting the conventional moral understanding of the society in which he lives. But he has some obligation to challenge it when it claims the right to *impose* a particular interpretation of men's religious duties or when it sanctions the forcible appropriation of real physical goods from their legally accredited possessors, or when it attempts to claim religious sanctions for the corrupt desires of the powerful. The calling was an undertaking which under the best of terrestrial circumstances taxed the moral capacities of human beings to the limits. The political norms which Locke affirms are to be seen as insistences that conventional social morality has no right to make the assignment still more difficult. No human authority had a status which justified it in encroaching upon men's individual religious understanding. Similarly no human authority enjoyed a status which would justify it in treating a human being as a means to its own ends.[5] Equally no human authority could have the right to obstruct the provision

betimes in children, has taken little notice of their actions: and he who thinks that these two roots of almost all the injustice and contention that so disturb human life, are not early to be weeded out, and contrary habits introduced, neglects the proper season to lay the foundations of a good and worthy man' (*Some Thoughts concerning Education*, *Works* (1768), IV, 60). What needs to be done is to distinguish between 'the wants of fancy and those of nature' (*ibid.* p. 61).

1 'Covetousness, and the desire of having in our possession, and under our dominion, more than we have need of, being the root of all evil, should be early and carefully weeded out' (*ibid.* p. 64). Cf. *Two Treatises*, II, §37, ll. 1–2.

2 *Ibid.* II, §111, ll. 1–3.

3 Cf. Locke's account of the role of law: '...*Law*, in its true Notion, is not so much the Limitation as *the direction of a free and intelligent Agent* to his proper Interest, and prescribes no farther than is for the general Good of those under that Law. Could they be happier without it, the *Law*, as an useless thing would of it self vanish; and that ill deserves the Name of Confinement which hedges us in only from Bogs and Precipices' (*ibid.* II, §57, ll. 10–16).

4 The neatest identification of the battles which Locke was in fact fighting, in his own eyes, is perhaps his friend John Shute, Lord Barrington's testimony, 'You alone have vindicated the Rights and Dignities of human nature, and have restored Liberty to Mens Consciences from the Tyranny of human Laws and their own Passions' (letter to Locke, 30 November 1703, MS Locke c 18, fo. 101v).

5 For a possible exception to this rule see above, chapter 12.

of the physical prerequisites for keeping a man healthy in his calling.

The scope of conventional values is extremely wide but it is restricted rigidly by the law of nature. The market determines the just price.[1] But if a man's enthusiastic exploitation of the market were to lead another man to starve to death, it would be the exploiter, not the market, who was 'no doubt guilty of murder'.[2] In the same way the conqueror in a just war, who has no right whatever to interfere with the property rights in land of the most justly conquered (since their wives and children have rights to the physical prerequisites for their continued performance of their terrestrial duties), has unlimited rights of reparation over their monetary wealth.[3] Conventional values are protected by conventions inside political societies and in the state of nature. In the state of war, natural values are the only values which enjoy protection and they do so because although for men they are no more authentically values than are those of social convention, they are *God's* values for men. Locke's treatment here is certainly conceptually confused—money is as real an asset in the securing of consumption needs in a money economy as is land itself. But its relation to the satisfaction of human need is less direct than that of the physical factors of production. Money as a social

[1] The tension between Locke's position on this issue and the position of such a 'classical' exponent of natural law as St Thomas Aquinas should not be exaggerated. See Raymond de Roover, 'The Concept of the Just Price: Theory and Economic Policy', *Journal of Economic History*, XVIII, 4 (December 1958), 418–34.

[2] 'Venditio' (1695), MS Film. 77, p. 269.

[3] *Two Treatises*, II, §§183–4. No conqueror, however just, can have the right to more than the damage done to him by his enemy. The only right a conqueror can have is a right of reparation. For the significance of Locke's distinction between natural and conventional goods see his argument that even very heavy monetary loss could under no circumstances justify the appropriation of the land of the conquered. 'And if I have not taken away the Conqueror's Land, which, being vanquished, it is impossible I should; scarce any other spoil I have done him, can amount to the value of mine, supposing it equally cultivated and of an extent any way coming near, what I had over run of his. The destruction of a Years Product or two, (for it seldom reaches four or five) is the utmost spoil, that usually can be done. For as to Money, and such Riches and Treasure taken away, these are none of Natures Goods, they have but a Phantastical imaginary value: Nature has put no such upon them: They are of no more account by her standard, than the Wampompeke of the *Americans* to an *European* Prince, or the Silver Money of *Europe* would have been formerly to an *American*. And five years Product is not worth the perpetual Inheritance of *Land*, where all is possessed' (§184, ll. 9–22). For the context of the argument see above, chapter 13.

institution, too, is very closely linked to that 'desire of having more than we have need of' which is one of the most intrinsically corrupt of human motives.

It is not true that Locke regarded unlimited appropriation as the essence of rationality. The law of reason was a moral law and unlimited appropriation was at best a morally perilous calling. The social expression of the motive of covetousness in a money economy had accentuated many forms of human corruption. It had also led to a rise in the standard of living. Locke regarded the first development with disquiet and the second with some enthusiasm. The disquiet sprang from the damage done to the quality of men's moral performance and the enthusiasm came from the real benefits already secured[1] and perhaps at least as much from the possibility of a more egalitarian and happy society which the level of production made available.[2] All social institutions were to be judged on the extent to which they facilitated physical ease and purity of motive in men's performance in their callings. Covetousness and ambition, and pride which was the motor to both of them, were the major human vices, not because the distribution of power and wealth in this world was just but because to envy the situations of others in the world and to attempt to appropriate their wealth or status is an infringement of the duties of the calling. It is not the responsibility of an individual either to commend or to revile the structure of the society in which he lives, but merely to execute the duties of the station within it to which he is called, to the best of his ability.

There is an explanation of the curious contours of this attitude in the moral tradition in which Locke had been brought up as a child and in the effects of his own subsequent intellectual development upon the structure provided by it. It was a central fact of Calvinist theology, both in its radical development among the Saints[3] and *a fortiori* in its more conservative articulation in the Anglican church in the sixteenth and seventeenth centuries, that the intense religious individualism of the doctrine of the calling was intimately bound to the social discipline of the religious com-

[1] *Two Treatises*, II, §41.

[2] MS Film. 77, pp. 310–11.

[3] This has been stressed brilliantly recently in Michael Walzer, *The Revolution of the Saints* (London, 1966), *passim*.

munity. Social authority within the church community was given the most vivid religious sanction. The Christian egalitarianism of the calling was controlled firmly by a self-confident social and theological hierarchy, which carried the status of a divine provision for human needs. Locke's social experience as an adult was at no point restricted to a closed Puritan community and his intellectual experience from an early point in his life destroyed the epistemological basis for the religious authority of any human minister within the community. To turn a Church into a voluntary society *because* each man can and must know for himself is to dissolve the moral cement which bound together the Puritan community and to leave it as a series of individual human beings confronting their God in a social world which neither had made directly. The necessary individuality of the religious relationship became an epistemological axiom and the force with which it was asserted reduced all human authority to a purely instrumental status. The only dependable channel of moral insight was the faith of the individual in his God. This faith was non-rational and historically generated but it was not irrational. Christianity was 'reasonable', though unassisted human reason could not have construed its truths. But although it was not contrary to reason, it was in itself an emotional attitude as much as an intellectual position. Furthermore, because the autonomous emotional commitment was a prerequisite for cognitive competence in the most essential elements of the law of reason, no weight of conceptual complexity or sophistication in any other human being could be any sort of surrogate for it. There could be no normative expertise in religious knowledge because the incidence of faith was determined by the grace of God and the individual's experience of faith was a necessary and a sufficient condition[1] for a grasp of religious duty adequate to secure his salvation.[2]

[1] It was of course the grace of God and not an individual's conviction that he had been vouchsafed this which was a sufficient condition. Cf. the chapter 'Of Enthusiasm', inserted into the fourth (1700) and subsequent editions of the *Essay concerning Human Understanding* (see IV, XIX, esp. §12: 'Firmness of persuasion, no proof that any proposition is from God').

[2] The only status which this left open to the priest is the performance of ceremonial functions and the provision of an intelligible series of the appropriate texts. Men appropriately form voluntary religious societies to provide themselves with a richer and more intricate religious culture and there is no doubt that this culture

This dissolution of the religious community as the *locus* of moral authority for human beings converts the priesthood of all believers into the primary definitional mode of all human duties. The calling loses the moral status of external definition by a divinely sanctioned external order and is reduced to drawing its status solely from the authenticity and force of the moral effort of the individual consigned to it. The complete individualization of religious duty evacuates human social organization and its hierarchy of all value except its contingent convenience.

In this sense the secular 'Lockean' liberals of the contemporary United States are more intimately than they realize the heirs of the egalitarian promise of Calvinism. If the religious purpose and sanction of the calling were to be removed from Locke's theory, the purpose of individual human life and of social life would both be exhaustively defined by the goal of the maximization of utility. However, it does not seem plausible that Locke would have supposed the maximization of utility to have been generated by the existing power structure and particular social structure of seventeenth-century England. Gross social inequality was compatible with equality of religious opportunity and since it was equality of religious opportunity which really mattered, and since social inequality was a singularly intractable feature of his experience and he was by disposition something of a political quietist, this social inequality became a target only when it entrenched upon the callings of individuals. It seems clear that Macpherson is right to see Locke as ascribing the remediably oppressive features of seventeenth-century English society not to the system of capitalist production itself but to economic scarcity and, we must surely add, to the moral corruption of the ruling class.[1] But it is inept to see in him the convinced lyricist of the moral sufficiency of *any* system of economic production.

If we wish to grasp *why* labour should be the title of the industrious and rational, it is essential to remember that the duty of

can do them some service (especially since so few of them can at present read Greek and Hebrew or indeed read at all; see above, p. 224, n. 4). But it can have no more *authority* over them than they choose to ascribe to it and hence under no circumstances can acquire the right to coerce them.

[1] See above p. 236, n. 1. See also, for example, *Two Treatises*, I, §58, ll. 21–2: '...Cities and Palaces, where those that call themselves Civil and Rational, go out of their way, by the Authority of Example.'

labour was central not only to the capitalist system of production and exchange but also to the Calvinist doctrine of the calling. It was the moral sufficiency of the calling as the definition of the terrestrial components of human duty which Locke assumed throughout his mature writings. We can grasp it most delicately in the conception of the moral purpose of his own life which he implicitly advances at intervals in his writing and correspondence. 'I think', he wrote to his friend William Molyneux on 19 January 1694, 'every one, according to what way Providence has placed him in, is bound to labour for the public good, as far as he is able, or else he has no right to eat.'[1] Not even old age and ill health justifies a 'lazy idleness'.[2] Providence had placed him in the calling of a scholar. The duty of the scholar was to study. This could often be an autonomously delightful activity but, when it was pursued merely for its delights, it no longer amounted to labour in the calling and became simply recreation.[3] The proper end of it remained firmly the attainment of salvation[4] and its character had to be judged in terms of its contribution to the pilgrim's progress.[5] Terrestrial utility was not to be ignored[6] but

[1] *Some Familiar Letters between Mr Locke and Several of his Friends*, *Works*, IV, p. 296. For the converse of this attitude, the insistence that the industrious had a right to be treated well, see Damaris Masham's letter, 'People who had been industrious, but were through age or infirmity passed labour, he was very bountiful to, and he used to blame that sparingness with which such were ordinarily relieved, as if it sufficed only that they should be kept from starving or extreme misery whereas they had, he said, a right to live comfortably in the world' (printed in M. Cranston, *John Locke: A Biography* (London, 1957), p. 426). Cf. C. B. Macpherson: 'One can detect a shade of difference in his attitude towards the employed and the unemployed' (*The Political Theory of Possessive Individualism* (Oxford, 1962), p. 226).

[2] *Some Familiar Letters*, *Works*, IV, 296.

[3] 'Study', MS Locke f 2, p. 87, printed in Peter King, *The Life of John Locke* (London, 1830), I, 171.

[4] 'Heaven being our great business and interest the knowledge which may direct us thither is certainly so too so that this is without peradventure the study which ought to take up the first and chiefest place in our thoughts' (MS Locke f 2, p. 100, King, *Life of Locke*, I, 180–1).

[5] '...our pilgrimage through this world'; 'the next thing to happiness in the other world, is a quiet prosperous passage through this' (MS Locke f 2, pp. 91 and 100, *ibid.* I, 174, 181). Cf. John Donne, 'Those are the two great works which we are to doe in this world; first to know that this world is not our home, and then to provide us another home, whilest we are in this world' (*The Sermons of John Donne*, ed. George R. Potter and Evelyn M. Simpson (10 vols. Berkeley, Calif., 1953–62), II, 307).

[6] 'That which seems to me to be suited to the end of man and lie level to his understanding is the improvement of natural experiments for the conveniences of this

it was conceived in terms compatible with the demands of the next world. Men were owned by God. They were vessels sent on a voyage by him and the duty of prudence to which they were subject was a duty to maintain their capacities at their fullest in order not to rob their owner of their services.[1] Recreation is not merely legitimate; it is mandatory because it is a necessary condition for living out the full term of their service.[2] Were it not for this physical necessity of rest, 'we should set ourselves on work without ceasing'.[3] Some men's callings provide little opportunity for study,[4] though all have time enough to study as much as they need to understand. Those who inherit wealth and as a result do not have a particular calling thrust upon them by economic necessity, are no less obliged to find work to do.[5] Those whose particu-

life and the way of ordering himself so as to attain happiness in the other—i.e. moral philosophy which in my sense comprehends religion too or a man's whole duty' (MS Locke f 2, p. 135, King, *Life of Locke*, I, 198); '...the principal end why we are to get knowledge here is to make use of it for the benefit of our selves and others in this world' (MS Locke f 2, p. 115, *ibid.* I, 182). Cf. Donne on '*Here we have no continuing city, but we seek one to come*': 'we seeke it not here, but we seeke it whilest we are here els we shall never finde it' (*Sermons*, II, 307).

1 See esp.: 'we rob God of so much service'. 'He that sinks his vessel by overloading it though it be gold and silver and precious stones will give his owner but an ill account of his voyage' (MS Locke f 2, p. 115, King, *Life of Locke*, I, 183).

2 MS Locke f 2, p. 115, *ibid.* I, 182–3; and 'Recreation', MS Locke f 3, pp. 351–7, *ibid.* II, 165–9.

3 MS Locke f 2, p. 114, *ibid.* I, 182.

4 'Those who have particular callings ought to understand them; and it is no unreasonable proposal, nor impossible to be compassed, that they should think and reason right about what is their daily employment.' 'Besides his particular calling for the support of this life, every one has a concern in a future life, which he is bound to look after. This engages his thoughts in religion; and here it mightily lies upon him to understand and reason right. Men, therefore, cannot be excused from understanding the words, and framing the general notions, relating to religion, right. The one day of seven, besides other days of rest, allows in the Christian world time enough for this (had they no other idle hours) if they would but make use of these vacancies from their daily labour, and apply themselves to an improvement of knowledge with as much diligence as they often do to a great many other things that are useless, and had but those that would enter them according to their several capacities in a right way to this knowledge' (*Of the Conduct of the Understanding*, *Works*, IV, 154).

5 '...if those who are left by their predecessors a plentiful fortune are excused from having a particular calling in order to their subsistence in this life. 'Tis yet certain that by the law of God they are under an obligation of doing something' (MS Locke f 2, pp. 101, 114, King, *Life of Locke*, I, 181). See also *Conduct of the Understanding*, *Works*, IV, 155. The obligation which they are under is the obligation to be of some *use* to their fellow men—'Labour for labour-sake is against nature' (*ibid.* p. 161).

lar calling is simply to study what is useful for themselves and their fellow men have labours available to them as all-enveloping in extent as the poorest peasant, and unless they display some measure of medical prudence, they are considerably less likely than the 'frugal laborious country man' to complete the full distance of their pilgrimage.[1] Provided that they display such due physical prudence, the moral standing of their lives depends on the labour which they expend rather than on their intrinsic intelligence or social distinction. There is moral complacency as well as appropriate intellectual modesty in Locke's famous self-description in the *Essay concerning Human Understanding*, as an 'under-labourer',[2] and equal moral assurance in his self-description in his introductory note to his *Paraphrase on St Paul's Epistles* as gleaning after other great labourers had harvested the fields.[3] Both cases were in his eyes equally cases of appropriate labour, apt to do good to his fellow men.[4] Any man who laboured strenuously in his calling during his passage through this world was observing the law of reason. The industrious and rational were to be found among Calvinist peasants in France before the Revocation of the Edict of Nantes[5] as much as among the residents

[1] MS Film. 77, p. 310.

[2] 'The commonwealth of learning is not at this time without master-builders, whose mighty designs, in advancing the sciences, will leave lasting monuments to the admiration of posterity; but everyone must not hope to be a *Boyle* or a *Sydenham*; and in an age that produces such masters as the great *Huygenius* and the incomparable Mr. *Newton*, with some others of that strain, it is ambition enough to be employed as an under-labourer in clearing ground a little, and removing some of the rubbish that lies in the way of knowledge' (Epistle to the Reader).

[3] 'There is nothing, certainly, of greater concernment to the peace of the church in general, nor to the direction and edification of all christians in particular, than a right understanding of the holy scripture. This consideration has set so many learned and pious men amongst us, of late years, upon expositions, paraphrases, and notes on the sacred writings, that the author of these hopes the fashion may excuse him from endeavouring to add his mite; believing, that after all that has been done by those great labourers in the harvest, there may be some gleanings left...' (*A Paraphrase and Notes on the Epistle of St Paul to the Galatians*, *Works*, III, 290).

[4] Cf. MS Locke f 2, 101 (King, *Life of Locke*, I, 181). A man 'will never be very happy in himself nor useful to others without [*sc.* prudence]. These two are every man's business.' See also *ibid.* p. 182. Frank Manuel has emphasized how close Newton was to this assessment of the business of an intellectual and how far the conception directed the scope of his studies in Frank E. Manuel, *Isaac Newton, Historian* (Cambridge, Mass., 1963), *passim*.

[5] '...more might be brought to be rational creatures and Christians (for they can hardly be thought really to be so, who, wearing the name, know not so much as the very principles of that religion) if due care were taken of them. For, if I mistake

of Thanet House and altogether more than among the colleges of Oxford and the manor houses of England.

There are two types of differential rationality which Locke recognized. One of them was the central category of human moral experience, those who lived according to the law of reason and laboured in their calling, as opposed to those who, through sin, lived out their lives in vicious self-indulgence. There is every textual reason to believe that Locke supposed both of these to be found in every class in seventeenth-century English society. Indeed there is no reason to believe that he supposed this differential to be correlated in any way whatever with the class structure of the society. The other form of differential rationality was the distinction between those capable of sophisticated analysis in any field of human endeavour and those not so capable. This was in practical terms a distinction of great significance but its bearing on Locke's conception of English social structure is not easy to identify. The clearest point perhaps is that one necessary condition for this type of rationality is literacy. The illiterate cannot analyse issues of any great complexity.[1] However, literacy is very far from being a sufficient condition for this achieved 'intellectual' rationality. The moral qualities of authentic concern for the truth and of persistent effort are also prerequisites. The comparatively Utopian division of labour commended in his note of 1693 suggests that he did feel a certain uneasiness about the social relationship between these two types of differential rationality.[2] It is perhaps most appropriate to read this scheme as a social programme for converting the second type of differential rationality from a morally arbitrary to a morally justified distribution.[3] The

not, the peasantry lately in France (a rank of people under a much heavier pressure of want and poverty than the day-labourers in England) of the reformed religion, understood it much better, and could say more for it, than those of a higher condition among us' (*Conduct of the Understanding*, *Works*, IV, 155). The extent of Locke's acquaintance with the French Calvinist community dated from his travels in France: see *Locke's Travels in France 1675–79*, ed. John Lough (Cambridge, 1953), and was maintained by extensive correspondence and further acquaintanceship during the period of his stay in Holland.

[1] There are repeated references in the *Essay concerning Human Understanding*, the *Conduct of the Understanding*, and the *Reasonableness of Christianity*, to the special difficulties of the illiterate in cognitive matters.

[2] See above, chapter 17.

[3] The qualifications which he makes (MS Film. 77, pp. 310–11) in order to preserve 'the distinction that ought to be in the ranks of men' indicate neatly the *emotional* ambivalence of his commitment to the egalitarianism of his own ideas.

equalization of the social opportunity to study would make the resulting differentials in human comprehension a result of God's genetic provision and differential human moral effort. The political implications of such an attitude make Locke a very distinctive figure. He cannot be read, like his brilliant pupil, the third earl of Shaftesbury, or Henry St John,[1] as a lyricist of an aristocracy of aesthetes dominating a natural rural hierarchy. Neither, on the other hand, can he be read simply as Defoe, for instance, is appropriately read as the uninhibited apologist for the new commercial relations, for the 'projectors'. Despite the egregiously pervasive commercialism of his metaphors, justly noted by Macpherson,[2] and despite his own extensive investments, he at no point in his works devotes extended moral enthusiasm to the role of the merchant or industrial producer. His emotional attitude towards such men was complaisant enough but they belong almost entirely to the areas of his life in which he performed services for others and drew dividends from the slave-trading companies but from which he sheepishly averted his eyes when he came to elaborate a coherent morality. It is clear that he exploited the resources of these new economic relations, just as they exploited him. But it is not at all clear, despite Macpherson, that they succeeded in exploiting his purely intellectual energies to any great degree. By simplifying so much the complexity of Locke's intellectual position, Macpherson fails to grasp the powerful ambivalence of its meaning in its historical situation. There is a sense in which Henry Yorke was right, when he made his famous speech on Castle Hill in Sheffield with *Locke on Government* in his hand, to believe that he had on his side 'the Spirit of John Locke'.[3]

But, if this account of the historical meaning of Locke's theories is correct, there remains a biographical problem on which it has only been possible to touch briefly and at intervals. Why was it that John Locke of Pensford, Westminster School,

[1] For Shaftesbury's social ideal see his *Characteristicks of Men, Manners, Opinions, Times* (5th edition, Birmingham, 1773) I, *passim*, esp. pp. 237–8. There is a fine presentation of Bolingbroke's thought in Isaac Kramnick, *Bolingbroke and his Circle* (Oxford, 1968). There was of course a considerable difference in the actual political commitments of Shaftesbury and Bolingbroke.

[2] Macpherson, *Possessive Individualism*, pp. 225–6.

[3] *The Trial of Thomas Hardy for High Treason...taken down in shorthand...*(London, 1794–5), III, 241. See *The Spirit of John Locke Revived* (Sheffield [? 1794]).

Christ Church, Thanet House, France, Holland, and Oates should have come to adopt these theories? It is unlikely that we shall ever be able to answer this question with much conviction because so little of the relevant evidence is available. But it is perhaps worth concluding with a short sketch of the highly conjectural explanation which has been implicit throughout this account. Both Von Leyden and Abrams have seen the crucial development in Locke's intellectual life as an epistemological insight which he derived at some point between 1660 and 1664 or at the latest 1667 and which set him off on a career of continuing inquiry into the scope and limitations of human knowledge, particularly religious and moral knowledge, in which he persisted up to the time of his death. There can be no doubt that this does represent the crucial break in Locke's intellectual development, though it is perhaps still obscure in causal terms just why it happened.[1] But in itself the elaboration of the implications of this break (performed recently with great skill and sensitivity by Abrams) does not suffice to explain the full concrete development of Locke's political and social attitudes. To fill out this explanation it is necessary to regress to a more vulgar level of observation.

Locke was brought up by a Puritan father in Somerset.[2] He rose in society largely by his own efforts, by a combination of diligence and a capacity to display just enough social deference to satisfy the great. He was in many ways an arrogant, impatient, hot-tempered, and chronically anxious man. It is clear that he often did not find at all attractive the attentive deference appropriate to his social status or the measured cadences and bland assurance appropriate to his eirenic interpretation of the duty of the intellectual. The carefully restrained aggression bursts out into vitriolic assault upon a legitimate intellectual prey. And no one is *such* a legitimate intellectual prey, has so surely abandoned the law

[1] See above, chapters 2–4. Abrams in particular provides an elegant rationale for the development. But, while the evidence is certainly not in direct conflict with his reading, it is also insufficiently rich and precise to establish at all points that his account is the way that Locke's interests *did* in fact develop.

[2] All the relevant biographical information here referred to is conveniently available in Maurice Cranston, *John Locke: A Biography* (London, 1957). On Locke's early upbringing see especially the quotation from Damaris Masham's letter printed *loc. cit.* p. 12.

of reason, and entered into a state of war with him, as a man who attacks him or even presses him upon an issue which causes him intellectual embarrassment. The diligence, both intellectual and practical, which he undoubtedly did manifest also had its costs. He was a chronic invalid from his forties onwards and the most emotional moral reproaches which we can find him addressing to himself seem to arise from the realization that his driven, compulsive self-dedication to study had caused this physical damage.[1] He did not live at ease among his fellow men.[2] The haggard eyes of the final portraits record the lasting threat of failure in his efforts to wring ease and happiness from the recalcitrant world.

Calvinism was a religion which demanded ceaseless effort from its adherents but at least in return it provided a determinate structure in their social setting for their lives. The force of Locke's sceptical intelligence and the trajectory of his social mobility broke down the given structure of the religious community but it left him initially with nothing in its place except the earliest social values he had learnt, diligence and self-control. These values he knew by feeling, by faith, and it was these, the 'oracles of the nursery',[3] whose meaning he was to interpret with ever greater epistemological sophistication for the remainder of his intellectual career. Throughout the rest of his life two conceptions of substantive morality nudge against one another in uneasy rivalry. One of these is purely secular, a matter of terrestrial utility at the

[1] Cf. MS Film. 77, pp. 310–11.

[2] Cf. for example: 'Tell not your business or design to one that you are not sure will help it forwards. All that are not for you count against you. For so they generally prove either through folly, envy, malice or interest' (Lingua *94*, MS Film. 77, p. 38, King, *Life of Locke*, II, 81–2), and the repeated insistence throughout the works that those who do not believe in God cannot be trusted at all, the extraordinary importance of oaths in securing social order, the endless need for caution, and the often mean or vicious tone of parts of the correspondence.

[3] Ironically, his own analysis applies directly to himself: 'Who is there almost that hath not opinions planted in him by education time out of mind, which by that means come to be as the municipal laws of the country which must not be questioned, but are there looked on with reverence as the standards of right and wrong truth and falsehood, when perhaps those so sacred opinions were but the oracles of the Nursery or the traditional grave talk of those who pretend to inform our childhood who receive them from hand to hand without ever examining them. This is the fate of our tender age which being thus seasoned early it grows by continuation of time as it were into the very constitution of the mind which afterwards very [*sic*] difficulty receives a different tincture' ('Study' (1677), MS Locke f 2, p. 125, King, *Life of Locke*, I, 188).

social level and of manipulative attention to current social values in order to maximize the influence and power of the individual.[1] The other is heavily concerned with individual salvation, defined largely in theological terms,[2] and incorporates the first morality as a dutiful subsidiary. The first morality does have some authentically Hobbesian characteristics. Why, then, did Locke under the impulse of his growing epistemological scepticism and his successful social ascent not simply discard the theological morality and adopt the secular 'Hobbesian' variant? The explanation that Locke *believed* in God, while clearly true, is in itself merely to beg this question. The problem is to grasp what there was in God for Locke, what essential service he performed in making sense of Locke's life. It should not be difficult in these terms to make out why Locke did not become a gay and careless libertine. There simply was never a point in his early life when he enjoyed the sort of autonomous social security and status which could make such a role self-sufficient. There was too much at stake for too long in his struggle to make a place for himself in the world to provide him with such assurance. He needed to levy too many claims on others, and even more importantly had levied too many on himself and suffered too much anxiety to feel confident in a world in which any manoeuvre which paid off was morally appropriate. From one perspective it might be just to observe that he was never

1 See, for example, 'that which would be no vicious excess [*sc.* in] a retired obscurity may be a very great one amongst people who think ill of such excess because by lessening his esteem amongst them it makes a man uncapable of having that Authority and doing that good which otherwise he might. For esteem and reputation being a sort of Moral Strength whereby a man is enabled to do as it were by an augmented force, that which others of equal natural parts and natural power cannot do without it, he that by any intemperance weakens this his moral strength does himself as much harm as if by intemperance he weakened the natural strength either of his mind or body and so is equally vicious by doing harm to him self' ('Virtus', MS Film. 77, p. 10, King, *Life of Locke*, II, 95). The obligation seems in form to have been an instance of the duty of prudence. See MS Locke f 2, p. 101, King, *ibid.* I, 181.

2 'There is, indeed, one science (as they are now distinguished) incomparably above all the rest, where it is not by corruption narrowed into a trade or faction, for mean or ill ends, and secular interests; I mean theology, which, containing the knowledge of God and his creatures, our duty to him and our fellow-creatures, and a view of our present and future state, *is the comprehension of all other knowledge directed to its true end*; i.e. the honour and veneration of the Creator, and the happiness of mankind. This is that noble study which is every man's duty, and every one that can be called a rational creature is capable of' (*Conduct of the Understanding*, *Works*, IV, 166; my italics).

so devout as when levying claims on others.[1] But in a sense the more important point may be that he was never so devout as when he reflected on the strain of his own struggles and it was not until he had become distinctly ill physically, in fact until the period of his visit to France, that he made any serious attempt to work out the naturalistic ethic in a fashion which confronted the dilemmas exposed in the *Essays on the Law of Nature*. To set this out crudely, the Lockean social and political theory is to be seen as the elaboration of Calvinist social values, in the absence of a terrestrial focus of theological authority and in response to a series of particular challenges. The explanation of why it was *Calvinist* social values which Locke continued to expound is that he was brought up in a Calvinist family. And the reason why he *continued* to expound them is that his own experience was too dominated by 'uneasiness', too anxious, to make a self-confident naturalism a tolerable interpretation of the world. A 'state of licence' did not seem an enhancement of liberty but simply a destruction of security.[2] His own psychology and his own biography conspired to retain him within the inherited theological framework and in consequence the honesty and force of his thought were devoted to making such sense as could be made of this framework instead of to replacing it.

But to present the explanation in this fashion is to betray a damaging residual historicism. The reason why Locke failed to become Hobbes was that he was not only born a Calvinist and subject to acute status aspirations but also very neurotic. But what of the reasons why Hobbes never became Locke? The instinctive answer that Hobbes was less neurotic, could accept the bleak reality of the world as it is, is to congratulate Hobbes on the maturity of his adaptation and the good taste of the allegiance to the way of the future which this manifested. We felicitate him for his striking resemblance to ourselves. But it is important to insist on how much better the adaptation may have been to the life of Chatsworth than to that of the London slums or even the Yorkshire villages of his day. In accepting his interpretation of the

[1] Cf. Hooker on Calvin, 'Divine knowledge he gathered, not by hearing or reading so much, as by teaching others' (*The Works of that Learned and Judicious Divine Mr. Richard Hooker*..., ed. John Keble (2nd edition, Oxford, 1841), I, 128).

[2] *Two Treatises*, II, §6, ll. 1–2.

world, Hobbes was accepting as true an interpretation of the lives of most men which might have made them simply unendurable. It may be that he could furnish an altogether more accurate and coherent explanation of the world and man's place in it than Locke could. It may be a sufficient causal explanation of the fact that Locke did not emulate this feat that his own personal need for reassurance was more demanding than that of Hobbes. But it is also the case that his anxieties forced him to preserve a coherence for the lives of other men than himself. There may be a certain socially insulated heartlessness, besides the poise, in such a maturity as that of Hobbes in the society in which he lived and a certain residual sensitivity to the needs of others, besides the personal weakness, in such a neurosis as that of Locke. In this perspective, the answer to the question of why Hobbes did not become Locke (avoided that awful fate) may need a more nuanced treatment. In this endeavour it is just to note that, despite his gross personal meanness and his expansive moral insensitivity, Locke *did* continue to take seriously the problem of preserving rationality for the lives of all men. It was because self-preservation was in Locke's eyes so grossly inadequate as a continuing human end that he could not abandon the majority of mankind to the careers of naturalistic deprivation which were all that the economy could make available to them. As he worked away in his declining years at the *Reasonableness of Christianity* and the *Paraphrases of St Paul's Epistles* he was keeping a kind of faith with the majority of his fellow men with which the more benign Hobbes had scarcely troubled himself, labouring to preserve for all men that ease to be won from labour which could alone confer rationality upon their lives.

However corrupt Locke's motives for writing the *Two Treatises of Government*, the structure of ideas in that work kept the same faith. In his relationship with God every man was prised loose from the tangle of seventeenth-century social deference. The meanest cowherd, as much as the first Earl of Shaftesbury, participated in and helped to constitute the ethical legitimacy of the political community. Only in a relationship which so completely and explicitly extricated men from the pressures of their contemporary society could it have been possible, in seventeenth-century England, to confer on the individual a moral status which would enable him to call into question the moral legitimacy of his society. It was not as an economic producer, a proprietor of his labour, but only as a recipient of the commands of God, that Locke could consider a man in this way as set over against his society and his family. In the relationship with God, there was given to every man an Archimedian point outside the realm of human contingency from which the rational individual could judge the world and act upon it. No society in history has yet met the critical standard which this feat set up, though many more sophisticated and secular figures than Locke have pretended brazenly that their society did or does so.

19

CONCLUSION

For Professor Macpherson Locke's significance lies in his role as one of the great systematizers of 'possessive individualism', a doctrine once historically appropriate to the new bourgeois order but one which now threatens to rivet upon the generations which have escaped from their necessity the immemorial shackles of scarcity.[1] The key to this doctrine is a belief in the rationality of unlimited desire. It sees the essence of man as lying in a infinity of consumption, an infinity of appropriation. In place of traditional, more especially Christian, conceptions in which this relentless libidinal drive was considered a psychological curse, to be 'fought down' to the best of men's abilities, concupiscence has become sanctioned, indeed espoused as *the* rational mode of human existence.

I have tried to question the felicity of inflicting this role upon Locke by pointing out his persisting adherence to a conception of rationality firmly premised upon the reality of an after life. In a calculus of rational choice in which infinite satisfactions are available in another world and only the most discomfitingly finite pleasures accessible in this one it would indeed be remarkable if the decisions judged rational turned out to be a series constructed solely from the full set of immediate terrestrial desires which it was in principle possible to satisfy. Something historically astonishing has taken place when the Calvinist conception of the calling has become assimilated to the duty of a member of a contemporary capitalist society to yearn ceaselessly for consumption. Adapting Hume's reasoning on miracles, we may suggest that where 'the fact, which the testimony endeavours to establish,

[1] Professor Macpherson has given a more extended account of the theoretical perspective in which his analysis of Locke's thought in *The Political Theory of Possessive Individualism* (Oxford, 1962) is set in three studies, *The Real World of Democracy* (Oxford, 1966), 'The Maximization of Democracy', *Philosophy, Politics and Society*, ed. Peter Laslett and W. G. Runciman, 3rd series (Oxford, 1967), and 'Democratic Theory: Ontology and Technology', *Political Theory and Social Change*, ed. David Spitz (New York, 1967).

partakes of the extraordinary and the marvellous; in that case, the evidence resulting from the testimony, admits of a diminution, greater or less, in proportion as the fact is more or less unusual'.[1] If Locke had combined his chilling vision of the calling[2] with a conception of the human essence in terms of the moral rationality of infinite appropriation he would have taken on a task of conceptual reconciliation of truly miraculous perversity. The testimony which Macpherson can adduce in support of his interpretation of Locke's intellectual assignment seems inadequate to establish that Locke had conceived such a curious ambition. A more economical hypothesis might be that Locke was simply not addressing himself to the issue which Macpherson judges him to have been treating in the *Two Treatises*.

In itself this insistence, if accepted, merely requires minor historical amendment of the place held by Locke in the saga of possessive individualism. But there is one perspective from which it may be of more significance in the uncomfortable moral history of liberalism. Locke saw the rationality of human existence, a rationality which he spent so much of his life in attempting to vindicate, as dependent upon the truths of religion. Theology was the key to a coherent understanding of human existence. I have argued throughout that a defensible theology is a necessary condition for the cogency of many of his arguments and that there is every reason to believe that Locke himself would have assented to this judgement. If, then, Locke is not judged to have possessed a defensible theology, it is hardly remarkable (and again we have no reason to suppose that Locke himself would have dissented from this judgement) that the residue of his thought should provide no coherent account of human rationality.

Locke perhaps was not much interested in the sort of freedom meant by Macpherson,[3] but it is not clear that his lack of interest

[1] David Hume, *An Enquiry concerning Human Understanding*, ed. L. A. Selby-Bigge (2nd edition, Oxford, 1902), section x, part 1, 89, p. 113.

[2] See above, chapter 18, and especially the claim that if it were not for the necessity of rest to maintain physical existence, 'we should set ourselves on work without ceasing' (MS Locke f 2, p. 114, Peter King, *The Life of John Locke* (London, 1830), 1, 182). This seems an odd norm to extract from a utilitarian calculus.

[3] See Macpherson, *Possessive Individualism*, p. 262. It is not that Locke was not confused about the freedom open to the labouring classes, just that he was at least as confused about the extent and limits of the freedom open to himself.

had anything except in the most brutally *ad hominem* of terms to do with the class state. Freedom of thought he set some little store by, a professional interest for an intellectual, though the freedom, needless to say, was not to be extended to atheists. But freedom of thought was required not because of any exuberant taste for the Promethean delights of unrestrained speculation, a matter at best of licence rather than liberty, but because it was a necessary condition for the pursuit of religious truth. Furthermore, religious truth itself was valued not for its formal properties but because it too was in its turn a necessary condition for religious practice, for the correct understanding by human beings of their duties to God. The correctness of this understanding would not only enable men to articulate true religious propositions but, through its action on their will, enable them to translate these into right actions in their lives. Freedom of thought was necessary to make intelligible to all men the crudest of practical syllogisms. The human mind was to be made free in order that men might grasp the more clearly their ineluctable confinement in the harness in which, ever since the delinquencies of their first ancestor, God had set human beings in the world. For only in this recognition, bitted, bridled, yoked, could they tame their pride and set all their strength to haul the immense weight which God had chosen to attach to them. Even with the recognition, their exertions on earth were near to being a labour of Sisyphus. But, through dutiful acceptance of the yoke in their lives, they could earn the only possible, though happily the surpassing, ease of the world to come.

It is perfectly correct to observe, as Macpherson does, that Locke's political theory has the effect of turning the acceptance of the existing distribution of economic power (or something close to this) within a class state into a duty even for the most deprived. But it has this effect not because Locke consecrates infinite desire as morally rational, but because the sacrifice of immediate sensual gratification which such social passivity requires from the deprived is compensated by the availability of a concrete style of life which transmutes all their suffering into rationality. Their acceptance of an existing social structure is predicated not on the moral status of this social structure but on the triviality of the rewards forgone by the poor when set against the grandeur of the opportunities which *any* stable social structure must leave available to the devout Christian. The only sort of social structure subject to rational resistance as a whole is one which claims rights over individuals which are formally incompatible with their discharge of Christian duties or which explicitly denies the religious equality of all men.

It has been the classic trope of liberalism, as Macpherson argues, to give an account of the human essence which presents the subjection of the individual to the market economy as essentially non-coercive, as offering a freedom as extensive as could be compatible with the nature of the external world. Marxists have sneered tellingly at the ludicrous mendacity of this claim, though they have as yet, as Macpherson agrees, scarcely succeeded in elaborating in concrete terms an unequivocally less coercive alternative. In this perspective the structure of Locke's thought may perhaps retain a certain potential embarrassment for the simpler devotee of liberalism. For in two separate ways it scarcely fits the dimensions of the secular theory. In the first place there is no reason whatever to suppose that Locke did perceive the subjection of the individual to the market as a non-coercive experience. The cause of his acceptance of the propriety of this subjection may well have been, in terms of his own psychology, his class situation, but the reason in terms of his theory why it must have seemed acceptable was simply that the tribute paid by the wage labourer to accumulated private capital was altogether less relentless in its experiential exactions than the tribute which he owed to God. The coerciveness of wage labour pales into insignificance before the boundless repression demanded by the calling.[1] Secondly, and more importantly, the injunction to take existing economic and social inequality, within limits, as given was judged rational in terms of a concrete doctrine of the nature of the good life. Because he could give such an elaborate and specific account of how men should live, of what actions they should perform, because he could give such concrete descriptions of a mode of life which could be experienced as emotionally viable and conceived as rational by those who adopted it, he had no need to yearn for egalitarian social

[1] An opinion then, as now, presumably more plausible to the gentry than to the wage labourer. But Locke did have, or thought he had, some sociological evidence of its realism in the most unpromising conditions. See *Conduct of the Understanding*, *Works* (1768), IV, 155, cited above, p. 254.

change. It was not necessary to change the world to enable each man to change himself. Wherever there was the will, there was the way. All this did not make egalitarian social change necessarily undesirable, but it did make it all too conveniently dispensable.

The rationality of this mode of life did not depend upon the rationality of infinite desire. Indeed it provided specifically for the development and exercise of those powers of the individual which Locke conceived it to be morally appropriate to exercise. Rational action was tied logically to the strenuous discharge of a series of duties to God. Hence the disappearance of this framework of religious belief would dissolve the concrete structure of rational human action. In its place there would be left only the confusing abstractness of the utilitarian calculus. Instead of being instructed to keep their hands off the property of others in return for the knowledge of how to live, the labouring classes must be instructed to keep their hands off the property of others in return for what they could get out of the economy. The sum of what they have extracted has of course increased greatly and fairly steadily over the last century, but the ratio of the total product distributed to them has hardly grown as dramatically. The idea of a unitary moral theory (as opposed to a unitary legal account) of political obligation is in many ways an exceedingly superstitious one. Nothing which we know at the moment about the distribution of opportunities and coercions among the majority of the population of any state today suggests that it would be rational to assess these as implying an unequivocal obligation to obey the state, though no doubt most of the time most people have adequate prudential reasons for doing so with a purely exploitative intention and no doubt on many particular occasions it would be grossly immoral for particular individuals not to do so.

Any theory of political obligation with holistic ambitions must depend upon a concrete theory of rational human action and any theory of rational human action with holistic ambitions must depend upon the creation of a form of society in which all men could knowingly adopt it.[1] The period between the disappearance

[1] I am here accepting the analysis of the character of a viable social morality set out by Alasdair MacIntyre in his *Secularization and Moral Change* (London, 1967). See also his *A Short History of Ethics* (London, 1967).

of a religious basis for rational political obligation, which has in large part already come about, and the emergence of a form of humanly rational society which has assuredly not yet come about and which may indeed never do so, has been and largely remains in the societies of the West a period of bourgeois political theory. The mendacities of this theory have long been displayed. Their present relative obfuscation is a result as much of tedium and imaginative exhaustion as of indignant disagreement with this claim. Few now suppose these societies to be particularly admirable and such discomfort as is still felt can be readily solaced by noting the contrasting mendacities widely touted in other parts of the world. It has even become common to feel a discreet self-satisfaction at our own superior honesty with ourselves, our capacity to recognize and admit the presence of sundry motes and beams in our own eyes. At least we have no *illusions* about the state of Denmark. The celebrants of the 'end of ideology' have espoused in effect the politics of *Candide*.

To place the political theory of Locke will not help to dissipate this faintly miasmic confusion but it does provide an image for the oddity of our situation. We have, it seems, come to accept in the broadest of terms the politics of Locke but, while doing so, we have firmly discarded the reasons which alone made them seem acceptable even to Locke. It is hard to believe that this combination can be quite what we need today.

BIBLIOGRAPHY

A full bibliography would be out of place in a work of this character. The checklist which follows contains all works cited in the text, all work on Locke from which I am conscious of having learnt directly, whether in agreement or disagreement, and such secondary writing on the history of ideas as I have found helpful in formulating the perspective aimed at in this book, together with a number of recent articles on Locke's political thought which do not appear in Mr Laslett's most recent edition of the *Two Treatises* (2nd edition, Cambridge, 1967). For earlier work, prior to 1967 and not cited here, Laslett provides an excellent list which can be supplemented for American commentaries by Richard H. Cox, *Locke on War and Peace* (Oxford, 1960). A helpful indication of the sort of intellectual materials available to Locke himself can be obtained from the catalogue of his library edited by John Harrison and Peter Laslett, or more extensively from the Wing *Short Title Catalogue*. Specifically political writings can be approached through the notes or bibliographies of such widely available scholarly works as those of J. W. Allen, W. H. Greenleaf, Otto Gierke and P. Zagorin. Besides the Bodleian collection of Locke manuscripts listed below there are Locke materials of varying importance in the British Museum, Public Record Office, Somerset Record Office, Houghton Library of Harvard University, Beinecke Library of Yale University, Newberry Library, Chicago, Huntington Library, Pasadena, California, and New York Public Library; and the remainder of Locke's library is for the most part in the possession of Mr Paul Mellon at Oak Spring, Virginia. I have been given the most generous access to all of these, but they are not included in the bibliography because I have not cited them directly in the text.

BIBLIOGRAPHY

Aaron, Richard I. *John Locke*, 2nd edition, Oxford, 1955 (1st edition, 1937).

Aarsleff, Hans. 'The State of Nature and the Nature of Man in Locke', *John Locke: Problems and Perspectives*, ed. J. W. Yolton, Cambridge, 1969.

Abrams, Philip. *John Locke as a Conservative: An Edition of Locke's First Writings on Political Obligation*, unpublished Ph.D. dissertation, Cambridge, 1961.

A Just and Modest Vindication of the proceedings of the Two last Parliaments...(anon.), London, 1681.

Althusser, Louis, *Pour Marx*, Paris, 1966.

Anscombe, G. E. M. *Intention*, Oxford, 1957.

Anscombe, G. E. M. 'Modern Moral Philosophy', *Philosophy*, XXXIII, 124 (January 1958), 1–19.

Anscombe, G. E. M. 'War and Murder', *Nuclear Weapons: A Catholic Response*, ed. Walter Stein, paperback edition, London, 1963, pp. 45–62.

Anscombe, G. E. M. 'A Note on Mr. Bennett', *Analysis*, XXVI, 6 (June 1966), 208.

Aquinas, St Thomas. *Summa Theologiae*, Latin and English edition, ed. T. Gilby, O.P., 60 vols., London, 1964.

Armstrong, Robert L. 'John Locke's Doctrine of Signs', *Journal of the History of Ideas*, XXVI, 3 (July–September 1965), 369–82.

Aronson, Jason. 'Shaftesbury on Locke', *American Political Science Review*, LIII, 4 (December 1959), 1101–4.

Arrow, Kenneth J. *Social Choice and Individual Values*, 2nd edition, New York, 1963.

Bacon, Francis. *The Physical and Metaphysical Works of Lord Bacon*..., ed. Joseph Devey, London, 1860.

Baldwin, Alice M. *The New England Clergy and the American Revolution*, reprint, New York, 1958 (1st edition, 1928).

Barnes, Annie S. *Jean Le Clerc (1657–1736) et la République des Lettres*, Paris, 1938.

Barrington, John Shute, Lord. *The Rights of Protestant Dissenters. In two parts*..., London, 1704.

Behrens, B. 'The Whig Theory of the Constitution in the Reign of Charles II', *Cambridge Historical Journal*, VII, 1 (1941), 42–71.

Bennett, Jonathan. 'Whatever the Consequences', *Analysis*, XXVI, 3 (January 1966), 83–102.

Berlin, Sir Isaiah. 'Hobbes, Locke and Professor Macpherson', *The Political Quarterly*, XXXV (1964), 444–68.

Blackall, Offspring. *The Divine Institution of Magistracy and the gracious Design of its Institution. A Sermon Preach'd before the Queen...*, London, 1708.

Blackall, Offspring. *The Lord Bishop of Exeter's Answer to Mr Hoadly's Letter...*, London, 1709.

Blake, William. *The Complete Writings of William Blake...*, ed. Geoffrey Keynes, London, 1966.

Bodin, Jean. *The Six Bookes of a Commonweale*, trans. R. Knolles (1606), ed. K. D. McRae, Cambridge, Mass., 1962.

Bonno, Gabriel. *Les Relations Intellectuelles de Locke avec la France...*, University of California Publications in Modern Philology, XXXVIII, 2, 37–264, Berkeley and Los Angeles, Calif., 1955.

Boswell, James. *Boswell in Holland 1763–64*, ed. Frederick A. Pottle, London, 1962.

Bourne, H. R. Fox. *The Life of John Locke*, 2 vols., London, 1876.

Brogan, A. P. 'John Locke and Utilitarianism', *Ethics*, LXIX, 2 (January 1959), 79–93.

Brown, Louise Fargo. *The First Earl of Shaftesbury*, New York, 1933.

Brown, Stuart M., Jr. 'The Taylor Thesis: Some Objections', *Hobbes Studies*, ed. K. C. Brown, Oxford, 1965, pp. 57–71.

Burnet, Thomas. *The Sacred Theory of the Earth: Containing an Account of the Original of the Earth...*, London, 1684 (trans. of 1681 Latin edition).

Calvin, Jean. *Institution de la Religion Chrestienne*, ed. Jean-Daniel Benoit, 5 vols., Paris, 1957–63.

[Cary, John.] *A Vindication of the Parliament of England in Answer to a Book Written by W. Molyneux...*, London, 1698.

Cassirer, Ernst. *The Platonic Renaissance in England*, trans. James P. Pettegrove, London, 1953.

Cherno, Melvin. 'Locke on Property: A Reappraisal', *Ethics*, LXVIII, 1 (October 1957), 51–5.

Christie, W. D. *A Life of Anthony Ashley Cooper, First Earl of Shaftesbury 1621–1683*, 2 vols., London, 1871.

[Claude, M.] *Les Plaintes des Protestans, cruellement opprimez dans le Royaume de France*, Cologne, 1686.

[Clement, Simon.] *An Answer to Mr. Molyneux, his Case of Ireland's Being Bound by Acts of Parliament in England...*, London, 1698.

Condillac, Abbé Étienne-Bonnot de. *Essai sur l'Origine des Connoissances*

Humaines, 2 vols. Amsterdam, 1746, *Oeuvres Philosophiques de Condillac*, ed. Georges Le Roy, 3 vols., Paris, 1947–51, I, 1–118.

Condorcet, Jean-Antoine-Nicolas de Caritat, Marquis de. *Esquisse d'un Tableau Historique des Progrès de l'Esprit Humain*, ed. O. H. Prior, Paris, 1933.

Costello, William T., S.J. *The Scholastic Curriculum in Early Seventeenth-Century Cambridge*, Cambridge, Mass., 1958.

Cox, Richard H. *Locke on War and Peace*, Oxford, 1960.

Cox, Richard H. 'Justice as the Basis of Political Order in Locke', *Nomos VI. Justice*, ed. Carl J. Friedrich and J. W. Chapman, New York, 1963, pp. 243–61.

Cragg, G. R. *From Puritanism to the Age of Reason, A Study of Changes in Religious Thought within the Church of England 1660 to 1700*, paperback edition, Cambridge, 1966 (1st edition, 1950).

Cranston, M. *John Locke: A Biography*, London, 1957.

Davis, David Brion. *The Problem of Slavery in Western Culture*, Ithaca, N.Y., 1966.

Day, J. P. 'Locke on Property', *Philosophical Quarterly*, XVI, 64 (July 1966), 207–20.

de Jouvenel, Bertrand. *Sovereignty, An Inquiry into the Political Good*, trans. J. F. Huntington, Cambridge, 1957.

de Jouvenel, Bertrand. *The Pure Theory of Politics*, Cambridge, 1963.

De Marchi, E. 'Locke's Atlantis', *Political Studies*, III, 2 (June 1955), 164–5.

de Roover, Raymond. 'The Concept of the Just Price: Theory and Economic Policy', *Journal of Economic History*, XVIII, 4 (December 1958), 418–34.

Dewhurst, Kenneth. *John Locke (1632–1704): Physician and Philosopher. A Medical Biography*..., London, 1963.

Divine Institutes of True Religion and Civil Government...(anon.), London, 1783.

Dodge, Guy Howard. *The Political Theory of the Huguenots of the Dispersion*, New York, 1947.

Donne, John. *The Sermons of John Donne*, ed. George R. Potter and Evelyn M. Simpson, 10 vols., Berkeley and Los Angeles, Calif., 1953–62.

Douglas, David. *English Scholars 1660–1730*, 2nd edition, London, 1951 (1st edition, 1939).

Dunn, John. 'Consent in the Political Theory of John Locke', *The Historical Journal*, X, 2 (July 1967), 153–82.

Dunn, John. 'The Identity of the History of Ideas', *Philosophy*, April 1968.

Dunn, John. 'Justice and the Interpretation of Locke's Political Theory', *Political Studies*, February 1968.

Dunn, John. 'The Politics of Locke in England and America in the Eighteenth Century', *John Locke: Problems and Perspectives*, ed. J. W. Yolton, Cambridge, 1969.

Edwards, John. *Some Thoughts Concerning the Several Causes and Occasions of Atheism, Especially in the Present Age*..., London, 1695.

Edwards, John. *Socinianism Unmask'd. A Discourse Shewing the Unreasonableness Of a Late Writer's Opinion Concerning the Necessity of only One Article of Christian Faith:*..., London, 1697.

Elton, G. R. *The Tudor Constitution*..., Cambridge, 1960.

Feiling, Keth. *A History of the Tory Party 1640–1714*, Oxford, 1924.

Figgis, John Neville. *The Divine Right of Kings*, paperback edition, New York, 1965 (1st edition, 1896).

Filmer, Robert. *Patriarcha and other Political Works of Sir Robert Filmer*, ed. Peter Laslett, Oxford, 1949.

Foxcroft, H. C. *The Life and Letters of Sir George Savile, Bart., First Marquis of Halifax*, 2 vols., London, 1898.

Friedrich, Carl J. *Constitutional Reason of State, The Survival of the Constitutional Order*, Providence, R.I., 1957.

Furley, O. W. 'The Whig Exclusionists: Pamphlet Literature in the Exclusion Campaign, 1679–81', *Cambridge Historical Journal*, XIII, 1 (1957), 19–36.

George, Charles H. and Katherine. *The Protestant Mind of the English Reformation 1570–1640*, Princeton, 1961.

Gibson, James. *Locke's Theory of Knowledge and its Historical Relations*, reprint, Cambridge, 1960 (1st edition 1917).

Gierke, Otto. *Natural Law and the Theory of Society 1500–1800*, trans. E. Barker, paperback edition, Boston, 1957 (1st edition of translation, 1934).

Goldwin, Robert A. 'John Locke 1632–1704', *History of Political Philosophy*, ed. Leo Strauss and Joseph Cropsey, Chicago, 1963, 433–68.

Gomezio de Amescua, D. Balthassare. *Tractatus de Potestate in Seipsum*..., Mediolani, 2nd edition, 1609 (1st edition 1604).

Gough, J. W. *Fundamental Law in English Constitutional History*, Oxford, 1955.

Gough, J. W. *John Locke's Political Philosophy*, reprint, Oxford, 1956 (1st edition, 1950).

Gough, J. W. *The Social Contract, A Critical Study of its Development*, 2nd edition, Oxford, 1957 (1st edition, 1936).

Greenleaf, W. H. *Order, Empiricism and Politics. Two Traditions of English Political Thought 1500–1700*, London, 1964.

Gwyn, W. B. *The Meaning of the Separation of Powers. An Analysis of the Doctrine from its Origin to the Adoption of the United States Constitution*, Tulane Studies in Political Science, IX (1965).

Haber, Francis C. *The Age of the World: Moses to Darwin*, Baltimore, 1959.

Halévy, Elie. *La Formation du Radicalisme Philosophique*, 3 vols., Paris, 1901.

Haller, William. *The Rise of Puritanism*, paperback edition, New York, 1957 (1st edition, 1938).

Hardy, Thomas. *The Trial of Thomas Hardy for High Treason...taken down in shorthand...*, 4 vols., London, 1794–5.

Harrison, John and Laslett, Peter. *The Library of John Locke*, Oxford Bibliographical Society Publications, N.S. XIII, Oxford, 1965.

Hazard, Paul. *La Crise de la conscience européenne*, Paris, 1961 (1st edition, 1935).

Hexter, J. H. 'The Loom of Language and the Fabric of Imperatives: The Case of *Il Principe* and *Utopia*', *American Historical Review*, LXIX, 4 (July 1964), 945–68.

Hill, Christopher. *Puritanism and Revolution, Studies in Interpretation of the English Revolution of the Seventeenth Century*, paperback edition, London, 1962 (1st edition, 1958).

Hill, Christopher. *Society and Puritanism in Pre-Revolutionary England*, London, 1964.

Hoadly, Benjamin. *Some Considerations Humbly offered to the Right Reverend the Lord Bishop of Exeter...*, London, 1709.

Hobbes, Thomas. *Leviathan: or The Matter, Forme and Power of a Commonwealth Ecclesiasticall and Civil* (1651), ed. Michael Oakeshott, Oxford, 1946.

Holdsworth, Sir W. S. *A History of English Law* (16 vols., 3rd edition, London, 1923).

Hooker, Richard. *The Works of that Learned and Judicious Divine Mr. Richard Hooker...*, ed. John Keble, 3 vols., 2nd edition, Oxford, 1841.

Hume, David. *An Enquiry concerning Human Understanding*, ed. L. A. Selby-Bigge, 2nd edition, Oxford, 1902.

Hume, David. *Essays Moral, Political and Literary*, London, 1903.

Hume, David. *A Treatise of Human Nature*, 2 vols., London, 1911.

Hume, David. *Dialogues concerning Natural Religion...*, ed. Norman Kemp Smith, 2nd edition, London, 1947 (1st edition, 1935).

James I. *The Political Works of James I*, ed. C. H. McIlwain, Cambridge, Mass., 1918.

Jenkins, J. J. 'Locke and Natural Rights', *Philosophy*, XLII, 160 (April 1967), 149–54.

Jones, J. R. *The First Whigs, The Politics of the Exclusion Crisis 1678–1683*, London, 1961.

Jordan, W. K. *Philanthropy in England, 1480–1660*, London, 1959.

Kearney, H. F. 'The Political Background to English Mercantilism, 1695–1700', *Economic History Review*, 2nd ser., XI, 3 (April 1959), 484–96.

Kendall, Willmoore. *John Locke and the Doctrine of Majority-rule*, 2nd edition, Urbana, Ill., 1959 (1st edition, 1941).

Kendall, Willmoore. 'John Locke Revisited', *The Intercollegiate Review*, II, 4 (January–February 1966), 217–34.

Kenny, Anthony. *Action, Emotion and Will*, London, 1963.

King, Peter, Lord. *The Life of John Locke*..., 2 vols., second edition, London, 1830.

Kliger, S. *The Goths in England*, Cambridge, Mass., 1952.

Kramnick, Isaac. *Bolingbroke and his Circle*, Oxford, 1968.

Krieger, Leonard. *The Politics of Discretion: Pufendorf and the Acceptance of Natural Law*, Chicago, 1965.

Laing, R. D. *The Divided Self: An Existential Study in Sanity and Madness*, London, 1960.

Lamprecht, Sterling Power. *The Moral and Political Philosophy of John Locke*, reprint, New York, 1962 (1st edition, 1918).

Larkin, Paschal. *Property in the Eighteenth Century with Special Reference to England and Locke*, Cork, 1930.

Laski, Harold J. *The Rise of European Liberalism*, paperback edition, 1962 (1st edition, 1936).

Laslett, Peter. 'Locke and the first Earl of Shaftesbury', *Mind*, no. 241 (January 1952), 89–92.

Laslett, Peter. 'John Locke, the Great Recoinage and the Board of Trade, 1695–1698', *William and Mary Quarterly*, 3rd ser. XIV, 3 (July 1957), 370–402.

Laslett, Peter. 'Market Society and Political Theory', *The Historical Journal*, VII, 1 (1964), 150–4.

Laslett, Peter. *The World We Have Lost*, London, 1965.

Le Clerc, Jean. *Lettres Inédites de Le Clerc à Locke*, ed. Gabriel Bonno, University of California Publications in Modern Philology, LII, Berkeley and Los Angeles, 1959.

[Leslie, Charles.] *The Case of the Regale and of the Pontificat Stated*..., n.p. 1700 [? 1701].

[Leslie, Charles.] *The New Association of those Called Moderate-Church-Men...*, Part II, London, 1703.

[Leslie, Charles.] *The Finishing Stroke, Being a Vindication of the Patriarchal Scheme of Government, in Defence of the Rehearsals...*, London, 1711.

Letwin, William. *The Origins of Scientific Economics, English Economic Thought 1660–1776*, London, 1963.

Locke, John. *Lovelace Collection of the Papers of John Locke* (with subsequent additions) = MS Locke, Bodleian Library, Oxford.

Locke, John. *Commonplace Book, 1661* = MS Film. 77. (This is in the possession of Arthur J. Houghton, Jr. and is cited with his kind permission.)

Locke, John. *Ragionamenti sopra la moneta l'interesse del danaro le finanze e il commercio soritti e pubblicati in diverse occasioni dal signor Giovanni Locke, Tradotti la prima volta dall'inglese con varie annotazioni* [by Francesco Pagnini and Angelo Tavanti], 3 vols., Firenze, 1751 (copy in Bibliothèque Nationale).

Locke, John. *The Works of John Locke in Four Volumes*, 7th edition, London, 1768.

Locke, John. *Original Letters of Locke; Algernon Sidney; and Anthony Lord Shaftesbury*, ed. T. Forster, London, 1830.

Locke, John. *The Correspondence of John Locke and Edward Clarke*, ed. with a biographical study by Benjamin Rand, London, 1927.

Locke, John. *An Essay concerning the Understanding, Knowledge, Opinion, and Assent...*, ed. Benjamin Rand, Cambridge, Mass., 1931.

Locke, John. *An Early Draft of Locke's Essay...*, ed. R. I. Aaron and Jocelyn Gibb, Oxford, 1936.

Locke, John. *Locke's Travels in France 1675–1679...*, ed. John Lough, Cambridge, 1953.

Locke, John. *Essays on the Law of Nature*, ed. W. Von Leyden, Oxford, 1954.

Locke, John. *Two Treatises of Government...*, ed. Peter Laslett, Cambridge, 1960.

Locke, John. *An Essay concerning Human Understanding*, ed. J. W. Yolton, 2 vols., London, 1961.

Locke, John. *A Letter concerning Toleration*, Latin and English Texts..., ed. Mario Montuori, The Hague, 1963.

Locke, John. *Two Tracts on Government*, ed. Philip Abrams, Cambridge, 1967.

Long, P. *A Summary Catalogue of the Lovelace Collection of the Papers of John Locke in the Bodleian Library*, Oxford, 1959.

Lough, John. 'Locke's Reading during his Stay in France (1675–79)', *The Library* (December 1953), pp. 229–58.

Lovejoy, Arthur O. *The Great Chain of Being, A Study of the History of an Idea*, paperback edition, New York, 1960 (1st edition, 1936).

MacIntyre, Alasdair. 'A Mistake about Causality in Social Science', *Philosophy, Politics and Society*, ed. P. Laslett and W. G. Runciman, 2nd ser. Oxford, 1962, pp. 48–70.

MacIntyre, Alasdair. *A Short History of Ethics*, London, 1967.

MacIntyre, Alasdair. *Secularization and Moral Change*, London, 1967.

McLachlan, H. *The Religious Opinions of Milton, Locke and Newton*, Manchester, 1941.

McLachlan, H. John. *Socinianism in Seventeenth-century England*, Oxford, 1951.

Maclean, A. H. *The Origins of the Political Opinions of John Locke*, unpublished Cambridge Ph.D. dissertation, 1947.

Maclean, A. H. 'George Lawson and John Locke', *Cambridge Historical Journal*, IX, 1 (1947), 69–77.

Macpherson, C. B. *The Political Theory of Possessive Individualism*, Oxford, 1962.

Macpherson, C. B. *The Real World of Democracy*, Oxford, 1966.

Macpherson, C. B. 'The Maximization of Democracy', *Philosophy, Politics and Society*, 3rd ser., ed. P. Laslett and W. G. Runciman, Oxford, 1967.

Macpherson, C. B. 'Democratic Theory: Ontology and Technology', *Political Theory and Social Change*, ed. David Spitz, New York, 1967.

Manuel, Frank E. *Isaac Newton, Historian*, Cambridge, Mass., 1963.

Marx, Karl. *Theories of Surplus Value*, Part I, Moscow, n.d.

Meinecke, Friedrich. *Machiavellism. The Doctrine of Raison d'État and its Place in Modern History*, trans. Douglas Scott, London, 1957.

Miller, Perry. *Errand into the Wilderness*, paperback edition, New York, 1964 (1st edition, 1956).

Mintz, Samuel I. *The Hunting of Leviathan*, Cambridge, 1962.

Molyneux, William. *The Case of Ireland's Being Bound by Acts of Parliament in England Stated*, Dublin, 1698.

Monson, Charles H., Jr. 'Locke and his Interpreters', *Political Studies*, VI, 2 (1958), 120–33.

Montesquieu, Charles-Louis de Secondat de. Composition manuscript of *L'Esprit des Loix*, Bibliothèque Nationale, nouvelles acquisitions français 12832–6.

Montesquieu. *Œuvres Complètes de Montesquieu*, publiées sous la direction de M. André Masson, 3 vols., Paris, 1950–5.

More, Sir Thomas. *The Complete Works of St. Thomas More*, IV, *Utopia*, ed. Edward Surtz, S. J. and J. H. Hexter, New Haven, 1965.

Moulds, Henry. 'John Locke's Four Freedoms Seen in a New Light', *Ethics*, LXXI, 2 (January 1961), 121–6.

Naudé, Gabriel. *Considerations Politiques sur les Coups d'Estat*, par Gabriel Naudé, Parisien. Sur la Copie de Rome [Paris], 1667.

Nelson, Benjamin N. *The Idea of Usury: From Tribal Brotherhood to Universal Otherhood*, Princeton, 1949.

Newton, Isaac. *The Correspondence of Isaac Newton*, Cambridge, 1959–.

Ogg, David. *England in the Reigns of James II and William III*, Oxford, 1955.

Ogg, David. *England in the Reign of Charles II*, 2 vols. paperback edition, Oxford, 1963 (1st edition, 1934).

Paley, William, M.A. *The Principles of Moral and Political Philosophy*, London, 1785.

Parry, Geraint. 'Individuality, Politics and the Critique of Paternalism in Locke', *Political Studies*, XII, 2 (1964), 163–77.

Passmore, J. A. *Ralph Cudworth: An Interpretation*, Cambridge, 1951.

Passmore, John. 'The Idea of a History of Philosophy', *History and Theory*, supplement 5, 'The Historiography of the History of Philosophy', pp. 1–32.

Perkins, William. *The Workes of That Famous and Worthy Minister of Christ in the Universitie of Cambridge, Mr. William Perkins*..., 3 vols. London, I, 1635, II, 1631, III, 1631.

Petzäll, Åke. 'Ethics and Epistemology in John Locke's Essay concerning Human Understanding, *Göteborgs Högskolas Årsskrift*, XLII, 2 (1937).

Pitkin, Hanna. 'Obligation and Consent', *American Political Science Review*, LIX, 4 (December 1965), 990–9, LX, 1 (March 1966), 39–52.

Plamenatz, John. *Consent, Freedom and Political Obligation*, Oxford, 1938.

Plamenatz, John. *Man and Society. A Critical Examination of Some Important Social and Political Theories from Machiavelli to Marx*, 2 vols. London, 1963.

Plumb, J. H. *The Growth of Political Stability in England 1675–1725*, London, 1967.

Pocock, J. G. A. *The Ancient Constitution and the Feudal Law*, Cambridge, 1957.

Pocock, J. G. A. 'Burke and the Ancient Constitution: A Problem in the History of Ideas', *The Historical Journal*, III, 2 (1960), 125–43.

Pocock, J. G. A. 'Machiavelli, Harrington, and English Political Ideologies in the Eighteenth Century', *William and Mary Quarterly*, 3rd ser. XXII, 4 (October 1965), 549–83.

Polin, Raymond. *La Politique Morale de John Locke*, Paris, 1960.

Polin, Raymond. 'Justice in Locke's Philosophy', *Nomos VI, Justice*, ed. Carl J. Friedrich and J. W. Chapman, New York, 1963, pp. 262–83.

Pollock, Sir F. and Maitland, F. W. *The History of English Law...*, 2 vols., Cambridge, 1895.

Powell, Sumner Chilton. *Puritan Village, The Formation of a New England Town*, paperback edition, Garden City, N.Y., 1965 (1st edition, 1963).

[Proast, Jonas.] *The Argument of the Letter concerning Toleration, Briefly Consider'd and Answer'd*, Oxford, 1690.

[Proast, Jonas.] *A Third Letter concerning Toleration: in Defense of the Letter concerning Toleration, briefly Consider'd and Answer'd*, Oxford, 1691.

[Proast, Jonas.] *A Second Letter To the Author of the Three Letters for Toleration. From the Author of the Argument of the Letter concerning Toleration Briefly Consider'd and Answer'd*, Oxford, 1704.

Pufendorf, Samuel von. *De Jure Naturae et Gentium Libri Octo* (Londini Scanorum, 1672), Carnegie Classics of International Law Series, ed. W. Simmons and trans. C. H. and W. A. Oldfather, 2 vols., Oxford, 1934.

Robbins, Caroline. *The Eighteenth-Century Commonwealthman...*, Cambridge, Mass., 1959.

Roberts, Clayton. *The Growth of Responsible Government in Stuart England*, Cambridge, 1966.

Rothkrug, Lionel. *Opposition to Louis XIV, The Political and Social Origins of the French Enlightenment*, Princeton, 1965.

Ryan, Alan. 'Locke and the Dictatorship of the Bourgeoisie', *Political Studies*, XIII, 2 (June 1965), 219–30.

Salmon, J. H. M. *The French Religious Wars in English Political Thought*, Oxford, 1959.

Sanderson, Robert. *XXXVI Sermons...*, 8th edition, London, 1689.

Schlatter, Richard. *Private Property: The History of an Idea*, London, 1951.

Schochet, Gordon J. 'The Family and the Origins of the State in Locke's Political Philosophy', *John Locke: Problems and Perspectives*, ed. J. W. Yolton, Cambridge, 1969.

Seliger, M. 'Locke's Natural Law and the Foundation of Politics', *Journal of the History of Ideas*, XXIV, 3 (July–September 1963), 337–54.

Seliger, M. 'Locke's Theory of Revolutionary Action', *Western Political Quarterly*, XVI, 3 (September 1963), 548–68.

Shackleton, Robert. *Montesquieu: A Critical Biography*, Oxford, 1961.

Shaftesbury, Anthony Ashley Cooper, 1st Earl of. *Shaftesbury Papers*, MSS. Public Record Office, 30/24/VI—.

Shaftesbury, Anthony Ashley Cooper, 1st Earl of. *Some Observations concerning the regulating of Elections for Parliament, found among the Earl of Shaftesbury's Papers after his death..., A Collection of Scarce and Valuable Tracts (=Somers Tracts)*, ed. Sir Walter Scott, 13 vols., 2nd edition, London, 1809–15, VIII, 396–403.

Shaftesbury, Anthony Ashley Cooper, third Earl of. *Characteristicks of Men, Manners, Opinions, Times*, 3 vols. 5th edition, Birmingham, 1773.

Shaftesbury, Anthony Ashley Cooper, third Earl of. *The Life, Unpublished Letters, and Philosophical Regimen of Anthony, Earl of Shaftesbury, Author of the Characteristicks*, ed. Benjamin Rand, London, 1900.

Shaftesbury, Anthony Ashley Cooper, third Earl of. *Second Characters of the Language of Forms*, ed. B. Rand, Cambridge, 1914.

Sherlock, William. *The Case of the Allegiance Due to Soveraign Powers, Stated and Resolved, According to Scripture and Reason, and the Principles of the Church of England...*, London, 1691.

Shipton, Clifford K. 'Elisha Williams', *Sibley's Harvard Graduates*, V, Boston, Mass., 1937.

Singh, Raghuveer. 'John Locke and the Theory of Natural Law', *Political Studies*, IX, 2 (1961), 105–18.

Skinner, Quentin. 'Hobbes's Leviathan', *The Historical Journal*, VII (1964), 321–33.

Skinner, Quentin. 'History and Ideology in the English Revolution', *The Historical Journal*, VIII, 2 (1965), 151–78.

Skinner, Quentin. 'The Limits of Historical Explanations', *Philosophy*, XLI, 157 (July 1966), 199–215.

Skinner, Quentin. 'The Ideological Context of Hobbes's Political Thought', *The Historical Journal*, IX, 3 (1966), 286–317.

Smith, Constance I. 'Filmer and the Knolles Translation of Bodin', *Philosophical Quarterly*, XIII, 52 (July 1963), 248–9.

Sprott, S. E. *The English Debate on Suicide from Donne to Hume*, La Salle, Ill., 1961.

[Stevens, W.] *The Life of the Author* in *The Theological, Philosophical and Miscellaneous Works of the Rev. William Jones...*, 12 vols., London, 1801.

Straka, Gerald M. 'The Final Phase of Divine Right Theory in England, 1688–1702', *English Historical Review*, LXXVII, 305 (October 1962), 638–58.

Straka, Gerald M. *Anglican Reaction to the Revolution of 1688*, Madison, Wisconsin, 1962.

Strauss, Leo. *Natural Right and History*, Chicago, 1953.

Strauss, Leo. 'Locke's Doctrine of Natural Law', *American Political Science Review*, LII, 2 (June 1958), 490–501.

Strauss, Leo. *The Political Philosophy of Hobbes*, paperback edition, Chicago, 1963 (1st edition, 1936).

Tanner, J. R. *Tudor Constitutional Documents*, Cambridge, 1922.

Taylor, Jeremy. *Ductor Dubitantium, or The Rule of Conscience in all her general measures*..., 2 vols. London, 1660.

Taylor, Jeremy. *The Rule and Exercises of Holy Living*, reprint, London, 1907.

Thomas, Keith. 'The Social Origins of Hobbes's Political Thought', *Hobbes Studies*, ed. K. C. Brown, Oxford, 1965, pp. 185–236.

Tierney, Brian. *Medieval Poor Law, A Sketch of Canonical Theory and Its Application in England*, Berkeley and Los Angeles, 1959.

Troeltsch, Ernst. *The Social Teaching of the Christian Churches*, trans. Olive Wyon, paperback edition, 2 vols., New York, 1960 (1st edition of translation, 1931).

Tuveson, Ernest Lee. *Millennium and Utopia, A Study in the Background of the Idea of Progress*, paperback edition, New York, 1964 (1st edition, 1949).

Urbach, E. E. 'The Laws regarding Slavery as a source for social history of the period of the second temple, the Mishnah and Talmud', *Annual of Jewish Studies*, I (1963), 1–94 (first printed in Hebrew in *Zion*, 1960).

Ussher, James. *A Body of Divinity, or The Summe and Substance of Christian Religion*..., 3rd edition, London, 1648.

Van Schaack, Henry C. *The Life of Peter Van Schaack, Ll D*..., New York, 1842.

Viano, Carlo Augusto. 'I rapporti tra Locke e Shaftesbury e le teorie economiche di Locke', *Rivista di Filosofia*, XLIX (1958), 69–84.

Viano, Carlo Augusto. *John Locke: Dal Razionalismo all'Illuminismo*, Turin, 1960.

Vico, Giambattista. *La Scienza Nuova Seconda*, ed. Fausto Nicolini, 3rd edition, Bari, 1942.

Viner, Jacob. '"Possessive Individualism" as Original Sin', *Canadian Journal of Economics and Political Science*, XXIX, 4 (November 1963). 548–59 (and subsequent controversy with Macpherson *ibid.* pp, 559–66).

Voltaire, François-Marie Arouet de. *Lettres Philosophiques* (1734), edition critique...par Gustave Lanson, 2 vols., 3rd edition, Paris, 1924.

Von Fürer-Haimendorf, Christoph. *Morals and Merit: A Study of Values and Social Controls in South Asian Societies*, London, 1967.

Von Leyden, W. 'John Locke and Natural Law', *Philosophy*, XXXI (1956), 23–35.

Von Leyden, W. 'On Justifying Inequality', *Political Studies*, XI, 1 (1963), 56–70.

Waldman, Theodore. 'A Note on John Locke's Concept of Consent', *Ethics*, LXVIII, 1 (October 1957), 45–50.

Walzer, Michael. *The Revolution of the Saints. A Study in the Origins of Radical Politics*, London, 1966.

Warrender, Howard. 'Hobbes's Conception of Morality', *Rivista Critica di Storia della Filosofia*, anno XVII, fac. IV (October–December 1962), 434–49.

Weber, Max. *The Protestant Ethic and the Spirit of Capitalism*, trans. Talcott Parsons, paperback edition, New York, 1958 (1st edition of translation 1930).

Western, J. R. *The English Militia in the Eighteenth Century*, London 1965.

Weston, Corinne Comstock. *English Constitutional Theory and the House of Lords 1556–1832*, London, 1965.

Wilbur, Earl Morse. *A History of Unitarianism in Transylvania, England and America*, Cambridge, Mass., 1952.

Willey, Basil. *The Eighteenth-Century Background*, paperback edition, Harmondsworth, Middx., 1962 (1st edition, 1940).

[Williams, Elisha] 'Philalethes', *The essential Rights and Liberties of Protestants. a seasonable Plea for The Liberty of Conscience, and The Right of private Judgement, In Matters of Religion*...Boston, 1744.

Wisdom, John. 'Gods', *Logic and Language. First and Second Series*, ed. Antony Flew, paperback edition, Garden City, N.Y., 1965, pp. 194–214.

Wood, Antony. *The Life and Times of Antony Wood, antiquary, of Oxford, 1632–1695*: ed. Andrew Clark, 7 vols., Oxford, 1891—.

Woodhouse, A. S. P., ed. *Puritanism and Liberty*..., London, 1938.

Yeats, W. B. *The Collected Poems of W. B. Yeats*, New York, 1956.

Yolton, J. W. *John Locke and the Way of Ideas*, Oxford, 1956.

Yolton, John W. 'Locke on the Law of Nature', *Philosophical Review*, LVII, 4 (October 1958), 477–98.

[Yorke, Henry?] *The Spirit of John Locke Revived*, Sheffield [? 1794]. (Copy in Library of Congress.)

Young, Edward. *An Apology for Princes, or The Reverence due to Government. A Sermon*..., London, 1729.

INDEX